Portraits in British History

THE DORSEY SERIES IN HISTORY

Editor
GENE A. BRUCKER
University of California at Berkeley

Portraits in British History

RONALD POLLITT, Ph.D.
Associate Professor of History
University of Cincinnati

HERBERT F. CURRY, Ph.D.
Associate Professor of History
University of Cincinnati

 1975

The Dorsey Press   *Homewood, Illinois   60430*
Irwin-Dorsey International   London, England   WC2H 9NJ
Irwin-Dorsey Limited   Georgetown, Ontario   L7G 4B3

First Printing, February 1975

ISBN 0-256-01679-8
Library of Congress Catalog Card No. 74–24454
Printed in the United States of America

For
C. William Vogel

Preface

THIS book is designed to supplement textbooks ordinarily used in introductory courses in British history. Unlike most such auxiliary works, it features neither documents nor essays on problems of historical interpretation. Rather, it comprises 15 biographical essays, for we are convinced that one of the most fruitful ways of studying the past is to view it as human experience on the most elemental level, as biography.

Textbooks and lectures, of course, treat in some detail the lives of monarchs and statesmen, and they allot extensive attention to the unidentifiable millions who, in the aggregate, give force to great historical movements. Thus, students learn of the far-reaching impact of decisions taken by great individuals and they are also exposed to the influence of mass movements and historical forces. Students have less opportunity, however, to become acquainted with the men and women of British history who were neither at the peak of the societal pyramid nor at its base, but who still made important contributions to Britain's evolution. Although these persons are frequently mentioned in textbooks, they are usually given little more than passing mention. We think that examining their lives offers unique insights into the fabric of British history.

Because there is not sufficient information about the medieval period, we have included essays on two early kings. With these exceptions it is the less prominent figures who people our book: the "overmighty" subject, the physical scientist, the authoress, and the colonial governor. Through investigating their lives and the worlds they lived in, we hope to enable students to deepen their understanding of British history.

Throughout the preparation of this book we have received help from many friends, colleagues, and students, and we cannot mention all of them here. There are, however, a few individuals to whom we are especially thankful, and we wish to acknowledge their part in the preparation of the manuscript: Gene Brucker, University of California, Berkeley; Bentley Gilbert, University of Illinois at Chicago Circle; Stanford Lehmberg, University of Minnesota; William Maehl, University of Oklahoma; Pamela Pollitt, Wright State University; and Ruth Noll,

Jill Patrick, and Janet Thompson, University of Cincinnati. Matters of judgment and the inclusion of any errors in the text are, of course, solely the responsibility of the authors.

January 1975   RONALD POLLITT
                                                                       HERBERT CURRY

Contents

Portraits in British History

Chapter 1

ALFRED THE GREAT:
The Foundation of
the English Monarchy

J∪ST after Easter, in late March of 878, young King Alfred of Wessex
sought refuge on the Isle of Athelney in the remote marshes of
southern England. Barbaric Danish raiders had begun menacing his
kingdom before he had come to the throne, seven years earlier, and since
January they had been pillaging at will over almost all of his realm.

Athelney was at the same time a nadir and rebirth for the old English
monarchy. There, the young King devised plans for the recovery of
Wessex. His comrades-in-arms made forays from the Isle to harrass the
surrounding Danes and to inform the English ealdormen, or nobles.
that their sovereign planned a new and, it was hoped, victorious battle.
With a coordination attesting both the loyalty of his men and the administrative ability of the King himself, Englishmen from Somerset and
Wiltshire met their sovereign at "Egbert's stone," bordering the two
counties. There, as described in the Anglo-Saxon of Alfred's biographer
Asser, they "were fain of him," or rejoiced enthusiastically in their monarch. Under Alfred's inspiring leadership the reconquest of England
was begun.

King Alfred, the savior of Anglo-Saxon civilization, was himself descended from barbarian marauders. According to the royal genealogy,
the West Saxon dynasty had been founded by Alfred's Germanic ancestor
Cerdic, who had landed near Southampton some 400 years before. On
the ruins of Roman England, which he and his followers had helped
to destroy, Cerdic had established a primitive pagan kingdom south
of the river Thames. By the time Alfred was born in 849 this Kingdom
of the West Saxons had been Christianized and included most of southern England.

The Britain of King Alfred was a primitive, undeveloped land. Everywhere, four centuries of vandalism and neglect had brought devastation
to the physical remainders of Roman Britain. Only ill-kept roads, a few
crumbling walls, and broken tiles stood as shattered records of the provincial urban culture that had characterized Britain during the 400 years
of Roman rule. The Anglo-Saxons themselves were little more than sub-
sistence farmers. Few in number and technologically unsophisticated,
they had made few enduring marks on the countryside. They built only
rarely of stone, even royal and noble residences were small and of rough
timber construction, and the peasant majority lived in crude huts made
of mud and wood. Much of the land was still covered with scrub or
inundated by water, and in southern Britain a virtually uninhabited
band of forest ran, 30 miles wide, for 120 miles across the island. It
. was a rich, attractive land, but in Alfred's time it still showed few permanent traces of human activity.

Yet, the Anglo-Saxons had created a flourishing Christian literary culture and artistic work of great beauty. In the 7th and 8th centuries
great monastic schools in Kent and at York had attracted pupils from
all of northern Europe. Outstanding scholars, like the Venerable Bede,

had written fine Latin prose, and abbeys and churches had been adorned
with beautiful books and paintings. Through the universal church and
through far-reaching commercial activities, the English were in regular
communication with the continental and Mediterranean societies and
the sources of classical culture. It was this new Anglo-Saxon civilization,
laboriously being cultivated and acutely vulnerable, that the new waves
of Danish attacks threatened to obliterate.

The Danes, or Vikings, were Scandinavian pirates. A people of tremendous vitality and terrible ferocity, they brought fire and devastation
to western Europe for hundreds of years. Their ships reached as far
as America in the West and Russia in the East, and they planted permanent colonies in Ireland, Gaul, and Sicily. In the 9th century they raided
the continent unhindered and undertook to conquer all of Britain. Pagan
and unlettered, they presented a deadly challenge to the hard-won and
insecure Christian culture of Anglo-Saxon England.

Like the Europeans of the 19th century, whose industrial base enabled
them to dominate the world, the Danes possessed an advanced naval
and military technology which made them superior to any forces they
encountered. Their graceful ships had strong keels, oars, and sails and
could outfight, outmaneuver, and outlast any other warships in western
Europe. They were also things of frightful beauty, with swift lines,
and figureheads carved into images of dragons and birds of prey. Militarily, the Danes wore more and better armor, defended themselves
with long shields instead of round ones, and had developed incomparable skill in wielding long-handled battle-axes. Above all, they built
forts, defensive bases on land, from which they sallied out to kill and
to plunder and to which they retired for safety. Virtually impregnable,
the forts withstood all attack and constituted a major innovation in
the fighting tactics of the Dark Ages.

The Danish society was predatory in outlook, glorifying violence,
adventure, and loot, and as in many warlike societies, this military orientation exerted a determining effect on social organization. Men sailed
and fought together in distinct groups, and the captain of a ship's crew
was also the leader of the war band. He and his seamen warriors were
bound to each other by close ties of personal loyalty and self-interest.
The men followed their captain's lead and prized his life above their
own. In turn, the captain not only had to be a daring and successful
commander but also was expected to reward his men regularly with
splendid gifts.

The Vikings had launched their first destructive probes at Britain
in the 790s, 50 years before Alfred was born. They sacked the rich
monasteries at Lindisfarne, Jarrow, and Iona in the north, and landed
briefly in the south on the coast of Dorset. In the 830s their attacks
began in earnest. These followed a uniform pattern. Every spring the

Danes landed on the unprotected coasts of eastern and southern Britain, built forts, stole horses, and raided until the autumn, when they sailed home. Eventually they began spending the winters, so that they might begin raiding earlier in the next year. Inevitably the prostrate country-side yielded less and less plunder; local authority, failing of defense, began to disintegrate; and in reaction, the nature of the Danish purpose began to change. Families and chattels accompanied the pirates and, as the portable booty diminished, captains began rewarding their men with land. The new aim was permanent conquest, and a substitution of Viking rule for the government of the Anglo-Saxon kings. Like the Anglo-Saxons before them, the Danes would find a new home in Britain. Between 865 and 870 most of the northern English kingdoms were vanquished and by 870 the pagan host was poised for a determined attack on the South.

Alfred grew to manhood while the ominous new purpose of the Danes took form and became clear. The fourth son of King Ethelwulf of Wessex, he was of double royal descent, for both his father and his mother, Osburth, claimed Cerdic as ancestor. Indeed, they traced their origins to the great god Woden himself, a traditional pretension of Anglo-Saxon royalty. Very little is known about Alfred's youth. Undoubtedly, like all young men of high birth, he wore a short tunic belted at the waist, with leggings and furs in the winter and cloaks and jewels on special occasions. He lived successively in the royal manors at Wantage, Chippenham, Wilton, and Winchester and, according to Asser, especially enjoyed hunting wolves, deer, and wild boars. He received training in the military arts and seems to have shown more interest in learning than most young Saxon men. He mastered reading and writing when he was 12 and committed much Saxon poetry to memory. As a young prince he participated in the activities of the court and spent evenings in the king's great hall listening to sagas of glorious feats in battle. From childhood he experienced the discomfort and pain of ill health. Until, legend has it, he was cured by prayers at two holy shrines in Cornwall, he suffered from *ficus*, or hemorrhoids. Then, at the age of 20 he was stricken dramatically during the course of his wedding feast. The nature of this malady is uncertain; 20th-century physicians have suggested either kidney stones or inflammation of the bladder. Neither herbal remedies nor prayers brought cure and, to the end of his life, Alfred's health remained uncertain and he was frequently in pain.

The most prominent events in Alfred's childhood were two trips that he made to Rome in 853 and 855. They were symbolic of the uniquely close association between the West Saxon dynasty and the Christian Church. Of all the kings in England, the West Saxon monarchs were the most consciously and, it would seem, sincerely Christian, and Alfred's father Ethelwulf was an especially devout son of the church. The church, in turn, consistently supported him in his policies and wars.

Controversy and legend surround the major occurrence of Alfred's visit to the Holy City in 853. Pope Leo IV wrote Ethelwulf that he invested the young prince as a "spiritual son . . . in the manner of Roman Consuls." In the ceremony he placed a diadem on the child's head. Later chroniclers and Alfred's biographer Asser interpreted this act as a coronation, a prescient distinction indeed to be conferred upon the fourth son of the King of Wessex. It was probable that the Holy Father wished merely to honor the son of the devout King of Wessex, who was holding the frontiers of Christendom against the pagans. Whatever impression the ceremony made on the boy at the time, Alfred seems later to have attached to it a prophetic significance that especially hallowed his kingship to him.

Alfred's voyages also placed into sharp relief the perils that beset Christendom. On the way to Rome his suite crossed a Channel beset by heathen pirates and a continent ravaged by pagan Danes, and reached a Holy City that was under constant pressure from Islamic marauders. Everywhere, the followers of Christ were under attack. Alfred's world was a world on the defensive, a civilization under threat of annihilation.

King Ethelwulf died in 858, when Alfred was nine years old. The Anglo-Saxon kingship was elective, and the nobles of Wessex chose Alfred's older brothers to succeed Ethelwulf: first Ethelbald, who died in 860, and then Ethelbert, who ruled until his death in 866. When Ethelwulf's third son Ethelred came to power in 866, he called his 17-year-old brother to share in his councils, and young Alfred became the new king's trusted second-in-command. Ethelred and Alfred cooperated with the King of Mercia, on the northern border of Wessex, in joint defense against the Danes and, about 868, the ties between Wessex and Mercia were strengthened when Alfred married a Mercian woman, the Lady Ealhswith. She was of royal blood, and the alliance buttressed the claims of Alfred's descendants to be rulers of all England.

The alliance with Mercia did not forestall the Danes, and in December 870, they launched an invasion of Wessex itself. Provocatively, they constructed earthworks near a royal manor at Reading and set out to begin the conquest of the southern English kingdom. From the first, their raiding parties encountered firm resistance, and early in January of 871 King Ethelred and his brother Alfred led the royal army to Reading. Their attempts to storm the Danish ramparts failed and they finally retreated down the ridge of the Berkshire downs. The Danes pursued and, in leaving the security of their fortress, took the risk of open battle. The battle occurred at Ashdown, not far from the Great White Horse which had been cut into the chalk soil of the downs more than a thousand years before, during the early Iron Age of Britain. It was at Ashdown that Alfred first won fame as a courageous and gifted military commander. The Danes drew up in their traditional "boar's head" formation on the side of a hill. In front stood the two kings and their closest retainers, marshalled into a wedge. Behind, in support, were arrayed the lines of the Danish noblemen and their followers. The tactics were simple: the royal band would attack and break the English force and then the men of the second line would enter the fray to finish them off. The English matched the Danish configuration, King Athelred commanding their wedge and Alfred leading their second line.

Asser's description of the battle was written more than 20 years later and at second hand, but it appears from his muddled account that the English battle plan was unusual. Instead of an engagement focusing on a clash between the opposing royal bands, the English planned to bypass the Danish Kings and bring their entire force to bear on the Danish second line, thus surrounding and isolating the Danish royal wedge.

On the morning of the battle, the Danes began moving sooner than the English had expected, while King Ethelred was still hearing Mass. Piously, he refused to leave the altar before the service was finished, thus endangering the English plan of battle. Alfred impatiently seized the initiative. Placing himself in command of the wedge, he led the English warriors uphill toward the Danish battle-axes. The unorthodox tactics worked. The Danish Kings were taken off guard and cut off from the bulk of their army, one king and five earls fell on the battlefield, and only a small fraction of the force escaped. The victorious English pursued them until they regained the safety of their fortress at Reading. Clearly, Alfred's audacity and presence of mind had been the determining elements of the English victory, and his triumph at Ashdown won him the reputation as the finest English warrior of his day.

The Danes persisted in their campaign, however, and the English met defeat twice more before King Ethelred died in April. He left two young sons, but boys were incapable of leading a Wessex at war. Accordingly, with popular acclaim, the hero of Ashdown assumed the crown. Alfred continued the attempts to dislodge the invaders, but they were reinforced by new bands from across the channel. Consistently, the honors of battle went to the Danes. At the end of the year, his kingdom devastated and his armies disheartened, Alfred sued for peace. In return for tribute, the Danes agreed to evacuate Wessex.

Yet, although the year 871 ended in defeat for Wessex, it was also critical for the Danes. In the nine major engagements of the year they lost one king, nine earls, and countless other fighting men. Wessex offered the stiffest opposition they had encountered in Britain. Rather than risk an attempt to push the conquest of the south to an early conclusion, they turned back to consolidate their winnings north of the Thames. Determined resistance in the nine battles of 871 gained for Wessex a five-year respite before the Danes would renew their pressure. How this time was to be used was up to the new king.

The Kingdom of Wessex possessed virile traditions which provided firm bases for the powerful united community that Alfred began to build. The society of his land was in many ways more corporate than individualistic in nature. His people were welded together by strong personal ties originating in their Germanic past, bonds that served to promote stability and cohesion in a society that had few effective legal or governmental restraints. Like the peoples of pre-European Africa, the Anglo-Saxons were united by strong ties of kinship. Kin groups, which usually included all blood relatives to the extent of fourth cousins, helped pay court fines, revenged wrongs in blood feuds, assisted their members in times of need and held them to the rules of society through tenacious cultural sanctions. Outside a kindred, a man was virtually defenseless before the chaotic forces of a young and vigorous society.

Augmenting the authority of the kin groups and, in fact, steadily moving to replace it, were the principles of lordship. In origin, lordship was similar to the relationship which bound the Danish fighting men to their captains, and it stemmed directly from the military foundations of Anglo-Saxon society. Like the Danes, the Anglo-Saxons had been raiding bands of barbarian conquerors four centuries before and, like the Danes, the warriors were united by powerful sentiments of personal loyalty. A lord was a king, or a nobleman, whose military prowess attracted fighters, mostly lesser nobles, who swore binding oaths of fealty to their commander. In return the lord undertook to arm his men, to care for them, and to reward them with feasting and gifts. A lord's fighting men made up his comitatus. At Ashdown the royal force heading the Danish army was the combined comitatus of two Danish kings, and it faced the comitatus of King Ethelred of Wessex.

It is difficult to overestimate the importance of the patterns of reciprocal loyalty in the comitatus. Conversion to Christianity made little impression on them. After all, Christ himself had his 12 apostles. Centuries of settled society tended to introduce elements of civilian government, as commanders in wars became also ealdormen, or governors, of provinces, but the ties between lord and man remained invulnerable. They were constantly glorified as ideals in song and story and were the central inspiration of secular Anglo-Saxon literature. In *Beowulf*, which provides many insights into Anglo-Saxon mores, they were exalted as the worldly ideal of old English society. Beowulf possessed characteristics of heroic caliber: courage and unsurpassed proficiency in war, loyalty to his chief, generosity to his companions-in-arms, and a deep concern for justice. In epic form, *Beowulf* offers a paradigm of Anglo-Saxon society.

Thus, superimposed on the kindred was the aristocratic code of the kings and chiefs, each leading a comitatus. The men of the comitatus followed their leader with unquestioning obedience and loyalty, died for him willingly in times of war and advised him in times of peace. The leader protected them and, in Anglo-Saxon England, rewarded them with land. This institution was fundamental to Alfred's Wessex, to the Danes who threatened it, to the Germans described by Tacitus eight centuries before, and it became the inspiration for the feudal system and the chivalric code of the high middle ages that followed.

The relationship between the lords and the masses of the peasantry, or ceorls, was not exalted in song and story and it is not nearly so clear. It was also neither completely developed nor universal in the fluid society of Alfred's England. Probably the majority of English peasants were still free and independent men but, because of the insecurity produced by the Danish raids, many ceorls had placed their lands under the protection of a lord. At first the obligations they incurred were primarily military, as the ceorls composed the lower ranks of the armies, but eventually the lord's control seems to have produced a net of duties that bound the ceorls to him in other social, economic, and legal ways. Ceorls could change lords if they wished, and for most of the peasantry the kindred, not lordship, was still the vital mainstay of organized life. Nevertheless, whatever the pattern, the kin group or a variety of lordship, close personal ties and obligations formed the very foundations of existence for all men in Alfred's Wessex.

Alfred was sustained by the cohesive nature of Anglo-Saxon society. It can be argued, although some historians disagree, that Alfred, as king, was the supreme lord of all the people of Wessex. Whether this was the case or not, he could draw extensive, if ill-defined, authority from the ancient concepts of kingship which derived from the past of his people. Alfred, as an Anglo-Saxon king, inherited his position rightfully from his royal forebears. He was the acknowledged leader in times of war and occupied an exceptional place in law, not above it, but above all other men under the law. A special aura surrounded him: He need not support his word with an oath, no one could fight or draw a weapon in his hall under pain of death, and breach of peace in his presence entailed very heavy penalties. He possessed a broad and general judicial power and acted as arbiter in cases of disputed legal decisions. Alfred's dignity was enhanced further by the sanctity of Christian anointment at a coronation ceremony, indicating that he ruled by divine permission. His powers were defined only vaguely, but theoretically they could be very extensive. An able and creative ruler like Alfred could make much of them.

From 871 until 875 the Danes left Wessex in peace while they ensured their mastery of the north, and when they turned back to Wessex, Alfred was the only Anglo-Saxon monarch still ruling in Britain. In 875 their attacks began in earnest, and by 878 the Danish King Guthrum had hounded Alfred to the marshes of southern England and had won the submission of great numbers of his people. It was at this point that Alfred rallied the men of Wessex from his base in Athelney. The English won the day at Chippenham. On one of the rare occasions that a Danish fort proved vulnerable, they forced King Guthrum to surrender.

In victory, King Alfred worked for a peace of reconciliation. Instead of perpetrating the wholesale slaughter which might have been expected as retribution for the devastation and humiliation the Danes had caused, Alfred took hostages and exacted from Guthrum a pledge to depart. He persuaded Guthrum to renounce the gods of his fathers and accept baptism. Shortly thereafter, the vanquished Danish ruler and 30 of his companions were guests of Alfred, and the triumphant King of Wessex himself stood as sponsor of the new followers of Christ.

Athelney, the victory that followed, and the conversion of a heathen king, came to be central to the Alfredian legend. Here indeed was the model Christian English monarch: brave and inventive in adversity, successful in battle, and magnanimous in peace. Alfred's terms of peace also demonstrated his vision and his grasp of the broad outlines of the perils facing his world. To Christianize was to civilize. If the Vikings could not be kept at bay, their destructive menace might be countered in another way, through conversion. Guthrum and his band then turned north of London to East Anglia where the Anglo-Saxons, even if they were under Danish rule, at least had a Christian king.

For more than ten years thereafter, except for isolated raids, the Danish menace to Wessex receded. Many of the Danes turned their energies to the Continent, where there was no Alfred of Wessex to thwart them, and those who remained in Britain began settling down in their new fatherland. In a few generations they were to become almost indistinguishable from their Anglo-Saxon neighbors.

In these years Alfred, only recently a royal fugitive at Athelney, initiated the reconquest of England. Using as an excuse the fact that King Guthrum of East Anglia had helped some Danish raiders, Alfred sent a force to occupy London in 886. This was the first sign to Englishmen that the lands they had lost might be regained, and London became a center of resistance for all who would oppose the Danes. True, Alfred acknowledged Danish rule in the North, in what came to be called the Danelaw, when he and Guthrum divided Britain into Danish and English parts along the old Roman road called Watling Street, but the recovery of London made that concession seem only a temporary expedient. Throughout the island, Anglo-Saxons recognized that the King of Wessex offered new hope and opportunity and, as the Anglo-Saxon Chronicle relates, "all English people that were not under subjection to the Danes submitted to him." This amounted to an acceptance, by all free Englishmen, of Alfred's overlordship, and it marked an important advance toward an united England under a single English sovereign. It also implied that Alfred's position as king was fundamentally different from that of earlier Kings of England. They, men like Egbert and Offa, had attained their positions and exercised their claims by force. Alfred's overlordship outside Wessex was not, and could not be, imposed by force. Rather, when Englishmen accepted Alfred as sovereign, they recognized voluntarily that he represented common aspirations and interests. It is a truism that the Danes forced Englishmen to unite, but it was the character and ability of King Alfred that made him an acceptable ruler of all Christian Anglo-Saxon England.

As the Vikings began encountering more opposition on the continent, they turned again to Wessex. Three hundred and thirty ships, carrying two great armies, their families, horses and possessions, landed in Kent in 892. For four years, occasionally helped by Danes resident in Britain, the Norsemen endeavored to capture the last independent English kingdom. They encountered a Wessex much more advanced militarily than the kingdom that Alfred had inherited, for in the 880s he had initiated a series of military changes that transformed his realm into the best defended state of his time. In creating a new military system, Alfred not only secured his own kingdom but also laid the foundations for the successes of his son and grandson.

As no ruler in Britain had perceived since the time of the Romans, Alfred saw that England's insular position might be turned to strategic advantage. The best way to defeat an invasion was to destroy the enemy army while it was still at sea. Accordingly, he had his craftsmen build ships of his own design which were twice as large as the Danish vessels. Powered by 120 oars, they were the fastest and highest ships built in Europe at the time. They were hard to maneuver, however, and the inexperienced seamen of Wessex were unable to exploit their potential fully. Unfortunately for Alfred's dreams of maritime power, the ships ran aground "very awkwardly" in the only recorded engagement of his fleet in 896. On that occasion the Danish fleet was routed, but it would still be a mistake to ascribe too much importance to Alfred's navy. His ships were ill-made and badly sailed, and his immediate successors did not continue his naval policy. Nevertheless, Alfred did arrive at the same concept of defense that English rulers in later centuries were to employ with brilliant success to counter threats from all the major powers of the Continent. In Alfred's crude and foundering warships lay the precocious germ of the Royal Navy that was to be a cause and a symbol of Britain's position as a dominant world power.

If the Vikings could not be kept from the soil of Wessex, they could be dealt with after they landed by adopting techniques copied from

their own tactics. When the Danes landed in Kent in 892 they captured
peasants who were building a new *burh* or fort, ordered by the King.
These burhs were to provide refuge for the peasantry, to control the
surrounding countryside, and to serve as centers of resistance. By the
time Alfred died, a protective ring of 30 burhs had been completed,
and almost all villages in Wessex were within 20 miles of a burh. Many
of them already were, or soon became, centers of government, religion,
and commerce, as well as defense. Unintentionally, Alfred's defensive
measures created the nucleus from which would grow many English
towns, or boroughs.

The burhs were not uniform in design. In some places, as at Bath
and at Winchester, they were built on the foundations of Roman walls.
Elsewhere, in the countryside, earthworks were constructed across the
ends of promontories. In other places a ditch or bank surrounded a
large square protected by a wooden stockade. Some burhs were very
large; the fortifications at Wallingford ran for 3,000 yards. Whatever
the configuration of the burh, Alfred ordered that each one be constructed, maintained, and garrisoned by the men of the district it
guarded. Assessments were made according to the acreage of farmland
attached to an estate or village, and a certain acreage had to provide
a specific number of warriors to man the wall. Sixteen soldiers, it was
thought, were needed to defend every 22 yards of wall.

In Alfred's later campaigns he called more and more on the noblemen
and their followers to do the fighting. Yet in times of universal peril,
the obligation to fight had to be universal. Traditionally the Anglo-Saxon
fyrd had answered this need. The fyrd was organized on a local basis
and contained every able-bodied man in a district. It was very amateurish, and its effectiveness was diminished by the reluctance of ceorls
to move far from their farms and their eagerness to return to them
before a campaign was over. It was largely the weaknesses of the fyrd
that had permitted the Danes to range freely over Wessex in 878. In
his reorganization Alfred took into account the needs of both farm and
defense; he simply divided his armed forces into two parts, ordering
one half to active duty while the other half remained at home on the
land.

It was, fundamentally, Alfred's ability to organize and his administrative vision that thwarted the Danish invasions of the 890s. The fighting
lasted four years. Nowhere could the enemy achieve a permanent base,
as they had in the past. Everywhere they encountered burhs and were
harried by an alert English army. The new military system of Wessex
kept them constantly on the move. Aside from a few young Danish
hotheads, their brothers already resident in England gave them little help, for the interests of the new invaders and those of the older
settlers no longer coincided. At one point the armies of Wessex even

chased the Danes far to the north and besieged them in the city of Chester. Finally, in the summer of 896 the Viking army disintegrated and most of the soldiers took their families to settle among their Scandinavian brethren in the North. Their attempt to win a new homeland in Wessex had failed. For the last three years of Alfred's reign his kingdom was at peace.

Alfred applied to civil government the same concern for system and organization that distinguished his handling of military problems. He, as king, was the government in a much more direct and immediate sense than were later monarchs after the Norman Conquest. In a very genuine way, he was king-chief, or king-father, the personal ruler of his people. The machinery of his central administration in Wessex was rudimentary, based solely on him and his court, and Alfred was always the mainspring of all activity.

In attendance at Alfred's court were two distinct groups of men, the members of his household and, periodically, leading prelates and noblemen of the realm. When the latter were present, the court was called a Witan. Generally, the household managed the day-to-day operation of the government and the Witan acted as a policy-making body. Alfred's household was, essentially, an expanded comitatus. So great was his military fame that young noblemen came from all over England to join his retinue. They, and his old companions-in-arms, constituted his bodyguard. In addition, the household included scribes and priests, minstrels and scholars, and men like the stewards and cupbearers who were directly responsible for managing the royal palaces, all waiting upon the King. During Alfred's reign the nature of the comitatus began changing. Where before the companions had been primarily personal dependents of the King, now they gradually became more and more involved in landholding, with the responsibilities of supervising large estates. Alfred acknowledged the importance of their new interests with the same good sense and organizational flair that he had applied to reforming the fyrd. He divided his companions into three groups and, under a system of rotation, each group spent one month in day and night attendance on the King and two months managing their lands.

The financial arrangements of Alfred's government were direct and uncomplicated. He and his court were constantly traveling throughout the realm, stopping at royal estates and residences of ealdormen. In this way the King could live off his land while at the same time personally watching over his people. The tradition of mobile government had produced the rule that all subjects were obligated to offer hospitality to the King and his suite. This came to be called *feorm*, or food rent, and it was equivalent to the quantity of provisions necessary to maintain the court for a day and a night. Occasionally the feorm was commuted to a money payment and so became an important part of the royal revenues. Alfred also received revenue from the tolls and from the law courts. It was a sign of the personal and simple nature of Anglo-Saxon government that Alfred made no distinction between the monies used for administration and the funds he spent for personal use. The royal treasure chests were in his bedroom and, heavily guarded, accompanied him on his travels.

Alfred brought order to the finances of his state. He assigned half of his revenues to God and half to the business of government. The half that went to the church he divided further into quarters; one each for monastic foundations, the palace school, the poor, and parish churches. He apportioned the secular half into thirds, for his household, for his workmen, and for gifts to foreigners.

In many ways King Alfred's government was government in miniature. This was due, in part, to the fact that many of the activities of modern governments were undertaken by subjects as obligations owed their sovereign. Alfred did not have to pay his army or finance the building and manning of burhs; these were duties his people were obliged to perform. Nor were royal officials or members of the royal family charges on his treasury; they received support rather from lands allotted to them. In the shires, which were taking definite form in his time, his will was implemented by his ealdormen. Great landholders, they did not receive salaries from Alfred's treasure chests. Personally loyal to Alfred, they did not require extensive bureaucratic supervision. They were the commanders of the fyrd, they saw to it that Alfred's orders were obeyed in the shires, and they supervised the conduct of local moots, or courts.

Much of the business of Alfred's court was judicial. It heard appeals from local moots, dealt with cases involving great men, and with matters directly affecting the king's position or his estates. So many cases came before Alfred, Asser noted, that he had to hear them even while washing his hands. Below God, of course, the King was the ultimate legal authority in Wessex, and Alfred seems to have had a keen understanding of the importance of law as a foundation for the stable and civilized polity he sought to create.

Accordingly, around 890 he revived a right of royal law-making that had not been exerted for a century. In the text of his laws he describes the procedure he followed:

> . . . I, King Alfred, collected [past laws] together and ordered to be written many of them which our forefathers observed, those which I like; and many of those which I did not like, I rejected with the advice of my councillors, and ordered them to be differently observed.

Alfred's laws, or dooms, provide a valuable insight into the character of the King as well as Anglo-Saxon society. His laws were not an universal code, like those of Justinian or Napoleon. As in most rudimentary societies, laws in Alfred's Wessex were looked upon primarily as being unwritten customs. They were written down only when ancient custom needed to be changed, reaffirmed, or interpreted. Hence, Alfred's dooms dealt with particular matters and did not make up a comprehensive system.

In Alfred's view, law was also a reflection of the divine will. Therefore, underlying custom and the laws issued by previous monarchs were the principles set forth by God in the Bible. The commandments the Lord gave to Moses and the injunctions of the Messiah were, he believed, at the very base of ethical human activity. Moreover, Alfred supplemented the old laws and customs of Wessex with those of Mercia and Kent, for he was not just a West Saxon ruler. He was the overlord of all free Englishmen.

His dooms were designed to promote order in a chaotic society where the kin groups still were accustomed to seek justice by force. Alfred now commanded all men to pursue restitution instead through the courts, and only if that means failed could they legally resort to the traditional blood feud. He set forth minutely the fines that might be imposed for infractions of the laws, from the keeping of vicious dogs, to stealing horses, to murdering a fellow man. More broadly, his dooms favored the new bonds of lordship over the old, potentially disorderly, links of the kindred. A person might fight for a wronged kinsman, Alfred ruled, but not if it involved fighting against his lord. Basic to his justice, too, was a strong sense of equality before the law: "Do not," he enjoined, "judge one judgement for the rich and another for the poor."

Whether as lawmaker or as a general, Alfred consistently worked to defeat the forces of anarchy and barbarism. He lived always with the painful consciousness that he and his people dwelt amid the wreckage of a superior civilization. The crumbling remnants of Roman Britain stood as constant reminders of decline from a glorious past. His trips to Rome had impressed him with the fact that his country was on the dark edge of a great, if decayed, European heritage. Even the small gains that Anglo-Saxon England had made had withered before the onslaught of the Viking raiders. Life was beset with uncertainties, monasteries were plundered, the Anglo-Saxon literary tradition had deteriorated, and even knowledge of Latin was disappearing.

Alfred fought a rearguard action to preserve what could be salvaged. He also struggled to restore what had been lost. Like Charlemagne, he believed that the key to recovery lay in understanding the literature and thought of the past, that through the writings of Christian antiquity the present might be understood more clearly and inspiration might be found for building a better future.

With the clarity of purpose and pragmatism that characterized his other activities, Alfred devised and inaugurated a practical educational program. Through it he hoped to provide Englishmen with information that, as he himself wrote, "it was most needful for men to know." Great works of the past would be translated from Latin into Anglo-Saxon. Then, as many English youths as possible would attend school until they were able to read English writing and, through Alfred's translations, learn from the superior wisdom of the ancients. The young men destined for the priesthood would remain in school to learn Latin, while those entering secular life would leave their studies. The benefits of the program were to be manifold. Alfred knew that educated men were needed in all callings if the English kingdom were to advance, and that an instructed people would present a better defense against pressure from the heathen. He also believed that knowledge that was widespread would not be destroyed as easily as scholarship that was concentrated in just a few monastic centers.

Beginning in the mid-880s the court of the warrior King became a center of learning, as Alfred recruited scholars from northern Gaul and Germany, from Mercia, and from Wessex itself. Most famous of these was the Welsh priest Asser, who became Alfred's intimate friend and admiring biographer. He also became Alfred's teacher, for the King regretted his own ignorance as much as he rued the illiteracy of his people. Late in November of 887, under Asser's guidance, the 38-year-old monarch began to pick out and translate words and sentences from the Latin Bible. Thereafter, whenever he had free time during the day, or during the night when he could not sleep, he worked on his Latin. Alfred also directed the labors of his scholars personally and, as his proficiency grew, prepared several translations himself. Between 892 and his death in 899 he produced versions of five Latin books. Linguists have disagreed about how much assistance he received, but they concur that the King wrote at least four of the works almost entirely by himself. He would go to his scholars for help when he could not puzzle out the Latin satisfactorily; they would explain the sense of the text as best they could, then he would write the English version alone. The series included the histories of Orosius and Bede, the handbook of Pope Gregory, and the philosophies of Boethius and St. Augustine.

It is unlikely that the translation of Bede's *Ecclesiastical History* was Alfred's, but his preparation of Pope Gregory's *Pastoral Care* and Orosius's *Universal History* is undisputed. Gregory's *Pastoral Care* is a major work on Christian stewardship, and it was used by religious leaders, especially parish priests, for centuries. Designed as a handbook of spiritual guidance, its teachings also constituted an excellent dissertation on the nature and responsibilities of secular authority. As such, his precepts did not differ significantly from Alfred's conception of the duties of a Christian King who, like bishop or priest, was also the responsible and loving father of his people. Alfred believed that dissemination of Gregory's principles among his bishops, abbots, and ealdormen would elevate the quality of ecclesiastical and secular leadership throughout his realm. Since Gregory emphasized the church's duty to educate laymen, his teachings also reinforced Alfred's educational program. An Anglo-Saxon copy of *Pastoral Care* was sent to each bishop, each with a costly bookmark. Two copies survive.

Alfred's translation of *Pastoral Care* followed the original text literally. His rendering of Orosius's *Universal History* was more impressionistic and original. Orosius wrote the *History* in the 5th century. It is a turgid and fact-ridden tirade against the heathen, and it celebrated the natural disasters that had punished them throughout history. Alfred condensed and simplified the annals and augmented them with information of his own. He illustrated points with examples from his career as a soldier and administrator and added a whole new section describing the geography and peoples of northern and central Europe in the 9th century. Much of the new information he secured directly from Scandinavian sailors and merchants who visited his court, and his additions transformed the *History* into the best, and almost the only, work of geography in the Dark Ages.

In his last years Alfred turned from the substantial disciplines of history and geography to the more ephemeral realm of philosophy and religion. His translations of Boethius's *Consolation of Philosophy* and St. Augustine's *Soliloquies* stand as testaments to his ethical convictions and religious beliefs. Boethius was a Roman aristocrat in the service of the Gothic conqueror of Rome, Theodoric. Charged with treason, he wrote the *Consolation of Philosophy* in 524 while in prison awaiting his uncertain fate. Rebelling against the caprices of fortune, he ultimately found solace in the concept of a One Supreme Good that transcends all human misfortune and pain. Through the ages the work has stood as an inspiring palliative for the anguish of the human condition. The principle that it advanced, that man possesses resources that enable him to surmount worldly vicissitudes, was also a common one in Anglo-Saxon literature and it was natural that Alfred should be attracted to the general theme of the work.

The Latin of the original is very elaborate, and the philosophical terms and reasoning are complex. Even with the help of his scholars, Alfred could not comprehend fully nor transcribe faithfully the sophisticated Roman dialectic for the more primitive 9th century, so much had learning declined since Boethius's time. So gleaning from Boethius what he and his scholars could and enriching the substance with his personal observations and experience, Alfred created what amounted to a new book. Although Boethius's Christianity has been questioned, Alfred did not doubt that the Roman aristocrat's One Supreme Good was the Christian God. The book is permeated with his faith in Christ's way, and Alfred made its message accessible to his people by using a clear and simple style and citing examples from familiar everyday Anglo-Saxon life. God, wrote Alfred, is like an axle, carrying the wagon of humanity to the heavenly Jerusalem, where men may bask in his presence free from the terrors of Viking raids. Or, he compares God to a floor and a roof which, like a house, shelter the souls of men. In such ways Alfred brought Boethius's and his own teachings to a homely level for the instruction and inspiration of his people.

Alfred described his last book, the *Soliloquies* of St. Augustine, as a collection of "Blossoms." Augustine composed the *Soliloquies* while he was still a young man in the late 380s, and it antedates his more famous *Confessions*. He presented it as an internal dialogue between his spiritual and rational selves, as they debated the question of immortality and the way in which the human soul can learn God's will. Much of the dialogue amounted to very dull and complicated Latin argument; Augustine was, after all, a teacher of rhetoric at Milan. But he was also preparing for his baptism by Ambrose, and the *Soliloquies* testify to his joy at finding ultimate truth and eternal life in the Christian God. This was undoubtedly what drew Alfred to the *Soliloquies;* like Boethius, Augustine had found certainty and comfort in submission to the will of God. Alfred's translation was as direct as he could make it and, as in all his later works, was supported by examples from contemporary Anglo-Saxon life. Some of these, in fact, are of considerable historic importance as descriptions of the institutions and mores of 9th-century England.

In this manner, Alfred prepared for his people's instruction accounts of their Christian past and demonstrations of the truths of their Christian heritage. He did not, like Charlemagne, generate a renaissance, and his policy did not even produce a very substantial increase in literacy among English laymen. Times were too hard, teachers were in short supply, and then, as later, not all men appreciated the value of learning history, philosophy, and religion. Yet, his educational program was well-conceived and practical, and his own translations stand as monuments to his abilities and character. They have become major sources for the history of his life and times. Through them he still speaks directly, not only to his own people, but also to the people of all succeeding generations.

The magnitude of Alfred's literary achievement must not be underestimated. To master Latin was difficult enough, but to render it into Anglo-Saxon was more challenging still. English prose was as yet an unformed and rudimentary medium. The expression of subtle ideas, even the construction of complex sentences, was new to English and, in many ways, beyond its capabilities. Alfred struggled not only with Latin but also with his native language. In doing so, he gave it fresh vitality and sophistication. The importance of the *Anglo-Saxon Chronicle,* the fundamental account of events in pre-Norman England, demonstrates the impetus that Alfred gave to Anglo-Saxon prose. Under his encouragement it became more complete and regular and, during the 890s, copies began to be distributed throughout England. Alfred's own works were still being copied long after the Norman Conquest; the *Soliloquies* has been preserved only in a manuscript of the 12th century.

To attempt a final assessment of the character and importance of a man so far removed in time and in outlook from the 20th century as Alfred, is to risk misrepresentation. Of necessity, few materials have survived the 11 centuries that intervene between Alfred and the present. The most important of them is the *Anglo-Saxon Chronicle,* a contemporary narrative history. A kind of diary, it contains annual entries that relate the events of the preceding 12 months. Sometimes it is merely a bare statement of fact; at others, it includes detailed accounts and commentaries on events of the day. Seven versions still exist, one dating from late in Alfred's reign. Some insight into the King and his time also may be gained from Alfred's laws and a few land-grant charters and coins. Asser's *Life of Alfred,* the first biography of an English layman is, of course, fundamental.

Moreover, the sources, meager as they are, must be used with care. Human nature might be eternal, but men are formed by their times. An admirer like Asser might well have been blind, consciously or not, to certain aspects of Alfred's character, and might have valued or condemned qualities that later ages judged differently. Asser is a valuable source for events and for atmosphere. He may, perhaps, be believed when he writes that Alfred was a good husband to the Lady Ealhswith and a beloved father to his five children, but his other judgments must be suspect. One recent biographer believes that Alfred was a humble man, and another has written of his conservatism and his sense of stewardship and continuity. He might have been like that, but no one can be certain.

Only the record can tell and, stripped of the accretions of legend and uncritical adulation, the record still indicates greatness. By inspirational leadership, the example of personal bravery and imaginative innovation, Alfred led the men of Wessex to military victory and laid the foundations for an united England under his dynasty. He was also a hard-working administrator who brought order to government and law. Certainly he was the most effective ruler in all of Europe since the days of Charlemagne. A man of action, he was also a contemplative man. Believing profoundly in the truth of Christianity, he was also intellectually curious. Above all, he possessed a strong sense that a king must be the responsible father of his people.

Let him speak for himself as, in a preface to the *Soliloquies*, he tells a parable of man's building a shelter on earth so that he might pass to an eternal home in God:

> I gathered for myself stout poles and upright beams and cross-beams, and handles for all the tools which I could work, and pieces of wood for bolts and for slanting supports, to use for all the structures which I knew how to build, the fairest pieces of timber, and as many as I could carry. I neither came home with a single load nor did I want to bring home the whole forest, even if I could have carried it. In each tree I saw something that I required at home.
>
> So I advise everyone who is strong and has many wagons to make his way to the same forest where I cut those upright beams, and fetch for himself more there, and load his wagons with fair twigs, so that he can weave many a fine wall, and raise many a beautiful house, and make a goodly estate, fenced within its own land; and may dwell therein pleasantly . . . .
>
> But He who taught me, to Whom the wood was pleasing, He can give it to me to live more pleasantly, both in this transitory dwelling by this road while I am in this world, and also in the eternal home which He has promised us. . . . I believe . . . that . . . He will make this road better for me than it has been before; that, especially, He will so enlighten the eyes of my understanding that I can find out the straight road to the eternal home, and to the eternal mercy, and to the eternal rest which is promised to us by the holy fathers. So be it.

But Alfred's enduring fame will rest primarily on his prowess as a warrior. At his death in 899 there were still two Englands, Danish and Anglo-Saxon. In the following years a strong Wessex, under Alfred's son and grandson, went on the offensive. By 954 Alfred's grandson Edred had completed the reconquest begun two generations earlier and was recognized as King of all England. The organizational and military base, and the traditions of leadership which made this accomplishment possible, had been created by Alfred. For this reason, if for no other, Alfred earned the title, "the Great." In the long line of English sovereigns, only Alfred of Wessex bears that distinction.

SUGGESTED READINGS

Aside from Asser, there are three good biographies of King Alfred. Charles Plummer's *The Life and Times of Alfred the Great* (New York: Oxford University Press, 1902) is somewhat dated and heavy with the trappings of Victorian scholarship. A thorough if simplistic and uninterpretive account may be found in Eleanor Shipley Duckett's *Alfred the Great* (Chicago: University of Chicago Press, 1956). Best of all, for its readability and analysis, is H. R. Loyn's

Alfred the Great (London: Oxford University Press, 1967). For a broader understanding of Anglo-Saxon England, the work of F. M. Stenton, *Anglo-Saxon England*, 2d ed. (New York: Oxford University Press, 1947), and of Dorothy Whitelock, *The Beginnings of English Society* (Baltimore, Md.: Penguin, 1952), are fundamental. The results of more recent scholarship, especially in the social, agricultural, and institutional areas, may be found in Peter Hunter Blair, *An Introduction to Anglo-Saxon England* (Cambridge: Cambridge University Press, 1956), and D. P. Kirby, *The Making of Early England* (London: B. T. Batsford, 1967).

Chapter 2

HENRY II:
The Angevin Empire

H ENRY PLANTAGENET, King of England, Duke of Normandy and Aquitaine, Count of Anjou and Maine, and overlord of Britanny, Wales, Scotland, and Ireland, founded the Angevin Empire and became the most powerful ruler in western Europe. Throughout a career marked by ambition, ruthlessness, tragedy, and success, he stamped English medieval history indelibly with his will. Feared and respected by those who knew him, Henry II's powers seemed preternatural to many of his contemporaries. St. Bernard of Clairvaux, for instance, referring to the wife of one of Henry's ancestors who reputedly flew out of a chapel window during mass and disappeared, wrote of the Plantagenet family, "From the Devil they came, to the Devil they will go." Absurd though the prediction may seem in the 20th century, it nevertheless demonstrates the impact that King Henry II had on his age.

Henry was born at Le Mans on March 5, 1133, his mother being Matilda, the heiress of King Henry I of England, who also ruled Normandy. The boy's father, Count of Anjou and Maine, was Geoffrey Plantagenet, so named because of the sprig of *planta genesta,* "broom plant," which he wore in his hat. Under ordinary circumstances, young Henry could have expected to inherit Anjou and Maine and spend his life challenging the suzerainty of the King of France. But the circumstances of his boyhood were not ordinary. Through his mother's claim to the Kingdom of England and the Duchy of Normandy, and his father's ambition to extend the boundaries of his counties, Henry Plantagenet grew up believing that a significant part of western Christendom was his by right of birth. From the age of nine, he actively campaigned with his parents to secure this patrimony.

After the death of King Henry I in 1135, England and Normandy were seized by Henry Plantagenet's uncle, King Stephen, who usurped his half-sister's right of succession. In response, Matilda and Geoffrey formulated a simple but effective strategy to unseat Stephen. Matilda organized an Angevin party in England and attacked Stephen there, while Count Geoffrey launched an invasion of Normandy in the name of his son. For over a decade the Plantagenets struggled with the usurper, Geoffrey conquering Normandy in 1144 but Matilda failing to make progress in England. In 1147 she finally abandoned her hopes of becoming a queen and retired to Anjou, never to return to England. Her 14-year-old son was left to decide whether or not he should settle for Normandy and accept the loss of a kingdom.

Henry soon made it clear that he intended to continue the war against Stephen. In 1149, the young Plantagenet carried out an abortive invasion that served notice of his policy, and two years later his hand was strengthened considerably. Count Geoffrey died, and the resources of Anjou and Maine descended to Henry to complement his Norman holding. One year later, the Angevin married Eleanor, Duchess of Aquitaine, who, though older than Henry and the former wife of the French King

Louis VII, brought as her dowry an immense tract of land in central and southern France. In five years, Henry Plantagenet had gone from a Norman Duke to a Prince who controlled lands stretching from the English Channel to the Pyrenees, and from this power base the Angevin launched his final attack on King Stephen.

Landing on the Hampshire coast with 2,000 men on January 6, 1153, Duke Henry soon forced Stephen to come to terms. In the resulting Treaty of Winchester, signed in November 1153, two decades of civil war in England ended with a Plantagenet victory. King Stephen accepted Henry and his heirs as rightful successors to England's throne, and in return the Angevin agreed to do homage to Stephen as monarch. Satisfied with the agreement, Henry returned to France in 1154, and in the autumn he received word that Stephen had died at Faversham. Accompanied by his wife and his two younger brothers, Henry Plantagenet took six weeks to return to England, and on December 19, 1154, he was crowned King, in London, by the Archbishop of Canterbury. Henry, now King, Duke, and Count, was 21 years old when he became the most powerful feudal lord in western Europe.

The man who founded the Angevin Empire was in many ways an extraordinary individual. Physically, Henry Plantagenet was of average height, but his stocky, heavily muscled figure indicated that he was a warrior of great strength. He also seems to have been a relatively handsome man whose red hair and beard, gray eyes, and sharp features gave him great presence and marked him as a dominating figure. Although not unusual in appearance and dress, King Henry did possess some peculiar emotional characteristics. The King had the capacity to change his moods instantly and without much provocation, and many a courtier suffered profound abuse when his amiable sovereign turned mysteriously into a dangerous, shouting man with wild, bloodshot eyes. In moments when anger completely overcame him, the King was capable of destroying everything breakable in a room and ending his outburst by rolling on the floor, chewing the rushes. Oddly enough, his contemporaries never seemed to be disturbed by Henry's behavior, probably because it never resulted in anything so serious as murder. They simply ascribed his attacks of rage to the bequest of his grandfather, Henry I, who was also renowned for an inability to control himself.

The Angevin's appearance and station naturally made him popular with women throughout his domains, and Henry, particularly in the last half of his reign, took his share of mistresses. Some of his more famous affairs were with the sister of the Earl of Clare and also with Alice de Stafford. But in 1173, the year of Queen Eleanor's imprisonment, King Henry took his most famous mistress, the "Fair Rosamund." Inexplicably, this affair was singled out as especially significant, despite the fact that it had no discernible importance, and balladeers, poets, and authors ever since the 12th century have labored over Henry II's "undying" love for Rosamund. Alfred, Lord Tennyson, for example, even went so far as to make Rosamund a ward of Thomas Becket, placing her, disguised as a monk, at the scene of Becket's murder. Perhaps we should be thankful that Jean Anouilh seemed to be unaware of Rosamund when he wrote his play about Becket.

Henry II was, perhaps more than any other English king, a man who loved the business of governing, and he had a restlessness of spirit and a boundless energy that enabled him to pursue his vocation relentlessly. Always on the move, the King kept his Court in a state of continual semi-exhaustion by riding about his lands. Even when he settled down, he stood or paced about, forcing his weary companions to stay on their feet. Yet, despite his constant movement in governing his domain, King Henry seemed to love hunting more than anything else. He delayed one of the most important meetings of his reign, with Thomas Becket at Northampton, for a whole day so that he could go hawking. He also spent what was then a small fortune, £56, to send a ship to Norway to buy falcons when he heard that some especially well-trained hunting birds were for sale there.

Perverse in his habits, dangerous to friends and enemies alike, seemingly possessing an abundance of all human weaknesses and strengths, Henry Plantagenet had the kind of quicksilver personality that is impossible to summarize. His vices made him perhaps too human, and his virtues raised him above many of his peers. Beyond his character traits his significance lay in his ability to formulate policies and then implement them. That, despite all of his petty concerns and passions, was what the founding of the Angevin Empire rested on, and Henry II began to make use of this ability from the moment he was crowned King of England.

Much of Henry II's work in the years immediately following the coronation was dictated by circumstances. After nearly 20 years of sporadic warfare, England was second only to Aquitaine in needing the monarch's attention, so at his crowning he laid the groundwork for what he thought were necessary changes. Like his predecessors, King Henry swore in his coronation oath that he would give equitable and merciful judgments and also keep the peace. These promises alone had proven too vague, however, when Henry I took the throne, so he had supplemented them with an important constitutional innovation: the issuing of a charter of liberties in which the monarch put himself under the law by pledging to revoke "evil customs" and return to the superior law of the past, the law of King Edward. Since Stephen had issued a similar charter, Henry II did too, and while he realized that it limited his power, he also knew that the extent of the limitation depended largely on the personal forcefulness of the ruler. That was the nature of feudal monarchy, and no prince knew it better than Henry Plantagenet.

Personal indeed was the character of Henry II's government, and its function was confusing even to those who administered it. After determining to his own satisfaction that royal power had been eroded during Stephen's reign, King Henry set about re-creating a viable government for the realm. Despite superficial confusion, he succeeded admirably. Since the King was the source of all authority, he was naturally the focal point of the government; but primitive communications demanded that much of the royal authority be delegated. Accordingly, a large number of what effectively were ministers without portfolio were attached to the sovereign administratively and charged with implementing the royal will in the monarch's absence. Known as *familiares regis*, these men advised Henry, acted as his voice in judicial matters, represented him in the provinces, and generally served as vehicles for the transmission of royal authority.

In a kind of loose line organization, the ruler and his familiares were supported by a more formalized governmental structure. Consisting of the Royal Household and the Justiciar, these bodies supervised the details of government. The Royal Household, with its domestic and administrative agencies, accompanied the King on his perpetual journeys around Britain and Europe. It stood constantly ready to see that Henry's letters were written, his food was prepared, his chapel was ready for service, his bodyguard was at full strength, and all of the hundreds of daily needs in the life of a King were met. The Justiciar's office, in contrast, remained in England and was usually located at Westminster, where its responsibilities were, in the broadest sense, judicial. Ruled by the Justiciar, this office consisted of the *Curia Regis apud Westmonasterium*, overseeing legal and financial affairs, and the Chief Forester, whose Justices of the Forest maintained the royal hold over England's woodlands. Between King, familiares, the Household, and the Justiciar, the delineation of power and responsibility was vague; but the stability of the Justiciar's organization combined with the flexibility of the familiares enabled Henry II to develop a government that functioned effectively. Though it baffled the Plantagenet's contemporaries and defies modern attempts at categorization, it worked.

The ability of Henry II to establish a stable regime depended to a great extent on his selection of officials in the first months of his reign. The most important office, that of Justiciar, posed the greatest problem, for while Henry wanted to appoint Richard de Lucy, one of King Stephen's servants, the King understood that to make a commoner Justiciar would offend the great barons. Henry took the path of least resistance. He appointed de Lucy and Robert, Earl of Leicester, as co-Justiciars and got what he wanted, while keeping the nobility happy. Although it was viewed with only moderate interest at the time, the Plantagenet's next assignment of office was to have far-reaching importance. On the recommendation of Theobald of Canterbury, the King installed Thomas Becket as his Chancellor.

Thanks to the film *Becket*, millions now think of Henry's Chancellor as a Saxon, but in truth he came from a respectable, if undistinguished, Norman family. Born in Rouen, Thomas Becket's father moved to London, where he became a successful merchant and served as sheriff of the City. Becket himself was educated both in England and Paris, had worked as a clerk for London's sheriffs, and ultimately entered the household and became the favorite of Archbishop Theobald. By appointing Becket as Chancellor, Henry II was convinced that he had acted wisely. Thomas's competence was certainly a point in his favor, but beyond that he held out the promise of improving Crown relations with both London's oligarchy and the Church. Moreover, the monarch soon learned that Becket was personable, a boon companion, and a close relationship developed between the two that in time was to lead Henry II into a serious miscalculation.

In a matter of weeks, Henry and his officers formulated a program of reform and reorganization aimed at consolidating the Angevin power in England. At a Great Council meeting at Oxford early in January 1155, the King issued proclamations designed to enhance his sovereign authority by ordering that mercenaries be expelled from the realm and that all castles erected without royal permission be destroyed. Many barons secretly scoffed at the commands, no doubt thinking how King Stephen had futilely sought the same goals; but they soon learned that Henry meant to be obeyed. During the spring and summer months mercenaries returned home under intense royal pressure, and simultaneously the King's men besieged and destroyed unauthorized castles. By the beginning of October the monarch felt that his command of England was so strong that at a council meeting he seriously discussed a project to conquer Ireland. The plan ultimately was shelved after the King's mother wrote from Anjou vigorously opposing it. In the end it was just as well that Henry did not commit himself to an Irish campaign, for shortly thereafter his attention was required by the bane of the Plantagenets: interfamilial warfare.

According to Count Geoffrey's will, Henry's younger brother, also named Geoffrey, was to inherit Anjou and Maine when the eldest son became King of England. Having built his empire through planning and action, Henry had no intention of giving away a strategic part of it to his brother, so after his coronation the King ignored Geoffrey's demands for the county. The result was a minor revolt that began early in 1156 which, because of its potential for growth, required Henry's presence in France. Accordingly, the King crossed the Channel with a small force, added more troops in Normandy, and then invaded Anjou. By seizing rebel strongholds with machinelike efficiency, King Henry soon crushed the rebellion and humbled his younger brother. Fortunately for Geoffrey, the experience was less painful than it probably should have been, for the people of Nantes, at the suggestion of King Henry, offered the Dukedom of Britanny to the defeated brother. What had looked like a serious political disturbance in the King's empire thereby turned into a further expansion of Angevin power. Within two years Geoffrey was dead and Henry assumed the overlordship of Britanny. He kept it until the end of his reign.

King Henry's year-long campaign in 1156 was profitable beyond the addition of lands. It gave him a reputation for strength and success, and it provided the kind of stability that he needed in his empire so that he could address himself to some pressing questions in England. Foremost was the matter of the realm's currency, which was in short supply and debased as a result of the maladministration of King Stephen. The monarch called in all of the old coins, had them melted down, and then reissued purer ones, the famous "short cross" pennies that have been described as the best English currency minted up to that period. Additionally, the sovereign and his officers turned their attention to the Crown revenues, which were much lower than they should have been according to the tax base. A series of reforms, dealing largely with the collection of taxes, combined with the institution of a new impost, generously described as a "gift," soon raised the treasury balances and eased the pressure on the royal purse.

Finally, in 1158, the King decided that it was time for his eldest son, also called Henry, to marry, and after some discussion it was determined that a match with the French royal house would be most promising. Doubtless King Henry thought that he might also add the Capetian lands to his empire, for Louis VII did not have a son at the time. If nothing else, the union would surely ease tensions between Henry II and King Louis and reduce French pressure on the Angevin lands. Since the negotiations for the marriage were likely to be delicate, Henry II sent his Chancellor, Thomas Becket, with an impressive escort to Paris. Becket's embassy led ultimately to a satisfactory arrangement for the marriage of Prince Henry to Princess Margaret, Louis's eldest daughter, and though the ceremony was not performed until 1160, Henry Plantagenet had accomplished a great deal in the less than two years he spent in England after Geoffrey's revolt. The King's decisive action proved wise, for his Chancellor had scarcely departed for Paris when the monarch was forced once again to look after his continental domain.

Outwardly, Henry II's return to France in the summer of 1158 appeared to be to suppress a revolt that began in Britanny after Duke

Geoffrey's death, but in view of the fact that the King had little trouble in asserting his authority, his campaign must have had other motives. Trouble in Aquitaine, notorious for the violence and independence of its barons, certainly was another reason for Henry to visit his continental lands, but more importantly, he seems to have wanted to expand his holdings to the Mediterranean by conquering Toulouse. Excepting Ireland and Wales, the expedition to the south of France was Henry's only attempt to expand by force of arms, and despite all of his ingenuity, it failed. Too determined a foe in the Count of Toulouse, the opposition of King Louis, reliance on mercenaries, and overextended communications—all combined to deprive the Plantagenet of victory. But there was one result of the campaign that proved a portent for future developments in western feudalism. On the advice of Becket, the King permitted his English and Norman knights to pay a fee, five shillings, to escape service so far from their own lands. This was one of the earliest cases of exacting a cash payment in lieu of feudal service. It took the Angevin over four years to learn that he could not conquer Toulouse; and while all of that time was not devoted exclusively to the southern campaign, he learned a valuable lesson from his experiences. When Henry II landed in England in January 1163, after nearly a five-year absence, he was convinced that naked military aggression was rarely worth the cost.

What is easily the best-known and most controversial series of events in Henry II's reign began almost two years before he returned to England, for in April 1161, Archbishop Theobald of Canterbury died. An aggressive nature blended with sober judgment had enabled the prelate, after 22 years of struggle, to establish the see of Canterbury as supreme in the English Church. The issue of his successor consequently posed a most important question for the King. Perhaps if he had been present in England, the monarch might have been more cautious in choosing a new archbishop. Possibly if Henry had not known that the Holy Roman Emperor had smoothed relations between church and state by making the Archbishop of Mainz his Chancellor, the outcome would have been happier for all concerned. But as it was, Henry, plagued by military, financial, and diplomatic problems, took the logical and seemingly advantageous step of selecting his Chancellor, Thomas Becket, as a replacement for Theobald. Becket was not even a priest, and he did point out at the time that he and King might disagree in the future. Ignoring the warning, the King forged ahead. He expected Becket to help him restore the relationship of church and state that had existed in the reign of Henry I: a provincially autonomous church acknowledging Rome but directed by Canterbury and protected from foreign influence by the Crown. By asking too much of his Chancellor, Henry II committed an error in judgment that was to plague him throughout the rest of his life.

Much of the conflict that followed Henry Plantagenet's decision had its roots in the peculiar character of the English Church and its complex ties with the Crown. In William the Conqueror's time the King was effectively head of both state and church, but he paid little heed to the actual functioning of the religious institution. Instead, he permitted the Archbishop of Canterbury to run the church, and viewed the sovereign's role as one of securing England's status as an *alter orbis* of Rome by preventing papal interference in the realm. Under the impact of reforms instituted by Pope Gregory VII, the Conqueror's attitude was called into question by the Papacy, and both William Rufus and Henry I had been compelled to give way gradually to Roman pressure in matters such as lay investiture. While finally accepting a compromise, by requiring prelates only to do homage for their lands, Henry I indicated that he was willing to negotiate outstanding differences between the Papacy and the Crown in England. But he made it clear that although he would allow the Papacy more authority in England, he still reserved the right to uphold the broad and customary royal prerogatives concerning the English Church. Papal legates, for instance, visited the *alter orbis* usually whenever the Pope wanted them to, but occasionally Henry I denied them entrance simply to show that he had both the power and the right to do so.

Exactly how much these Crown rights over the church were eroded during the reign of Stephen cannot be ascertained, but one thing seems clear. Stephen did not understand the delicate nature of the Anglo-Norman relationship between church and state; he viewed the papal reforming movement as largely an attack on what he construed to be his proprietary rights over England's Church. Unwilling to negotiate, he reacted violently to even the most innocent suggestions of change. Moreover, he frightened English prelates by viciously persecuting the bishops of Salisbury and Lincoln; and, unable to fathom the reasons for monarchical rights over the church, he bequeathed to Henry II a terribly confused relationship. What exactly was the Crown's responsibility relative to the church? What powers did it entail and what was their purpose? How far should the King go in asserting the uniqueness of the English Church and protecting its independence? These were some of the questions that Henry Plantagenet hoped Becket would help him answer after the Chancellor was elected to the see of Canterbury.

During the spring of 1162, the Plantagenet instructed his officers in England to take the necessary steps to insure Becket's election. By May the monks of the cathedral chapter at Canterbury had voted as their sovereign desired. Becket still had not taken holy orders, so his consecration as Archbishop was delayed until June, but on the second day of that month he was installed in the cathedral. Virtually from the start of his tenure of office, Becket indicated that Henry would have been well-advised to listen to warnings of possible differences between them. The new Archbishop's first significant act was to resign from all of his secular offices, leaving no question about where he would stand should any conflict between church and state arise.

Even though he was far from England, the meaning of Becket's resignations was probably not lost on King Henry. When he returned to his island domain early in 1163, he began to notice subtle changes in his former Chancellor. True, Becket was friendly enough to the King, as he had been for years, but there was a certain indefinable distance in his attitudes, a stiffness that Henry did not recall noting in the early days of his reign. For the moment, Becket's personality shifts did not trouble the ruler, for he had matters of more immediate importance that concerned him. There were questions of land tenure and shrinkage of the lands of the royal demesne that had occurred during the civil wars, questions that could be put off no longer. Also, there were financial problems stemming from fluctuating revenue and excessive expenditure by the royal household. To resolve these issues King Henry called a council to meet in London in March 1163.

At the meeting the more serious matters were dealt with successfully, but there was one issue, not discussed at length in the council, that troubled the monarch. This was the problem of the "criminous clerks," which grew in prominence during the remaining months of the year. Simply stated, criminous clerks were clerics who had committed serious crimes, such as rape, murder, or robbery, but who by virtue of their position could be tried only in ecclesiastical courts. Since the most serious punishment that these courts could impose was defrocking, King Henry thought that more needed to be done to discourage clergymen from committing crimes. Henry II was shocked when he learned that since the beginning of his reign over 100 clerics had invoked the doctrine of benefit of clergy to escape punishment by lay courts. Inasmuch as he wanted to reform the legal system anyway, and the criminous clerks also held potential for serving as an example of the royal relationship to the church, the King decided to act immediately. His determination was to lead him into the greatest of the many crises of his reign. It precipitated his long and bitter quarrel with Becket, which quickly turned from a disagreement over a principle into a clash of personalities.

Claiming that he was merely reviving practices that had fallen into disuse during his predecessor's rule, Henry II began his campaign against the felonious clerks in the summer of 1163. He cited a phrase in canon law concerning wayward clerics, "let them be handed over to the secular courts," as his authority for dealing with the individuals in question. The Archbishop, interpreting the King's maneuver as one designed to bring the church under Henry's thumb, denied both the claim and the authority. Instead, the prelate argued that the clergy had always judged their own offenders, that defrocking was quite sufficient punishment for any clerical crime, and finally he cited the work of the great canon lawyer, Gratian of Bologna, who wrote, "God judges no man twice in the same matter." The weakness in the royal case lay in Henry's claim of a false precedent; benefit of clergy was common in the time of Henry I and had grown to the proportions of a national scandal during Stephen's rule. Moreover, the Plantagenet could not prove that defrocking was insufficient punishment. Yet, Becket's plea was equally weak, for he misunderstood the King's proposal. While the Archbishop's citation of Gratian was correct, he overlooked the fact that Henry did not propose to try anyone twice; rather he wanted the church to try, convict, and defrock, and then turn the offender over to lay officers for punishment. No mention was made of a second trial, so double jeopardy was never really an issue, except for Becket's desire to see it as one. Since neither side was clearly in the right, and the Archbishop thought that he was defending the church from a Plantagenet assault, the question rapidly took on dimensions that had nothing to do with prosecuting an average of less than ten felonious churchmen a year.

Publicly, the first clash between Henry and his erstwhile Chancellor came at a council meeting early in October 1163. The monarch, pointing out that the loss of holy orders was a weak deterrent to crime, demanded that the church honor his claim to punish the guilty. In his answer, Becket described the royal request as an innovation and ominously begged Henry not to pursue this course and inaugurate a dangerous struggle between the government and the church. King Henry, changing his tack, attempted to trick the prelate by pleading that the clergy agree to obey the "royal customs," but Becket saw through the ruse and agreed on behalf of the church with the reservation to obey "saving their order." Although frustrated by Becket's tactics at the meeting, King Henry soon received help from an improbable source. Pope Alexander III, who under ordinary conditions would have supported the Archbishop, felt constrained instead to back the Plantagenet. The existence of the anti-Pope, Victor IV, made it impossible for him to challenge the English King, since he needed Henry's friendship. As a result, the Pontiff sent letters to Becket ordering him to submit to the monarch's orders, and early in January 1164, the Archbishop informed Henry that he would comply with the royal demands. The King, conscious of the impact of Becket's public opposition to the Crown, insisted that the prelate submit publicly; and a meeting was arranged near Salisbury to resolve the dispute.

At the meeting, Henry Plantagenet was at his devious best, for he hoped to capitalize on the Pope's injunction to Becket. On the evening of January 25, 1164, all of the concerned parties came together and the Archbishop promised to yield to the King's stipulation. The barons and the bishops, satisfied that the quarrel was ended, went to bed thinking that a costly struggle had been averted, but it was a false security. The next day, Becket was presented with a document to sign that left him stunned, for King Henry had commanded all of the barons old enough to remember his grandfather's time to draw up a code containing the ancient customs and practices of England. This code, known as the Constitutions of Clarendon, effectively enmeshed the church's judicial system in a royal net, and Becket, after reading the document, categorically refused to put his seal to it. Claiming that the Constitutions were not time-honored English practices, but rather sinister innovations, the Archbishop would do no more than reluctantly assent to the proposal verbally. Henry II, on the brink of victory, had gone too far, for he had driven his former friend into a position that made any future compromise impossible.

There were 16 clauses in the Constitutions of Clarendon. Five were singled out by Becket as utterly unacceptable. Two of these clauses aimed at taking cases involving lands held by the clergy out of ecclesiastical courts and placing them under the jurisdiction of lay courts. Two others dealt with preventing legal appeals beyond the Archbishop of Canterbury's court to the Papal Curia and with keeping English clerics resident in England. The last clause brought up the issue of criminous clerks, and required that churchmen who pleaded benefit of clergy and were found guilty in a church court should then be turned over to the secular authorities after defrocking. The Archbishop found these clauses so repugnant that he was determined to have his verbal agreement to the Constitutions abrogated, and to accomplish this he decided to stop saying mass until the Pope absolved him from his oath to obey the document. This tactic overlooked the difficulties of Pope Alexander, who promptly sent a letter ordering Becket to resume celebrating mass but said nothing about the requested absolution. His rebellious spirit rising, the Archbishop then tried to flee from England; but he failed twice and accomplished nothing more than alienating King Henry further.

Henry II was a dangerous and vengeful enemy, and he set about destroying Thomas Becket. First, the King began supporting opponents of the prelate by exploiting the traditional rivalry between the Archbishoprics of York and Canterbury, and then he used the Crown's influence to develop an anti-Becket party among the higher clergy. Moreover, he tried to humiliate the Archbishop by bringing him before royal courts on a series of petty charges, but Becket countered by appealing his case to the Papal Court. By November 1164, however, the Archbishop had taken all the royal harassment that he could stand; and having no other choice than to flee or give in, he left the country.

When news of Becket's flight reached the King, his companions thought that they would be subjected to the greatest of all Plantagenet rages. Instead, Henry was quietly reflective, for he had anticipated the Archbishop's escape and had already decided that Becket's exile was the best solution to the impasse. A royal embassy was sent to plead King Henry's case before Pope Alexander, himself an exile because the anti-Pope had taken Rome. While Alexander let it be known that he was sympathetic to Becket, no active measures were taken against Henry. Disappointed with papal timorousness, the Archbishop temporarily retired to the abbey at Pontigny, where he stayed until the summer of 1166. Henry II, pleased with Alexander's inaction, turned his efforts back toward the questions of legal reform that had begun the controversy.

For English history, the Archbishop's exile had ramifications far beyond the struggle between King and prelate. Throughout 1165 Henry II had his officials collect data, study the various aspects of England's legal system, and formulate some important policies of change. Early in 1166 all of this effort came to a climax when the Court, meeting again at Clarendon, promulgated the Assize of Clarendon. Although not as famous as the Constitutions, the Assize of Clarendon had substantial impact, for it was primarily responsible for establishing King Henry's reputation as a founder of English Common Law. The aim of the document was not, as has sometimes been claimed, to bring the administration of justice totally under royal control, but rather it was designed to eliminate lawlessness in England so far as that was possible in the 12th century. Henry's principal instruments to achieve this were the itinerant justices.

Usually important courtiers, these justices served the dual purpose of forming a link between local and central government and also increasing the effectiveness of the legal system. Armed with royal commissions, they traveled about the country, authorized to hold trials concerning questions of the King's judgment-cases beyond the competence of the shire courts and the sheriffs. Since the justices reported to the Curia Regis apud Westmonasterium, they extended the judicial authority of that body throughout the realm. But their powers did not end with legal supervision. They also saw that the King's will in financial matters was obeyed, and frequently they played key roles in levying and equipping troops in the shires. Although the personnel of this body changed often, nearly all of Henry's familiares served as itinerant justices. There was a coherence to their activity that was vital to Henry II, for by expanding the power of the Crown they made it pervasive in England; that was perhaps the Plantagenet's most notable achievement. Henry used the justices with discretion, however, for he carefully arranged their duties so that they would not infringe on the judicial prerogatives of the nobility. This was probably the wisest feature of his policy. Soon after the Assize of Clarendon was issued the quarrel with Becket flared up again. The King was to need all of the support that he could muster.

The last act in the tragedy of Henry II and Thomas Becket began in the late spring of 1166. The Archbishop, who up to that time had confined his attacks on the King to plotting, began to threaten to use his powers of excommunication and interdict. Henry, justifiably concerned, maneuvered through Pope Alexander to negotiate a settlement of the dispute. Months of tortuous discussions, futile meetings, and threats and counter-threats stretched into years. Despite the best efforts of the Pope, his legates, the barons, and the French King, Becket remained sullenly in exile and Henry II did not relax his defiant pose. By 1170, however, the royal cause turned sour, for Pope Alexander authorized his legates to use their power of interdict against the Plantagenet's continental domains. That finally moved the English King to bargain in earnest. At a meeting that began on July 22, Henry and his former Chancellor came to terms in what was tantamount to a royal surrender, for the monarch agreed to withdraw the parts of his judicial reforms that the prelate found unacceptable and also guaranteed Becket's safety. When the King and his adversary made peace there was general rejoicing except by the few who had profitted by the quarrel. Some of the more perceptive observers recorded doubts about the sincerity of the arrangement, and they expected it to collapse in much less time than it had taken to conclude it.

When the Archbishop returned to England after a six-year absence, King Henry stayed in Europe to attend to political issues. In a matter of weeks the monarch was receiving disturbing reports from his island kingdom about Becket's conduct. With incomprehensible tactlessness, Becket was taking reprisals against his enemies, and he showed little discrimination in choosing targets. The King probably expected Becket to excommunicate some barons and churchmen, but when he learned that all of the bishops who had participated in the crowning of his son had suffered the Archbishop's wrath he was nearly overcome with anxiety. That action reflected on the heir-apparent's coronation itself, possibly invalidating it; and since the crowning of the ruler's son in the King's lifetime was judged to be a quid pro quo for political stability, Henry's distress was understandable. At Christmas 1170, an unhappy Henry Plantagenet celebrated the festival in Normandy, and in the course of conversation with his barons he angrily condemned his retainers for letting him "be mocked by a low-born clerk." With this unthinking comment the monarch issued Thomas Becket's death warrant.

Four knights, reading more into the royal complaint than was really there, left the Court and rode hard for the Channel coast. There they boarded a ship for England and ended their unauthorized journey by stabbing the Archbishop to death in his own cathedral. As soon as their absence was noticed in Normandy Henry intuitively guessed their purpose and sent a party to overtake the knights and arrest Becket. The effort was, of course, in vain. On the first day of 1171 a messenger arrived in Normandy with news of the murder in Canterbury Cathedral. Henry II was prostrate with grief. For three days he neither ate nor spoke to anyone, locking himself in his chamber where he contemplated what had caused him to bring about the death of one of his oldest friends. He also pondered the impact that the crime would have on his authority. Ultimately he escaped punishment except for penance and a scourging at the hands of Canterbury's monks, but it is not difficult to imagine how bitter his thoughts must have been on his role in creating England's most revered martyr.

Perversely, 1171 marks both the high and low points of Henry Plantagenet's career, for Becket's death was offset by the expansion of the King's territorial control to its greatest extent. Since there was nothing more that he could gain on the Continent, and he badly needed to escape the spotlight that the murder had brought on him, Henry II turned his interest to the most troublesome and unlikely place in Europe: Ireland. There he hoped both to add land to his empire and to escape the almost unanimous censure that followed the murder. So, early in August, Henry returned to England to prepare for a campaign that began England's domination of Ireland for centuries.

Much of the conquest of Erin had been accomplished before King Henry decided to go there in person. Indeed, the extent of the conquest motivated him as much as anything in the campaign, for while the monarch was quarreling with Becket, an Irish chieftain named Dermot MacMurrough sought the aid of English barons in his attempt to become Ireland's High King. Specifically, he contacted Richard, Earl of Clare, a Welsh marcher lord of skill and ferocity, who agreed to support MacMurrough in return for Irish lands. In May 1169, the first contingent of English knights landed in Ireland, and just over a year later Richard of Clare joined them with reinforcements. Since the Norman-English were able warriors and the Irish were ill-organized and poorly equipped, much of the island fell under Clare's control with ease. By September 1170, MacMurrough and his allies captured Dublin, the center of Irish wealth and political power, and reports of the capture worried Henry II. He knew all too well the independent spirit of his marcher barons, and fear of Clare creating a rival kindom across the Irish Sea led the Plantagenet, with a strong army, to Milford Haven in the autumn of 1171.

After several delays caused by contrary winds, King Henry finally sailed from Wales on October 16, landing two days later on Ireland's south coast. The size of the royal army both impressed the Irish and intimidated Richard of Clare, who surrendered Dublin to King Henry and arranged for the Irish chieftains to do homage to their new ruler. With little more than a show of force, Ireland was thus added to the Angevin Empire; and, systematic administrator that he was, Henry II spent the winter months studying the character of his new prize and estimating how he could reorganize it to assure permanent possession.

It did not take the King long to decide that the Irish tribal leaders were unreliable in a feudal context and could be controlled only by threats of force. That led Henry to make Richard of Clare governor of Ireland with a powerful army at his disposal. A more stable form of control was sought by the King when he summoned the Irish clergy to meet him at Cashel, for he correctly guessed that the strongest and most constant force in medieval Irish life was the church. At the Council of Cashel in February 1172, Henry II persuaded the Irish churchmen to accept a body of regulations that brought Irish religious practices into line with those of the rest of Western Christendom. Additionally, the monarch granted a number of privileges to the Irish clergy in return for their swearing an oath of homage to him. These agreements at Cashel effectively put the Irish Church under English control, and the meeting was consequently instrumental in assuring England's subjection of the island.

When King Henry left Ireland on April 17, 1172, he calculated that the island could easily be turned into a major fief of the Crown. Whatever joy this realization brought him was, however, canceled by the purpose of his departure, for he had been summoned to Avranches in Normandy to face papal legates and give an accounting of his part in Becket's murder. This meeting, which the monarch feared because of the possibility of the Pontiff's censure, proved extremely dangerous for Henry and caused him to summon all of his wisdom, courage, and statesmanship to forestall a calamity.

Covering nearly 1,000 miles in a month in what his courtiers thought was an unnecessary rush to his doom, Henry II arrived at the cathedral of Avranches on May 21, 1172, to meet the legates. There he swore that he had neither ordered nor had knowledge of the plan to kill the Archbishop, and he submitted himself to whatever punishment the papal emissaries deemed just. Pope Alexander's ambassadors then pronounced their sentence. King Henry was ordered to revoke all new customs introduced in his reign, with certain clauses of the Clarendon Constitutions mentioned specifically. Superficially, it appeared that King Henry abjectly bowed to the Pontiff's will at Avranches, but in reality the formal settlement of the Becket controversy was largely a draw. The sovereign's acquiescence in revoking all new customs was really a sham, for Henry maintained that he had only revived his grandfather's customs at Clarendon, therefore there was nothing new to withdraw. Yet the Plantagenet did agree to affirm the immunity of the clergy from secular justice, and that manifestly was a victory for the Holy See. What appeared on the surface to be a tragic scene where the mightiest Prince in Christendom sought mercy at the hands of the Papacy was in reality a contest between equals where neither got the upper hand.

Because of the relatively light sentence imposed at Avranches, King Henry II was in a bouyant mood when he celebrated Christmas at Caen in 1172. His empire had survived what might have been a devastating blow, and with the inclusion of Ireland had even grown since Becket's demise. The Angevin territories were economically stable, and the royal officials carried out Henry's commands with an efficiency unrivaled in Europe. But under all of this security there was a current of strain in Henry II's holiday gaiety. His eldest son, Henry, known as the Young King since his coronation during the Becket quarrel, had declined to join the Plantagenet family at Christmas, preferring to hold his own celebration at Bonneville. King Henry suspected that his heir's behavior might be the symptom of a new outbreak of Plantagenet internecine struggle, and the monarch's concern was amplified by reports of plotting between young Henry and the French King. The Great Rebellion was about to begin, and the royal offspring were to give Henry II little rest for the remaining 16 years of his life.

Early in 1173 the Young King fled to Paris and joined forces with Louis VII. Deprived of real political power, and a monarch in name only, Henry II's heir determined to use force to satisfy his ambitions, and the French King was a most willing accomplice. Throughout his reign Louis had pursued the goal of expanding the Capetian lands at the cost of the Angevins, but never did he have an opportunity like the one that appeared in 1173. To compound Henry II's problems, his younger sons, Richard and Geoffrey, joined in the Young King's project, probably at the instigation of Eleanor of Aquitaine. The Queen herself even tried to make her way to Paris to improve the chances of success for the enterprise; but she was recognized despite her masculine disguise by one of King Henry's border guards and she was arrested. For years afterward Eleanor was kept in close confinement on Henry's orders to prevent her participation in further conspiracies. With the Queen's thwarted defection and reports coming in of the Young King's growing strength, Henry II realized that the Angevin Empire was in serious danger.

Soon after Easter, Henry's wayward son launched an attack in strength. In addition to his two brothers and the King of France, the Plantagenet heir counted among his supporters most of the important barons of Anjou, Britanny, and Aquitaine. A large number of the English feudal aristocrats also supported his cause. Only Normandy remained firmly under Henry II's control, but the King was nonplussed by the seeming disintegration of his government, for he was confident that he could use the base of Normandy to subdue the rebels. Had he not used Normandy as the foundation stone of the empire in the first place?

The array of forces opposing King Henry seems overwhelming, but that results from the projection of a total war mentality into the Middle Ages. Thanks largely to von Clausewitz, modern warfare centers on the desire to destroy the enemy's military capacity; but in the 12th century this concept occurred to political leaders only in a negative sense. Cautious almost to a fault when it came to military campaigns, medieval princes went to war most unwilling to risk their estates on the dubious outcome of a pitched battle. As a result, warfare consisted of nearly equal portions of bluff, threat, and laborious siege, with all-or-nothing commitments viewed as the path to a fool's destruction. All of the parties in the Great Rebellion, at least in the early stages, were of one mind on the subject of warfare, hence the Young King's campaign was one of maneuver, which his father found little trouble in countering.

After several months of such fighting, with most of the skirmishes proving that King Henry had not lost his capabilities as a warlord, the two sides sat down to do what the war had been started to accomplish, negotiate a settlement. In bargaining, Henry II had few peers, and his enemies were rightly cautious in the discussions. First, Henry II offered to give the Young King substantial revenues and castles in either England or Normandy. Then he suggested that Richard take half the revenues of Aquitaine, along with four major castles, while Geoffrey marry the heiress of the Duchy of Britanny. Considering that King Henry was winning the war, such as it was, the terms were more than generous, but his sons saw instantly that their father was trying to buy them off with revenues and castles while withholding what they really wanted: political power and independence. Urged by King Louis, who stood to profit from Angevin bickering, to reject the English monarch's proposals, the young rebels elected to renew the war in hopes of forcing their father into a more vulnerable position. They would have been better advised to accept the money.

Since the rebels were unable to make progress against King Henry in France, they shifted their main thrust to England. Hoping to conquer the kingdom and use it as a bargaining tool in future negotiations, they sent the Earl of Leicester across the Channel with a body of Flemish mercenaries to lead the attack on the King's loyal barons. Henry, confident in the ability of his English party to hold the island, remained in Normandy to watch over the rebel movements in France. His trust in the stability of the government he had constructed in England was vindicated on October 17, 1173, when the Earl of Leicester's army was annihilated at the battle of Fornham. Eschewing the caution that everyone else in the war observed so carefully, the Earl learned to his dismay that there were good reasons for restraint in medieval warfare. He not only lost his army, he also put the rebel cause in the greatest jeopardy. There was only one hope left now for the Young King: that King William of Scotland, the last important rebel ally, would be able to overcome Henry's forces.

The invasion of Northumberland by the Scots showed some promise, for it was opposed only by the Bishop of Durham, who combined the functions of churchman and royal agent in the north, and it realized some early successes in capturing strong points. Negotiated early in the winter and scheduled to last until April 1174, a truce between King William and the prelate took away much of the momentum of the drive. When the war was resumed, the English forces proved to be too much for the Scots. After losing a number of minor skirmishes and most of the castles that had fallen into their hands, the Scots were finally humiliated when King William was captured on July 13, 1174. The defeat signaled the end of the Great Rebellion, and a good index of Henry II's strength was that he could sit in Normandy and win a war fought hundreds of miles away.

In the final settlement, the Young King and his partisans suffered in varying degrees. Largely in an unsuccessful attempt to establish family unity, Henry II did not punish his sons, but rather granted them some of the revenues that he had offered a year earlier. The main issue of the war from the rebel point of view, political power and independence, was never considered by the Plantagenet as a possible concession, for he knew that if he diluted authority in his domains the Angevin Empire would crumble. Perhaps the harshest requirement of the settlement was directed at King William of Scotland. He was compelled to do homage to Henry II for his kingdom, his vassals were forced to make their oaths directly to the English King, and the Scottish Church was reduced to the status of a satellite of the English Church.

No doubt misnamed, for it was great only in the sense of Henry's victory, the Great Rebellion ended in utter defeat for the turbulent younger Plantagenets and their supporters. But in a peculiar fashion the King's victory was a hollow one. By failing to recognize and contend directly with the causes of the revolt, Henry II assured that it would be continually renewed in the years after 1174. Caught between his sensitivity as a father and the demands for political stability in his state, Henry II could neither bring himself to punish his children ruthlessly nor grant enough of their demands to pacify them. Accordingly, ugly family disputes entailing constant intrigue, the close imprisonment of Queen Eleanor, and periodic warfare were the Plantagenet's lot in the years following the revolt.

Henry II's triumph in 1174 meant that during the remainder of the decade his lands would be sufficiently peaceful so that he might once again turn his attention toward the reforms he thought necessary to strengthen his hold over the empire. Of all the schemes that were discussed by the King and his advisers, the best-known and most lasting concerned the administration of justice in England. Focusing on the itinerant justices, these legal innovations following the Great Rebellion proved to be one of Henry's most effective policies.

Although the itinerant justices were in the broadest sense a revival of an instrument used by Henry I, the Assize of 1166 made it possible for them to become vitally important to England's legal evolution. Indeed, the most recent biographer of Henry II rightly claims that what the justices accomplished between 1166 and 1179 began the era of English Common Law. Their achievement came in three basic steps. First, as a result of the Clarendon Assize the justices were authorized to hold "petty assizes" around the realm, principally to judge cases of land possession. Next, their powers were expanded to enable them to hear cases involving pleas of right, which concerned considerably more than land ownership; their sessions constituted, with certain exceptions, the sitting of the King's court in the provinces. Finally, in 1179, King Henry authorized the justices to combine a feature of the petty assizes, the use of a jury testifying to facts, with judgment of pleas of right. This final step was known as the "grand assize" of the itinerant justices, open to any action for right, and it spread the machinery of Henry's justice throughout England.

To simplify control of the justices, Henry Plantagenet was careful to see that their royal authority was counterbalanced to an extent by local restraints. The sheriffs, for example, were kept as an integral part of provincial justice, and juries of local men tended to prevent the justices from becoming too powerful. Moreover, the King checked his justices administratively. A total of 18 were appointed at any given time, and they were divided into groups of three each. Groups were then assigned to territorial areas containing between four and eight shires, where they would travel and hold their sessions during the year. The personnel of the groups changed often, as did their territorial assignments, so the threat of justices becoming regionally autonomous was negligible. King Henry's political sensitivity was never better demonstrated than in the case of the itinerant justices. By giving them Crown authority he extended his own power, and by cleverly limiting their strength he kept them as useful servants of the monarchy. Disorder was reduced, Plantagenet control was magnified, Common Law was firmly grounded in England's legal traditions, and the most important step to accomplish all of this came in the wake of the Great Rebellion's violence.

The tranquil years of the 1170's saw the Plantagenet King at the height of his powers. Firmly in control of his domains, skillful enough to inaugurate enduring changes in England's institutions, and internationally respected for his wisdom and leadership, Henry II of England was the foremost political figure in Europe. But in 1180 the historical tide abruptly turned against him. First, the Young King and his brother Richard began showing signs of restiveness. Then, the monarch's son-in-law, the Duke of Saxony, ran afoul of Emperor Frederick Barbarossa, was driven off his ancestral lands, and had to seek safety in Normandy. But above all, Louis VII, paralyzed by a stroke, was replaced by his son, Philip, later to be dubbed Augustus; and the new French ruler's attitude toward the Plantagenet was singularly hostile. Henry II, still young by modern standards, but an elder statesman in the medieval period, erred in evaluating the impact of these seemingly unrelated events. Confident that he could deal with any contingency, the English monarch underestimated the abilities of his young counterpart in France.

Philip Augustus, probably the greatest of the Capetians, was the foremost exponent of his dynasty's policy of expanding the territorial sway of the French Crown. Since the most serious obstacle to this goal was the Angevin Empire, King Philip decided to attack the Plantagenets by every means at his disposal. Weaker than his adversary, Philip realized that he would have to develop a technique other than simple force to achieve his object, and he found the solution to this problem in combining the elements of clever diplomacy and exploitation of the Plantagenet family dissension. Although Henry II scarcely intended to do so, he made King Philip's task easier by provoking his sons to rebellion; but this time the struggle was to be more than an exercise for the English monarch.

In the two years following Philip Augustus's accession, Henry's sons intensified their demands for a share in governing the empire. Henry suspected the French King of having a hand in the growing Plantagenet family troubles, but he could not do anything to stop Philip from meddling. King Henry could, however, undermine the apparent French policy by pacifying his children, and he bent his efforts toward that end by demanding that Richard and Geoffrey do homage to the Young King. The royal strategy backfired. Geoffrey grudgingly performed the act of homage, but Richard refused, and instead began fortifying his castles in anticipation of a renewal of civil war. When the conflict began early in 1183, Richard stood against the Young King and Geoffrey, with their father neutral for the moment. Since Richard was badly outnumbered, and Henry II was unwilling to let the Young King impose terms on his younger brother, the sovereign ultimately went to Richard's aid. Much to the French King's delight, the Plantagenet quarrel had in a few months turned into a chaotic struggle of brother against brother and father against son. The Angevin Empire was shaken once again to its foundations by Henry II's inept handling of his children.

Sympathizing with the Young King but supporting neither side, Philip of France waited patiently for the Angevin conflict to reach a stage where he could intervene advantageously. His ambition was frustrated in June of 1183, when the Young King died unexpectedly of a fever in the middle of a successful campaign. This event had a sobering effect on all of the Plantagenets, and within a month the civil war ended in reconciliation between Henry II, Richard and Geoffrey. While the end of the war disappointed King Philip as much as it pleased Henry II, it was really more of a truce than a peace, for Richard, the new heir-apparent, was even more ambitious than the Young King and his abilities were far greater.

Following his eldest son's death, Henry Plantagenet made a desperate attempt to bring permanent peace to his family. In the autumn of 1183, still unwilling to share real power, the English monarch met with his three remaining sons to arrange a distribution of his lands to take effect after his death. The central core of the empire, Anjou, Normandy, and England, was to go to Richard directly, and he was also to be overlord of the rest of the Angevin lands. Britanny was to be held by Geoffrey, and John, the youngest and King Henry's favorite, was to hold Aquitaine as a fief from Richard. Since the father did not consult his sons about these bequests, Henry's plan to smooth familial relations failed miserably. Richard, despite the fact that he inherited the entire empire, was enraged both by the requirement that he surrender Aquitaine and Henry's refusal to give him a voice in the government. Incapable of understanding the viewpoint of his heirs, the monarch demanded that Richard accept the arrangement. In answer Richard fled to Poitou and began massing troops to resolve yet another Plantagenet dispute with force. King Henry's last war was imminent.

In its early stages the struggle between Henry and Richard was more one of maneuver and negotiation than one of violence and bloodshed. Henry thought that he had been quite reasonable by extending an offer to give Aquitaine back to Richard and compensate John with Ireland. Still, the heir-apparent remained hostile, and when war broke out between Henry and Philip Augustus early in 1187, the Plantagenet judged Richard's attitude to be his family's greatest liability. King Henry's worst fears were confirmed during the summer when, during a truce, reports reached him that Richard had gone to visit King Philip and a friendship had evolved to the point where they ate together constantly and even slept in the same bed. The obvious folly of supporting a Prince bent on destroying the empire he was scheduled to inherit seems to have escaped Richard; he was apparently blinded to the French menace by his determination to force his father to grant concessions. Henry realized the danger but was unable to do anything to counter it. His only hope lay in a quarrel arising between his powerful enemies, and that never materialized.

Attacked throughout his empire by Philip, Richard, and rebellious barons, Henry II could only fight holding actions and, like Frederick the Great of Prussia six centuries later, wait for a miracle. As he was driven from one place to another, the mighty Angevin's sense of failure and humiliation rose until it blinded his judgment altogether. Finally, the English monarch decided to make a last stand on June 9, 1189, at Le Mans, the city of his birth. A French army drove him out, however, and the symbolism of flames consuming the city where the Angevin Empire had been born was not lost on Henry Plantagenet. As he fled north, his heel throbbing from a spear wound, the French did not bother to pursue, choosing instead to ravage the rest of undefended Anjou. On July 2, King Henry was approached by French and English barons and persuaded to make peace with Philip and Richard. Racked by fever from the blood poisoning that had begun in his wounded heel, Henry found the journey to the parley difficult. Scarcely able to sit on his horse, Henry II finally arrived at Coulombieres and agreed to the terms dictated by Philip Augustus and Richard.

The meaning of his surrender was probably apparent to King Henry, despite his semicomatose state. But the mightiest Prince in Europe was spared the agony of reflecting for long on the magnitude of his defeat. After the meeting he was put to bed immediately, and on the next day, July 6, 1189, he lapsed into a coma and died. "Shame, shame on a conquered King" were Henry Plantagenet's last words. He was interred at the abbey of Fontevrault where he still lies today.

Much of King Henry II's time and effort was expended outside of England. Indeed, half of his life was spent on the Continent and most of his statecraft was devoted to his European domains. Yet his importance to British history is such that he is usually viewed as one of the most effective English monarchs. In both foreign and domestic activity King Henry left an imprint on England that belies his dying words. Precedents were set for English claims to suzerainty over Scotland and Ireland during his rule. The historic connection between England and France that lasted until Mary Tudor lost Calais resulted principally from Henry's efforts, for while the Conqueror's Normandy was lost to Philip Augustus, Aquitaine remained in English hands until the 15th century. But Henry II's greatest achievement was a domestic one. Through legal and administrative reforms he increased the strength of England's feudal monarchy so that it became in fact what it was in theory: the touchstone of government. In the centuries that followed Henry Plantagenet's death his successors often found it necessary to modify what he had begun in law and government, but the basic elements of his creation, however, remained unaltered.

SUGGESTED READINGS

King Henry II has been the subject of several historians, but two recent biographies, though dissimilar, are the best sources of information about the first Plantagenet monarch. Richard W. Barber, *Henry Plantagenet* (London: Barrie and Rockliff, 1964), through relatively brief, is sound in scholarship and readable. Wilfred L. Warren, *Henry II* (Berkeley: University of California Press, 1973) is easily the most authoritative work on the subject. Ten years in preparation, well-written, and concisely organized, Warren's biography will no doubt be the standard work on Henry II for several years. Other works that may be consulted are: Amy R. Kelly, *Eleanor of Aquitaine and the Four Kings* (Cambridge: Harvard Press, 1950); David Knowles, *Thomas Becket* (Stanford: University Press, 1971); and Thomas M. Jones, ed., *The Becket Controversy* (New York: John Wiley & Sons, 1971), which provides several varying interpretations of Becket and his quarrel with Henry II.

Chapter 3

JOHN WYCLIFFE:
Discontent and Heresy

D OCTOR of Theology, Oxford intellectual, political propagandist, and religious reformer, John Wycliffe has for centuries been viewed as the first in a long line of "Protestant" reformers who shattered forever the unity of Christendom. For anyone who looks hard enough, all of the major elements of 16th-century Protestant doctrines can be found in Wycliffe's 14th-century writings. In them may be seen a denial of transubstantiation, criticism of the worldliness of the higher clergy, and attacks on the power of the Papacy. These, and other assertions in Wycliffe's voluminous writings tempt the student to conclude that Wycliffe's only misfortune was that of writing too early to be appreciated. Yet, to see Doctor John Wycliffe through the glass of 16th-century Protestantism is to misunderstand both the man and the times in which he lived, for Wycliffe is a more satisfactory medium through which to understand the complexities of late 14th-century England than he is a portent of things to come in the reign of King Henry VIII.

Although John Wycliffe looms as a most impressive figure in late medieval English history, and although the Wycliffe Society has done its best over the years to illuminate his career, very little is actually known about him. Most authorities agree that he was born in Yorkshire around 1330 to parents who today would be described as "middle class," and in 1360 he became lord of the manor of Wycliffe, reputedly under the overlordship of John of Gaunt, Duke of Lancaster and third son of King Edward III. The evidence to support these claims, however, is very much open to dispute, and nothing really is known about John Wycliffe until he reached middle age. Whatever training and experiences shaped him as a child and young man will probably never be known, and his humanity is reduced proportionately by our ignorance of the first half of his life.

The first time that John Wycliffe appears in the documentary record is in 1356, when he became a junior fellow of Merton College, Oxford. By then he had earned the Bachelor of Arts degree, and was to use his fellowship at Merton to study for the Master of Arts and theological degrees. Accordingly, when Wycliffe finally emerged historically he provided a good deal of information about himself by inference. His approximate age can be calculated from the fact that he took the first degree in 1356, and the award of a fellowship indicated that he was viewed as a promising student. But most importantly, it is appropriate that the first bit of verifiable data on Wycliffe should be so closely associated with Oxford University, for while he was famous as a political propagandist and aspiring reformer of the Church, he was above all else an Oxford don. That Wycliffe was primarily an academic, more specifically a Schoolman,[1] and spent most of his life in Oxford has frequently been ignored in favor of emphasizing his Court associations and heretical views.

---

[1] *Schoolman* was the term used in the medieval university system to describe a teacher of philosophy, logic, and theology.

When Wycliffe studied and taught at Oxford, it was one of the fore-most seats of learning in the Western world, rivaled principally by the University of Paris. Relatively small, with only six colleges, housing approximately 75 members, Wycliffe's Oxford was a university controlled by and operated for scholars who held bachelor's, master's, and doctoral degrees. The most distinguishing feature of the institution was the over-whelming impact of the Church on the university. Training was almost exclusively theological, and clerics from all over England and neighbor-ing countries went to Oxford to hear the lectures of the great Doctors of Theology and to read the manuscripts containing much of the corpus of medieval intellectual effort. The religious influence affected only the academic side of life at Oxford, for there was little Christian humility and less turning of cheeks among the resident scholars. Indeed, the university seethed with passions that contradicted the Christian teach-ings of forbearance and love, and antipathies were most pronounced between the two broad groups of resident clergymen, secular and regular.[2]

The six colleges with their 75 members were made up exclusively of the secular clergy who wielded great power in the university, but they were numerically unrepresentative of Oxford's intellectual commu-nity. Altogether, there were perhaps 1200 to 1500 clerics and laymen at the university at any given time, mostly living in privately owned halls that tended to be representative of the academic interests or geo-graphical origins of their residents. Thus some halls housed aspiring civil lawyers, while others were filled with West Countrymen, and still others with Irishmen. Unattached to colleges, these hall-dwellers were an odd mixture of regular clerics and laymen who had little reason to feel anything but anger and jealousy at the pretensions of the numeri-cally inferior secular clerics of the colleges. In the quarrels between secular and regular clergy, the attitude of the latter was exacerbated by the knowledge that not only did they have superior numbers; but that they also produced superior intellects. Robert Grosseteste, Bishop of Lincoln and Oxford's first Chancellor, was a regular cleric, as were Roger Bacon, Duns Scotus, and William of Ockham. Against these giants of Scholasticism, the secular clergymen offered with some embarrassment only the "Profound Doctor," Thomas Bradwardine, and later John Wycliffe, whom the monks thought did not quite measure up. What with the struggles between secular clerics, regular clerics, and laymen, the constant bickering between town-dwellers and student-scholars, and the place of Oxford's faculty in deciding the great questions of the day, it is easy to understand how John Wycliffe became the subtle,

---

[2] A secular cleric was one who lived and worked in the outside world and whose activity was not limited by a monastic rule, while a regular cleric was a member of a monastic community or religious order and adhered to its rule.

pugnacious, sensitive, and provocative figure who held such a prominent place in English history from 1371 to 1384.

Viewed as a promising young scholar, John Wycliffe was not expected to remain as a fellow at Merton College for long. The whole purpose of the fellowship was to free him to prepare himself for the Master of Arts examinations. He would then normally be granted a clerical benefice. From 1356 until 1360, Wycliffe followed this normal course of development, but in the spring of 1360 he deviated from the pattern. He was elected the third master of Balliol College. The move from Merton proved to be a wise one, for approximately one year later, on May 14, 1361, he was granted the most profitable "living" in the gift of Balliol College, the rectory of Fillingham in Lincolnshire.

The receipt of Fillingham meant that John Wycliffe had been given a church and flock for which he was responsible; but because he was interested in scholarship and not in the daily chores of a parish clergyman, Wycliffe never actually lived or worked at Fillingham. Since its only value to him lay in its capacity to provide revenue to enable him to work toward his theological degrees, Fillingham made Wycliffe a nonresident cleric. He became, and remained, what he was later to criticize as one of the worst features of the Church. Taking part of the money from his benefice, he hired a priest to substitute for him in Lincolnshire at a minimal salary. He then used the rest of the revenue to hire rooms in Queens College so that he could study for his Bachelor of Theology degree.

If anything, the acquisition of Fillingham proved to be more of a curse than a blessing for John Wycliffe, for while it enabled him to proceed toward his theological degrees, it also dragged him deeper into the corruption he became famous for attacking. The Lincolnshire "living" provided Wycliffe with £15 a year after the deduction to pay a curate, and as his accomplishments and prestige grew, so did the scholar's regard for himself and his dignity. Fifteen pounds a year seemed an inadequate stipend for a man of his promise and standing in the university, so he persuaded the Oxford authorities to nominate him for the award of a prebend and canonry[3] in York minister. This salary and position in York's cathedral obviously would have accentuated Wycliffe's nonresidence, but worse yet, it would also have made him a pluralist. On November 24, 1362, the Pope's reply to the nomination reached Oxford, and much to Wycliffe's disappointment he was denied the plum at York. Instead, the Papacy granted him the prebend and canonry of Aust in the collegiate church of Westbury-on-Trym near Bristol. It paid only £6 13s. 4d., which was pitifully little compared to York, but at least

---

[3] A prebend is the part of a church's revenue specifically allocated for the salary of a resident cleric, and a canon is a cleric serving in either a cathedral or a collegiate church.

it did not require residence. In 1366, when the Bishop of Worcester visited Westbury's collegiate church, he was appalled to learn that all five of the canons were absentees and only one had even bothered to provide a vicar. John Wycliffe was not the one.

Some authorities charge that Wycliffe's first two benefices only whetted his appetite for material reward. That instead of satisfying the relatively few material wants that a medieval scholar should have had, they aroused in Wycliffe not merely a desire for greater reward but something much more dangerous: a supremely arrogant inability to accept frustration in any of his ambitions. Indeed, one highly respected historian has suggested that Wycliffe's raucous and critical voice could have been stilled forever by a few well-timed bribes in the form of Church appointments. Preferring to coerce him, however, the ambitious scholar's superiors only aroused a pride and willfulness in John Wycliffe that in its expression was to create extensive difficulties for the already troubled late medieval Church.

Wycliffe's first major disappointment, and one that seemed to have vitally important personal consequences for the scholar, occurred in connection with the foundation of a small Oxford college, Canterbury Hall. Founded by Simon Islip, Archbishop of Canterbury, this college was inaugurated sometime in the early 1360s. Perhaps its most unique feature resulted from the optimism and good will of the Archbishop, for despite being a secular prelate himself, he designed the college as a mixed society of four regular and eight secular clerics. Moreover, in 1363 he made the monk Henry Woodhall the college's first warden and gave the regular clergy more than their full share of power in administering the college. For all his good intentions, Islip expected too much. The animosity between regular and secular churchmen that was general at Oxford quickly became the predominant feature of Canterbury Hall as well, and incessant quarreling between the two groups finally led the Primate to take steps to convert the college to an entirely secular institution in 1365. By December of that year Woodhall had been dismissed, and John Wycliffe was chosen by the Archbishop to replace the dispossessed monk. Wycliffe's experience at Balliol along with his steadily growing academic prestige made him a natural choice for the post; and because it promised to satisfy his new-found hunger for material reward and recognition, he took up the duties with zeal. Given the background of the appointment, he might have been more cautious with his emotional commitment to the job.

It was not enough that Islip designated Wycliffe as his choice to head the college. The appointment also had to receive the assent of King Edward III as well as that of Canterbury Cathedral Priory. Before these were secured, Simon Islip died, and Wycliffe's archiepiscopal benefactor was replaced by Simon Langham. The new Archbishop's major claim to notoriety was the fact that he was the only monk elected to Canterbury's see between the 12th and 16th centuries. On April 22, 1367, Langham reinstated the deposed monk Woodhall and ordered Wycliffe out of Canterbury College. Unused to such treatment, to say nothing of having little experience with frustrations in preferment, John Wycliffe took the prelate's order in the worst possible grace. Instead of quietly surrendering the college to the monks, he organized the other secular clerics into a determined group and elected to fight the Archbishop's decision. An appeal of the order was lodged with the Pope.

Wycliffe might have saved himself the time and trouble. He and the secular clergymen had no case, but they pressed the appeal despite that legal disability. As costs for the action mounted, Wycliffe showed how deeply he was involved in what he knew intellectually was a hopeless cause. Instead of giving up, he exchanged his rectory of Fillingham, relatively profitable in income, for the much poorer rectory of Ludgershall in Buckinghamshire. The money that he made on the exchange was used to finance the lawsuit, and it proved to be a poor investment. In 1371 the Pope ruled against Wycliffe's appeal and he was officially deprived of the wardenship. Although angry over his losses of Canterbury College and Fillingham, John Wycliffe never seems to have questioned the correctness of the papal decision; only the most religiously partisan historians of Wycliffe's quarrel with the Church see it stemming from this Papal ruling. The monks who had caused all of Wycliffe's grief, however, did not benefit from his objective reasoning as did the Papacy. In a fury, Wycliffe blamed all regular clerics for what had happened to him, and virtually overnight he became the leader of the secular clergymen in their continuing struggle with the monks at Oxford. In a matter of months John Wycliffe became the acknowledged chief academic enemy of monasticism at the university, and he never missed an opportunity to attack monks as individuals or in entire orders.

The first of two great watersheds in the career of John Wycliffe was 1371, when he not only lost his lawsuit over Canterbury's wardenship, and began his bitter struggle with the monks, but he also secured his Doctor of Theology degree and so was drawn by external forces as well as his own contentiousness into England's political life. His last truly theological, academic treatise, *On the Incarnation of the Word,* was produced in 1370, and thereafter his writings were first political and then heretical. Perversely, just as he reached the point in his academic career when he might have achieved the stature of a Grossteste or a Bacon, he put his skills at the disposal of lay politicians.

The temptation to blame Wycliffe's choice of political work on his frustration with the Canterbury College decision is great, but his motivation is not really that transparent. No doubt ambition played a part in his entering the political arena, but the peculiar atmosphere of the period contributed just as much to his fateful choice. After the death of his Queen in 1369, Edward III withdrew from ruling the country, leaving government in the hands of a largely clerical Council headed by William Wyckham, Bishop of Winchester. Wyckham's inability to solve the military and fiscal problems that accompanied the renewal of the Hundred Years' War in 1369 led to one of the gravest political crises of the century. A cabal of laymen led by John Hastings, Earl of Pembroke and close associate of the Black Prince, the heir to the throne, launched a campaign to drive Wyckham and his clerical colleagues from office. At about the same time that Wycliffe was receiving Pope Gregory XI's decision on the wardenship, Pembroke and his friends succeeded in forcing Wyckham's resignation. It was this combination of changing governments, military disasters, and fiscal difficulties that led ultimately to John Wycliffe's becoming a minor politician.

The lay Council that replaced Edward III's clerical advisers in 1371 should have known something about war and finance. It was dominated by the renowned warriors Pembroke and the Black Prince, but John of Gaunt, more political and less warlike, was also prominent. This new body proved, however, no more successful in solving problems than Wyckham had been. The English continued to lose ground militarily, and as costs mounted and the Council felt the strain of paying for the war, a tendency grew among the lay politicians to blame their difficulties on the Church. As Wycliffe was to point out, many of England's prelates were deeply involved in worldly affairs, and their activity created the impression that the late medieval Church was too concerned with temporal matters. The plausibility of this impression made the Church an ideal scapegoat for the troubled lay Council, and through the means of charge and counter-charge a quarrel developed between Church and state that approached in intensity the struggle between Henry II and Thomas Becket two centuries earlier. The two main points of contention were the questions of the Pope's right to tax England's clerics and his right to appoint or "provide" men for English Church offices. As a matter of course the Council cast around for intellectuals who might provide arguments to buttress the government's position, and the end result was Doctor John Wycliffe's entrance into government service as a political theorist cum propagandist.

As nearly as can be determined, the specific event that brought Wycliffe into government service was a complicated question of finance that arose in the Parliament of 1371. A tax totaling £100,000 was to be levied to pay for the war, with half coming from the commons and the rest from the clergy. Two Austin friars defended the government's position on this tax division by arguing, as Wycliffe did at some length in later writing, that it would be beneficial for the Church to pay the levy for she was too materialistic and this would help her back onto the path of righteousness. Moreover, the friars claimed that the Church's moral condition notwithstanding, it was the Crown's right to seize Church property when it was to be used for the common good of the country. While Wycliffe did not make the public plea for this position, it is likely that he was its author, for his later writing as well as his subsequent role in the affair suggest the seminal nature of his thought in developing the Council's stance and its defense.

After considerable debate, the Convocations of Canterbury and York agreed to pay the £50,000, and no sooner did they commit themselves to the Crown's demand than they received word that Pope Gregory XI needed £20,000 to fight a war in Italy. What had seemed to be resolved in the spring of 1372 thus became a major issue once again, for the Council forbade the Convocations to pay one farthing to the Papal collectors. In fact, they even ordered the arrest of one of Gregory's agents to show their determination. At the same time the government complained about the drain of English gold by nonresident French and Italian prelates, and in the process threatened the Pope with the terms of the Statute of Provisors of 1351, which authorized the imprisonment of Papal nominees and empowered the King to expel certain prelates and fill their places as he saw fit. Negotiations were instituted to bring about an amicable settlement of the outstanding issues, and in 1373 the Council sent a mission to the Pope at Avignon, led by the Dominican Bishop of Bangor, John Gilbert. Although Gilbert was singularly unsuccessful in persuading the Pope that he was being unreasonable, he did arrange for a conference to be held at Bruges in the spring of 1374 so that the issues could be finally settled. This Bruges conference led to John Wycliffe's first official government assignment.

In reward for past services and as a promise of better things to follow, Wycliffe was given a new and valuable benefice before he crossed the Channel. On April 7, 1374, he was granted the rectory of Lutterworth in Lincolnshire, and he surrendered Ludgershall without qualms, for his new "living" was roughly equal in value to the lost Fillingham. It was a promising start for the new government servant. Unfortunately the award was not a good omen for the Bruges conference. Leaving England on July 27, 1374, and returning on September 14, Wycliffe went to Bruges as principal assistant to England's chief negotiator, John Gilbert. While it was not known exactly what part John Wycliffe played in the discussions, there is little doubt that the embassy failed. None of the outstanding issues between the English government and the Papacy were settled, and another conference had to be arranged to reach an agreement. Apparently the Council thought that Wycliffe's skills were best used in propaganda rather than in negotiation, for he was not assigned to the second English delegation that went to Bruges.

The Council's decision to use Wycliffe exclusively as a propagandist seems reasonable in view of the nature of his writing in the early 1370s. His particular concern was the theory of lordship, and his pronouncements on the subject show indirectly how the lay politicians could view Wycliffe as a valuable proponent and still be unhappy with him as a diplomat and negotiator. He said exactly what they wanted to hear about political power and said it much more convincingly than they could.

The question of lordship, which was really at the heart of the quarrel between the lay Council and the Church in the 1370s, was hardly new in the 14th century. In varying forms, the question went back historically to the Papacy of Gregory VII, but Wycliffe's era saw some of the most extreme expressions of exactly what lordship was and how it was exercised. Giles of Rome, for instance, articulated the Ultramontane theory of lordship, which stated that the only just form of lordship was derived from the Roman Church. Obviously, this view was an extreme Papalist one, for it subjected all temporal rulers to the Pope. Other philosophers argued, however, that lordship depended less on the Church as a medium for just rule than it did on the lord's being or not being in a state of grace. Richard FitzRalph, Archbishop of Armagh, was also concerned about lordship, and in his great book *On the Poverty of the Savior* he pointed out that conditions for just lordship applied equally to temporal and religious lords. Moreover, he made a special plea for reform of the monastic orders by the Church, claiming that the monkish lords were mostly corrupt and undeserving of the power of lordship. A copy of FitzRalph's book appeared in the library of Merton College, Oxford, in 1356, the first year of Wycliffe's fellowship there, and it probably went a long way toward shaping John Wycliffe's final theory of lordship.

Not really original in his thought on the subject, Wycliffe simply adapted the ideas of his predecessors on lordship to his own needs. Wanting to provide the Council with an argument that would enable them to tax the Church and to intimidate with threats of discipline any prelate who might oppose the government, Wycliffe culled bits and pieces from the works of earlier thinkers and synthesized them to reach the desired conclusion. Ultimately, he reversed the order of priorities of Giles of Rome, arguing that in the chain of power from God to the temporal lord the Church was at best peripheral, for the ruler's state of grace was the key factor in the validity of his lordship. Wycliffe then proceeded, like Marsiglio of Padua, to deduce the rest of his clever theory from the Incarnation, by arguing that the priest represents Christ's humanity and the temporal ruler Christ's divinity. It followed logically that it was the prince's duty, one of the responsibilities of lordship, that he correct the faults of the Church in his realm.

Although it was not until 1379 that Wycliffe produced this theory in final written form, it had been articulated as early as 1373, when two Benedictines, Ughtred Bolton and William Binham, had engaged Wycliffe in debate over his theory of lordship. Wycliffe's significance as a government spokesman can perhaps best be seen in the fact that he replaced Ughtred Bolton as second-in-command to Bishop Gilbert on the Bruges embassy when it crossed the Channel in the summer of 1374.

The failure of the Bruges conference coincided with several other English defeats to make the theorizing of John Wycliffe of little use to the Council by 1375. With English armies unable to make headway in France, the Church inexorably winning its quarrel with the Council, finances still in a crisis state, the King lapsing into utter senility, and the Black Prince dying, John of Gaunt decided that it was time to cut his losses. In March of 1375 Lancaster went to Bruges to negotiate a truce in the war and also to come to an agreement with the Church. Taking the form of six papal bulls dated September 1, 1375, Gaunt's settlement with the Pope was a thinly veiled surrender of all conciliar claims. On the two principal issues over which the quarrel had raged, provision to English Church offices and clerical taxation, the Papal negotiators refused to make any substantive concession. John of Gaunt, desperately in need of peace with the Church, accepted the terms of the concordat; and when he returned to England, he received nothing but abuse for his statesmanship. Lay criticism of the Bruges concordat was such that when the "Good Parliament" met on April 28, 1376, Gaunt and his associates were attacked viciously in the Commons. Several officials were impeached for corruption, and the Parliament petitioned the King to remedy the abuses in the English Church. Although his assessment of the government's weakness was correct, Lancaster clearly miscalculated public reaction to the dispute between Council and Church.

If Gaunt and the Council suffered defeat and humiliation in 1375, John Wycliffe, the government's intellectual champion, paid, at least so far as he was concerned, a greater price for his support. First, there was the frustration of the Lincoln prebend. As early as 1371, Pope Gregory XI had tempered his decision against Wycliffe in the Canterbury college wardenship case by promising him the first available prebend at Lincoln Cathedral. In 1373 the Pontiff repeated his promise to the Oxford scholar. Yet in 1375, when the rich prebend of Caistor fell vacant, Wycliffe was shocked to learn that the Pope had given it to the illegitimate son of Sir John Thornbury, who was a mercenary soldier serving the Pope in Italy. Because of his pride and his belief in his own right to the reward, John Wycliffe overlooked the plausible explanation that the Pope forgot his promise under the incessant drone of thousands pressuring him for benefices. Instead, the irate scholar chose to believe that Gregory's action was part of a conspiracy designed to punish Wycliffe for supporting the Council, and rumors that someone at the Papal Curia was also trying to deprive him of Lutterworth and Westbury only served to buttress his sense of persecution.

Wycliffe's worldly ambitions received a further setback in 1375 when the vacant bishopric of Worcester was filled. For two years the scholar had considered himself a candidate for the post, so his disappointment was great when Worcester along with Lincoln and Hereford were given to other aspirants, all government servants like Wycliffe, apparently without him being considered. The result was that Wycliffe's sour attitude toward the Church was reinforced by a jealous hatred of England's higher clergy.

The attack of the Good Parliament on John of Gaunt gave Wycliffe his first chance to vent his frustration on someone, for the attack was led by the man Gaunt had deposed, William Wyckham. By October of 1376 the Parliament had been dismissed, and Gaunt, furious at having suffered humiliation at Wyckham's hands, determined to avenge himself. Calling a Great Council, the angry Duke first negated most of the acts of the Parliament. He then turned on Wyckham, charging him with malfeasance of office for the period prior to 1371. In the subsequent "trial," Wyckham was found guilty and saddled with an immense fine, avoiding confinement in prison only by virtue of his status as a cleric. Master John Wycliffe, already a Crown servant and having no reason to love the prelates of the Church, played a major role in the attack on Wyckham.

The historical record is fairly clear about Wycliffe's part in the assault on William Wyckham in 1376. Indeed, it provides the first conclusive data that Wycliffe was actually in the employ of John of Gaunt, Duke of Lancaster, for on September 22, 1376, shortly before Wyckham's condemnation by the Great Council, John Wycliffe was called to appear before the Council at the behest of John of Gaunt. The purpose of the summons was simple; Wycliffe was to make the rounds of London's pulpits preaching against Wyckham and in favor of Gaunt's revived anticlerical policies. Accepting the assignment did considerable harm to Wycliffe's reputation. Many powerful individuals, especially in the Church, who earlier had viewed Wycliffe as a brilliant, if renegade, scholar, now began to refer to him as nothing more than a clerical employee of the Duke of Lancaster.

Wycliffe's participation in Lancaster's attack on William Wyckham was a serious mistake, for Wyckham, unable to defend himself, soon found a champion in the person of William Courtenay, Bishop of London. Noble by birth and popular in the City, Courtenay had the ability, connections, and resolution not only to defend Wyckham against Gaunt's attack, but he also singled out John Wycliffe as the chief supporter of Lancaster deserving of attention.

Courtenay's first opportunity to take the field in behalf of the beleaguered Wyckham came in February of 1377, when Wyckham as Bishop of Winchester was summoned to the Convocation of the clergy scheduled to be held in St. Paul's. Gaunt and the Council specifically forbade Wyckham to come within 20 miles of the King; but when, at Courtenay's insistence, the Archbishop of Canterbury ordered Wyckham's attendance and he complied, Gaunt knew that his party had suffered a reversal that was potentially dangerous. As Lancaster suspected, the easy victory encouraged Courtenay to launch an offensive on behalf of Wyckham. His target was Master John Wycliffe, who at the time was not only one of Gaunt's leading partisans but also had been attacking with some vigor the worldliness of the higher clergy.

The thrust of Courtenay's offensive was not very subtle. Using the writings and teachings of Wycliffe, especially on the subject of clerical and civil lordship, Courtenay accused the scholar of holding questionable opinions and demanded that he be examined as a possible heretic. None of the other prelates were willing to cross Courtenay for the sake of John Wycliffe, so the scholar's trial was scheduled for February 19, 1377, at St. Paul's.

On the appointed day Master Wycliffe arrived to face his judges and defend his opinions in the Lady Chapel situated at the east end of the cathedral. John of Gaunt left no doubt about his support for Wycliffe. The Duke not only provided four Doctors of Theology, one from each of the mendicant orders, but he also showed up in person with numerous followers, hoping to overawe the judges. Gaunt's plan to thwart the prelates and save Wycliffe worked, but not exactly in the manner the Duke expected. First, a dispute erupted between Courtenay and one of Lancaster's supporters, Henry Percy, Marshal of England, and after much verbal abuse on both sides tempers were ragged. In this tense atmosphere, Percy then provided the spark for an explosion when he invited Wycliffe to be seated so that the trial could begin. Bishop Courtenay immediately objected, pointing out that unless he were physically disabled the accused must stand before his judges. This merely revived the earlier quarrel between Courtenay and Percy, but soon John of Gaunt himself intervened and threatened the Bishop with physical violence. Courtenay's popularity was such that the Londoners witnessing the spectacle were provoked beyond endurance by Lancaster's behavior. An uproar began that held all of the potential for turning the trial into a bloodbath, and only the escape of the Lancastrians from the cathedral prevented a serious confrontation.

With all of the name-calling and threatening, the reason why prelates, Londoners, and Lancastrians had come to St. Paul's, to examine the possible heresy of John Wycliffe's opinions, was largely forgotten. In fact, the trial never even began, for Percy and Courtenay were at each other's throats well before the official proceedings could get under way.

It is, of course, possible that everything worked out precisely as John of Gaunt had intended. The Duke clearly set out to save his scholarly ally, and the tempestuous diversions at the trial may have been planned to see that Wycliffe ran no risk of condemnation as a heretic. This interpretation, however, probably credits Gaunt with too great a capacity for planning and stage management, for he could not predict with any certainty what Courtenay would do under goading. What caused the tumult notwithstanding, the result was manifestly favorable to John Wycliffe. His writings were not examined by a hostile court, there was no indication that the trial would be rescheduled, and he seemed to be high in the Duke of Lancaster's favor. The trial was nevertheless a loss for the Lancastrians and, consequently, for Wycliffe, for he had been called to London to help Gaunt in his struggle with Wyckham and Courtenay, and he had ended up in great peril and on trial himself. Considerable effort had to be exerted by his patron to prevent a judgment that would have been disastrous for both Wycliffe and the Lancastrian cause. It was hardly a conclusion designed to raise Wycliffe's stock in the estimation of the lay politicians.

Lancaster's rescue of Wycliffe at St. Paul's was, however, only a respite in the attack on the Oxford scholar. Although the trial instigated by Courtenay was not revived, other dangers arose to confront Wycliffe, most notably from his old monastic enemies, the Benedictines. Working diligently to prepare for the Council a critique of bullion payments to the Papacy, Master Wycliffe was unaware that a more serious offensive than Courtenay's was being mounted against him, for the Benedictines did not confine their work to England. Knowing that the scholar enjoyed the protection of Gaunt, then the most powerful man in the island, the monks struck instead in the Papal court with a plan to have the Pope accomplish Wycliffe's destruction.

Actually, the Benedictine offensive was more than a monkish plot to even the score with their chief persecutor at Oxford. Two of the leading figures in the attack were Thomas Brinton, the Benedictine Bishop of Rochester and a close associate of Courtenay and Wyckham, and Adam Easton, a Hebraic scholar soon to become a cardinal. Resident at Avignon and a close confidant of Pope Gregory, Easton was the fulcrum of the Benedictine plan. On November 18, 1376, he had written a letter to Abbot Litlington of Westminster Abbey informing him that a proceeding on the charge of heresy had been instituted against John Wycliffe at the Papal Curia. Easton requested that the Abbot collect all of the writings of Wycliffe and then forward them to Avignon for evaluation. Litlington was made to understand that there was substantial interest at the Papal Curia in Wycliffe's writings on lordship, which were incidentally to have been the basis for Courtenay's examination at St. Paul's earlier in the year.

Considering the normal amount of time consumed by Papal red tape in the medieval period, the action against John Wycliffe developed with unusual speed. By May 22, 1377, Pope Gregory XI had received from Easton and his associates a list containing 50 suspect propositions taken from Wycliffe's writings on lordship, and on the same day the Pope issued several bulls condemning 18 of the propositions specifically. But, the Papal condemnation was not based on the doctrinal impact of Wycliffe's writings. The Pontiff noted that the writings were not yet judged heretical, but rather were condemned as erroneous principally because they were politically unsound. In short, they affected Church government but did not concern Church doctrine, and the author was possibly anarchistic, but until further evidence was produced he was not subject to the normal punishment for heresy. Still, the bulls were sent off, apparently with the intent of silencing and humiliating Wycliffe.

Altogether there were six Papal bulls concerning Wycliffe that emanated from Avignon. One was sent to King Edward III, and it informed him of the finding of the Curia and requested that he cooperate with the Church authorities in whatever final decision was reached in the case of the errant scholar. Another bull was sent to Oxford University. It directed the school's officials to hand John Wycliffe over to the Church's investigators and also to cooperate in obliterating the erroneous teaching of Wycliffe. The remaining bulls were sent to the English prelates charged with investigating the case in detail, most notably Simon Sudbury, Archbishop of Canterbury, and William Courtenay, Bishop of London. These churchmen were directed to examine the teaching and doctrines of Wycliffe closely, to ascertain if he had actually taught the erroneous tenets, to determine if he had wandered beyond simple error in his speculations, and if so, to extract a confession from him, imprison him, and send the confession to the Pope for further action. Superficially, it appeared that Wycliffe's enemies had snared him neatly through the intermediary of the Papacy; but there was one development that they could not foresee. Most of the threat of the bulls was mitigated by the fact that they took so long to be delivered to England. Arriving as they did late in December 1377, they became just another minor part of the political confusion gripping the country, for Edward III had died the preceding June and instability was paramount in the early months of Richard II's minority.

Because of the confused political situation, the scholar's enemies decided that they were not in a position to arrest him at the moment, so they contented themselves with ordering him to appear at St. Paul's in 30 days for examination. Oxford's faculty did nothing to make Courtenay and his associates think that even this gesture would be acknowledged, for the university officials made it clear that they viewed the attack on Wycliffe, Oxford's foremost scholar at the time, as a violation of the university's charter and rights. The furthest Oxford's Chancellor was willing to go was to ask Wycliffe if he would undergo a voluntary house arrest, which he did, confining himself to his rooms in Queen's College to await the next move by Courtenay.

John Wycliffe seemed unconcerned about the forces arrayed against him at the end of 1377. Opposed by virtually all of England's bishops and the Pope as well, the Oxford don calmly wrote, preached, and lectured as he had for years. He was not, however, totally immune to the pressure. As the time of his hearing at St. Paul's drew nearer, he began to worry about plots against his life, and finally he refused to appear at the cathedral. By March of 1378 Wycliffe's fears seem to have been assuaged sufficiently so that he agreed to appear before the bishops and answer their questions. His only qualification was that he make his appearance at Lambeth Palace rather than at St. Paul's. When the prelates agreed to the new meeting place and a royal safe-conduct was secured, presumably by Gaunt, Wycliffe presented himself for trial readily at the end of March.

Wycliffe's Lambeth Palace trial was less dramatic than the one at St. Paul's two years earlier, but the result was remarkably similar. All of the same elements met at the archiepiscopal palace; the bishops, the Lancastrians, and the mob. Before the trial could actually begin, the mob started a small disturbance which was fanned into a major riot. John Wycliffe and his supporters escaped unscathed, and the scholar's enemies, denied their prey once again, accepted defeat as gracefully as possible. Unable to examine Wycliffe and presumably condemn him, the bishops ordered him to cease advancing the opinions cited by Pope Gregory. Explaining that Wycliffe's views tended to fuel dissension in the Church and also upset the laity, the prelates publicized their empty sentence and Master Wycliffe returned victorious to Oxford. For the second time in two years the most powerful churchmen in the island had tried to silence the Crown's intellectual champion unsuccessfully. It is consequently understandable how Wycliffe's feeling of invincibility could lead him into a false sense of security in the months following his Lambeth Palace triumph early in 1378.

As it turned out, Wycliffe's escape at Lambeth was the high point of his invulnerability, for a series of momentous events began at approximately the same time that were to affect his position dramatically. Foremost of these events was the death of Pope Gregory XI in 1378, which led to a major alteration in the institutional structure of the Church. One Pope, Urban VI, was installed at Rome, while another, Clement VII, took office at Avignon; the Great Schism had begun. The Schism had a detrimental as well as a beneficial effect on Wycliffe's career. On the one hand, the weakness of the Papacy made it possible for him to escape pontifical censure because of his role as a government spokesman. Both Popes were anxious to refrain from offending the English government. On the other hand, the lack of Papal leadership against Wycliffe left his suppression up to the prelates of England's Church. Led by Courtenay, the English higher clergy launched their third attack on Wycliffe after 1378, and thanks largely to the rashness of his theological pronouncements their work was made easier for them.

If 1371 was an important year in John Wycliffe's life because it was then that he turned from scholarship to politics, the year 1378 was all the more significant, for during that year he turned from orthodoxy to heresy. Moreover, he won a number of influential disciples to his heresy and started the movement, Lollardy, that most scholars view as the foundation of English religious nonconformity. Before 1378, Wycliffe could, despite his arrogance and the many enemies he made, have submitted himself to his ecclesiastical superiors and in all likelihood he would have been welcomed back into the fold. He chose instead to go well beyond his political teaching, already condemned as erroneous by the Church, and attack the central core of Christian doctrine. By so doing he made himself unique and assured his place in British history, for few before him had so deliberately set up their own judgment on the essential mysteries of Christianity in defiance of the collective wisdom on the subject articulated by the Roman Church.

In formulating an explanation for John Wycliffe's lapse into heresy a number of factors must be borne in mind. Certainly his personality was of key importance, for he appears to have been by nature pugnacious, ambitious, and proud. His profession only exaggerated these traits, for the life of an Oxford don in the 14th century was hardly calculated to temper his inability to admit mistakes or his bent toward intellectual arrogance. Nor can Wycliffe's relationship with his peers and superiors be forgotten, for by 1378 his reaction to nearly any statement by a monk or prelate was reflexive and argumentative. But perhaps the most interesting explanation offered to date for the intensity with which Wycliffe adopted and defended heretical positions is a medical one. Proposed by K. B. McFarlane, this medical analysis points out that since Wycliffe had his first major stroke in 1382, then he probably suffered from hypertension by 1378. That being the case, the course of the disease was such that much of the behavior of his heretical period, such as frenetic activity, overwork, and elevated sensitivity to criticism, may well have been somatic in origin. In short, the scholar was ill and his hypertension contributed to his working himself steadily deeper into heresy from 1378 until 1384.

In its earliest stages, Wycliffe's heretical writings took the form of a number of treatises made public during the year 1378. The character of these early works points out the progressively radical development of the scholar's views. First, there was a provocative tract entitled *On the Truth of Holy Scripture.* In this Wycliffe argued that the Bible should be interpreted literally, which in itself was bordering on heresy but hardly a novel concept. For decades before John Wycliffe was born scholars had debated the merits of literal interpretation, the debate having been resolved by the affirmation that the collective wisdom of the Church superseded the literal meaning of Scripture. Wycliffe rejected the Church's interpretation of the Bible out of hand, however, and claimed that the only source of Christian truth was the Bible. It followed logically from Wycliffe's premise, that Scripture meant what it said and that the Bible could be read with profit by everyone. Accordingly, he suggested in the treatise that the Scriptures be translated into English, for few outside the Church and the university knew Latin. It would appear that in this first of his heretical treatises Wycliffe was, while sketching an outline of the doctrine of the priesthood of all believers, also deprecating the importance of the priestly office and, by implication, those who held it.

John Wycliffe's next tract was, in its way, even more radical and hence heretical, for it rejected the concept of free will upon which most of the edifice of medieval Christianity was constructed. Entitled simply *On the Church,* this second treatise was a grim, predestinarian explanation of man's chances for salvation, which Wycliffe seems to have viewed as slender. Taking some of his arguments from his near-contemporary, Thomas Bradwardine, and others from as ancient an authority as Augustine, Wycliffe proposed that the only true Christian Church was the one composed of those chosen by God for salvation, the elect. All others, no matter what they did, were doomed to an eternity of damnation.

To round off his literary efforts in 1378, Master Wycliffe produced another treatise that had the ring of his earlier political writing. This work was labeled *On the Office of King,* and in it Wycliffe refined and finally wrote down what he had been lecturing about for nearly a decade at Oxford. Specifically, he claimed that Kings were, despite their temporal status, superior to Popes, for the former were vicars of God while the latter were by their own admission merely vicars of Christ. Wycliffe thus endowed rulers with supreme power in their realms, and given his withdrawal from politics, it is unclear why he bothered to stir up the enmity that this tract brought him. The only reasonable explanations are that either he hoped to curry favor with the lay authorities in case his writings got him into too much trouble, or he seriously thought that he had exposed the true structure of political relationships, or he simply fell victim to his own rhetoric and could not stop himself from expressing ideas as they occurred to him.

John Wycliffe's writings of 1378 were, however, merely a prelude to his more serious heretical production of the following year, for in

1379 he focused his attention on the central mystery of Christianity: the Eucharist. It seems that the Eucharist had always troubled Wycliffe, even before he began his career as a renowned controversialist; he could not, despite his leaning toward the Realist side in the Realist-Nominalist controversy,[4] reconcile himself to the problems inherent in transubstantiation as they related to appearance and reality. Throughout most of his adult life, including the period of his deepening alienation from the Church in the 1370s, Wycliffe accepted the Eucharist as an unexplained mystery and declined to speculate on it. Then, in 1379, in *On the Eucharist* he denied the Real Presence as then officially defined by the Church, committing himself to perhaps the most dan_gerous possible heresy. His action is made all the more difficult t' understand by the explanation he offered for his position. He objected, for instance, to transubstantiation because it placed too much reliance on the priest and thus made him too important in the unfolding of the mystery. He also objected to the concept because it subjected the body and blood of Christ to the possibility of accident and indignity at the hands of humans. Finally, he complained that because it was a mystery which could not be explained or understood, it therefore encouraged men to be idolatrous. Supporting his position with arguments that the Gospels gave no ground for believing in transubstantiation, and that the concept was relatively recent in historical origin, John Wycliffe concluded his treatise on the Eucharist by proposing a new doctrine of his own making. Called "receptionism," this doctrine stated that the nature of the wafer and the wine depended entirely upon the state of grace of the communicant receiving it.

Wycliffe's writing on the Eucharist was probably the most important of all his voluminous literary production. His critics were quick to point out that his views really made no sense by any logically recognizable standard, and it seems reasonable to conclude that although he was confident in his criticism of the sacrament he was unable to explain why he thought that he was right. Yet, Wycliffe's writing on the Eucharist is of crucial significance in the history of Christianity, for behind the muddled criticism is a methodology that pleaded for a return to the purer faith and practice of the early Christians. In this, if in nothing else, John Wycliffe is the intellectual predecessor of the Protestant reformers of the 16th century; and it is his use of the historical method rather than his criticism of the Church's corruption that makes him so consequential.

For nearly two years, John Wycliffe suffered little for his writings.

---

[4] The advocates of Realism in this philosophical controversy maintained that abstract or universal terms had objective reality, while the Nominalists held that such terms were necessities of thought and convenient to language, having no corresponding realities.

But by 1380 the views that he espoused, especially on the Eucharist, had caused both a broadening and deepening of criticism against him at Oxford. Indeed, he had gone so far and offended so many that even his reputation as the university's foremost scholar could not save him from official action. By the last months of 1380 the Chancellor of Oxford, William Bardon, who had opposed Wycliffe's radical teachings without effect privately, instituted an official investigation of the scholar's views. Bardon appointed a commission of 12 Doctors of Theology, 6 friars, 4 secular clerics, and 2 monks, and instructed them to examine Wycliffe's writings on the Eucharist. By a close vote of seven to five the commission notified Chancellor Bardon that Wycliffe's views on the Eucharist were, in their opinion, erroneous and probably heretical. They had not the power, of course, to declare the views heretical on their own authority. This decision proved to be a critical one for John Wycliffe, for not only was it the first time that a case had gone against him; it went against him in Oxford, which he had always thought to be the safest of sanctuaries.

While Wycliffe's reaction to the decision may have been one of distress, his behavior revealed only anger and defiance. Informing Bardon that no report of a commission was going to compel him to change a view that he knew in his conscience was correct, Wycliffe appealed the decision. He did not, however, appeal to any ecclesiastical authority, but following his own theory of civil dominion he appealed to the King. Sensing danger, John of Gaunt responded to Wycliffe's appeal on behalf of Richard II by riding in person to Oxford and attempting to persuade the scholar to bow to the commission's decision. Although the evidence is incomplete, what followed approached a compromise. Wycliffe declined to recant his condemned opinions. Indeed, on May 10, 1381, he published a tract entitled *Confession* staunchly defending his views. Yet, shortly after the publication he left Oxford for voluntary exile at Lutterworth. Bardon was happy to see him leave the university, Wycliffe was content with having sustained his rejection of the commission's decision, and Gaunt, apparently the author of the settlement, had given the Crown a reason to ignore the embarrassing appeal.

Having to exile himself from Oxford was not the only indignity Master John Wycliffe had to suffer in 1381. First, many of his more enthusiastic lay supporters began exhibiting signs of faltering loyalty to his cause. His once extensive and powerful lay backing then melted away almost entirely when, coincidentally with his move to Lutterworth, the Peasant's Revolt began. Most historians agree that Wycliffe either was not responsible for the revolt or his culpability was very indirect, but his contemporaries and critics were not so generous in their judgments. They saw a direct connection, for example, between his teaching that the Bible should be read and interpreted by all, which easily translates into enjoining people to think for themselves, and the demands of the peasants for relief from the burdens of manorialism. To make matters worse, the leader of the revolt, a priest named John Ball who had a history of troublemaking, was rumored to have been Wycliffe's student for two years and thus to have been inspired by his teacher to lead the rebellion. These kinds of accusations drove away Wycliffe's remaining lay supporters who were suffering property losses in the revolt. John Wycliffe was thus left at the beginning of 1382 with only a small group of followers, largely clerics and scholars. Though small in number, they were sufficient to ensure the maintenance and spread of Wycliffe's teachings, and it is as much to them as to his own writings that Wycliffe owes his significance in religious history. They are known as the Lollards.

Originally, the term Lollard referred to any heretic or person of suspected religious views, and literally it meant "mumblers." But the followers of Wycliffe gave the term a greater specificity of meaning by making it possible to identify it, rightly or wrongly, with proto-Protestantism. Divided into two distinct groups, an "intellectual" one at Oxford and an "emotional" one near Leicester, these earliest Lollards were diverse in skills and aims. The Oxford group, which was determined to keep alight the flame fired there by Wycliffe, was led by such men as Nicholas Hereford, John Aston, and Lawrence Steven, all well-educated and capable of debating the Wycliffite doctrines with the best of the Schoolmen. In contrast, the Leicester group consisted of a combination Lollard school and conventicle organized by a zealous layman, William Smith, and an ill-educated and unbeneficed priest, William Swinderby. All of the subtlety and talent of the Oxford group was of little use, for that group was the logical target of the English Church when a decision was finally made to stamp out what John Wycliffe had started. Because of the Church's counteroffensive, the future of Lollardy belonged to the Smiths and the Swinderbys.

With Wycliffe in voluntary exile at Lutterworth in 1381, and his more fervent disciples at Oxford rashly propagating his doctrines at the university, it did not take long for the Church to carry forward the work of Bardon's commission. The only stimulus needed was some determined leadership, and that presented itself in 1382 when William Courtenay was elevated to the Archbishopric of Canterbury. The new Primate had as one of his highest priorities the eradication of Wycliffe's views, and since they were being expressed most clearly and persuasively by the Lollards at Oxford, Courtenay attacked Wycliffe's disciples.

The Archbishop's strategy was simple and effective. On May 17, 1382, he appointed what came to be called the "Earthquake Council" and scheduled it to meet at the house of the Blackfriars in London for the purpose of rooting out Lollard heresy. Since the most dangerous Lollards were thought to be those in residence at Oxford, they were chosen for the Council's attention. In proceeding against the Oxford Lollards Courtenay selected 24 propositions from the writings of John Wycliffe, never naming the scholar specifically. The Primate then charged the Lollards with propounding the suspected views and ordered the Council to determine the orthodoxy of the propositions. Why John Wycliffe was not charged along with his Oxford disciples is a question that cannot be answered with certainty. It seems likely that a bargain was struck between Courtenay and Gaunt, giving the Archbishop a free hand in suppressing the Lollards, provided he left the author of their heresy, John Wycliffe, to rest in the peace and quiet of Lutterworth.

In later years, Wycliffe's partisans were to claim that the "Earthquake Council" was packed by Courtenay with regular clergy to secure a decision acceptable to the Primate. That is not so, for the Council was a fair mixture of regular and secular clerics. The body's decision was, however, largely what Courtenay desired. Fourteen of the propositions examined were declared erroneous, and the remaining ten were pronounced heretical. Wycliffe's teachings on, for instance, the Eucharist, the Papacy, confession, and the owning of property by clerics, were found to be undoubtedly heretical, and Courtenay was given the theological justification for smashing the Lollards whenever and however he chose. Shortly after the Council gave its decision, an earthquake shook London, and what normally would have been called the Blackfriars Council received its more dramatic "Earthquake" appellation.

Armed with his Council's judgment, the Archbishop descended on Oxford in the late summer of 1382, calling on the leading Lollards to recant their heresy. Some, like Nicholas Hereford, fled rather than submit to the Primate's demands. Others, Aston for example, made their peace with the Archbishop and were reconciled to orthodoxy. By the last days of November Oxford's Lollards had either been reconciled or driven into hiding, and the intellectual heart of the movement had effectively ceased beating. John Wycliffe, it is true, was still untouched at Lutterworth, and he was still writing furiously in the same angry and heretical vein, but there were now no bright young clerics at Oxford to appreciate the thrust and subtlety of his discourses. Nicholas Hereford's vernacular translation of the Bible, the first to be rendered into English, was nearing completion by the end of 1382, but Hereford could not appear publicly without serious risk. Courtenay clearly had won the third round of his struggle with John Wycliffe, for the Archbishop had reduced Oxford's proud Lollards to impotence and left his old adversary to fume irrelevantly in rural Lincolnshire.

As a movement, Lollardy was badly wounded by the loss of leadership that accompanied the Oxford purge. The head of Lollardy had been cut off, but the body continued to live through men like Smith, Swinderby, and their Leicestershire followers. The scholarly heresy that

Courtenay systematically obliterated was replaced by the semieducated, emotion-laden Lollardy, dominated by pious, well-meaning laymen and unbeneficed clergymen, that was to continue on into the 15th century.

Master John Wycliffe was not required to witness in detail the destruction of the movement he initiated. While the "Earthquake Council" was deciding that many of his doctrines were heretical or erroneous, Wycliffe suffered a massive cerebral hemorrhage that left him too ill to comprehend what was being done to his disciples except in generalities. Recovered, the scholar found himself unable to break the habits of a lifetime, and his remaining months were spent at Lutterworth writing defenses of views that few of his contemporaries were fated to read. On December 28, 1384, just over two years after his first stroke, he suffered a second one while he was hearing mass. Completely paralyzed, the scholar lived for three more days, expiring finally on the last day of 1384. Having never been excommunicated, despite his being the author of at least ten heretical positions, Master John Wycliffe was buried in consecrated ground near his church.

So long as the Great Schism lasted, the Roman Church could not afford to take the drastic measures against Wycliffe that his defiance merited. Even the spread of his teaching to Bohemia, where it inspired John Hus to inaugurate a similar movement, was insufficient to prod the troubled Church to move against the memory of Wycliffe. But when the Council of Constance met to heal the breach in the Church, one of the first items of business after the settlement of the Papal tiara on Martin V was the extinction of heresy, and the man at the top of the Council's list for attention was John Wycliffe. That he had been dead for over 30 years seemed to disturb the Council not at all. His writings were examined, his teaching was condemned on 300 counts, and he was declared a manifest heretic. In 1415, Philip Repingdon, Bishop of Lincoln in whose diocese Wycliffe's body rested, was ordered by the Council to exhume the scholar's remains, burn them, and cast his ashes on the nearest stream. A reformed Lollard himself, and one of the closest followers of Wycliffe at Oxford, Repingdon ignored the exhumation order. His successor, Richard Fleming, also suspected of having Lollard sympathies, resisted the order for as long as he thought prudent and then finally had some bones dug up and burned that may or may not have been Wycliffe's. Thus in the spring of 1428, Master John Wycliffe suffered the only indignity that the Church could inflict on him.

For British history, John Wycliffe's significance depends to a very great extent upon how the scanty information available about the man is approached. Without much difficulty he can be seen as a source of the Protestant Reformation, for most of his doctrines anticipated in one way or another the major views of the 16th century reformers by 125 years. Yet to see in John Wycliffe an archetype of Luther, Calvin, or Zwingli is to do the Oxford scholar a serious disservice. Although his personal ambitions and disappointments loomed large in the course of his career, he was almost entirely a creation of the historic forces that dominated the last half of the 14th century.

Three great developments, political, social, and ecclesiastical, all made possible the career of John Wycliffe and stimulated him to action, and it is as a mirror of these developments that Wycliffe assumes importance in British history. Politically, his career coincides with the last years of Edward III, a forceful monarch who bequeathed to England a devastating war with France and lapsed into senility many years before his death. The result, underscored perfectly by Wycliffe's political activity, was a power struggle between lay and clerical politicians that ultimately settled itself into a controversy between church and state. Creating a political turmoil that manifested itself in nearly every sphere of activity in England, this crisis in leadership was not really resolved until the Lancastrian Revolution of 1399 carried Henry IV into power. Socially, the career of John Wycliffe follows closely after the visitation of the Great Plague to England, for the scholar's first fellowship at Merton was awarded a mere seven years after the disease first appeared in the British Isles. The sociopsychological impact of a kingdom losing between 25 and 50 percent of its population in a matter of months was the temporary weakening of institutional authority and discipline, and it allowed Wycliffe to act with relative impunity so long as he did not threaten the Crown or property rights. In ecclesiastical affairs there can be no doubt that the condition of the Roman Church, first troubled by the Babylonian Captivity and then by the Great Schism, made possible the evolution and spread of the scholar's teachings. If the Papacy had been under less stress to maintain the support of the English, then the Popes might have been more energetic in dealing summarily with Wycliffe. As it was, the Papacy was compelled by temporal considerations to make light of the serious religious threat posed by him, and in consequence he escaped all Papal action except the censure of Gregory XI.

It was, then, as a weather vane for his own time rather than as a prophet for momentous events in the future that John Wycliffe became a character of consequence in British history. His career accordingly is an illustration of the great pressures that strained the fabric of English society during the last half of the 14th century.

SUGGESTED READINGS

Though dated, the standard biography of John Wycliffe is Herbert B. Workman's *John Wyclif* (Oxford: Clarendon Press, 1926), 2 volumes. Two more recent accounts are Kenneth B. McFarlane, *John Wycliffe and the Begin-*

nings of English Nonconformity (London: English Universities Press, 1952), and Joseph H. Dahmus, The Prosecution of John Wyclyf (New Haven: Yale Press, 1952). Valuable studies of Wycliffe's political theory and his intellectual development in the context of Oxford Scholasticism are, respectively, Lowrie J. Daly, The Political Theory of John Wyclif (Chicago: Loyola Press, 1962), and John A. Robson, Wyclif and the Oxford Schools (Cambridge: University Press, 1961). Of the many works providing background information for Wycliffe's career, some of the more useful are: George M. Trevelyan, England in the Age of Wycliffe (London: Longmans, 1909); Margaret Deanesly, The Lollard Bible (Cambridge: University Press, 1920); and H. Kaminsky, "Wyclifism as Ideology of Revolution," Church History, 1963, pp. 57–74.

Chapter 4

WARWICK THE KINGMAKER:
The Last "Over-Mighty" Subject

RICHARD NEVILLE, Earl of Warwick, is best known as the "Kingmaker," and the title reveals the main thrust of his career. His interests and actions were essentially political and it was in that sphere that he established his significance for British history. Powerful, ambitious, proud, and resourceful, Neville superficially appears to be just another feudal noble who sought, as had so many of his class before him, to limit the power of his overlord and expand his own autonomy. But to see so little in the "Kingmaker" is to underestimate him, for he personified many of the features that gave a unique character to 15th-century England. Frequently seen as one of the more dreary times in England's history, the years between the Lancastrian Revolution and the Tudor succession were ones that saw the beginnings of modern government under Edward IV, great social changes stemming from the effects of visitations of the plague, and a lengthy civil war between the houses of Lancaster and York that caused periodic economic confusion. Yet, the career of Richard Neville, though obviously political, reveals a great deal about 15th-century England that does not pertain to wars, plots, and shifting power balances. The kind of society that produced a Neville, the quality of leadership in central government that permitted him to function, and the economic structure that financed his adventures are all revealed clearly, if indirectly, in the activities of England's only "Kingmaker."

Born on November 22, 1428, just 19 days after his grandfather, the Earl of Salisbury, was killed at the siege of Orleans, Richard Neville virtually began life as a political asset to the Yorkist party. His father, Richard, Earl of Salisbury, was the closest ally and brother-in-law of Richard, Duke of York, whose claim to the throne rested on direct descent from Edward III. Knighted at a young age, Richard Neville quickly became an instrument in the Yorkist drive to strengthen their position in the realm, for in 1439 he married the daughter of Richard Beauchamp, Earl of Warwick. While Beauchamp never became the ally that the Yorkists had hoped for, the marriage nevertheless proved fortuitous. Through the deaths of his father-in-law and brother-in-law, Richard Neville inherited all of the Beauchamp estates in the Midlands and on the Welsh border. On July 23, 1449, the scion of the Neville house was created Earl of Warwick through his wife's right to the title. By virtue of his social standing, economic strength, and political connections, the 21-year-old Neville had in 11 years become one of the most powerful men in England.

The rise of the new Earl of Warwick could not have come at a more propitious time for the Yorkist party. By 1450, it was obvious that England had lost the war with France, and hundreds of soldiers returning from the Continent were swelling the ranks of noble partisans in the Yorkist-Lancastrian rivalry. Domination of the weak-willed King Henry VI by his French wife, Queen Margaret, and her ally, the Duke of Somerset, threatened the Yorkists with the power of the central government. Jack Cade's rebellion in the spring of 1450 indicated the seriousness of discontent on all levels of English society, for followers of the man calling himself "Mortimer" included knights, merchants, and peasants. Under the circumstances, the Yorkists felt keenly the value of Warwick's added strength to their cause, particularly when the new Earl appeared in London with 3,000 troops to support his uncle in the autumn of 1450. But a military test of strength between the contending houses was delayed for nearly five years by the threat of armed uprisings, governmental instability, and the confusion that accompanied the conclusion of the French war.

By the spring of 1455, the Duke of Somerset made the fateful decision that precipitated the Wars of the Roses.[1] He called a secret conference at Westminster, invited only his adherents, and plotted a strategy that was designed to force the Yorkists into a military confrontation. Accordingly, Somerset had King Henry call a council of peers, ordering them to meet at Leicester toward the end of May to deal with what Somerset characterized as "threats to the King." Since the only peers who did not receive invitations were York, Salisbury, and Warwick, it was obvious who were supposed to constitute the threat to the sovereign. Realizing that the challenge he had expected for so long had finally come, the Duke of York conferred with his supporters and elected to lead an army to the meeting at Leicester to dispute the allegations of Somerset and settle the issue between the two houses by force of arms if necessary.

Because of his great resources in men and supplies, Warwick figured prominently in this gathering of the first great Yorkist army. Both economically, through his control of vast tracts of land, and psychologically, through his status as a feudal warlord, Richard Neville could summon thousands of men, farmers who knew how to fight, to support him in a military venture. In later years, Warwick was to strip his estates all over England of able-bodied men to construct armies, but in 1455 he had not learned how to wring the most out of feudal loyalties. Assembling 1,000 men in Warwickshire, he marched east to meet his father and uncle, and when Neville joined forces with them on the Leicester road the Wars of the Roses began. In the vanguard of the Duke of York's contingent was a boy of 13, York's eldest son, Edward, Earl of March. At the time, Warwick scarcely noticed his young cousin, but in a few years their relationship was to shape England's history in the middle decades of the 15th century.

Upon learning that the King, Somerset, and a Lancastrian army had taken up defensive positions in the town of St. Albans, the Duke of York and his allies cautiously approached their sovereign. They notified

---

[1] First appearing early in the 19th century, the name "Wars of the Roses" is perhaps the best known phrase describing the Lancastrian-Yorkist struggle.

Henry VI by messenger that they had come to refute the charges of Somerset; but when their appeal for an audience was rejected they decided to attack. By dividing his force into three units, York hoped to smash through the strong Lancastrian defenses of St. Albans and seize the King. The assault of York and Salisbury, however, made no headway; and just as it appeared that a decisive Lancastrian victory was inevitable, one of Warwick's captains took the initiative and saved the day. By probing the defensive line, he discovered a weak point and ordered his archers to attack the position. Soon, the streets of the quiet town were filled with Yorkists, all wearing the red jacket and ragged staff insignia that marked them as Warwick's men, and the Lancastrians found themselves surrounded. Although he had nothing to do with the initial breach of the defense, Warwick immediately took advantage of the turn in the battle, clearing a path through the streets so that his archers could fire into the marketplace. There, surrounded by a wall of armored Lancastrians, stood the befuddled king; and as Warwick ordered his men to "Spare the commons" and "Aim for the Lords," the elite of the Lancastrian aristocracy were slaughtered. Henry VI, left amid the carnage of his bodyguard, was taken prisoner.

Warwick's part in the victory increased his prestige immensely. In a single day, he had become the foremost warrior in England, and he did not hesitate to use his fame in capitalizing on the victory politically. With Somerset slain and the king in the hands of the Duke of York, a Yorkist government was quickly formed, and Warwick, in a position to claim virtually any of the high offices of state, chose what many regarded as a post far below his dignity. He asked his uncle to appoint him Captain of Calais, an office formerly held by the Duke of Somerset and thought to be dangerous because of constant French pressure to seize that last foothold of the English in Europe. Despite its disadvantages, Richard Neville had chosen the post with an eye to the future, for he saw in it the keystone to political power not merely in England, but also in northwestern Europe. It was ideally situated for influencing England's foreign policy, which proved to be Warwick's all-consuming interest, and it also held out the promise of a safe refuge if the Lancastrians managed to regain power. Neville's evaluation of the importance of the post was vindicated many times in the years after he assumed the office in 1456.

Warwick's first impression of Calais was not a favorable one. The physical defenses of the city were virtually in ruins and the few soldiers manning them were unreliable because of poor food and lack of pay. To make matters worse, the city was under constant threat of attack from the sea, for there was no appreciable English fleet available to defend that vulnerable flank. Neville was exhilarated by the challenge. Located as it was between the states of England, France, and Burgundy, Calais appeared to him as a dangerous but decisive enclave holding all of the potential necessary to enable him to rise to true greatness. All, in Warwick's view, that Calais needed to become the touchstone of northwestern European political life was some firm leadership and an infusion of money and supplies. The Earl soon saw that the city got both.

In the fall of 1457, Richard Neville began his great work of strengthening Calais. First, he persuaded his uncle to appoint him to the special office of Keeper of the Seas for three years so that he could shore up the naval defenses of the city. Then he secured the entire tonnage and poundage subsidy, excepting only that from the ports of Sandwich and Southampton, to finance his activities as Keeper of the Seas. Warwick then gathered and equipped a fleet at Calais, and by the spring of 1458 he decided that he was strong enough to act. Upon receiving news that 28 Spanish ships were making their way up the Channel, Warwick launched the first offensive from Calais in many years. In the ensuing battle, fought on May 28, 1458, the Yorkist Earl won a dramatic victory against great odds. His mariners killed over 200 Spaniards and captured six of their great ships; and many thought that the triumph was the greatest English naval victory in nearly a century. Richard Neville's reputation as a warrior spread throughout western Europe, and his ambition and his pride in his flair for leadership grew proportionately. As he had suspected, the Captaincy of Calais gave him the opportunity to enhance his power and prestige.

While Warwick received the acclamation of his Kentish sailors and paid a diplomatic visit to the Duke of Burgundy, the Lancastrians were building their strength in England. Richard Neville scarcely noticed the subtle changes in England's political condition until the spring of 1459, when he learned that Queen Margaret was working to deprive him of his coveted Captaincy. But even that news he dismissed as inconsequential rumor. It proved to be a serious error in judgment.

By the summer of 1459, it had become apparent in England that the Lancastrians were strong enough to unseat the Yorkist administration, and both York and Salisbury made no secret of their concern. Summoning Warwick back from Calais, they mustered their forces for another confrontation with the supporters of Queen Margaret, but their efforts were too late. On October 13, 1459, all three of the Yorkist leaders, meeting at Ludlow with their troops, were challenged by a superior Lancastrian army, and rather than fight a hopeless battle, they fled. Separating to confuse the pursuit, the Yorkists went to their most secure places of refuge: the Duke of York to Ireland, and the Nevilles, along with Edward of March, to Calais. Queen Margaret took control of Henry VI once again, and, along with him, the government. The Lancastrians had regained power in a surprisingly easy bloodless coup. York and his supporters were not, however, defeated, and they still had considerable strength to draw upon. The Duke was very popular in Ireland, where he enjoyed a regal reception when he arrived from Ludlow, and Warwick, safe at Calais, had command of an impregnable bastion from which the Yorkists could launch an invasion of England at their convenience.

Political expedience and Warwick's growing ambition dictated that any plans for a Yorkist reconquest exclude the Duke of York, for Richard Neville was dissatisfid with his uncle's leadership. While Richard of York relaxed in Ireland, Warwick worked tirelessly in Calais, and by the summer of 1460 he had collected enough men and supplies to mount an attack on the Lancastrians. When his forces landed in England they found a fertile recruiting ground in the southern counties. Within a few weeks, the Yorkist strength was such that they met and defeated an enemy army near Northampton, once again capturing King Henry VI. A few days later, led by the Earl of Warwick, the Yorkists entered London with the hapless king and set up the second Yorkist government in five years. However, this time it was an altered Yorkist government, for the Duke of York was conspicuous by his absence. It was closer to a Neville administration, with Warwick directing affairs and his brother George, Bishop of Exeter, becoming Lord Chancellor. Sulking in the north of England, the defeated Lancastrians predicted that Warwick's ambitions would lead to a Yorkist split and thus provide the followers of Queen Margaret with a golden opportunity. Their assessment of the situation was accurate.

In the autumn of 1460, the Duke of York left Ireland and finally appeared in England, entering London with a great retinue and preceded, much to the horror of the more cautious Yorkists, by a banner emblazoned with the royal arms. Leaving no doubt that he had returned to depose Henry VI and make himself king, the Duke of York shattered Warwick's control of the realm. Throughout the Wars of the Roses the issue had always been which side would control the crown, never who would usurp it, and the Yorkist chieftain, motivated no doubt by years of frustration as well as fear of the Queen, had muddled an already confused struggle for power with his claim to the throne. Neither Yorkists nor Lancastrians could, in the fall of 1460, assess the impact of York's tactics, but both knew that the Duke had injected a dangerously novel element into the power struggle.

More than anyone else, the Earl of Warwick reflected the confusion created by his uncle's claim. Outwardly, he embraced and entertained York with the greatest respect, but beneath the veneer of Yorkist solidarity Neville was deeply troubled by the possibility of King Henry's deposition. Personally, he was concerned because York's usurpation would destroy the Neville hold on the government, but his greatest concern was political. He was astute enough to realize that York's ambitions would ultimately split and destroy the Yorkist party. This perception, after a few days of apparent friendship, led to a great quarrel between the Duke and Warwick, with York refusing to deny his claim to the throne.

Warwick, who had led the party for over a year and was responsible for recapturing control of the realm, was not put off so easily by the Duke's argument of legitimacy. Enlisting the aid of his cousin, York's eldest son, Edward, Warwick kept pressing the Yorkist leader day after day to abandon the claim to sovereignty. Finally, the pressure achieved its purpose when the Duke responded positively to the argument that his interests would be best served by a compromise. The result was an arrangement worked out through Parliament whereby the Duke of York was recognized as heir to the throne and given the titles of Prince of Wales and Protector of England. The Duke's new status notwithstanding, Warwick had made his point, for the issue in the struggle remained control of King Henry, and the Yorkist party was still solidly behind the cause of the White Rose.

Richard Neville's successful compromise did not come any too soon. Early in 1461 the Yorkists in London heard that the Duke of York's army, which had gone north to meet the revived Lancastrians, had been destroyed in the battle of Wakefield. The magnitude of the disaster was increased by further information that both York and his second son, Edmund, had been slain. For Warwick, the Yorkist defeat was both a personal and a political calamity. His brother, Sir Thomas Neville, was killed in action; his father was captured, dragged from prison, and summarily beheaded by a Lancastrian mob. The heads of all the Yorkist leaders were placed above the gates of York city, indicating both the harshness of the era and the bitterness of the struggle. The Duke's head was subjected to some grisly Lancastrian humor by being capped with a paper crown.

Despite his grief at the loss of father, brother, uncle and cousin, Richard Neville thought first of the precarious Yorkist position and his own greatly increased resources through the inheritance of Salisbury's earldom. As the Lancastrians swarmed over the north of England, recruiting men and preparing for a march on the capital, Warwick and Edward of March gathered their levies and formulated a strategy for meeting the onslaught of Queen Margaret. At the beginning of February, the Lancastrian horde marched through the Midlands, pillaging as it passed, and while York's eldest son led one force out to meet Queen Margaret, Warwick took command of another army, hoping to catch the Lancastrians in a pincer movement. On February 12, Warwick left London with his troops, but by the time he reached St. Albans he abandoned the pincer strategy and decided instead to take up a defensive position, which left the initiative to the Lancastrians. It was a grave error for the man who enjoyed the reputation of being England's foremost warrior. At St. Albans Warwick was outmaneuvered and his army routed by the Queen's men, and the Yorkist leader was forced to flee westward to join forces with Edward, who was marching hard to head off the enemy drive on London. Warwick finally met his cousin at Chipping Norton, and at the council of war that followed, the groundwork was laid for Richard Neville to become a "Kingmaker." Edward of March asked his Neville cousin, "Where is the King?" "You are the King," was Warwick's reply, thinking that he could control Edward and finally conceding that only a change of dynasty would resolve the dispute. With that, the Yorkists committed themselves to a fight to the death with the Lancastrians. The Kingmaker and his protégé were to win, not as a result of their own strategies, but through forces beyond their control.

The subsequent Yorkist triumph resulted principally from luck. First, the citizens of London, whom Warwick and March had expected to surrender meekly, elected to defend the capital against Queen Margaret and her looting followers. Then, with only the ill-organized City levies barring her path to success, the Queen unaccountably held back her forces. While she waited, presumably for the City troops to change their minds, the Yorkists acted decisively. Upon hearing of London's defiance, Warwick and March rode hard for the capital, and on February 26 their advance column entered the city. The next day the Kingmaker and his cousin followed their vanguard. For the first time in the dynastic struggle, London had freely given its allegiance to a party, and the Earl of Warwick's prestige and personality were instrumental in obtaining the Yorkist victory.

Neville wasted little time in capitalizing on his party's success. Calling upon all of London's citizens to gather at Paul's Cross on the morning of March 4, 1461, Warwick took a crucial step in the dynastic struggle: he proclaimed a Yorkist King with great pomp and ceremony. But this Yorkist King was not the bitter, blustering, and frustrated Duke of York; it was his son Edward, Earl of March, who rode from Paul's Cross to Westminster Hall and took up his duties as King Edward IV.

Warwick's kingmaking and Edward's regal pretensions made many Londoners and the Yorkist supporters nervous, for there was still a Lancastrian army moving with impunity throughout the island. Leaving St. Albans when the Yorkists entered London, Queen Margaret, the King, and their followers had moved northward, settling finally at York to await the inevitable Yorkist thrust that would decide the question of who was really King. Richard Neville, acutely aware of the Lancastrian threat and determined to secure what he had created, acted conclusively. Leading an army, the ranks of which held many sympathetic Londoners, the Kingmaker marched northward, and soon his cavalry screen reported the enemy drawn up in battle formation between the villages of Saxton and Towton. What most observers thought would be the crucial battle in the bloody struggle between Lancaster and York was soon to begin.

Superficially, the Lancastrians appeared to be the superior force. Queen Margaret had managed to field an army of 25,000 men, the largest force ever assembled in England for a battle, and the preponderant majority of the island's nobility were visible in the Lancastrian vanguard. In contrast, the Yorkists had one third fewer men, less than half a dozen noble leaders, and to make matters worse, 4,000 of their troops were still marching to join the army facing Queen Margaret. Despite his inferior position, Warwick elected to attack, and as he did, the battle was decided by a stroke of fortune; the wind, which had been driving snow into the faces of Neville's men, changed, blinding the Lancastrians. The Kingmaker took advantage of this change in the weather to launch an assault, and the enemy gradually retreated before the Yorkist host. At that point the missing Yorkist troops arrived and were immediately sent to the attack. They proved to be the decisive factor. Within an hour the Lancastrian lines wavered and then broke, the Queen's men fleeing for their lives. As the bridges over streams became jammed, troopers in full armor tried to escape by swimming, only to be drowned in the ice-choked water. When dusk came to the battle of Towton the supporters of the house of Lancaster lay strewn over the gory fields. The King and Queen, their son, and the Dukes of Exeter and Somerset escaped to find temporary refuge in the city of York, but 10,000 of their followers were not so fortunate; they lay dead on Towton field or at the bottom of the streams that fed the river Aire.

With the Lancastrian party in ruins, King Edward and his allies returned to London to form a government and prepare for the Yorkist coronation. Warwick, who had played so singular a role in his cousin's success, did not, however, ride back to the capital. He, with his brother Lord Montagu, remained in the north to hunt down the remaining Lancastrians and destroy their strongholds. The Kingmaker, who was confident that he had created a Yorkist dynasty, now proposed to secure it militarily and politically. Enjoying the fruits of victory, the offices, lands, and adulation, would have to wait until he finished the task that had consumed so much of his time and energy for so long.

It took the Earl of Warwick nearly four years to achieve his goal. Despite their defeat, the Lancastrians still held three nearly impregnable northern castles and the leadership of the party remained at large, stirring up discontent. Yet, the sheer weight of Yorkist power ultimately decided the issue of controlling the north. Her hopes at their lowest ebb, Queen Margaret struck a bargain with King Louis XI of France wherein he agreed to supply her with arms and men in return for the eventual surrender of Calais. With this she launched a futile offensive against the mighty Earl in the autumn of 1462. Her tiny force was so frightened, however, by the reports of Neville troops arrayed against them that they fled before fighting. The Queen and her son made their way to France and Louis XI's protection. When a Yorkist force captured the pitiful King Henry VI in Lancashire and sent him to captivity in the Tower, Warwick's task in the north was finished. The Kingmaker returned to Court to begin the great work for which all of his efforts had been merely a prelude: directing England's government by controlling the man he had made a King.

While pacifying the north, Richard of Warwick contemplated what course England should take now that she had a stable government. He particularly considered the relationship of England to the other states of Europe, and like many powerful men before and after him, he saw himself even more triumphant in the diplomatic arena than he had been on the battlefield. Thus Warwick was lured inexorably into backing an adventurous foreign policy that ultimately destroyed him.

Calais, and Warwick's hold on it, seems to have been the base for his concept of a proper diplomatic arrangement for England. As Captain of the city, he was conscious of an independence that a more sober man might have thought illusory. Perhaps, as his most recent biographer has suggested, Warwick hoped to use his control of Calais and his friendship with King Louis of France to carve out a sovereign state for himself in continental Europe. He might also have intended to use his Calais-inspired foreign policy simply as a means of demonstrating to himself and all England that his control over King Edward was absolute. Whatever Neville's motives, the policy that he formulated was antithetical to the traditional English diplomatic stance that had its roots in the origins of the Hundred Years' War. Instead of maintaining the alliance with Burgundy, with all of its economic benefits, Warwick proposed to effect a rapprochement with France. It was this innovative foreign policy that was foremost in the Kingmaker's mind when he returned to the Court of Edward IV in 1464.

Accustomed to command, responsible for the final Yorkist victory, and the most powerful subject in the realm, the Earl of Warwick had no reason to suspect that the inexperienced young King would not acquiesce in his cousin's diplomatic plans. After all, the Earl had put Edward on the throne, and the Neville family had been the truest and most effective servants of the cause of the White Rose. Yet, when Warwick approached King Edward with his scheme for a French alliance he found the monarch noncommittal. Attributing the King's attitude to an inability to comprehend brilliant planning, the Kingmaker assumed that he had only to press his case and make it more lucid to secure the royal assent. Could it be, the Earl speculated, that King Edward was sympathetic to the policy but found the prospect of the prerequisite marriage to a French princess distasteful? As Richard Neville rode toward Reading in the autumn of 1464 to attend a Great Council, he mused over the King's reactions, but he was confident that in the end he would win out as he had so many times before.

So far as the Kingmaker was concerned, the Council meeting at Reading was merely a formality. The Lords spiritual and temporal would assemble with the sovereign, discuss and approve Warwick's plan for a French alliance and marriage, and then the Earl would leave for the Court of Louis XI to negotiate the details of the agreement. Before the Council met formally, however, King Edward called his closest advisers together to explain his real motive for summoning the peers. Richard Neville opened the meeting by raising the question of the King's marriage, meaning of course the French marriage, and Edward's response stunned the assembly. The King conceded that he wanted to be married, but went on to state that he would not have a Valois princess. Instead, he intended to marry an Englishwoman, Elizabeth Woodville, the daughter of Lord Rivers. In the silence that followed, the Kingmaker realized the magnitude of his defeat, for the King had not only rejected Warwick's plans and advice, he had chosen to marry an obscure widow whose husband had died fighting for the Lancastrians. The insult was almost more than the Neville patriarch could bear, but he said nothing for the remainder of the meeting.

Warwick's chance to vent his rage came shortly after the assembly, when he confronted Edward in the royal apartments. The interview that followed could only have occurred in the confused atmosphere created by the dynastic struggle, for few times in British history has a sovereign prince been so abused by a subject who was substantially more powerful than the King himself. The Kingmaker, his anger mounting as he talked, insulted Edward IV grossly and poured scorn on the proposed marriage. Referring principally to the political idiocy of the match, Warwick predicted that it would bring the wrath of all subjects down on the Crown, and the Earl meant, of course, that his own wrath would be foremost. Moreover, Neville charged the King with ingratitude and reminded him that he would not be sitting on the throne had it not been for the expenditure of Neville blood and treasure. With that, the Kingmaker strode out of the room, gathered his retainers, and without royal leave departed for his stronghold of Middleham Castle in Yorkshire. Throughout the tirade, King Edward had remained silent, but his resolve to marry Elizabeth Woodville and through her to raise a Court party to counterbalance the power of the Nevilles remained unshaken. Edward knew full well that his cousin had made him a King, but he also realized that in order to rule he would have to rid himself of the smothering blanket of Neville domination.

Warwick's fury in the wake of the King's announced marriage nearly drove the Earl into military opposition to the royal policy. The Kingmaker's first reaction, for instance, was to dispatch a letter to the French King that led the wily Valois to think that his noble English friend intended to destroy Edward IV and make himself monarch. But in the quiet vastness of the north country, Warwick's anger subsided, and he informed Louis XI that while he intended to continue pressing for a rapprochement with France, he had no inclination to precipitate a civil war. Apparently Neville decided to wait and see exactly what impact the Woodville marriage would have on England's power structure, for reason told the Earl that Edward's decision could just as easily have been one of impulse as one of policy. Accordingly, the Kingmaker remained aloof in Yorkshire, feasting his retainers, corresponding with Louis of France, and receiving messages assaying Edward IV's plans from Neville agents at Court.

As news arrived of the growing Woodville influence over the monarch, Warwick felt the gulf widen between him and his cousin, and the Earl was too experienced a politician to remain inactive in the face of a threat to his power. Alternatives to inaction were plentiful, but only two were attractive to the Kingmaker: to raise an outright rebellion against his sovereign, or to outmaneuver the boy he had put on the throne. Of the two, Richard Neville found the latter most promising, for England in the last half of the 1460s was a conspirator's paradise.

The House of York itself was the most fertile ground for sowing a plot against the Yorkist King, for his younger brother George, Duke of Clarence, openly resented Edward's supremacy and was infuriated by the arrogant Woodvilles. Clarence thus was the keystone upon which Warwick began to build a conspiracy aimed at King Edward. Promising Neville support to the angry royal Duke in an ill-defined plan to unseat Edward, the Kingmaker then looked to his own family to forward the plot. Warwick's brother George, who had been elevated to the Archbishopric of York and held the office of Lord Chancellor, readily agreed to support the plan. The other Neville brother, John, who had been granted the Earldom of Northumberland, was less responsive, and, torn between loyalty to his brother and obedience to his King, Northumberland ultimately rejected the Kingmaker's overtures. At that early stage Warwick was unruffled by his brother's recalcitrance, for the Earl only intended to mount a threat to Edward. For that purpose, the Archbishop was the only essential supporter beyond the Duke of Clarence himself, for the Kingmaker's strategy was to marry his daughter, Isabel, to George of Clarence and then use his son-in-law, who was heir-apparent, to force the King back under the Neville shield. The Lord Chancellor was only too happy to oblige Warwick, for he was an ambitious prelate who viewed his assignment of securing a papal dispensation for the proposed marriage as an ideal means of also obtaining a Cardinal's hat for himself. Before the plot could develop further, however, King

Edward surprised the Kingmaker by agreeing to the suggestion that Warwick be sent on an embassy to negotiate a treaty with the Valois King. Warwick thought that Edward had finally come to his senses and decided to adopt the Neville foreign policy, so he suspended his plans for Clarence and prepared for a meeting with Louis XI. So desperate was Richard Neville to vindicate his French policy that it apparently never occurred to him that Edward IV might be hatching a counter plot.

In reality, King Edward was taking a calculated risk, for by the spring of 1467, when he agreed to Warwick's embassy, he had already decided on a pro-Burgundian alliance and dispatched envoys to the Court of Count Charles. Warwick's mission thus was a sham, designed to dupe the powerful Earl and the King of France, but Neville did not realize this when he left London in May of 1467 to meet with King Louis. So far as Neville was concerned he had only to persuade the French monarch to grant certain economic and political concessions that would force Edward IV to accept a French treaty. It was toward securing those concessions that Warwick bent all of his efforts when he met Louis XI at the village of La Bouille. King Louis, already displaying the traits that were to win him the title of "Universal Spider," played shamelessly on the English Earl's vanity, promising him by thinly veiled hints a sovereign principality in Burgundian territory. The Valois ruler furthermore met nearly all of the demands Warwick made for a treaty, thus giving him the means to force Edward to accept a Neville diplomatic concept. The Kingmaker never guessed that Louis was only trying to buy time and prevent an Anglo-Burgundian alliance, which, with the lone exception of the Earl of Warwick, all of the major parties knew was in the offing.

Armed with agreements and promises, the Kingmaker returned to England overflowing with satisfaction. He was, however, soon deflated, for the extent to which he had been tricked was quickly revealed to him. First, he heard reports of rumors that he had gone to France to come to terms with the exiled Queen Margaret and was consequently a traitor. Then, he noted the smug looks of the Burgundian envoys at Court and realized that Edward's true policy had always been pro-Burgundian. But the crowning insult came with the news that his brother George had been dismissed from the Lord Chancellorship, which all astute courtiers viewed as a prelude to the fall of the house of Neville. Richard Neville's general reaction to all of this crushing news was, however, curiously egomaniacal, for what disturbed him most was the humiliating way Edward had sent him out of the realm to pull off his coup. In short, the Kingmaker was initially angry with himself for being taken in, but he soon turned his fury outward onto the Yorkist monarch and his Woodville allies.

Returning to the north of England to escape the leers of his enemies at Court, Warwick revived his plans for a conspiracy with George of Clarence. The Earl also began sounding out his retainers to discover where they would stand in a conflict between the monarch and his mightiest subject. As Warwick slowly gathered his forces, he kept a close watch on events in London through his agents, and by the beginning of 1468 reports began to arrive in Yorkshire that gave the Kingmaker hope that armed rebellion would not be necessary. King Edward, the Earl's spies reported, had gone too far in rejecting his cousin and wooing the Burgundians, for Charles the Rash, now Duke of Burgundy, was proving a reluctant ally. First, he protracted the negotiations for his marriage to Edward IV's sister far too long for comfort, and then he demanded economic concessions for Burgundian goods in England that, when granted by Edward, seemed to be rousing the hostility of London's merchants and artisans. This, thought Warwick, was only a natural turn of events, for had not Charles of Burgundy been a fervent Lancastrian; should he not demand a high price for giving his friendship to the Yorkists? Although the price of Duke Charles's alliance was high, King Edward paid it, and despite growing unrest in the kingdom, he secured his Burgundian association by sealing it with the marriage of his sister, Margaret, to Charles the Rash in the summer of 1468.

Throughout the last months of 1468, Richard Neville steadily gathered his forces and rejoiced at news of how seriously his cousin's policy had alienated his subjects. By the spring of 1469 Warwick was, with the support of King Louis, ready to use force to erase the insults dealt to the house of Neville by King Edward. Whether or not he intended to go so far as actually to place George of Clarence on the throne is difficult to judge, but whatever else he planned, the Kingmaker meant to purge the Court of Woodvilles and restore himself to a position of dominance. Kept by his grandmother's illegitimacy from becoming King by right of blood, Richard Neville's self-image and ambition would allow him nothing less than the privileges and respect due a maker of Kings.

By 1469 Warwick was so experienced in political subterfuge that, despite his determination to avenge the wrongs done to his family, he gave no hint of his plans. During the first months of the year he was comradeship itself to King Edward, and the monarch returned Neville's good humor by granting lands and revenues to the Earl and his brothers. It appeared that Edward had succeeded in reducing the Kingmaker's strength, for there were no recriminations or cries of betrayal by the Nevilles. But as spring turned to summer, Warwick's plan of revenge was completed. In April, he agreed to the sovereign's request that he go to Calais to inspect the English boundaries, and Edward apparently had no idea that by then hundreds of the Earl's followers were ready for a rising that would restore Neville control of England.

The key man in Warwick's plan was Sir John Conyers, a northern adventurer who had adopted the alias of "Robin of Redesdale," and as Warwick prepared to embark for Calais, "Robin" began an ostensibly popular uprising in the north. At first, King Edward thought that his local officials could contain the disturbance, but as the weeks passed it became apparent that it was more serious than he had thought. Reluctantly, King Edward decided to gather a small force and go north in person to put down the rebels. As Warwick, his brother George Neville, the Duke of Clarence, and the Earl of Oxford all arrived at Canterbury on July 4, Warwick's agents began spreading the rumor that King Edward was illegitimate and that Clarence was the rightful heir of the Duke of York. A week later, the Archbishop of York married Warwick's daughter Isabel to George of Clarence, and on July 20, 1469, the Kingmaker and his party marched on London at the head of a large retinue. While the King and his small force fruitlessly pursued the clever "Robin," Warwick entered London and completed the first phase of his well-planned coup d'etat.

In the capital, Warwick and Clarence proclaimed that they intended to join the King in putting down the rebels, and when news came that Edward's men were deserting, the conspirators mustered their troops and marched north. His force reduced by defections, the monarch was in no condition to resist the Kingmaker's might, so when the mail-clad Archbishop of York found King Edward at Olney and suggested that they ride in company to Warwick's camp the King immediately agreed. Edward IV had been completely outwitted by his cousin, so he elected to cooperate with Warwick and wait for an opportunity to redress the balance of power. Consequently, when King and Kingmaker met at Coventry all was smiles, for the ruler understood the need to dissimulate and the Earl was magnanimous in victory. Warwick, after all, only wanted to control the monarchy and restore Neville power and prestige, and Edward's only thought for the moment was to stay alive.

With the capture of the monarch, the Kingmaker thought that he had realized once again the principal war aim of the Wars of the Roses: control of the government through domination of the sovereign. By the high summer of 1469, however, this proved to be an outmoded concept, for the Earl soon learned that despite Edward's imprisonment in Warwick Castle, the country did not fall mutely into line behind Neville leadership. Edward IV jovially signed all documents placed before him, but throughout the realm some men demanded the King's release, others attacked their neighbors, and effective government ceased to exist. Warwick had miscalculated, for while he had control of the sovereign's person, he had failed in the minds of England's subjects to secure the authority to rule. The Kingmaker's tactics had been flawless but his strategy was faulty, and by September he had resigned himself to the ultimate failure of his conspiracy. He was not, therefore, surprised when Edward rode to York and was met by a large part of the nobility and a loyal army. The king returned to London, and there was nothing Warwick could do to stop him, for despite Neville power and planning the English people wanted Yorkist stability, not the grand stroke of a master conspirator.

Actually, Warwick's loss was not as great as it seemed, for while King Edward controlled London and the southeast, the Kingmaker still held most of the rest of England. The result of their struggle was a stalemate, for neither could rule without the other. By October 1469, this fact led Edward to seek a settlement with his cousin, and he invited the unhappy Earl to attend a meeting of the Great Council at Westminster so that they could reach an agreement. Warwick accepted and was greeted cordially by the King and his advisers. The reconciliation was marked by pardons for all of the Kingmaker's allies and a formal betrothal of the monarch's daughter, Elizabeth, to Richard Neville's brother, John. Neither the King nor his mightiest subject had, however, really forgotten the events of the preceding months; and it was only a matter of time until Warwick was back plotting once again, chasing the elusive goal of dominating the Crown.

In January 1470, one of Warwick's kinsmen began feuding with a neighbor in Lincolnshire, and this led the Kingmaker to formulate another conspiracy aimed at King Edward. Prodding his relative secretly to raise an open rebellion, the Neville chieftain hoped to take advantage of the trouble to destroy Edward IV and elevate George of Clarence, but in that, too, the Earl was frustrated. On March 4, 1470, the Lincolnshire rising began, and the Warwick-Clarence coalition hoped that the King could be lured into their trap as easily as he had been a year earlier. Edward IV did not repeat his previous mistake, however, and when he left London to put down the rebellion it was at the head of a powerful army. To add to the problems of the plotters, few men showed an interest in joining Warwick's forces. Indeed, many of his followers disappeared when they learned that another attempt to unseat King Edward was in progress. Within two weeks, the Kingmaker's chief agent in Lincolnshire, Sir Robert Welles, was captured and had confessed, revealing the depth of Neville's and Clarence's involvement in the uprising. Once again, Warwick received news of defeat, and he rode for Manchester where, with the help of Lord Stanley, he intended to gather an army for a final trial of strength with his cousin.

On the Manchester road, the Kingmaker discovered that Stanley would not fulfill his promise of aid. Warwick's plans for war quickly turned to preparations for flight, for he was now reduced to escaping and waiting for another opportunity. With the vanguard of the royal army hot in pursuit, Warwick, Clarence, and a few hundred of their

followers arrived at Exeter on April 10, and there they secured a small
fleet to carry them to the perennial haven of exiled Yorkists, Calais.
In the best tradition of romantic escape, Warwick's party sailed away
just as the King's men arrived, and the Kingmaker was again forced
back into reliance on the Captaincy of Calais to recoup his fortunes.

As Richard Neville's small fleet sailed up to Calais Roads, he no
doubt reflected on how everything of importance to him seemed to
begin and end with that English enclave in France. But this time his
reflections were interrupted by cannon fire and shot splashing around
his fleet. Unbelievable though it seemed, the garrison of Calais was
actually firing on the vessels of their Captain. Warwick guessed correctly
that Edward had sent orders to Lord Wenlock, the garrison commander,
to deny the Kingmaker's party entry into the city. Since he had nowhere
else to go, the Earl anchored out of range of the guns and began considering his alternatives now that Calais was denied him. After rejecting
all of his options, Warwick was nearly ready to negotiate with King
Edward when he received a secret message from Lord Wenlock explaining that a plan was afoot to trap the Earl's party between an English
fleet and a Burgundian army. That news brought an urgency to the
Kingmaker's situation, and it led him finally to commit himself to a
course of action that was as dangerous as it was promising. Richard
Neville, for years champion of the Yorkist cause, decided to seek the
support of Louis of France and become a Lancastrian.

Early in June, the arrangements for a meeting between Warwick
and Louis XI were completed, and the great Earl and his now useless
son-in-law traveled to the French King's castle near Amboise. Richard
Neville was greeted more like an independent prince than a landless
fugitive by the Valois ruler, and whatever doubts the English peer may
have had about supporting the Lancastrian revival disappeared. When
Warwick and his men left Amboise on June 12, the grandest Neville
plot of all had been hatched, for the French monarch had agreed both
to support the Kingmaker's invasion of England with men and supplies
and to arrange a reconciliation with the exiled Queen Margaret and
her son, Prince Edward.

Louis's role as mediator between the Lancastrian Queen and her
erstwhile Yorkist enemy was hardly an easy one, but Louis XI was
a master persuader. By pointing out the hopelessness of Margaret's position without Warwick's help and flattering her without restraint, the
French sovereign finally managed to achieve his purpose. Margaret
agreed with great reluctance to place the fate of her house in the
hands of the Kingmaker, and on July 22, 1470, Richard Neville knelt
before Margaret of Lancaster and begged her forgiveness. Yet, Warwick
the scheming realist was never better than on his knees before the exiled
Queen, for the price of his service was the marriage of his daughter

Anne to the Lancastrian heir-apparent, Edward, Prince of Wales. War-wick, unable to take the throne for himself, would, at least if all went well, have the satisfaction of being the grandfather of a King.

After the public ceremonies, Warwick, Margaret, and Louis began planning the Lancastrian invasion of England. The scheme called for the Kingmaker to land in the West Country with a small band of troops; Jasper Tudor, who was the half-brother of Henry VI and the Lancastrian Earl of Pembroke, would rally the Welsh to their cause; and messengers would be dispatched to alert the followers of both Lancaster and Neville to muster their men-at-arms. Altogether, it was a sound plan, for Warwick and Margaret judged their supporters to command nearly half of England's resources in men and supplies. Thus when the Kingmaker and his men landed at Plymouth and Dartmouth in mid-September their optimism rose with each hour that they marched on English soil.

For once, Richard Neville's sense of impending triumph did not mis-lead him. As he marched on Exeter, all of Devon rose in support of the cause of Lancaster, and messengers brought news that similar reac-tions were occurring in even marginally Lancastrian areas. It seemed that the Kingmaker's well-advertised aim of freeing King Henry from the Yorkist usurper was more popular than anyone had thought that it would be in 1470.

King Edward was not, however, shaken by his cousin's initial success. In Yorkshire when the news of the invasion came, Edward hurried south, gathering an army as he traveled, and he relied on Warwick's own brother, John, now Marquess of Montagu, to provide the bulk of the royal army from the north of England. For a few days it appeared that Edward's confidence in Montagu had been judiciously placed, for the Marquess dutifully mustered his men and marched to join his King. But when Montagu reached Doncaster, the Neville blood and the impu-dence of the Woodvilles proved too much for him; John Neville declared for his brother and Lancaster, and King Edward, caught between two hostile armies, was compelled to flee. With a small band of loyal follow-ers the Yorkist sovereign took ship at Lynn and sailed toward refuge with his Burgundian ally, abandoning his realm to Warwick and the Lancastrians. Amazingly, even for a period of striking political turns, Richard Neville rode into London, led the dirty, mad Henry VI out of his cell in the Tower, proclaimed him the rightful King, and ensconced him in the apartments so recently occupied by Elizabeth Woodville. Again, Warwick had made a King.

Neville's brilliant political stroke inaugurated what is usually known as the "Re-Adeption" of King Henry VI, and, brief though it was, Henry's return to power raised the Kingmaker higher than he had been in the days of 1461–62. Indeed, the revived Lancastrian government was a barely disguised Neville administration, for the state offices that Warwick did not take for himself he bestowed on his brother George and his ally, Sir John Longstrother. Doubtless the post that the Earl coveted above all others was that of King's Lieutenant of the Realm, which gave him what he had always sought: the power to rule without reigning. Yet Warwick, now over forty, had determined to extend Neville control past his own death, and he thought he had accomplished that with a Parliamentary statute. Early in December 1470, an Act was passed declaring Henry VI the true King and vesting the succession in his male heirs. Failing the continuation of Henry's issue, the Crown was to pass to George of Clarence and his heirs. Since both Henry's son and Clarence were married to the Kingmaker's daughters, the Neville line would remain dominant in England.

The satisfaction of being King's Lieutenant and providing for the future was well-balanced by the problems Warwick faced in governing the country. Foremost, Richard Neville had to worry about pacifying his former Lancastrian enemies and at the same time finding some way to guarantee the good faith of Queen Margaret once she arrived in England. The Earl also had to neutralize the Yorkist threat that still loomed both in England and from Burgundy. Under the circumstances, Warwick's policy was the wisest that he could have adopted. He chose to be moderate and to make a concerted appeal to moderates of both parties, hoping to build a base of support for himself that would keep the radical fringes in check. During the first few months after his coup it appeared that his policy had succeeded, for, while Queen Margaret lingered in France and behaved suspiciously, England was tranquil.

As time passed, however, England's tranquility seemed to the Kingmaker to have a hollow and sinister character. By February 1471, Neville wondered continually about the meaning of so much inaction. Why was Queen Margaret wasting time at Honfleur? Was there any truth to the rumors that his cousin Edward was gathering an invasion fleet in Burgundy? Why were the Lancastrians in England so courteous and yet strangely distant? Most importantly, what was wrong with the English people? They were obedient enough, but they lacked the signs of enthusiasm that would tell their new governor that he was accepted rather than tolerated. The answers to all of Warwick's questions were soon to come.

Early in March, when the Kingmaker was at Warwick Castle, news arrived that Edward had landed at Ravenspur with 2,000 men and was marching on York. Since the North Country was the heart of Neville territory, Warwick hoped that his cousin would be destroyed long before a royal army could be assembled, but in that hope he underestimated the exiled monarch. Using the same tactics that the founder of the Lancastrian dynasty had used in 1399, announcing that he had returned only to claim his Dukedom, the Plantagenet prince staved off an attack by the dour Yorkshiremen and persuaded them to open the gates of York to his army. From that base, Edward then marched south to confront Henry VI's Lieutenant of the Realm. At that point the Duke of Clarence, no doubt anxious to save his own skin, tried to mediate in the quarrel between Warwick and Edward, and, while he found his brother willing to negotiate, the Kingmaker spurned all offers of a reconciliation. The antagonism between Richard Neville and Edward IV, fueled over the years by intrigue, betrayal, and Woodville arrogance, thus was left to be resolved by force.

On Saturday night, April 13, 1471, most Englishmen slept peacefully. But near the town of Barnet just north of London a few thousand steel-clad soldiers were restlessly active. Inspecting their arms and planning their tactics, they prepared to decide the issue of whether England would be ruled by a prince of the royal blood or by a feudal adventurer.

In the first faint light of Easter Sunday, 1471, Warwick's army of Neville retainers and Lancastrians stood in ranks blocking the London-Barnet road, and facing them, unseen for the moment, were the Yorkist levies of King Edward IV. The Yorkists attacked the Kingmaker's positions with a desperation remarkable even for these civil wars, but at first they made no progress. Warwick, leading the defense, issuing orders, and joining in the hand-to-hand fighting, had placed his troops so well that Edward's men could not penetrate the Neville line. As Yorkists fell by the score in futile attacks, the Kingmaker began to sense victory, but then his Lancastrian allies dashed his hopes.

On the right flank of the Kingmaker's position his brother John stood firm, fending off one attack after another. Expecting to administer the coup de grace to Edward, Warwick ordered the Lancastrian Earl of Oxford, until then held in reserve, to march around the right of the line with his cavalry and attack the Yorkists from the flank and rear. Obediently, Oxford led his troopers off into the fog, but he turned to the attack too soon and mistakenly assaulted John Neville's men. At first, Montagu's soldiers thought that they had been outflanked by the Yorkists, for the emblem of Oxford was similar to that of York. When they discovered, however, that their assailants were Lancastrians, they cried "Treason," thinking that Oxford had changed sides. In the resulting panic the Kingmaker's line broke, and Richard Neville, never closer to a decisive victory, was left struggling in heavy armor trying to find a horse and effect an escape. He almost succeeded. Lumbering across the bloody ground toward a likely mount, he was recognized by a band of Yorkists who, ignorant of Edward's order that his cousin's life be spared, rode Warwick down, tore open the visor of his helmet, and killed him with a single dagger thrust. Six weeks later the remaining

Lancastrian force under Queen Margaret and her son was destroyed at Tewkesbury. Edward IV, restored to his throne, was never again seriously threatened by a Lancastrian rebellion.

Today, nothing remains of England's only "Kingmaker." After the battle the bodies of the Earl of Warwick and his brother, John of Montagu, also slain at Barnet, were carried to St. Paul's Cathedral. There, they lay naked in rude coffins for two days so that the English people could see that haughty Neville aristocrats would never again disturb the realm. Edward then allowed his cousin's faithful retainers to convey the bodies to Bisham Abbey where they were buried alongside their parents and their brother Thomas. During the destruction of the monasteries under Henry VIII, Bisham Abbey and all of its monuments were demolished. Ironically, both Lancaster and York in the person of this second Tudor King were responsible for removing the last traces of the man who had meant so much to both houses.

Even Warwick's carefully laid plans for the future came to nothing. His daughter Isabel, married to the unpredictable Duke of Clarence, gave birth to both a son and a daughter. The boy, as Earl of Warwick, was judicially murdered by Henry VII, and the girl, Countess of Salisbury, suffered the same fate at the hands of Henry VIII. The Kingmaker's daughter Anne, however, did become a Queen, but it was hardly the Queen that her father saw in his schemes. After the death of her first husband at the battle of Tewkesbury, she married Edward IV's youngest brother, Richard, Duke of Gloucester. In 1483, when Gloucester assumed the Crown as Richard III, Anne Neville became a Queen. But her moment of glory was short-lived, for she died before her husband was killed at Bosworth Field. The Kingmaker's strategems, always carefully thought out, seemed destined to be thwarted by what another political adventurer, Otto von Bismarck, later called "intangibles."

The centuries have dimmed the significance of Richard Neville, but his place in Britain's history is unique. Some scholars have called him an aberration, the product of a turbulent period begun by the Lancastrian Revolution and ended by Henry Tudor in 1485. Others, preferring to emphasize the dynamism of human frustration, have characterized Warwick as the personification of a force that strives without purpose. He could neither wear a crown nor control those who did, so his ambition, founded as it was on the quicksand of dynastic politics, consumed him. Warwick the Kingmaker may have been all of the things that historians have thought him to be, or none of them, but in the evolution of British history his role seems clear. Looking to the past, he was the complete feudal noble, resourceful, warlike, autonomous, an entity more powerful than his sovereign lord, Yorkist or Lancastrian. Yet he also anticipated the politician's domination of the future with his skill at intrigue and manipulation. Out of joint with time, Richard Neville stands as a repository of the forces that gradually changed England from a medieval to a modern state.

SUGGESTED READINGS

For a general outline of developments in the 14th and 15th centuries, Vivian H. Green, *The Later Plantagenets* (London: Arnold, 1955), provides a sound framework. A more specific scholarly study is Ernest F. Jacob, *The Fifteenth Century* (Oxford: Clarendon Press, 1961), which deals with the period 1399 to 1485. The only modern biography of Richard Neville is Paul M. Kendall, *Warwick the Kingmaker* (New York: Norton, 1957). Paul M. Kendall, *Louis XI* (New York: Norton, 1970), also provides insights into Warwick's activities. Other works, though dated, that might be consulted are: James Ramsay, *Lancaster and York* (Oxford: Clarendon Press, 1892), 2 volumes; and Cora Scofield, *The Life and Reign of Edward IV* (London: Longmans, Green, 1923).

Chapter 5

SAINT THOMAS MORE:
Conflict and Change
in Henrician England

Perhaps the most striking feature of Henry VIII's long rule was the strange blend of old and new, medieval and modern, that it produced in England. Examples of this characteristic of Henrician England are legion. The King himself insisted on being viewed as a mystical, anointed monarch rather than a chief executive, but he continually behaved like a wily modern politician. Of his two chief ministers, one was a prelate in the tradition of medieval government and the other was a bureaucrat scarcely distinguishable from any other powerful civil servant. One of the better examples of this duality apparent in Henry VIII's England was, Thomas More, for his entire career seems to have been a juxtaposition of medieval and modern elements. In religion he championed orthodoxy yet agitated for extensive reforms based on the revelations of Christian humanism. His views on government, especially social policy, were most enlightened, perhaps even radical; but he never in his public career challenged the theory of divine right monarchy. Perhaps most significantly, he strove with all of his considerable ability to rise in the material world, reaching the Chancellorship of England; then he baffled his friends and most of his family by turning his back on economic and political success for the sake of an abstraction. In many ways Thomas More, who defied Henry VIII and died for his stance, embodied the principal characteristics of the second Tudor's reign more clearly than any of King Henry's most prominent and loyal subjects.

A native Londoner, Thomas More was the only surviving son of John More, a City barrister, and Agnes, his first wife. Thomas's birth on February 7, 1477, coincided with the printing of the first book in England by William Caxton, and the combination of events proved fortuitous: More made his reputation as one of England's finest Renaissance scholars through the printed word, and Caxton made the spread of More's learning possible. The More family was undistinguished in origins, being wealthy, respectable Londoners who made a living primarily through the law. Thomas's education, accordingly, trained him for a legal career, and as a boy he was sent to St. Anthony's in Threadneedle Street, London's foremost school. He acquired two of his most useful skills, debating technique and a command of Latin, at St. Anthony's.

At the age of 12, Thomas More left school and, as was customary with young men of his class, entered the service of a great nobleman both to learn manners and to attract the attention of powerful men at Court. In More's case, the great nobleman was a cleric rather than a member of the feudal aristocracy; John Morton, a Cardinal, the Archbishop of Canterbury, and the Lord Chancellor, was the first Tudor sovereign's principal adviser and confidant. Young Thomas More could not have found a more auspicious place to learn the ways of the world, and his opportunities were enhanced by the Cardinal's fondness for this new member of his household. Morton seems to have been struck by the intelligence and maturity of young More and took especial pains with his education, making no secret of his belief in the boy's potential for greatness. Perhaps the most valuable training that More received at Lambeth Palace was in manners, for the Cardinal and his servants put little stock in the elaborate forms of late medieval chivalric behavior. They emphasized poise, gentleness, and consideration for the feelings of others, traits that were to characterize Thomas More throughout his life.

By the time More had reached the age of 14, the Cardinal decided that the boy had learned all that he could at Lambeth, so he was sent up to Oxford to complete his education. Ironically, More enrolled in Canterbury Hall, where more than a century earlier a dispute over the mastership of the college had started John Wycliffe on the road to heresy. During young Thomas's residence, the college was run by the Benedictines, and the Cardinal's protégé found life at one of England's two great universities austere at best. The food was poor and there was little of it, and his father sent money infrequently, assuming that his son would spend it on drink and licentious living. Consequently, Thomas More lived frugally at Oxford and spent most of his time filling in the gaps in his knowledge of the seven liberal arts. He may also have had his first exposure to the Greek language and its literature at Oxford, for Canterbury College was the center of Greek learning in England.

After two years, More left Oxford at the insistence of his father and returned to London to take up the study of law. The barrister's son first entered New Inn, an Inn of Chancery, and performed brilliantly. He then went on to Lincoln's Inn for further training, and in a relatively short time became, much to his father's delight, another More active in the ranks of London's barristers-at-law. Thus at the age of 18, Thomas More was called to the bar, but there is some question about the intensity of his desire to practice law. His interests, on the threshold of manhood, seem to have been evenly divided between the law, the "new learning," as the study of classical literature and language was called in England, and the religious life. While he remained a practicing barrister throughout his life, his other two concerns progressively eclipsed the law. His respect for England's laws never diminished, and his professional practice was scrupulously honest, but his intellectual curiosity was attracted by more subtle and less worldly matters.

While he was a student at Lincoln's Inn, Thomas More found himself more drawn toward the religious life than toward his legal studies. He frequently stayed at the Charterhouse in London, operated by Carthusian monks, and there he began wearing a hair shirt, shared the monk's simple meals, slept as they did on boards, and meditated. These experiences eventually led More to contemplate taking holy orders. His father was very disturbed when he learned of his only son's desire to become a priest, for he naturally wanted More to continue the family legal tradition. Ultimately, the father's concern was relieved when Thomas More decided against the priesthood because he felt himself too subject to worldly desires. His stay at the Charterhouse was hardly wasted, however, for his adolescent religious experiences helped shape him into a devout adult for whom Christianity was a great deal more than simply formal practice. In addition, More's association with the Charterhouse led him to learn Greek so that he could study the Scriptures more intelligently, and that introduced him to the Renaissance humanism that was just making an impression on England.

A product of 15th-century Italy, humanism grew out of the revival of interest in the literature and language of ancient Rome and Greece. In its early years, the movement concerned the collection and study of ancient manuscripts, which led to a new appreciation of classical pagan culture. But by the last decade of the century, when England received its first extensive exposure to Italian humanism through the lectures of John Colet at Oxford, the thrust of the movement had changed. Under the influence of Lorenzo Valla in Rome and the Neoplatonic revival in Florence, Italian humanism had developed a serious interest in Christianity and the religious literature of antiquity. Indeed, early in the 1490s this interest was combined in Florence with the emotionalism of Savonarola's preaching to produce a rejection of much of the secular spirit of the early Renaissance. It was this form of humanism that made a deep impression on Colet when he studied in Italy for two years, and it was articulated unmistakably by him in 1496 when he presented his lectures on the Epistles of St. Paul after his return home. This Christian-oriented humanism from north Italy gave definite character to the movement in England. It made the English brand of humanism essentially religious in interest, but certainly did not prevent the exploration of other subjects and the appreciation of many of the facets evident in the secular phase of the Renaissance.

Humanism was one of the avenues through which More rose to prominence in Tudor England, and his scholarly career was enhanced by personal relationships with some of Europe's foremost intellectuals. In 1499, he met and befriended the greatest humanist of northern Europe, Erasmus of Rotterdam. Both More and Erasmus were deeply impressed by each other and, though Erasmus was ten years More's senior, he was convinced that the young lawyer would be one of England's most renowned scholars. Ironically, it was through More's arrangement of a visit to Eltham that Erasmus met an eight-year-old boy, the future King Henry VIII, from whom the Dutch scholar expected much and received little. When More met Erasmus, the young lawyer was also developing close ties with some of England's most famous humanists. William Grocyn and Thomas Linacre both taught him Greek and encouraged his studies of the classics and the commentaries on the Scriptures. Indeed, these two pillars of the English Renaissance seemed to view the youthful barrister as more of a peer than a student, for in 1501 Grocyn asked More to lecture on Augustine's *City of God* in his church of Saint Lawrence Jewry. The crowds who heard the lectures were struck by More's learning and sensitivity to Augustine's meaning. Within three years, Thomas More was recognized as one of Europe's most promising humanists when he produced a series of Greek epigrams translated into Latin. His co-translator and close friend, William Lily, ranked in stature with Grocyn and Linacre, and he is still admired as an early master of one of England's finest schools, St. Paul's.

In 1505, the 28-year-old More firmly established his reputation as a scholar with a translation of *The Life of John Picus, Earl of Mirandula*. In a gesture that both gives an insight into More's personality and stands as a portent of what was to come, More presented a gift copy of the book to a friend, Joyeuce Leigh, a nun in the convent of the Poor Clares outside London. She treasured the copy and remained More's close friend throughout her life. Her brother, Edward Leigh, when he became Archbishop of York, worked closely with Henry VIII in reforming the Church and dispossessing the monastic orders.

While devoting time to scholarly endeavor and religious contemplations in these years, More also worked hard at his profession. In the process, he did what most of his peers either did or would like to have done. In 1504, for instance, he was elected to the House of Commons; his work in the Parliament remains as a sample of Thomas More's attitude toward arbitrary authority. Pleading the high cost of his eldest daughter's marriage to the Scottish King, King Henry VII asked the Commons for £90,000, which everyone knew was far in excess of the actual cost of the wedding. When the request was made, More spoke so eloquently and forcefully against it that the Lower House agreed to give the King only £40,000. Henry VII was so angered by the work of "this beardless boy" that he arrested More's father on a false charge and held him in the Tower until he paid a fine of £100. The son, fearful of a more direct royal attack, made plans to flee to the Continent, but when it became apparent that Henry VII would be satisfied with the elder More's punishment, Thomas elected to proceed with his plans to marry.

Thomas More's choice of a wife seems odd in some respects, for it apparently was governed by his sensitivity to the feelings of others rather than by his personal preferences. Between his studies, law practice, and meditation, More had found time to visit on several occasions the home of John Colt in Essex, principally to pay court to one of

Colt's three daughters. Originally, the young lawyer showed an interest in the second eldest girl, because she was the prettiest, but upon considering the matter he switched his choice to the eldest daughter. His reasoning was simple. He determined that it would be a terrible humiliation to the eldest girl to have her younger sister chosen over her by a suitor, so rather than be responsible for distressing her he married her. They immediately set up housekeeping in the London district of Bucklersbury, and shortly thereafter the Mores were visited by Erasmus, who cooperated with Thomas in translating some of the works of Lucian and also noted the happy relationship of the newlyweds. They had one child a year from 1505 until 1509.

1509 was a crucial year in the life of Thomas More, for it saw the accession to England's throne of King Henry VIII. Along with most of his countrymen, More was happy to have a new ruler, and he celebrated the event by presenting a long and complimentary poem to the second Tudor sovereign. At the same time, Erasmus decided to make his third visit to England, and since he planned to stay with More, he thought a good deal about him while traveling from Switzerland to Calais. It struck the Dutch scholar that More's name in Greek, *Moros*, meant fool, and taking that thought as his theme, Erasmus wrote his most famous work, *Moriae Encomium*, or *Praise of Folly*, at More's house and dedicated it to his English host. More was flattered by Erasmus's sentiment, and considered the book witty and thoughtful, for he, too, was deeply concerned about the need for reform evident in the Church.

In the first two years of Henry VIII's reign, however, Thomas More found himself far too busy to devote very much time to scholarship or the problems of the Church. In 1510, he was appointed an Under-Sheriff of London, and soon discovered that he would have to spend most of his time earning his princely salary of £400 a year. The Under-Sheriff was the chief legal officer on the staff of London's sheriff and was charged with collecting evidence, prosecuting cases, and supervising the bureaucratic details of his office. More proved an excellent choice for the position; he quickly became a public figure in the capital, and his reputation for honesty and impartial justice was still discussed in the City long after his death. This appointment proved to be the start of his political career, for it soon brought him to the attention of the Crown, but his good fortune was marred by tragedy. Less than a year after accepting the Under-Sheriff's post, his wife died, leaving him to care for their four young children. It apparently was concern for the children as well as loneliness that led More to remarry within a month of his first wife's death. His second wife, a widow named Alice Middleton, proved a good choice, for she reared his children as though they were her own and kept such an efficient household that More was able, once he had settled into his City job, to renew his interest in scholarly work on a part-time basis.

The first result of More's return to scholarship was a fragmentary history of the reign of King Richard III, which has been severely criticized in recent years. Apologists for the last Plantagenet ruler claim that More's history is distorted at best, relying on information gleaned from the arch protagonist of the Tudor cause, Cardinal Morton, and written to curry favor with Henry VIII. Reasonable though some of these arguments may be, More's principal biographer argues that, for all its faults, the *History of Richard III* began modern historical writing in England, for it was logically organized, used the available evidence judiciously, and sought to entertain as well as educate.

More's return to scholarship was interrupted in the spring of 1515 when he was sent to Flanders with a trade embassy. The task held little promise for Thomas More aside from the royal attention that it indicated, for he felt that his expense money was inadequate and that he was being needlessly deprived of his family's company. Yet, the visit to Flanders proved to be the stimulus for More's best-known literary production, for during his six months in the Low Countries he conceived and began writing *Utopia*. This much misunderstood book, which gave the adjective "utopian" to the English language, was begun as a learned prank, but it ended up as one of the 16th-century's most thoughtful commentaries on human activity. Ranging from politics and economics to religion and manners, *Utopia* was very close chronologically to another famous work that dealt with similar subjects, Machiavelli's *The Prince*. But where *The Prince* delineated the growth of European statecraft for the future, *Utopia* harked back to such medieval ideals as community, duty, and the majesty of law. Inasmuch as More portrayed the Utopians as being ignorant of property rights, he has been admired by some Marxist writers, but Thomas More was not a socialist. In his book he simply asked the question: How can pagans, lacking the teachings of Christianity, behave so much more reasonably than contemporary Europeans?

More's embassy to Flanders was the first indication of royal favor, and on May Day 1517, he was again brought to the King's attention during the "Evil May Day" riots in London. These disturbances resulted largely from an excess of xenophobia on the part of London's apprentices, and while the riots began as attacks on alein residents, they soon involved many of London's citizens. In his capacity as Under-Sheriff More was directly involved with these disorders, at one point nearly stopping the rioters singlehandedly by confronting them and using his eloquence to persuade them to go home. The Under-Sheriff might well have talked the riot to an end had not one of his aides, with an untimely threat of force, sent the apprentices rampaging off again to burn and pillage. In the end, the disturbance was put down by troops who arrested many of the rioters and drove the rest to cover. A London legend, however, soon grew up to the effect that Thomas More not only quelled the riot, but also persuaded the King to grant pardons to most of those arrested, and the legend is at least partly true. Thomas More was the official most responsible, through tireless effort, for ending the disturbance, and he did intercede with the King to have most of the harsh sentences imposed on the rioters reduced. His work in the crisis can only have impressed Henry VIII with his composure and ability.

It was less than six months after the riot of 1517 that Thomas More entered the service of King Henry; in the autumn of that year he went on another embassy, this time to Calais. His official appointment, however, did not come until July 22, 1518, when he resigned as London's Under-Sheriff to take up his duties as an officer of the crown. Erasmus good-naturedly chided his friend about becoming a "courtier," but in fact More was one of the few men in the royal service who was not a courtier insofar as the word can be taken to mean a fawning lackey. His first appointment by the King was crucial, for he was sworn to the King's Council, the body that advised the ruler and executed his decisions. Next, as a special sign of favor, Henry Tudor appointed More to one of the most sought-after positions at Court, the Mastership of the Court of Requests. A noteworthy Master of Requests because of the care he took to see that the poor were given justice, More benefited from the revenues of the post, for it was one of the most profitable in the royal service. Although salaried by the crown, the Master of Requests also received fees that were legally and traditionally paid for the adjudication of cases. While this practice of supplementing salaries was common throughout the bureaucracy, there was no position, except possibly that of Master of the Court of Wards, that received more in additional income than the Mastership of Requests. More was certainly not a corrupt judge, who accepted bribes and granted favors, but there is no doubt that he took his supplementary fees with a clear conscience and used them to build his mansion at Chelsea.

Thomas More's chief value to King Henry seems to have been as an adviser and ambassador extraordinary. It was in the latter capacity, in 1520, that More went to France to help arrange the details for the famous meeting between Henry VIII and Francis I on the Field of the Cloth of Gold. At the same time, the Master of Requests led an English delegation that met with a group of the Hanseatic merchants in Calais and Bruges to settle commercial disputes between the two parties. The talks at Bruges afforded More an opportunity to meet once again with his old friend Erasmus, who was then in the service of Emperor Charles V as a courtier. It was the last time that the two met face to face, for events on the Continent and in England made further personal contact impossible between two of Europe's most respected scholars. Three years earlier, the Augustinian monk Martin Luther had begun the movement in Germany that was to embroil Erasmus in a series of time-consuming theological controversies. In England, Cardinal Wolsey's inept diplomacy laid the groundwork for failures in England's foreign policy that were to trap Thomas More between his conscience and King Henry's will.

More's success in arranging the meeting with the French King and settling the disputes with the Hanse merchants raised him even higher in King Henry's esteem, and in 1521, as a sign of royal favor, More was knighted and appointed to still another important crown office, the post of Under-Treasurer. Even though More was technically subordinate to the Duke of Norfolk, the Lord Treasurer, he was responsible for most of the crown's financial matters. The duties of the office were demanding, but the importance of the work was a sure indication that the King intended to advance him further in the near future. Any pleasure More derived from this sign of royal confidence was, however, diminished somewhat by events in 1521. Early in the summer, the Duke of Buckingham was executed in one of the better-known examples of Tudor "judicial murder." More was appalled by this perversion of the law. But more important to the new Under-Treasurer were developments in Germany and the responses they provoked in England. At the Diet of Worms, Martin Luther had indicated that he would not be reconciled to the Roman Catholic Church, and his supporters, particularly some of the powerful nobles of the Holy Roman Empire, made Luther's movement a serious threat to the unity of Christendom. Thomas More was deeply troubled by Luther's activity, and so also was his monarch. The King began writing a book defending the sacraments of the Church against Lutheran attacks, and he called frequently on More, renowned for his grasp of theology and law, for assistance and advice. Many years later, when Thomas More was accused of being the author of King Henry's defense of the sacraments, he pointed out that he had only counseled the King, who was the sole author. He could not resist, however, stating that while Henry was writing the book More had warned the King against ascribing too much power to the Papacy; since this was the principal reason why More was being accused, his interrogators lapsed into an embarrassed silence.

For helping the King write the book that earned him and his successors the title of *Fidei Defensor,* Thomas More was taken even more into the royal confidence. Cardinal Wolsey, who had been administering England for nearly a decade and was answerable only to King Henry, was told to familiarize More with the details of all of his policies and negotiations. Naturally enough, most Court observers viewed this as evidence that More was being groomed to succeed Wolsey. A shrewd politician, the Cardinal interpreted the instructions similarly and resented both the royal command and Thomas More. At about the same time, More was assigned the difficult task of preparing England for the coming war with France. As Under-Treasurer, he assumed chief responsibility for the financial details of mobilization, and he was charged additionally with compiling a census of all resident French aliens in the realm and seeing that they were interned when the war broke out.

Thanks to Wolsey's diplomacy, a war between England and France seemed imminent in the first months of 1523, so writs were issued summoning a Parliament to provide money. On April 15, 1523, the Parliament met, the only one called during the 14 years of Cardinal Wolsey's tenure as chief minister, and since it was vital that the Commons cooperate and support the crown's foreign policy, great pains were taken by the Cardinal to influence the choice of Speaker of the House. Thanks partly to Wolsey's politicking, but more to his own reputation, Thomas More was elected Speaker, and both the government and the Commons were pleased with the choice. In presenting himself to the King as Speaker, More began his speech in the usual manner by declaring himself unfit for the position, but as he continued it became apparent that there was something quite unusual about the new Speaker's presentation, for he made a historic claim, that of the right of the Commons to free speech, before he finished. Not realizing that he was listening to the foundation of one of Parliament's most cherished rights, the King let the speech pass unchallenged and instructed More to ask the Commons for a grant of £800,000, or a fifth of all taxable property, to support the war. The Commons promptly refused the grant, thinking no doubt that four shillings of every pound was too stiff a price to pay for a few castles in France. But after much debate and a series of persuasive arguments by the Speaker, the members relented and gave the King his fifth. One of the members, a new man named Thomas Cromwell, first met More in the sessions of this Parliament.

The Anglo-French war dragged on inconclusively for two years. The English were unable to do more than capture an occasional castle or town, and the French were too distracted by their struggle with the Hapsburgs in Italy to bring the full weight of their strength to bear on the English invaders. Personally, Thomas More thought that the war was deplorable, for, like Erasmus, he was convinced that war was the most costly and least successful means of resolving a dispute. Indeed, his Utopians never fought wars, but rather used their wits to sow sufficient discord among their enemies that none was ever able to attack them. Yet, despite his personal feelings about war, Thomas More knew perfectly well that as a crown servant he was bound to serve the King in war as in any other enterprise of state. Since his objections to the

French war were philosophical and did not involve conscience, there was no inner conflict for him, so he served King Henry loyally and to the best of his ability.

By 1525, the government had spent all of the money raised to finance the French war, and the English participation was so reduced that a negotiated peace seemed to be the only possible outcome. Things looked bleak for Cardinal Wolsey, author of the manifestly unsuccessful policy that had led to the conflict; so to remain in power he elected to change sides, allying England with the erstwhile French enemy against the Imperialists. Both the Cardinal's judgment and timing proved to be wrong, for just as he was about to complete the betrayal of the Emperor, the Imperial army defeated the French at the battle of Pavia and captured King Francis I. Wolsey determined to attempt to salvage something from his mistakes, so he proposed that an embassy be sent to Spain to negotiate the partition of France with Charles V. He asked the King to send Thomas More, for the Cardinal thought that it would be well to have any potential successor out of the country when Henry Tudor realized the magnitude of Wolsey's diplomatic blunders.

Accordingly, King Henry asked his Under-Treasurer to lead the embassy to Spain, but More demurred, claiming that his frail health would not be able to stand the strain. No doubt More's health was in the back of Wolsey's mind when he suggested him for the mission, but his plans were thwarted by the King. Loath to risk the life of one of his most esteemed Councillors, Henry VIII acceded to More's request and sent instead Cuthbert Tunstall, Bishop of Durham, and Sir Richard Wingfield, Chancellor of the Duchy of Lancaster. As it turned out, More's fears were well-founded, for both ambassadors fell ill with a fever, and Tunstall hovered on the brink of death for several weeks. Wingfield, who in reality was More's replacement, died, vindicating both Thomas More's fears and his suspicions of Wolsey's motives for recommending him.

The death of Wingfield and the conclusion of the French war accelerated More's rise in the government considerably. As Wolsey incurred the wrath of England's taxpayers by attempting to extort from them an "amicable grant" to continue the war, the Under-Treasurer rose steadily higher in the King's favor. During the summer of 1525, for instance, King Henry paid a surprise visit to More at his new mansion in Chelsea, and left no doubt about his plans for More when he walked through the garden with his arm around the Councillor's shoulders. King Henry rarely displayed such signs of affection, and their talk seems to have been of grave matters, for shortly thereafter More was sent to France as chief of the delegation that negotiated a settlement to the war. Thomas More received a pension of 150 crowns for his efforts in the discussions, but that was as nothing compared to the other rewards that Henry VIII gave him. First, Wingfield's death had left the Chancellorship of the Duchy of Lancaster vacant, so the King gave the post, rich with rewards and heavy with duties, to More. Then, perhaps with an eye to his Councillor's love of learning, Henry nominated More for the High Stewardship of Cambridge University, which complemented his holding the same post at Oxford. Both appointments increased Sir Thomas's power and prestige substantially, and by the end of 1525 he was so high in the favor of the King that of 20 Councillors, he was one of four who were required to be in constant attendance on the monarch. At this point in his career, there was nothing remaining for Thomas More to aim at but the highest of all Crown offices, the Lord Chancellorship.

More's political rise did not significantly alter his manner of living. He kept in close touch with most of Europe's prominent humanists, counting among his correspondents Bude in France, Vives in Spain, and, of course, Erasmus, who in the late 1520s was settled in Switzerland. It was More's relationship with Erasmus that led to a series of portrayals of him and his family by one of northern Europe's finest artists, for in 1527, Hans Holbein arrived in England with a recommendation from Erasmus and was housed as a guest of the Mores at Chelsea. The result was a number of paintings and drawings that depicted Thomas More and his household at the height of his power. Most notable is a portrait of the King's Councillor that shows More in the robes of a minister of state with the power softened by the thoughtful face of a scholar. But most dramatic is an india ink drawing of the entire More family, including the patriarch, John More, his son and daughter-in-law, and all of their children. This drawing, sent to Erasmus as a gift, is now in Basel, and its most striking feature is the serenity of the More household that Holbein captured so successfully.

When Holbein sketched the More family, Cardinal Wolsey, his hold on King Henry slipping away, opened proceedings in what came to be known as the King's "great matter." The Cardinal's action proved to be one that led to his own destruction and Thomas More's as well. While Wolsey set about smoothing the way for an annulment of the King's marriage, Henry Tudor began soliciting the opinions of England's learned men concerning his marital problem. One of the first that he questioned was his Chancellor of the Duchy of Lancaster, Sir Thomas More. The interview led to the first serious disagreement between ruler and subject.

In their initial conference about the annulment, Henry explained his problem and presented the arguments for invalidating the marriage. He then asked More's opinion of the issue, and, somewhat to the King's surprise, the Councillor declined, claiming that he was not competent to advise the monarch in such a weighty matter. Henry VIII was not so easily put off, and when he pressed More for a reply, the distraught adviser begged for more time to consider the question. This the King granted, instructing More to confer with Bishops Tunstall of Durham and Clerk of Bath and then report back to him. Deeply disturbed by the King's probing, and fearful of the results of this development, More consulted both Tunstall and Clerk and also carefully studied all of the sources pertinent to the issue that he could find. He then reported back to King Henry that neither More himself, nor the bishops, nor the Council were qualified to advise the King in the matter. He did refer his sovereign to writings on the subject by Jerome and Augustine and other of the Church Fathers, but this predictably left the monarch dissatisfied.

While Henry VIII was pressing More to support annulment, the troops of Emperor Charles V, now England's enemy thanks to Wolsey's diplomacy, captured and sacked Rome. In the process, Pope Clement VII was trapped in the Castel Sant' Angelo, and since Charles V was the nephew of England's Queen Catherine, these events did not augur well for the possibility of obtaining a Papal annulment. Indeed, the threat to the Papacy by the Imperialists was the death blow to King Henry's chances of a favorable ruling from the Holy See in his "great matter." So he dispatched a delegation to France led by Cardinal Wolsey that was instructed to ratify an Anglo-French treaty and obtain Wolsey's appointment as Vicar General of the Church. Sir Thomas More crossed the Channel as second-in-command of this unpromising embassy, and while the French treaty was ratified, the mission failed to have the English Cardinal created Vicar General. At the end of August, when the embassy returned to England, Thomas More reported to King Henry, who realized that he would never be able to rid himself of Queen Catherine by traditional means. Accordingly, Henry began once again to put pressure on More to aid him in disposing of the Queen, but More resisted, claiming as before that the issue was beyond his competence. Yet, knowing that the question of the King's marriage was the most vital issue of Henry VIII's reign, More did not expect to be able to stave off the royal demand for cooperation indefinitely.

In 1528, Wolsey put all of his hopes into the Anglo-French alliance and pressed ahead with the war against Charles V. The Cardinal's aim was to administer such a serious military defeat to the Emperor that he would lose his hold on the Papacy; then Pope Clement might listen to reason in the case of the King's marriage. Once again, the Cardinal was frustrated, for not only were the allies unable to defeat the Imperialists, but the war proved very unpopular in England, where disruption of commercial ties with the Low Countries produced economic hardships. Consistent in his beliefs, Sir Thomas More opposed the war personally while working for victory officially. All of these events provoked him to outline his concerns in his famous "three wishes." While walking with his son-in-law, William Roper, on the bank of the Thames, he began talking about the great issues of the day, and stated his hopes that: Christian Princes would be at universal peace rather than at constant war; the errors and heresies of the Church would be eliminated, and Christendom settled back into a uniformity of religion; and the question of the King's marriage would be "brought to a good conclusion." The first two of these wishes were never fulfilled, and the last, curiously enough, was, although it was not the conclusion that Sir Thomas had in mind.

Shortly after More's talk with Roper, in 1529, all of his fears materialized. First, Cardinal Wolsey's foreign policy was wrecked when the Imperialists and the French opened negotiations that led to the Peace of Cambrai. The French pointedly neglected to inform their English allies of these discussions, and King Henry hurriedly dispatched More and Tunstall to Cambrai to look out for England's interests as best they could. Under the circumstances, Sir Thomas More and his colleague were not expected to accomplish much, but in fact they worked so successfully that the Duke of Norfolk declared openly that More had saved England from humiliation and disaster at Cambrai. More did gain a voice for England in the discussions, and he was at least partly responsible for the 13 years of peace that followed.

His work at Cambrai proved to be relatively insignificant, however, in comparison to what was taking place simultaneously in England. As More negotiated with the Germans and French, the Italian Cardinal Campeggio, Papal Legate to England, adjourned the trial of the King's marriage that he and Wolsey had been conducting in London. In the storm that followed this bitter disappointment for Henry VIII, Wolsey lost first the King's favor and then all of his state offices, and he was sent to York to assume his neglected duties as Archbishop. When King Henry summoned a Parliament, later to be dubbed the "Reformation Parliament," everyone at Court wondered who would be chosen to replace the fallen Cardinal. Thomas More's return from Cambrai three weeks after the calling of Parliament was soon to answer the question of Wolsey's successor, for it led him to the pinnacle of his career when Henry chose him to be the next Lord Chancellor.

On October 25, 1529, Sir Thomas More was made the chief judicial figure and foremost Crown official when the Great Seal of England was delivered to him. Given the differences between the King and his Councillor over the issue of the annulment, it might reasonably be asked why Henry chose More and why More accepted the post. The monarch, for his part, really had little choice, for he was determined not to have a cleric, which eliminated Bishops Tunstall and Fisher, and the Council, led by the Duke of Norfolk, opposed the appointment of Henry's brother-in-law, the Duke of Suffolk. Sir Thomas More, in contrast, had the support of virtually everyone of importance; he was even named by Wolsey as the only fit man for the Chancellorship. More's acceptance of the Great Seal was to him a matter of duty, for it would have been a grave insult to the King to refuse the office. Additionally, it satisfied the ambition that had made possible his rise through the ranks of government over the years. Henry VIII also gave Sir Thomas his word that he would not trouble him with business related to the annulment.

Parliament met a few days after the new Lord Chancellor took office and, standing at the King's right hand during the opening session, acting as the monarch's voice, More explained to the Lords and Commons the purpose of their summons. They were convened, he said, essentially to reform abuses in the Church, and he included in his speech a vicious attack on Wolsey, who was depicted as both guilty of mismanaging the King's affairs and responsible for the corruption in the Church. More has been criticized for his comments on the Cardinal, but in all fairness to the Chancellor, it must be noted that he spoke as the sovereign's voice and the sentiments expressed were not necessarily his own. His speech was well received by the Parliament, partly because of the content, and partly because most of the members of both houses knew More and respected him; and none were more receptive to his words than his four sons-in-law, who were members of the Commons. But this "Reformation Parliament," despite its warm response to the new Chancellor, was potentially dangerous to More, and he was well aware of the fragile nature of his position.

Throughout 1530, Henry Tudor kept his promise not to involve More in his marital difficulties, but the death of Cardinal Wolsey on November 4, 1530, strained relations between the King and his servant. The anticlerical feeling that swept England in the wake of the Cardinal's death was reflected in the Parliament, and Thomas More found it progressively more difficult to remain aloof from the annulment proceedings. The Lord Chancellor never spoke in opposition to the annulment, but, as pressure on him mounted, he made it clear that he opposed the royal policy. More was saved from being completely engulfed in the "great matter" by a timely proroguing of Parliament by King Henry, but, promises aside, the monarch never relaxed his pressure on the Lord Chancellor to support his cause.

When Parliament resumed its work in May 1532, a political and economic offensive against the Church in England began. Taking the form of the famous Supplication Against the Ordinaries, the assault was aimed at forcing the clergy, represented by the Convocation of Westminster, to declare the King the head of the Church. Henry VIII's desire for the headship did not originate in theological considerations, for he wanted control so that he could have his marriage to Queen Catherine annulled with a semblance of legality and be free to remarry. After some maneuvering, the Parliamentary threat worked, and the clergy surrendered to King Henry by acknowledging him as their new spiritual overlord. On the following day, May 16, 1532, Sir Thomas More resigned the office of Lord Chancellor of England. The carefully calculated resignation ended his political career and set him on a course that led to the executioner's block on Tower Hill.

More's retirement came as no great surprise, for his disagreement with the Crown's ecclesiastical policies was common knowledge. But his resignation was lamented by people great and humble, for his reputation as a judge was one that was soon to grow to legendary proportions. In 1597, for instance, Sir John Harrington described More as a "worthy and uncorrupt magistrate," and that sentiment expressed most accurately why his retirement 65 years earlier was regretted by the English people. Famous for his honesty, his belief in the majesty of the law, and his scrupulously fair decisions, Sir Thomas More had, in the opinion of Londoners especially, much of the wisdom for which King Solomon was famous. One story best illustrates More's capacity for justice and wisdom. His wife had been given a small dog which, though she did not know it, had been stolen from a beggar woman. Upon seeing the dog in the arms of one of Sir Thomas's servants, the beggar claimed it as her own. Lady Alice disputed the claim. More, impartial as always, directed the beggar woman to stand at one end of the hall and his wife to stand at the other. He then ordered them to call the dog and, when it ran to the beggar woman, he decreed that she should keep it. The story was still current toward the end of Queen Elizabeth's reign, and was frequently cited as evidence of Sir Thomas More's judicial capabilities.

In retirement, Sir Thomas concentrated on managing his household on a severely limited budget and at the same time attempted to keep from drawing the attention of the government to himself. On a reduced income of £150 a year, he fed and clothed his family without great difficulty, but keeping out of the Crown's way proved impossible. For the first year after his resignation, he was left to study and write, but during that time Thomas Cromwell rose steadily in the King's favor, and Henry's "great matter" drew to a conclusion. On May 23, 1533, Thomas Cranmer, the new Archbishop of Canterbury, ruled in Henry's favor in the annulment proceeding, and nine days later Anne Boleyn was crowned as England's new Queen. More's old friends, Tunstall, Clerk, and Gardiner, tried to persuade the former Councillor to attend the coronation, sending him £20 to buy a gown for the occasion, but More refused to go. To the monarch and many of his advisers, Sir Thomas's attitude seemed potentially dangerous, for they thought that opposition to the government's policies from a man of More's stature might provoke widespread resistance. Consequently, during the following months Cromwell opened a campaign designed to force More, through fear of royal displeasure, to conform publicly to England's new order. The intensity of Cromwell's pursuit of the former Chancellor may have been personally motivated, because Sir Thomas, while in power, had frustrated the ambitions of Wolsey's erstwhile secretary. It is also possible that Cromwell, one of England's first great secular bureaucrats, was simply performing an assigned task to the best of his ability. Whatever the motives, Cromwell launched his attack on Sir Thomas More at Christmas 1533 when the Nine Articles were published. More was summoned before the Secretary on a charge of having contradicted the Articles, and in a tense interview the retired Councillor denied the charge and proved that it was groundless. Cromwell was forced to search for other means to achieve his goal.

The Secretary saw definite possibilities for pressuring More in the arrest of Elizabeth Barton, the Nun of Kent, on a charge of high treason in the autumn of 1533, for he learned that Sir Thomas had corresponded with the Nun. Seizing the chance, Cromwell had More brought before him again, this time on a charge of misprision of treason, or having known of the nun's crime and failing to denounce it. This accusation suited Cromwell's purpose admirably, for it was not a capital charge, but rather carried a sentence of imprisonment at pleasure, ideal for bending Sir Thomas to the Secretary's policy. But Cromwell's hopes were dashed once again when he failed to prove the allegation, for More, learned in the law, had taken great care to keep free of the Nun's activities and was able to prove it. This frustration was apparently more than Cromwell could bear, for on February 21, 1534, he had More's name included among those in a Parliamentary bill of attainder relating to the Nun's offense, and the former Chancellor promptly wrote a letter of protest to Henry VIII. The monarch, anxious to compel More to his policy only by legal means, appointed a commission to hear the accused's defense, and while More's interview with the commission was unpleasant for all parties, his name was ultimately withdrawn from the attainder. Sir Thomas More had escaped from the second of Cromwell's traps, but this time only through the monarch's intervention. The warning that the Duke of Norfolk gave him, *Indignation principis mors est,* "the indignation of the Prince is death," left Sir Thomas with no doubt that Secretary Cromwell would try again.

The third attempt came even sooner than More expected, for in March 1534, a Parliamentary Act of Succession was passed that required all subjects of King Henry VIII to swear an oath of loyalty to the offspring of Henry and Queen Anne. Innocent enough in itself, this statute and its oath proved to be Sir Thomas More's stumbling block, for the oath included a great deal more than simply swearing loyalty to the royal children. It required, in addition, recognition of the King's headship of the church and the illegality of his marriage to Queen Catherine, and the oath had teeth for those who refused to take it. They were automatically guilty of misprision of treason, and were subject to confiscation of all their property and imprisonment at the King's discretion. This Act sealed Sir Thomas More's fate, for it left him no chance to escape the wrath of King Henry and Secretary Cromwell.

On Sunday, April 12, 1534, More was visiting friends in London when he was accosted by a Crown messenger and given a summons to appear at Lambeth Palace before the Commissioners of the Oath. He returned at once to Chelsea, knowing that he had little time left to spend with his family, and that evening he brought intense gloom to his household with his farewell. Up early the next morning, he made his way to Chelsea Old Church where he heard mass, confessed, and received communion. He then went by boat to Lambeth Palace to face the Commissioners; he expected the interview to end badly, for he had determined much earlier that he could not take the oath.

For five days after Sir Thomas left Chelsea to face the Commissioners, his family heard nothing of his fate. Then, they received a letter from him explaining what had happened at the archiepiscopal palace. The statute and oath had been shown to him, More wrote, and he had readily agreed to swear to the succession of Henry and Anne's offspring, but he had refused to take the oath as it was written. Furthermore, he refused to tell the Commissioners why he would not swear the oath. Anticipating Sir Thomas's refusal, the Commissioners immediately had him committed to the custody of the Abbot of Westminster, who held him prisoner for four days and then turned him over to officers who escorted him to the Tower. More was, of course, very concerned about his dilemma, but he believed what he had told his family many times: the government could not harm him so long as he did not break the law, and at worst his silence would only bring imprisonment.

The ex-Chancellor's estimate of the situation was, for the moment, correct. Indeed, the Commissioners as well as the Council were baffled about what to do with More now that he was in the Tower, for their aim was to persuade him to swear the oath, not to remain in prison as an example of resistance to the Crown. The Councillors were so concerned about More's recalcitrance, that they even discussed at some length modifying the oath so that More could take it. This, some advisers argued, could be used to trick Sir Thomas into complying with the requirement, and then they could announce simply that he had taken the oath, omitting that it was a different one from that avowed by every other subject. King Henry, however, rejected this proposal, for he had decided that More must take the full oath, so the King's servants were ordered to persuade him to accept it.

Gravely misjudging the prisoner, Cromwell and his colleagues elected to apply further pressure in hopes of forcing Sir Thomas into conformity. First, they deprived him of all his writing materials, and he was reduced to smuggling out notes to his family written with a piece of charcoal. They also tried to break down his resistance by moving him to progressively more uncomfortable cells. When that failed, they tried to use his family to convince him to change his mind, sending his daughter Margaret to see him and expecting her to persuade him to take the oath. She did try in the autumn of 1534, but to no avail, for her father explained to her that if he took the oath dishonestly he would imperil his soul, and that he would not do regardless of the cost.

Sir Thomas More was not the only famous Englishman who refused to swear the oath and refused to state why he would not take it. John Fisher, Bishop of Rochester, too, was kept in the Tower on a charge of misprision of treason, and the silence of these two public figures worried the King's servants more with each passing week of 1534. By the end of the year, the government was so embarrassed and afraid that More and Fisher would precipitate widespread resistance that they sought further legislation from Parliament to use against them and anyone else who behaved similarly. First, the Act of Supremacy was passed, declaring without qualification that King Henry was Supreme Head of the Church. Then, a retrospective statute was passed that defined the oath more carefully, and it was followed by an Act of Attainder against More and Fisher for refusing to swear, but the law did not condemn them to death for their refusal. Finally, an Act of Treasons was passed, which made it high treason to deprive the King of his dignity, title, or the name of his royal estate. Passed with great difficulty and in an atmosphere of extreme tension, this last statute subjected anyone who denied the Royal Supremacy to a traitor's death, and the Commons was so concerned about the statute that they inserted the words "maliciously deprive the King" of his titles, in order to provide an escape for those who could not accept the oath and sought refuge in the law. Those two words, "maliciously deprive," though they were inserted to save the resisters, proved useless, for the Commissioners who began trying cases under the Treasons Act immediately voided the words and overrode the will of the Commons.

Early in the spring of 1535, a test case of the new Treasons Act was heard. More's old friend, John Houghton, Prior of the London Charterhouse, and three of his monks were charged with denying the Royal Supremacy and brought before a court where the Oath Commissioners sat as judges. Admitting that they had denied it, Houghton and his fellows claimed that they had not done so maliciously and pleaded not guilty to the charge. The judges promptly ruled that whoever denied the King's supremacy did so maliciously, effectively depriving the

Carthusians of any escape. Still, the jury wanted to find them innocent, for they realized that the judges were not competent to alter a Parliamentary statute, but Cromwell browbeat the jurors into returning the desired verdict. The monks were sentenced to make the traitor's journey to Tyburn, where they were to be hanged, disembowelled, and quartered.

On the day after the sentencing of the Carthusians, Sir Thomas More was visited in the Tower by Cromwell and other Councillors. They demanded, once again, that More take the oath; and when he refused they insisted that he tell them why he would not. That, as usual, he declined to do, and Cromwell, thoroughly exasperated, cut right to the heart of the matter when he pointed out that such action threatened the Crown and the peace of the realm by inspiring resistance on the part of others. Cromwell and the other Councillors made it clear that they thought the Carthusian denial was inspired by More's tactics, and while they were wrong in their judgment, they nevertheless viewed the breaking down of Sir Thomas's resistance as imperative for the success of the Crown's policy. Thomas More now realized that he had no chance to escape, and fully expected to follow the monks in the near future.

He did not have long to wait. On May 7, 1535, just one week after his interview with the Councillors, Sir Thomas was questioned again. Again, he refused "to meddle with such matters" as the King's supremacy and marriage, but his friend Bishop Fisher was less wise. When visited by Richard Rich, the monarch's Solicitor General, the prelate told Rich, after assurances that his statement would be kept confidential, that King Henry VIII was most surely not the Supreme Head of the Church. Two weeks later, news arrived in London that Bishop Fisher had been made a Cardinal by Pope Paul III. Henry Tudor, infuriated by Fisher's elevation and referring to the Cardinal's hat, said, "I will so provide that if he wear it, he shall bear it on his shoulders, nor any head shall he have to put it on." Richard Rich's confidence made the King's vow possible, and it furthermore outlined a tactic that could be used against the more cautious Sir Thomas. How much Bishop Fisher's red hat precipitated his and More's death is a moot point, for at the same time that it was awarded, the remaining monks at the Charterhouse copied the two prisoner's examples by resisting crown pressure. This seemed to exhaust the patience of the King and his advisers, and the monks were arrested, chained so that they stood upright, and then left to die of starvation standing in their own excrement. The government then turned its fury on Fisher and More. First, Cardinal Fisher was tried on June 17, before the same court that had condemned Houghton and his brethren, and the testimony of Richard Rich quickly brought a verdict of guilty and sentence of the traitor's death. Five days later, with the sentence commuted to beheading, John Fisher was executed and his headless body buried under the north wall of All Hallows Barking Church. His head was placed on London Bridge as a grisly warning to traitors.

With Fisher and the Charterhouse monks gone, More was the last remaining symbol of resistance to the Henrician changes in church and state. On July 1, 1535, he was brought to trial in Westminster Hall on a charge of treason. His defense was simple and irrefutable. More argued that he had committed no treason because he had not in word or deed denied King Henry VIII anything and claimed that if his silence concerning the oath were to be construed at all, it must be to the effect that he consented to the oath, not that he denied it. The maxim of the law, he pointed out, was known to even the dullest student: *Qui tacet consentire*, silence gives consent. Noting the jury's reaction to this devastating blow to the government's case, Sir Thomas began to think that he might be saved by his cherished law after all, but then Richard Rich came forward. Under oath, Rich stated that on the night of June 12 Sir Thomas had told him that Parliament was not competent to make the King head of the church, and while More denied Rich's claim, he realized that he was doomed. Yet, he showed more concern for Rich than himself, reportedly stating, "In good faith, Master Rich, I am sorrier for your perjury than for my own peril." After 15 minutes the jury returned a verdict of guilty, and Sir Thomas More was sentenced to the traitor's death.

Back in the Tower, More spent his last days scourging himself and meditating on death. King Henry, presumably out of gratitude for the former Councillor's services, commuted his sentence to death by beheading, and on Monday, July 5, 1535, Sir Thomas sent his last letter and his hair shirt to his daughter Margaret. The next morning, he was told by Thomas Pope, founder of Trinity College, Oxford, to prepare himself for death. Shortly thereafter, he was taken to the scaffold, recited the 51st Psalm, embraced and forgave the executioner, and made a brief speech, stating that he was the King's good servant, but God's first. Brief though it was, More's speech was one of the most thought-provoking ever given from an English scaffold, for in it he refused to acknowledge the supremacy of the state over the individual conscience. Characteristically, Sir Thomas More's last words were light rather than weighty. Carefully placing his beard out of the path of the axe, he commented that the beard had not committed treason. With that, the executioner struck off More's head, and, like John Fisher's, it was then placed on London Bridge. Sir Thomas's body was buried in the Chapel of Saint Peter Ad Vincula in the Tower.

Canonized four centuries after his death, Thomas More is perhaps best known to the public as a religious figure who died a martyr's death.

But historians generally seem interested in the end of More's life only insofar as it adds drama to his brilliant career. The career itself has attracted considerable scholarly attention based on a variety of specialized interests. Researchers who examine European intellectual development, for example, see in Sir Thomas a brilliant Renaissance humanist whose career was ended prematurely by his quarrel with Henry VIII. Political analysts, in contrast, view More as an able politician and consummate lawyer whose values were outpaced by the events of his time. While they admire Sir Thomas's conviction and courage, their sympathies really lie with the wave of the future represented by the King and Secretary Cromwell. Other scholars have examined More's career from the perspectives of reverence for the rule of law, sensitive and compassionate social theory, and even the conduct of diplomacy. Yet, all of the views of Sir Thomas More and his place in British history seem in varying degrees distorted, for they tend to overlook the paradoxical nature of his career. A forward-looking, sometimes uncannily modern, man in his support of learning, parliamentary privilege, efficient governmental administration, and the protection of the individual by law, Sir Thomas was concurrently temperamentally and philosophically conservative. He enjoyed discussing, or writing about, change as an abstraction, and he was comfortable with change, such as internal reform of the Church, which would restore lost virtues. But wrenching, violent alteration without precedent, which attacked the core of all his values and showed no promise of being predictable or controllable, distressed him beyond measure. Just as Cromwell could leap without hesitation into the English Reformation, so Thomas More balked because he was overwhelmed by the consequences of the leap.

In the end, More's conservatism proved to be the most powerful force in his life, for, unable to reconcile himself to the new beliefs and institutions of Reformation England, he chose to die rather than conform. The duality of Thomas More's personality, represented by the hair shirt of the Charterhouse and the Lord Chancellor's chain of office, symbolize an England that was part of Christendom and one that rose to leadership of the Protestant Reformation. Protestantism and progress, as Whig historians have never tired of telling us, made modern England possible, and More and his hair shirt had to go to make way for the aggressive secularism that Henry VIII, willing or not, bequeathed to his successors.

The impact of King Henry's legacy on British history can perhaps best be seen in a story that was told in England in the 1930s. A mother, with some pride, explained to her son, "You have not the honor of being descended from Sir Thomas More; but from Dame Alice, his second wife, through the Alingtons, you are descended." "Glad of that," quipped the boy, living proof of the heritage of Tudor secularism, "She was the only one of the crowd that had any sense."

SUGGESTED READINGS

In recent years, Saint Thomas More has been the subject of an award-winning play and movie, *A Man for All Seasons,* by Robert Bolt, and anyone interested in Saint Thomas should make every effort to read the play and see the movie. The sources of Bolt's triumph should not, however, be neglected in favor of the artistic production. Two biographies should be the starting point for further study of Thomas More. The first, by his son-in-law, William Roper, *The Life of Sir Thomas More* (London: Oxford, 1935), gives a valuable insight into More's personality. The great scholarly effort of Raymond W. Chambers, *Thomas More* (New York: Harcourt, Brace, 1935), also deserves the student's attention. Three more recent works might also be consulted. Richard S. Sylvester and Richard J. Schoeck, "Saint Thomas More," in the *New Catholic Encyclopedia* serves, among other things, to correct earlier errors concerning More's birth date. G. R. Potter, "The English Renaissance: Sir Thomas More," in *Renaissance Men and Ideas,* ed. R. Schwoebel (New York: St. Martin's Press, 1971), and Martin N. Raitiere, "More's *Utopia* and *The City of God,*" in *Studies in the Renaissance* (1973), give an added dimension to More's work as a humanist. The most thorough treatment of *Utopia* is Jack H. Hexter's *More's Utopia: The Biography of an Idea* (Princeton: University Press, 1952).

National Maritime Museum, London

Chapter 6

SIR JOHN HAWKINS:
The Expansion of England

John Hawkins does not appear at first glimpse to be very representative of the era of Queen Elizabeth I, for the last half of the 16th century is usually depicted as a vibrant period that saw the foundation laid for modern England. The individuals associated with the "golden age" of Elizabeth, such as the Queen herself, Lord Burghley, Francis Drake, the Earl of Essex, and William Shakespeare, were extraordinary people who had a dramatic impact on the shaping of British history. John Hawkins seems out of place in such company, even though he was well acquainted with most of the famous Elizabethans, for he had none of their flair or their capacity to make themselves and their acts seem to be of historic dimensions. An ordinary man with ordinary drives for recognition, prosperity, and respect, Hawkins seems more like a Victorian burgher than a passionate and aggressive subject of the first Elizabeth, and indeed he was more bourgeois in tastes and aspirations than he was aristocratic or intellectual. In fact, John Hawkins's very ordinariness is the most unusual feature about him, for despite all that is known of his career, he remains enigmatic as a person. Yet, he was an Elizabethan in the truest sense of the term, for in the course of a long life with wide-ranging interests, he exhibited time and again the traits for which the glamorous subjects of the last Tudor monarch were renowned: courage, intelligence, patriotism, inventiveness, and curiosity. Inept at advertising his achievements, John Hawkins has left only a straightforward record of his contribution to the England of Elizabeth. It is not much of an instrument to use in analyzing Hawkins's personality, but it reveals a great deal about England's development during one of the most colorful periods in her history.

Nearly everything in the circumstances of John Hawkins's origins seemed to point him inexorably toward the part he was to play in British history. A Devon man, Hawkins was born in Plymouth in 1532, and the time and place of his birth, as well as the economic interests of his family, dictated the nature of his career. Hawkins's birth coincided with the beginning of the English Reformation and took place in a part of the British Isles that quickly adapted to the new religion. He was thus reared in an atmosphere where hostility toward Catholicism and Spain, the leading Catholic state during Hawkins's adult years, was the norm. Young Hawkins's family relied on seaborne commerce for its livelihood; his father, William Hawkins, was an important Plymouth merchant, and his elder brother, also named William, learned the details of the family business when he was a boy. Thus Protestantism, commerce, and the sea, the elements that were to carry John Hawkins to a position of importance and responsibility in Elizabeth's England, were evident at his birth.

Two years before John was born, his father made a business decision that was to have far-reaching significance both for England and the Hawkins family. An enterprising man, the elder Hawkins determined in 1530 to expand his commercial outlets by adding Africa and South America to a list of mercantile contacts that already included France, Spain, Portugal, and their respective dependencies. Specifically, Hawkins planned to take English manufactured goods such as knives, cloth, and inexpensive jewelry to Africa, trade with the natives there for ivory, gold, and pepper, and then continue his voyage across the Atlantic to Brazil. There he hoped to secure a commodity nearly as valuable in England as precious metal, brazilwood. Used in dyeing cloth and in very short supply in the British Isles, brazilwood and the considerable profit to be made from it were probably what prompted Hawkins to initiate his innovative trade scheme. Ultimately, it meant a great deal more than merely a fortune made from the raw material for red dye, for the Hawkins voyage of 1530 proved to be the prototype of the "triangle" voyages that were to become so important in British economic and imperial history. Additionally, William Hawkins's Brazil venture served to inform Englishmen of the wide variety of products available in the New World while it aroused their curiosity about its seemingly endless store of curiosities.

The Brazil voyage of 1530 was such an unqualified economic success that it stimulated Hawkins to repeat it in 1531 and again in 1532. The second venture attracted the attention of Henry VIII by bringing back to England a Brazilian Indian chieftain who apparently fascinated England's ruler. With these three voyages and the approval of King Henry, William Hawkins inaugurated not only a trade with two far distant areas but he also laid the foundation for a general reshaping of England's foreign trade. To be sure, the European wool market remained predominant for the rest of the sixteenth century both in fact and also in the minds of most English businessmen, but the distant and novel foreign trade that was to make England an economic power and also lead her to acquire an empire was begun by commercial pioneers such as William Hawkins.

When John Hawkins was born, his father had just begun to trade with the New World, so the excitement normal to maturing in a commercial, seafaring family during the Tudor period was intensified. With the return of each Hawkins expedition from Brazil, new discoveries and observations were reported by the crews, and from earliest childhood young John Hawkins was indoctrinated with the adventure and glory of sailing to Africa and America. Given little formal education, John was, like his elder brother, expected to learn seamanship and the intricacies of the family business. When he reached adolescence John Hawkins was definitely unpolished in a courtly sense; but he was well-mannered, articulate, and quite prepared to assume his share of responsibility in increasing the family's fortune. By the time Edward VI succeeded to the throne, John and William Hawkins had substantially taken control of the detailed operation of the family business. Their father, confident that the modest commercial empire he had constructed was in capable hands, gave only general advice and devoted most of his time to public service as Mayor of Plymouth and representative of the city in Parliament. At an age when a modern child would be only half way through his education, John Hawkins was a ship captain and merchant responsible for valuable stocks of goods and large sums of money. His life was a cycle of lading goods, sailing to France, Spain, or the Canaries, exchanging or selling cargoes, and returning to Plymouth to start again. At any other time in British history before Elizabeth's reign, he probably would have made a comfortable career for himself by simply following the established nature of his business. However, his adult years coincided with a period that permitted ambition and ability to rise above the limitations of class and status. It was symbolically appropriate for his own career, as well as a sign of the times, that Hawkins adopted the motto "Advancement by Diligence."

Hawkins's first step away from the ordinary merchant's life, one that led eventually to his rise in the ranks of Elizabethan government and society, resulted from his business dealings. At the time of Elizabeth's accession, he was trading regularly with merchants in the Canary Islands, where Englishmen had held legitimate trading privileges since the signing of the Treaty of Medina del Campo. From one of his commercial contacts in the Canaries, a man named Pedro de Ponte, John Hawkins learned that a potentially profitable market for black slaves existed in Spain's American empire. Any foreigner who sought to exploit the market, however, faced what appeared to be insurmountable obstacles. Regulated by the Medina del Campo treaty of 1489, Anglo-Spanish commercial relations specifically gave each country free access to the other's European possessions. But Spain's New World lands, discovered after the signing of the treaty, were viewed by the Spanish to be beyond the terms of the agreement. In fact, the Hapsburgs rigorously prohibited trade with their American colonies, as did the Portuguese, and the only exceptions that were made to these prohibitions arose under carefully limited circumstances. Regulated by the grant of a special license called an *asiento*, these exclusions from monopoly control were given only to a small number of foreign nationals and permitted them to sell only specific products in designated parts of the Spanish empire. To complicate matters further, England and Spain were at peace and formally allied against Valois France. Thus, Hawkins risked incurring the wrath of both the Spanish and English governments if he acted on de Ponte's information without securing an *asiento*. Moreover, Hawkins did not have sufficient capital to finance such a costly and dangerous enterprise as opening a trade in black slaves with Spanish America. The difficulties inherent in the venture nearly caused Hawkins to abandon it, but just as he was about to make that negative decision his resolve was stiffened by information that he learned during a visit to London.

The Hawkins family could claim extensive contacts in the capital. As early as the 1530s, the Hawkins patriarch had established business ties with such a powerful man as Thomas Cromwell, and while Cromwell had been executed in 1540, the connections in London that he and others had given the Hawkins family had been cultivated assiduously. When he went to the capital in 1561 to discuss an expansion of trade with other merchants and secure capital for various enterprises, John Hawkins naturally utilized his family's influence. In the course of his discussions, the issue of opening a trade in slaves was introduced by the ambitious, young Plymouth merchant, and his first insight into solving the problems of beginning this new trade probably came from Hawkins's father-in-law, Benjamin Gonson, who was Treasurer of the Admiralty. First, Gonson informed his son-in-law that the question of England's alliance with Spain could be largely ignored. The Peace of Cateau-Cambrésis of 1559 had ended the Anglo-Spanish war against France, and the alliance had been severely strained by Spanish treatment of the English during the negotiations. Additionally, Gonson told Hawkins, the Queen and her advisers seriously questioned the right of the Spanish and the Portuguese to prohibit foreigners to trade in their empires. The Government rejected the Papal Line of Demarcation as the definitive division of the non-European world between Spain and Portugal, and the Queen furthermore took the position that the Iberian powers would have to occupy effectively these far-flung territories to have any reasonable claim to exclusive control over them. Gonson concluded that it should prove worthwhile to test the nature and extent of the Government's views on Spanish and Portuguese imperial control. Hawkins's discovery of the Crown's attitude, which seemed authoritative, given the relatively high administrative post of Gonson, solved the political problems relating to inaugurating a slave trade. Hawkins was still left with the question of how to secure enough money to finance the project.

Before the formation of the joint-stock company of limited liability, it would have been virtually impossible to raise the money that Hawkins needed to open the slave trade. However, the creation of the Muscovy Company, a model for corporate financing, had demonstrated the ease with which capital could be mobilized, so Hawkins decided to form a similar company and sell shares in the project. The touchy political implications of the venture prevented him from "going public," but he had little difficulty in finding investors. Some powerful London merchants were already engaged in a clandestine trade with West Africa, and they indicated an interest in subscribing. Since the accepted ethics of Tudor England did not prevent civil servants from also having extensive commercial interests, a number of government officials who were also merchants and interested in innovative trade elected to support the venture. Early in 1562 these prospective investors agreed to the terms outlined by John Hawkins, and a company, legitimate but not possessing a Crown license, was formed to finance England's first venture into the slave trade. Consisting of the Hawkins brothers, Benjamin Gonson and William Winter of the Admiralty, William Broomfield of the Ordnance Department, and the London magnates Sir Thomas Lodge and Sir Lionel Duckett, the company represented the upper strata but certainly not the top of the Elizabethan social order. Each man subscribed the same amount of money, with the understanding that the profits would be shared equally.

Convinced by nearly three centuries of thought affirming individual rights, the modern mind finds Hawkins's plan of selling people to make money particularly repulsive. But, to most Europeans of the 16th century there were no serious doubts about the morality of slavery. The black African, uncivilized in the European view and non-Christian as well, had at best an insignificant place in the Elizabethan perception of universal order, and thus was ideally suited for slavery. Harsh as it was, this view was the psychological foundation of all European colonial empires, which needed some plausible justification for exploiting most of the world's population for the benefit of Europe. Indeed, race had little to do with such reasoning, for the Elizabethan Englishman held the white, Christian Irishman in little more regard than the African and treated him with almost as little consideration. This attitude, unquestioned in the Tudor era, supported both slavery and colonialism for 200 years. Accordingly, the morality of selling black Africans probably never occurred to John Hawkins. If it did, he suppressed it and forged ahead with his project.

In the autumn of 1562 John Hawkins sailed out from Plymouth harbor, leading a fleet of four ships; it marked the beginning of 250 years of English traffic in slaves. First, he sailed to Teneriffe in the Canaries to pick up a pilot, Juan Martinez, who knew how to navigate the waters of the West Indies and who had been recruited for Hawkins by Pedro de Ponte. While there he also learned that de Ponte had written to planters in Spanish America informing them to expect Hawkins, and their replies had been ones uniformly anticipating a new supply of slaves. From the Canaries the Hawkins fleet sailed on to Africa, where, between Cape Verde and Sierra Leone, the English plundered Portuguese shipping. Two ships were captured intact and because of their quality were added to Hawkins's fleet, and their cargoes of ivory, gold, and other goods made the voyage a financial success long before a single slave was transported to the New World. Slaves were, however, also part of the cargoes captured by Hawkins, and soon he had collected 900 blacks, all that his fleet could carry, and he turned west to transact the main business of the venture.

Crossing the Atlantic on the second leg of the "triangle" inaugurated by his father, Hawkins and his seamen were the first Englishmen to witness the horrors of what was to become the infamous "middle passage" of the slave trade. Crowded into the holds of ships that were ill-prepared to contain them, and tended by men who were unequipped to care for their simplest physical needs, the Africans lived in suffocating heat, slept in their own filth, and died by the dozen. The survivors, naturally ignorant of their destination, learned their fate in April 1563, when the Hawkins fleet made its first contact with Spanish colonists in the New World. Hawkins's landfall was, as he had intended it to be, the island of Hispaniola. There, in the city of Santo Domingo, was located the government for the Spanish Caribbean islands and for the string of settlements across the northern coast of South America known as the Spanish Main. The English captain calculated that if he could trade successfully at Santo Domingo, where most of de Ponte's friends lived, there would be no difficulty bartering thereafter in the rest of the Spanish dominions.

From the first contact, the Spanish planters made it clear that they very much wanted to trade with Hawkins, for slaves were in short supply throughout Spanish America. But the colonists were worried about the King's prohibition against trading with unlicensed merchants, so Hawkins and the Spaniards worked out a plan whereby he threatened them with force unless they traded with him and they gave in to his demands rather than risk bloodshed. A brisk trade ensued, with the Spanish securing the much-needed slaves and the English filling the holds of their ships with hides, pearls, ginger, sugar, and other products of colonial America.

Within a few months, Hawkins had disposed of all the blacks, and he returned to England in August 1563. He had collected so much cargo that he found it necessary to purchase extra ships in America, and he sent two of these laden with hides for sale to Spain. Presumably, Hawkins's intent was to indicate to King Philip II by sending these ships that he and his English backers meant to trade in good faith and had nothing but peaceful intentions toward Spain. If amity and peace was what Hawkins was trying to communicate to Philip II with the "hide ships," he failed completely, for the Spanish King was furious at the violation of his mercantile empire, and he promptly ordered the seizure of the ships and their cargoes. Moreover, he dispatched orders to his colonial officials to prevent any future trade with the English at all costs. Despite the loss of two ships, the voyage was a remarkable financial success. The investors realized profits of better than 60 percent, and John Hawkins quickly became famous for his exploit.

The success of the first slaving voyage created considerable interest in organizing a second one, and in 1564 a new syndicate was formed to develop further this profitable new trade. Some of England's most powerful merchants and bureaucrats bought shares. Prominent London politicians and businessmen such as Sir William Chester, Sir William Garrard, and Edward Castlyn invested readily in the venture, and the middle level of government administration was represented again by Gonson and Winter of the Admiralty. Even the highest levels of Elizabethan society and political life indicated a strong interest in the project, for a number of Privy Councillors subscribed to the venture. Some of the more noteworthy were Sir William Cecil, the Queen's principal adviser; Lord Clinton and Saye, the Lord Admiral; and the Earls of Leicester and Pembroke, confidants of the Queen. Indeed, Elizabeth herself thought so much of the project that she subscribed a ship, the *Jesus of Lubeck*, which was valued at £3,000 and constituted the lion's share of the voyage's backing. Clearly, England's economic and political leaders saw the traffic in slaves as a permanent and profitable new feature of English business enterprise. Some of the craftier politicians, such as Cecil, may even at this early date have seen the trade as an important weapon against Hapsburg Spain, but this cannot be proven conclusively.

In October 1564, Hawkins sailed again for Africa with a larger and more powerful fleet of five ships. When he arrived he made what proved to be an unwise alteration of the tactics of the first voyage. Instead of simply stealing blacks from the Portuguese, as he had done in 1562, he tried to capture them by attacking African villages. He soon learned it was considerably less hazardous taking blacks from the Portuguese. Commanding 40 men, Hawkins fell upon a village in hopes of capturing the entire population, but his men scattered to search for gold as soon as the Africans fled, so the blacks regrouped and counterattacked. The Englishmen suffered heavy casualties. Seven men were killed, including the captain of one of the ships, and 27 others were wounded; only discipline and John Hawkins's defensive maneuvers prevented a wholesale slaughter. Acknowledging that the English still had a great deal to learn about slave catching, Hawkins reverted to his former technique of gathering slaves and began stealing them again from the Portuguese. He collected 600 Africans from the Iberian slavers, who appeared to be more skilled at capturing blacks than they were at keeping control of them. Hawkins then set course for America.

After reaching the New World in March 1565, he discovered that conditions had changed dramatically in two years. The planters were still anxious to barter for Hawkins's captives, but their colonial governors were bound by King Philip's injunctions to keep the English from trading. The Spanish colonial officials, however, let Hawkins know that they could be persuaded to overlook their monarch's orders if they were again subjected to threats of force. Consequently, Hawkins conspired with them to carry out a charade of violent intentions, vowing to reduce every town on the Spanish Main to smoking rubble if his demands were not met. After this bizarre but necessary formality was completed, a brisk trade took place between the English and the Spanish planters under cover provided by the feigned protests of King Philip's representatives. Despite these awkward circumstances Hawkins was able to complete another profitable series of exchanges and, in September 1565, his fleet arrived in England with all the holds filled with Spanish colonial products. This time, no ships were sent to Spain as English tokens of honorable intentions.

When the profits were finally divided, it became clear that the second slaving venture was even more profitable than the first had been, and there were again proposals to mount yet another voyage. But Hawkins was concerned about the hostility of the colonial governors, who were obviously under the strictest orders from Madrid to prevent the English from trading. Since Hawkins's risks were increased by Philip II's apparent determination to keep the English out of his empire, he decided to put off forming a new company in favor of negotiating with the Spanish for an *asiento*. For two years he discussed the matter with the Spanish Ambassador, Guzman de Silva, offering nearly everything in his power to secure a license. John Hawkins promised to pay all duties prescribed by law to King Philip, to police the Spanish Main and protect it from Huguenot corsairs, and even to serve with his ships in the Spanish struggle against the Turks in the Mediterranean. The Spanish Ambassador dealt suavely with Hawkins. Consistently polite and friendly, de Silva led the seaman to think for months that the cherished *asiento* was almost in his grasp, when in fact Philip II had no intention of granting Hawkins a license, and this the Ambassador knew full well. Eventually, Hawkins was told that the Spanish King refused to give him access to the New World trade, and he was both disappointed by Philip's decision and angry at the Ambassador's duplicity in wasting two years of his time on what had never really been a negotiable issue. Faced with what he construed as obstinacy, unreasonableness, and dishonest dealing, John Hawkins set about finding financial backing. Thanks at least in part to de Silva's attitude, he had decided to ignore the Spanish rebuff and mount a third voyage in 1567. In all probability, John Hawkins and his supporters hoped to show King Philip that it would be less costly to admit them to the slave trade than to support a military force powerful enough to keep them out. Although the third slaving voyage did teach Philip II a number of lessons that he might have learned at less cost, they were not exactly the ones that originally motivated the Hawkins syndicate.

The third voyage was by far the largest and most ambitious in terms of ships and men. The syndicate that financed the enterprise was, with a few new merchant investors, basically the same one that subscribed to the second slaving venture. But the third voyage differed profoundly from its predecessors. It was an unlucky one, and ended all hopes of founding a permanent slave trade during the reign of Elizabeth. From the moment that Hawkins's fleet of six ships, two of them Royal Navy men-of-war subscribed by the Queen, left Plymouth the expedition seemed headed for disaster. A few days after departing England a violent storm battered and nearly sank the ships, with Hawkins's flagship, the *Jesus of Lubeck*, saved from foundering only by the most desperate measures on the part of her crew. Separated by the storm, the ships rendezvoused according to a prearranged plan at the Canary Islands, but there more trouble awaited. The English fleet was nearly trapped and destroyed by the Spaniards in the harbor at Teneriffe, which contrasted sharply to the warm welcome that Hawkins and his ships had received there in the past. The further the English progressed on the venture, the greater the difficulties that beset them.

In Africa, Hawkins seemed to have forgotten what he had learned about slaving on his last voyage, for an attempt was made to capture blacks rather than secure them by some safer means. After several men were killed by poisoned arrows in a vain effort to collect a slave cargo, Hawkins tried a new and surprisingly successful tactic. Learning of a war between two black tribes, he allied with one of them on condition that he receive all prisoners of war as payment for his help. Finally, the fortunes of the third slaving venture improved. Hawkins and his allies quickly won the war, the suitable prisoners were consigned to the holds of the slave ships, and by the time the English fleet embarked on the now familiar middle passage the past misfortunes were forgotten. The voyage across the Atlantic was uneventful.

Upon arrival in America, however, Hawkins found the Spanish officials not only hostile, but also totally committed to preventing the English from trading with the colonists. In every port along the Spanish Main he found it necessary to coerce the planters into trading by the threat or application of force, for fear of King Philip's wrath exceeded the need to increase the colonial labor force. The effort of trading under such conditions proved both so dangerous and so time-consuming that it took Hawkins several months to dispose of his slaves, and it was with considerable relief that he set sail for England by the most direct route, the Florida Channel. As he approached the channel in August 1568, the hurricane season was beginning and his luck worsened. A violent storm came up suddenly and drove all but one of his ships westward across the Gulf of Mexico. The ships, particularly the *Jesus of Lubeck*, which had never been properly repaired after struggling through the Atlantic storm several months earlier, were so badly damaged by the buffeting winds that an ocean crossing to the British Isles was out of the question, so Hawkins took the only option available. He sailed into the Spanish harbor of San Juan de Ulua on the Mexican coast, the main port for Mexico City, and seized the anchorage. Knowing that the annual Spanish treasure fleet from Europe was due to arrive at any time, John Hawkins fortified his position in the harbor and hoped that he would have enough time to repair his ships and escape unscathed.

Within two days of Hawkins's entrance into San Juan, the Spanish flotilla appeared under the command of Don Martin Enriquez, the Viceroy for New Spain. Understandably, he bristled with hostility upon learning that the English were in the harbor; and when he learned that they had fortified their position, his rage grew along with his determination to eject them. At first the Viceroy threatened and blustered, but when it became apparent that Hawkins was fully aware of the strength of the English position, Don Martin adopted a different stratagem. Using all of his guile, the Viceroy negotiated a settlement with Hawkins which made it possible for the Spanish fleet to enter the anchorage, although they did so covered by English cannon. Don Martin then plotted in conjunction with Spanish land-based forces a surprise attack that clearly violated the terms of his agreement with Hawkins. Later, the Viceroy stated that since Hawkins had no right to enter a Spanish roadstead, much less seize and fortify it, then Don Martin was bound neither as a Spanish Crown official nor as a gentleman to honor a bargain made with a man who obviously was a pirate. John Hawkins, for his part, ignored the logic of Don Martin's claim and accused him of the basest treachery. Consequently, the attack on Hawkins's fleet at San Juan de Ulua contributed significantly to the growth of distrust between English and Spanish seamen, merchants, and, eventually, politicians during the remaining decades of the Tudor era. This mistrust, exacerbated later by religious conflict and war, did a great deal to shape the ferocity of future Anglo-Spanish encounters.

Treacherous or not, Don Martin's plan worked to perfection. A combined operation utilizing land and sea forces was launched simultaneously against the English fleet, and when the smoke had cleared, two English ships lay on the bottom of the harbor, two were limping away into the Caribbean, and hundreds of Hawkins's men were either killed, wounded, or captured. After a harrowing voyage across the Atlantic in which Hawkins and his remaining crew survived mainly by eating boiled leather, what was left of his most powerful slaving expedition reached England in January 1569. Compared to its predecessors, the third venture was a disaster of the first magnitude. Yet, it still returned a profit to the investors who supported it, for Hawkins had managed to carry away most of the treasure he had collected when he fled San Juan.

Profits did not, however, compensate Hawkins and his backers for the loss of goods, ships, and men. Englishmen were angered and embittered over what they interpreted as treacherous activity on the part of the Spaniards. Their response was intensified because the attack on Hawkins coincided with other events that pointed toward a Spanish policy aimed at crippling or conquering England. In 1569, the Catholic Earls of Northumberland and Westmorland led a rebellion against Elizabeth, hoping for Spanish support. At the same time, Philip of Spain's representative in the Netherlands, the Duke of Alva, had precipitated a civil war there by attempting to suppress Calvinism, and many Englishmen viewed this as both an indirect attack on English Protestantism and a veiled threat to England's wool market in the Low Countries. These events combined with an Anglo-Spanish trade embargo to reduce relations between the two countries to a dismally low point, where it remained for the duration of Elizabeth's reign. But despite the setbacks he had encountered, John Hawkins personally benefited substantially from his thwarted attempt to open a trade in "black ivory." He made an international reputation for himself as a daring mariner and entrepreneur, and most importantly, he made powerful friends and contacts among England's ruling class. Soon after his return from Mexico, those contacts and a unique set of circumstances led John Hawkins away from the world of seafaring adventure and into the murky, conspiratorial realm of counterespionage.

Sir William Cecil, Elizabeth's principal adviser and also a subscriber to the last two slaving voyages, was the man responsible for John Hawkins's involvement in intelligence work. A meticulous administrator of remarkable ability, Cecil had by the late 1560s developed both a deep suspicion of Spain and also the machinery, a crude and informal espionage network, through which he could test his suspicions. Given his background, Hawkins would appear to be an unlikely choice as an agent for Cecil, but the disaster of the third slaving voyage transformed the unlikely into a reality. Several of Hawkins's men captured at San Juan de Ulua provided the opportunity for their former captain to serve Cecil as an intelligence agent, and they did so by making Hawkins one of the key figures in the first major counterespionage coup of Elizabeth's reign. This came with the exposure of Roberto Ridolfi's plot of depose Elizabeth and replace her with Mary, Queen of Scots.

Shortly after Hawkins's defeat at San Juan, a select few of his captured men were sent to Spain to be questioned by the Inquisition. One of these prisoners, George Fitzwilliam, Hawkins's servant, gave his master the chance to assist in uncovering Ridolfi's conspiracy. Fitzwilliam was related to the wife of the powerful Spanish Duke of Feria, and through this connection Fitzwilliam persuaded the Spanish authorities to release him from prison. He then wrote to Cecil, requesting his aid in freeing the other English prisoners, who were ill-clad, starving, and suffering daily torment at the hands of their Spanish jailers. At this point it appears that Cecil nearly let the chance presented by Fitzwilliam slip away, for he referred the matter to Hawkins, who naturally had the greatest interest in freeing his men. Reflection on the uniqueness of Fitzwilliam's position, however, seems to have given Cecil an inspiration. Instead of simply passing the matter on to Hawkins, Cecil conferred with him about the possibility of taking advantage of Fitzwilliam's status to probe in some detail Spain's attitude toward England. Anxious to please the Queen's closest adviser, John Hawkins agreed to cooperate fully with Cecil's intelligence exploration, and in a short time he began a series of interviews with Guerau de Spes, the new Spanish Ambassador to England.

Hawkins informed de Spes in general, but unmistakable, terms that he was distressed by the unwillingness of Elizabeth's government to do anything to help him recoup the losses he had suffered in Mexico. He particularly let the Ambassador know that he was concerned about the fate of his men, who were being held prisoner; and he hinted that he would do anything to secure their release. That de Spes was taken in by Hawkins's transparent ruse is testimony to his incompetence as an ambassador, for rather than being suspicious de Spes embraced the potential English traitor with an innocence unbefitting his profession. Although he declined to be specific, the Ambassador let Hawkins know that a major Spanish plot against England was in the developmental stages, and that was all Cecil and Hawkins needed to lead them into a relentless pursuit of the details of the conspiracy.

For several months Hawkins in London and Fitzwilliam in Spain tried to learn the details of the plot, and early in 1571 all of the parts of the intelligence puzzle were finally pieced together. Fitzwilliam returned to England and reported to Hawkins, and in March Hawkins bluntly offered his services and fleet to the Spanish. Philip II responded favorably, and in April Fitzwilliam was sent back to Spain carrying Hawkins's terms. In an interview with the King, he made a concrete offer on behalf of his master. Hawkins agreed to commit all of his family's wealth, influence, and naval strength to a plan to assassinate Elizabeth, replace her with Mary Stuart, and restore Roman Catholicism as England's only religion. In return, Fitzwilliam asked simply that Hawkins's men be released from custody and suitable rewards be given to Hawkins's followers after the plan had succeeded. King Philip was suspicious, despite the affirmation of the Englishman's honesty by de Spes, and he demanded that Hawkins secure a guarantee of his integrity from the Queen of Scots before he would release the prisoners. With a letter to the Scottish monarch outlining the plot in general terms and written in invisible ink, Fitzwilliam hastened back to England.

When she received the letter, Mary Stuart at once vouched for Hawkins and committed herself to the conspiracy. She had never met the

Plymouth seaman, and really knew nothing about him, but like so many desperate prisoners she was always willing to support anyone who promised to release her from captivity. Carrying the Scottish Queen's certification of his master's character and good intentions, Fitzwilliam returned to Spain in July. By then the plan had been worked out to its last detail. The murder of Elizabeth was to be followed by a Catholic rebellion led by the Duke of Norfolk and combined with invasions of England from Spain and the Netherlands. John Hawkins's role in the plot was a relatively modest but nonetheless crucial one. He was to sail eastward in the English Channel and aid the crossing of the Duke of Alva's troops from the Low Countries. His departure from Plymouth would denude the western approach to the Channel and leave it open to the invasion from Spain. In return for this promise of treason, King Philip demonstrated his good faith by releasing Hawkins's men and sending them home to England.

The Ridolfi plot proved to be a fiasco, since all of its details were known to the English government through information supplied by Hawkins and Fitzwilliam as well as other sources. For his part, Hawkins expertly played the role of double agent, and simply used the abortive conspiracy to free his men and provide Cecil with concrete evidence for what he already suspected: that the Duke of Norfolk was a traitor and the Scottish Queen a desperate and dangerous prisoner. Ultimately, no attempt was made to kill Elizabeth, but there were two noteworthy developments that stemmed directly from the exposure of the plot. One was the arrest, trial, and execution of the Duke of Norfolk, England's premier nobleman, on a charge of high treason. The other was an affirmation of the value of judiciously collected intelligence information, which was proven to be vital in the formulation of policies. With the exposure of the Ridolfi plot, the confidence of the Queen and her advisers in the utility of a secret service grew so that an espionage apparatus came to be viewed as a valuable and normal part of governmental activity. Under the guidance of Cecil's ally, Sir Francis Walsingham, the Elizabethan intelligence network increased in importance and refined its techniques, and soon it was highly respected in European political circles for its thoroughness and reliability.

After his men were released and Ridolfi's plot was frustrated, Hawkins continued his charade of treason in an attempt to extract more information from de Spes about Spanish policies concerning England. Hawkins had, however, compromised his position so completely that even the gullible Ambassador refused to have anything further to do with him. His brief career in espionage thus ended, John Hawkins managed to combine his maritime experiences with his work for the Crown to develop what was perhaps the most significant phase of his career. Through his friendship with Cecil, and his close ties with Benjamin Gonson,

Hawkins became after 1571 steadily more involved in the affairs of the Royal Navy. Although he did not have a formal post at the Admiralty, it seems that Hawkins worked as an aide to Gonson after the exposure of the Ridolfi conspiracy, and in the process he learned a good deal about the administrative side of naval affairs. Hawkins showed a genuine talent for solving many of the problems faced by the naval bureaucracy in the 1570s. By becoming an administrator and effectively giving up the life of adventure that seemed to fit him so well, John Hawkins assumed a position of leadership in one of the least understood but most important phenomena of the Elizabethan period: the founding of the modern bureaucratic state.

An "administrative revolution" initiated by Thomas Cromwell in the 1530s matured substantially during Elizabeth's reign, and the Admiralty was one of the principal government departments indicating the extent of bureaucratic development. In 1578 John Hawkins became a part of this dynamic administration by contriving with Cecil to replace Gonson as Admiralty Treasurer. Once in office, Hawkins soon showed just how much he understood the principles of effective administration, and through his leadership and introduction of innovations, he made the Admiralty a model department of government. Before Hawkins took Gonson's place as Treasurer, the Admiralty was typical of Crown departments in its haphazard procedures and moderate corruption. By the time he left the office, the Admiralty had been transformed into a distinctly modern administrative organization, characterized by definite structures and systems, efficiency, and relative honesty. Thus, in an unassuming but distinctive way, John Hawkins played a part in creating general guidelines for Britain's civil service.

Hawkins's achievements in bureaucracy were not easily won. When he assumed his duties as Treasurer, Gonson, who was tired, worn down by the pressure of managing the Navy's finances and cowed by his more aggressive Admiralty colleagues, warned, "I shall pluck a thorn from my foot and place it in yours." The retiring Treasurer could not have been more serious. He viewed the post as a thankless one with little profit, many pains, and endless frustrations. Hawkins chose, however, to ignore the warning, for he was fresh, determined, full of new ideas based on his maritime experiences, and confident that he could cope with the forces that had so discouraged Gonson. Consequently, when Hawkins became Treasurer he inaugurated a stormy period in the administration of the Royal Navy. For the first few years, it seemed as though the Admiralty might be reduced to administrative impotence by the strains that he created, but Hawkins finally took command and streamlined the department so that it was able to equip and maintain the English fleet that defeated the Spanish Armada in 1588.

Hawkins faced two basic problems as a naval administrator. First, he had to eliminate the corruption that in his view reduced the Admiralty's effectiveness. Some of the naval bureaucrats were, for example, using timber purchased by the Crown for the Royal Navy to build their own private ships, and Hawkins determined from the outset to put a stop to such brazen malfeasance. What was perhaps worse was the problem that Hawkins faced in overcoming the conservatism of his colleagues, for that threatened to prevent him from applying the latest technological developments to the ships in order to give them physical superiority over any potential enemy. Eliminating embezzling at the Admiralty proved to be his most trying task, for the main offender was one of his former partners, Sir William Winter, Surveyor of the Ships and Master of Naval Ordnance. Hawkins struggled with Winter, a powerful merchant-bureaucrat with impressive political connections, almost continually for nearly ten years, and in the critical encounters the Treasurer emerged triumphant. But Hawkins's victories over Winter and others were not due entirely to his own skill. He had a valuable ally in Cecil, who had become the Lord Treasurer and had also been elevated to the peerage as Baron Burghley. In his campaign against entrenched graft, support from Burghley assured Hawkins of the implementation of his policies.

The reforms of John Hawkins dealt with several features of administration, but the most important concerned naval expenditures and were incorporated in an unusual agreement between Hawkins and the Crown usually known as the "First Bargain." This was a contract in which the Treasurer agreed to perform specified services for the Navy, such as supply sailcloth and timber, in return for a government guarantee that he could exercise the rights and enjoy the privileges of his office. In effect, Hawkins sought to take most of the responsibility for the Royal Navy's support, and the Queen agreed to give him a free hand so long as he maintained an effective fleet and saved the government money. The Treasurer's main proposal was to reduce the ordinary charges[1] for maintaining the ships from £6,000 to £4,000 a year, and, even with this reduction in expenditure, he promised to give the ships better care and equipment than they had had before his succession to office. While this pleased Elizabeth and her Councillors, it infuriated Hawkins's fellow officers, for they saw the cut in expenditure as a threat to their incomes. Two of the men who had the most to lose by the proposals, Sir William Winter and his brother George, organized an assault on Hawkins's position designed primarily to make it impossible for him to fulfill his part of the "First Bargain." Within two years the

---

[1] Ordinary charges were the costs in wages and supplies required annually by the Royal Navy to keep the warships in a state of military preparedness. Extraordinary charges were the costs incurred when the fleet was mobilized and sent on a mission at sea.

Admiralty became a battleground where bickering among angry department heads was the rule rather than the exception.

When the quarreling reached such intensity that it threatened to affect the military capacity of the fleet, Lord Burghley intervened to restore order in the naval administration and also to protect the Crown's advantageous contract with Hawkins. The Lord Treasurer appointed Sir William Winter to the command of a small fleet patrolling the Irish coast, ostensibly to keep out Spanish infiltrators. That kept Hawkins's principal enemy away from London for two years. George Winter died during his brother's absence, thus removing another of the Treasurer's obstacles at the Admiralty. Hawkins was left in peace to complete his reforms and prepare the Navy for a rumored Spanish attack on England. Shortly after Winter's departure the Treasurer reorganized the Navy's finances and began carrying out the technical changes that were to prove so vital in 1588. Most notably, Hawkins added a number of small reconaissance craft to the fleet and overhauled all of the ships, re-equipping them to put them in the best possible condition. Moreover, he completely rebuilt many of the larger ships along lines of the battleship *Revenge*, which was long and low, fast and maneuverable, and armed with heavy cannon that were designed to inflict maximum damage on enemy ships, rather than simply to kill soldiers on the decks. In the midst of the reconstruction program, Winter returned from Ireland, chastened and willing to work with his former enemy to prepare the fleet for the clash with Spain.

Throughout the 1580s John Hawkins worked to make England's navy a key factor in the growing struggle between Protestantism and Catholicism. During those same years he and a number of other Elizabethan administrators formulated the precepts which have been the general tenets for effective bureaucracy down through the years. Efficiency was elevated to the status of a principle upon which all administration was to be structured. Corruption, peculation, informality, and contempt for procedure were anathematized as dangerous luxuries that the state could not afford. Technology was recognized as the means by which material superiority over the state's rivals was to be achieved. John Hawkins had no experience in government when he became Navy Treasurer, but he brought to the job an honest approach and a passion for the efficiency that had always meant the difference between profit and loss in his business dealings. When he temporarily left the bureaucracy and returned to the sea in 1588, John Hawkins claimed that he was really only a simple seaman who could best serve the Queen from the quarterdeck of a warship. Regardless of whether or not this claim was an expression of false modesty, it was an inaccurate evaluation of Hawkins's contribution to Elizabethan government, for he was prominent among the small group of Crown officials who set new standards for the performance of civil servants. Additionally, his work at the Admiralty was of the greatest consequence in preparing England for her clash with Spain when it came in 1588.

When England faced the attempted Spanish invasion, Hawkins was 56 years old, well beyond middle age in the 16th century, and he suffered from chronic bad health. Still, when the greatest fleet ever assembled prepared to sail from Lisbon to subjugate England, he decided to leave the relative security of the Admiralty and return to the sea, which he thought was the only proper place for him in the crisis of 1588. Initially reluctant to accede to Hawkins's request to be given command of a ship, Queen Elizabeth finally gave way under the pressure of his continual pleading and appointed him as commander of the *Victory*. Accepting the post of Rear-Admiral of the English fleet, subordinate to Vice-Admiral Drake and Lord Admiral Howard, John Hawkins took command of his ship at Plymouth in the spring of 1588 and left the worries of the Admiralty to a deputy.

The defeat of the attempted Spanish invasion of England in 1588 was easily the most dramatic event of Elizabeth's reign. Indeed, it was a turning point in European history. For the English victory not only frustrated the Spanish design to restore England to Catholicism by force: it preserved the rebel Dutch state in the Netherlands and administered a humiliating defeat to Spain that had a devastating impact on her international prestige. From beginning to end, John Hawkins played an important role in assuring the English victory. As Navy Treasurer, he saw to it that the fleets were armed, equipped, manned and supplied. As a fleet commander, he sat in the councils of war that planned the successful strategy and tactics. As commander of the *Victory* he inspired his men through exhortation and example to work to the limits of their endurance and courage. When the battle was won, and the remnant of the Spanish fleet was fleeing into the North Sea on the long route back to Iberia, Hawkins returned to London, exhausted by his efforts. He was also deeply concerned over the prospect of having to prepare the detailed accounts of money spent by the Royal Navy when he resumed his duties at the Admiralty.

Instead of the recognition that he might have expected for his work, Hawkins received little but criticism from the Queen and her advisers, who bemoaned the "excessive" cost of beating the Spanish. The knighthood that he was given was a hollow honor, for it did not come from the Queen in an elaborate ceremony at Court. It was rather bestowed by the Lord Admiral during the battle in a ceremony where Hawkins was only one of several men thus rewarded. Feeling humiliated, Hawkins retreated into the cover of his age and physical infirmities and requested a one-year leave of absence from the Admiralty to prepare his accounts. This was granted, and after several months he developed a more stoical attitude about his treatment by the Crown, apparently deciding that what he took to be Elizabeth's hostility toward him was actually nothing more than an expression of concern over the cost of an extremely expensive military undertaking. This realization seems to have cheered him as well as motivated him to complete the dreary work on the accounts, for by the end of 1589 they were accepted by the Lord Treasurer and the Chancellor of the Exchequer as being in order. Yet, Gonson's words haunted Hawkins as he struggled with his books on expenses and inventories, and he found the "thorn in his foot" so painful that he decided to retire from public service. By 1590 he wanted nothing more than to be allowed to return to Plymouth where he could relax, supervise the family business, and live the life of adventure vicariously through his son Richard, who was fast becoming a mirror image of his father as a young man.

Despite his desire to leave Crown service, Sir John Hawkins was not permitted to retire, for in Tudor England public officials could not terminate their careers at will. Serving the state meant also serving the monarch in a curiously personal capacity, and consequently the ruler's leave had to be secured before any public office of consequence could be vacated. Since Elizabeth I was a demanding mistress who never let an able man escape her service except through death, she denied Hawkins's request for retirement and compelled him to remain at the Admiralty as Treasurer. He was to oversee the financing and equipping of fleets that were sent to capture Spain's annual bullion fleet from America in what amounted to an English naval offensive in the early 1590s. But the expeditions, usually commanded by young courtiers with little experience at sea, all failed to achieve their objective, and the failures drove Elizabeth into a steadily deepening fury, for she had no conception of the technical difficulties involved in trying to intercept and then capture the bullion fleet. By 1594, she had finally had enough of defeat and failure caused, in her estimation, by the amateurishness of her fleet commanders, and she called upon her most experienced sea captains to administer a coup de main to the Spanish treasure convoy. The plan that Elizabeth and her advisers developed was impossible principally because it was based on several erroneous assumptions. A fleet under the joint command of Hawkins and Drake was to be sent to America, carrying enough troops to occupy Panama. Its primary objective was to cut Spain off from her Peruvian treasure trove, but the plan entailed the destruction of as much Spanish colonial shipping as possible and the capture of as many major cities as the English could occupy. Since it assumed that the Spaniards had learned nothing about protecting their New World empire since Drake's spectacular raids of the 1570s, the plan was totally divorced from reality. It accomplished nothing positive, for it led to a momentous English military defeat and also brought about the deaths of the two most renowned Elizabethan seamen, Sir Francis Drake and Sir John Hawkins.

When he sailed from Plymouth in August 1595, Hawkins was 63 years of age, physically ill, mentally exhausted, and assigned an unwanted task that was all the more depressing because he knew that he could not perform it. The liabilities of the operation were overwhelming. His co-commander, Sir Francis Drake, was far too impulsive for Hawkins's taste. Even though they were distant relatives and even though Drake had learned his seamanship in Hawkins's service and the Treasurer admired his co-commander's courage, Hawkins deplored his carelessness in preparing for the expedition. Hawkins knew, for instance, that the number of men that Drake insisted on having closely quartered in his ships would breed disease, for as Treasurer he had pioneered the reduction of ship's crews to provide adequate living space and preserve health. To compound the difficulties, Hawkins knew that the number of ships in the fleet was inadequate for the mission. Above all, there were the greatly improved Spanish defense and communications systems in America, which Drake held in contempt, the Queen insisted did not exist, and Hawkins held worthy of great respect and a cautious approach. Then, shortly before sailing, Hawkins learned that his son had been captured in the Pacific while attempting a circumnavigation of the earth and was being held prisoner in Lisbon. Sir John Hawkins found the prospects of his assault on the Spanish disheartening indeed, and events proved his apprehensions to be well-grounded.

Quickly he was at odds with Drake, who had not stocked enough supplies for the voyage and demanded that Hawkins share his. When Hawkins refused, Drake insisted that the fleet sail to the Canary Islands and seize Grand Canary while he took on adequate stores. Hawkins argued against this, pointing out that it would both delay the voyage, making it vulnerable to a Spanish fleet known to be preparing to intercept them, and it would also give the Spaniards time to warn the colonies in the New World of the English approach. A council of war ultimately overruled Hawkins's objections, and the fleet sailed for the Canaries, which were supposed to be undefended. As it turned out, Hawkins was correct in all of his criticism, for the English were unable to seize even a loaf of bread on Grand Canary because of the improved defenses built by a Spanish government that had learned well from earlier attacks by English fleets. While Drake sought vainly for a weak point to attack, the Spaniards in the Canaries followed a prearranged plan and sent a ship to alert the American colonies to the English menace. Delayed, discovered, and short of provisions, the English sailed across the Atlantic humiliated by their experience and having considerably more respect for John Hawkins's opinions. Arriving in Guadaloupe at the end of October, they found themselves confronted by a fully prepared and well-defended Spanish empire. Every serious attempt by the English to capture a major city was repulsed, and the troops that were landed in Panama returned to the fleet in a few weeks after a decisive defeat by the Spanish. The expedition was a resounding failure, and Drake's death left the tattered remnant of the expedition to be led back to England by Sir Thomas Baskerville, the commander of the soldiers. Sir John Hawkins was spared from this series of catastrophic English defeats, for he died of a fever on the afternoon of November 12, 1595, just before the fleet launched a futile attack on Puerto Rico.

The death of Sir John Hawkins, occurring when it did and coupled with that of Drake, served to emphasize in part the greatness of the Elizabethan era, and it provided fuel for the accounts that later were written about this legendary "golden age" of England. Over a period of 15 years, from 1588 to 1603, nearly all of the great Elizabethans died, and with the passing of each one the dynamism, creativity, and accomplishment of the last Tudor's rule was cast into greater relief. First, the Queen's favorite, the Earl of Leicester, who championed a policy of aggressive diplomacy and military activity in conjunction with other Protestant powers, died in 1588. Then, in 1590, the dour Puritan Sir Francis Walsingham, whose administrative ability and skill at gathering intelligence made a permanent impression on English government, succumbed to kidney stones. With the deaths of Hawkins and Drake in 1595, the importance to England of both a military and a merchant fleet was highlighted, for both men played key roles in the maturation of the island kingdom's maritime interests. In 1598, the anchor of Elizabethan government, Lord Burghley, who had done so much in evolving sophisticated economic policies, administrative techniques, and national security measures, passed away. Finally, five years after Burghley's death, Gloriana died. Thus the era ended and Robert Carey was sent on a 400-mile ride to Scotland to tell James Stuart that he had become King of England. The real abilities of these and many more Elizabethans made such a great impact on British history that the reign of the last Tudor monarch is still viewed as an age of incomparable achievement in nearly every area of human endeavor.

In a relatively short time, the accomplishments of the Elizabethans were embellished, and in some cases exaggerated, so that a legend developed about the age that was part truth and part romance. Since it grew out of a need to create heroes and glorify a striking period in Britain's past, the creation of an Elizabethan legend took the form of making the Queen and her servants larger than life and their deeds virtually superhuman in scope. Yet, the excesses of the legend notwithstanding, it was based on events that actually occurred in the last half of the 16th century. The orientation of England toward the sea that came through exploration, the search for new markets for trade, and the invention of a new form of business organization to finance distant foreign trade were all part of the foundation of the legend. So were the diplomatic and military coups, based largely on the growing struggle with Spain, that were planned and carried out by the Queen and her ministers. The nurturing of an efficient governmental administration also was important in creating the legend, for it enabled the English to do with relative ease what it took their rivals great effort to accomplish. But most strikingly, it was the spirit of Elizabeth's subjects that created the legend. This spirit, characterized by courage, daring aggressiveness, and a flair for innovation, led the Elizabethans to perform the feats upon which the legend was founded. It was this spirit and the events that it brought about that led Shakespeare, in a burst of poetic nationalism, to refer to his country as a unique "sceptered isle" and a "seat of Mars." Because of the complexity of the Elizabethan age, it would be absurd to see all or even most of its outstanding characteristics in the career of an individual; but through the experiences of Sir John Hawkins, some of the spirit, the style, that made the time of the first Elizabeth so unique can be glimpsed.

As a young man, Hawkins was in the vanguard of the famous Elizabethan adventurers who made their reputations on the sea. His slaving voyages not only showed clearly the advantages of extending England's foreign trade to far-flung areas, but also challenged the Iberian monopoly of the non-European world. Moreover, he gave practical experience at sea to men like Drake and acquainted them with the fabled wealth of the Indies. Later, as an agent of Cecil's primitive intelligence apparatus, he provided the Crown with important evidence of the danger of Mary Stuart as well as the hostile attitude of Spain toward England. This enabled the government to prepare both diplomatically and militarily for the contingency of open war with Spain and proved the value of a well-organized secret service to the shaping of policies. In his capacity as a naval administrator, John Hawkins intuitively conceived and practiced many of the basic precepts upon which the modern bureaucratic state still operates. He also made a significant contribution to England's defeat of the Armada, which was probably the single most striking event in the creation of the Elizabethan legend.

Sir John Hawkins never achieved the historical stature of any of his great contemporaries for the simple reason that he was not a man of genius. Not only was he not a man of genius, he seemed incapable of appreciating it in others. Drake's impulsiveness, flamboyance, and defiance of odds, Hawkins viewed as irrational rather than as marks of extraordinary ability; and the wiliness, subtlety, and probing quality of Lord Burghley's mind seemed to be quite beyond the comprehension of Sir John Hawkins. He was, in short, an ordinary man propelled to the fringes of the Elizabethan center stage by events over which he had little control and to the challenge of which he responded with his best efforts. His career consequently raises a question of generalizing about the spirit of an historical epoch, for John Hawkins produces a nagging doubt about forming judgments on the basis of the extraordinary actions of a few gifted individuals. Francis Drake's circumnavigation of the globe was, to be sure, a stroke of genius; but does it tell us any more about the England of Queen Elizabeth I than John Hawkins's formation of a tiny joint-stock company to begin a trade in black slaves?

SUGGESTED READINGS

Considering the diversity of his career and the documentary material pertaining to him, it is odd that so little has been written about Sir John Hawkins. All of the general histories of the Elizabethan period mention him, but only three historians have deemed Hawkins a subject worth serious investigation. These are: James A. Williamson, *Sir John Hawkins* (London: Black, 1949), the only full-scale scholarly biography of Hawkins; Rayner Unwin, *The Defeat of John Hawkins* (London: Allen & Unwin, 1960), which deals primarily with the third slaving voyage; and Michael Lewis, *The Hawkins Dynasty* (London: Allen & Unwin, 1969), a general history of the Hawkins family.

Curators of the Bodleian Library

Chapter 7

"FREEBORN" JOHN LILBURNE:
Early English Radicalism

THE place of "Freeborn" John Lilburne in the history of Britain's Civil Wars remains unresolved after extensive historical debate. Since he founded the Leveller party, stood as a symbol of defiance to what he called tyranny, whether Stuart, Parliamentarian, or Army, and appeared frequently and dramatically during the period 1640 to 1655, Lilburne was obviously a prominent figure in the wars. But the nature of his prominence is a matter of disagreement, for nearly every historian who has written about the Civil Wars has a different perception of John Lilburne. Some see him as a congenital dissenter who could not be satisfied by any government or reform, and they dismiss him as one of the many neurotics who became public figures through the opening of opportunities in an era of crises. Others see Lilburne simply as a menace to the stable government that Cromwell and his supporters tried to build after the defeat of Charles I, and they portray the Leveller primarily as a causative agent in the harshness of Cromwellian rule. Still other scholars view "Freeborn" John as the most consistent figure throughout the Civil Wars in his positions on the broad issues of civil and religious liberty, over which the wars were ostensibly fought. To them, Lilburne not only remained uncorrupted by success and kept before him the goals which motivated the original party of rebellion, but he also began the tradition of modern English political radicalism which has caused so many significant changes in British life since the mid-17th century. Of these views, the latter appears most persuasive, for seeing in "Freeborn" John something more than a political aberration points the way toward a comprehension both of the Civil Wars and the broad historic phenomenon of radicalism that has flavored British political history for over 300 years.

There was nothing in John Lilburne's background to indicate that he would play a prominent part in one of the great events of British history. His father owned the small manor of Thickley Punchardon in county Durham, and his mother was the daughter of a minor household officer at Greenwich Palace. Born in 1615 at his father's manor, John was the third of four children. Throughout the reign of James I the Lilburnes lived principally in Durham, but during two periods before the death of the mother in 1619 they resided at Greenwich. Clearly, the Lilburnes were a more or less ordinary 17th-century landed English family, subsisting on agricultural income and enjoying some small benefit from contacts at the Court of the first Stuart King.

Little is known of the early life of John Lilburne. He received a brief and haphazard education, and in 1630, at the age of fifteen, he was sent away to learn a trade. It was a significant move, for he was sent to London to be apprenticed to Thomas Hewson, a clothier, and much of the drama of the rest of Lilburne's life developed from this first contact with the capital. The Lilburne family was generally Puritan in sympathy, but it was in London that John was first exposed to the various forms of Puritanism that were challenging most directly the authority of the King and the dictates of the Established Church. It was moreover in London that he became familiar with the municipal and central forms of government, and the methods that governments employed to maintain their power and exercise their authority. He also soon learned that London, with its throngs of people, great wealth, and abject poverty, and position as the seat of government, had an almost immeasurable capacity to influence the direction of the kingdom. Accordingly, the capital made a great impression on the 15-year-old boy from Durham.

John Lilburne's first few years in London were uneventful. He began to learn the fundamentals of the clothier's trade, and spent what little free time he had in company with other apprentices. It was from them as well as from Hewson that he learned of the conflict between the Puritans and the state church directed by William Laud, Archbishop of Canterbury. In 1634 he was part of the crowd that witnessed the cropping of William Prynne's ears for slandering the Queen. This event more than any other probably influenced his future, for it taught him two of the basic tenets that governed his public life: Martyrdom was perhaps the easiest road to fame, and a crowd was a powerful ally if manipulated correctly.

Two years after watching Prynne lose his ears, John found himself involved in his initial confrontation with authority. It was the first of many occasions which led, over the years, to his imprisonment under four separate English governments and his elevation to the status as one of the most loved and feared figures in the island. In 1636 Hewson introduced him to Doctor John Bastwick, a Presbyterian who was imprisoned in the Gatehouse for his lucid and persistent denunciations of the Anglican bishops. Very impressed by Bastwick, both as an individual and as a Puritan thinker, Lilburne decided to commit himself to the Puritan cause. His zeal led him into trouble within a year, for early in 1637 he took one of Bastwick's pamphlets to Holland to have copies printed and then smuggled back into England. Lilburne made, however, one serious mistake in his smuggling enterprise. He trusted a man named Chilliburne to aid him in circulating the illegal pamphlets, and that led to the first of his many clashes with the government.

In December 1637, Lilburne returned to England to help Chilliburne and others strike what he thought would be a blow for religious toleration. Instead, he was betrayed by Chilliburne, arrested by officers of the Stationer's Company, which licensed all printed matter in England, and was charged with several violations of the Stationer's monopoly. When brought before the Court of Star Chamber early in 1638, he had his first opportunity to put to the test the lessons he had learned from Prynne, Bastwick, and the other Puritan martyrs. He refused to swear the oath *ex-officio,* which required him to answer questions on oath that might easily incriminate him and lead to his indefinite imprisonment. He was the first man to refuse the oath before the Star Chamber, and while he doubtless learned the tactic from Puritans who had declined to take the same oath before the Court of High Commission, he nevertheless set a precedent that was to cause the major Stuart prerogative court many difficulties. John's action, however, only increased his troubles, for he was saddled with an additional charge of contempt of court.

John Lilburne's trial in February 1638, raised many of the issues that brought about civil war in England three years later. As both the judges and his supporters expected, John Lilburne refused both to plead and to recognize the legitimacy of the court. He even lectured the judges on what he claimed were his rights according to the laws and traditions of England. Unimpressed by his tactics and resenting his challenge to their authority, the magistrates simply declared him guilty of contempt. His sentence was harsh, even for the 17th century when punishment was ferocious and official brutality commonplace. He was fined £500, condemned to be whipped through the streets from Fleet Bridge to New Palace Yard, and finally pilloried. He was then to be returned to the Fleet Prison and kept there in close confinement until he agreed to swear the *ex-officio* oath required by the court. Within hours Lilburne's hearing and the sentence were being recounted throughout London, and the young apprentice who had taken his stand on his rights as a "free born Englishman" became a popular hero. He was immediately and affectionately dubbed "Freeborn" John, a title he retained for the rest of his life.

While lying in the Fleet awaiting his punishment, Freeborn John launched an offensive against his tormentors. It was a relatively novel attack, for it took the form of a propaganda campaign designed to win public sympathy for his cause. On March 12, 1638, he wrote a tract entitled "The Christian Man's Trial," explaining his side of the controversy with the court. This first of many Lilburne pamphlets was somewhat amateurish, but through it he learned the value of the printed word as a political weapon. In a relatively short time he polished his style and developed his gift for coining memorable phrases so that he soon became one of England's foremost political propagandists. His budding literary career was, however, interrupted by the court-ordered punishment. On April 18, 1638, he was taken to Fleet Bridge, stripped to the waist, tied to the back of a cart and marched slowly down Fleet Street into the Strand and finally to New Palace Yard in Westminster. At every third step, the public executioner lashed him across the back with a whip made of knotted ropes, and in the unseasonable early spring heat John Lilburne had little to keep up his spirit except the ecstasy of martyrdom and the enthusiastic support of the crowds who lined the way. By the time he reached the pillory his back was an ugly mass of welts, but he still had enough strength left to bow mockingly to the Star Chamber building and harangue the crowd from the pillory. Indeed, his speeches so incensed some officials who witnessed the punishment that they ordered him gagged. Freeborn John responded by reaching into his pockets and throwing copies of his pamphlet to the crowd. After two hours, he was taken out of the pillory and carried back, without medical assistance, to the Fleet Prison. There he was put in chains and kept in close confinement, his suffering relieved only periodically by the visits of two women who tended his wounds.

Most of the Londoners who had followed the Lilburne case guessed that the Star Chamber Justices intended him to die in prison, and this roused them to impotent fury. Instead of dying, however, Freeborn John surprised both his friends and his enemies by slowly recovering. In three months he was again writing pamphlets, more defiant than ever, and before the end of the year he had produced two virulent attacks on arbitrary government. As time passed, the conditions of his imprisonment improved gradually, and while he received no help from his family he seems to have been well cared for by friends and admirers. For the next two years he stayed in prison, writing, reading, and keeping abreast of developments in the country as best he could. During that time he learned of the rising discontent in London, the King's quarrel with his Scottish subjects, and finally the summoning of the Short and Long Parliaments in 1640.

The meeting of the Long Parliament led directly to the release of John Lilburne. On November 9, 1640, an obscure member of the Commons from Cambridge named Oliver Cromwell rose in the House to speak on the issue of political prisoners. When he concluded his speech, Cromwell tendered a petition for the release of Freeborn John and several others he characterized as victims of political persecution. The cases cited in Cromwell's petition were referred to a committee for investigation, and four days later the lower house ordered all of the captives specified in the document released from custody. They were ostensibly set free so that they could prepare their cases for adjudication by the Commons, but no one really expected the lower house to rule against men who were viewed popularly as martyrs of Stuart tyranny.

Three years in prison had served only to sharpen Freeborn John's political awareness and deepen his hatred for King Charles's government. Released from prison, he spent some of his time preparing for the hearing before the Commons, but most of his efforts were directed toward systematically criticizing the royal policies that had kept him confined. For nearly six months he went almost daily to Westminster, arguing with Crown officials and talking with his friends and supporters, until in May 1641, he allowed himself to be overheard making clearly treasonous and inflammatory statements about the monarch. Taken into custody again, Lilburne was brought before the House of Lords on a charge of high treason, but the Lords dismissed the charge on the grounds of contradictory testimony. At the same time the Commons voided Freeborn John's Star Chamber sentence and voted him reparations for his suffering. Thus on May 3, 1641, John Lilburne was a free man for the first time in over three years.

As though to celebrate his release and the possibility of an untroubled future, Freeborn John married shortly after the Parliamentary decisions. His bride, Elizabeth Dewell, possibly was one of the visitors who had cared for him in the Fleet Prison. While King Charles and his Parliament drifted steadily farther apart, John Lilburne settled down to earn a living and support his wife. Earning enough money to live on, however, was not a simple task in early Stuart England. Nearly every worthwhile trade was restricted by laws limiting the membership in producing and service companies; and, since John was now too old to go back to work as a clothier's apprentice, he decided instead to open a brewery, several of which were being founded in London at the time with minimal interference. One of Lilburne's wealthy uncles in Durham supplied most of the capital, and by the end of 1641 the brewery was in operation. Freeborn John appeared to have given up politics for beer.

Despite his new business interest, Lilburne could not ignore events occurring almost daily in the capital. As the King's chief adviser, the Earl of Strafford, was tried and executed, the Archbishop of Canterbury was imprisoned in the Tower of London, and the sovereign failed in his attempt to arrest the opposition leaders in the Commons, John Lilburne was drawn inexorably into taking an active part in the national quarrel. When the armed conflict finally began, Lilburne and thousands like him rallied to the defense of Parliament, thinking that its program of individual rights and religious toleration was worth the risks of rebellion. In the late summer of 1642 he enlisted as a captain of foot in a troop of infantry raised in the City of London by Lord Brooke, and for the next two and one half years he fought and suffered great privations for the Parliamentary cause. Freeborn John proved to be as good a soldier as he was a politician and propagandist; and along with his brother Robert, who rose to important commands in the New Model Army, John Lilburne proved a valuable acquisition for the forces of Parliament.

Lilburne's greatest talent, which indeed was a mainstay of his career, was a flair for leadership; and it was never more apparent than in his soldiering. At Edgehill, the first major battle of the war, he so distinguished himself by his courage that he won the confidence of Lord

Brooke as well as the admiration of London's citizen-soldiers. As a result, he was entrusted with carrying dispatches between the Army and the Parliament, and in this work he became familiar with both the political leadership in the Commons and the officers in the field. His career as a communications officer was, however, cut short early in the winter of 1642–43 when he was with a Parliamentary unit in the town of Brentford that was attacked by Royalist troops under Prince Rupert.

The battle of Brentford was not one of the major battles of the war, but for Freeborn John it encompassed the heights and depths of emotion. As the surprise attack developed, Lilburne was the only officer who remained calm, and through threats and his own example he rallied enough men to turn a rout into an orderly withdrawal. The young officer and his men gradually yielded ground, suffering serious casualties, while the rest of the force escaped. In the headlong flight through creeks and over hedges that followed the delaying action, Freeborn John's elation at having successfully led the defense was turned into despair and humiliation. Half-clothed and slightly wounded, he was found hiding under a bush by Prince Rupert's cavalry and was taken into custody. Carried to Oxford, he was not held as a prisoner of war, but rather as an accused traitor.

By this time, Lilburne had some familiarity with tribunals and prisons, and he was generally contemptuous of both. When brought before the court he treated it in much the same way as he treated the Star Chamber, denying its authority, claiming the rights of a prisoner of war, and even objecting to the court's reference to him as a "yeoman" instead of a "gentleman" in the indictment. He argued unabashedly with all the members of the tribunal, including Prince Rupert, and finally the judges tired of his antics and deferred his trial. While in prison, Lilburne spent most of his time trying to convert his Royalist guards to the Parliamentary cause. He made such a pest of himself that by the spring of 1643 it became public knowledge in Oxford that he would either be murdered or soon tried and found guilty. When this rumor reached London his friends in Parliament arranged an exchange of prisoners to save him, and in May 1643 he was released and returned to the capital as a hero.

Lilburne's capture had, in the custom of the time, freed him from his commitment to Lord Brooke's troop, so when he returned to London he was once again a civilian. This new status led several members of the Commons to try to enlist him as a political rather than a military ally, and they offered him a variety of administrative posts that promised wealth and ease. An incorrigible idealist, John Lilburne spurned their offers and instead reenlisted in the army. This time he offered his services to his old benefactor Oliver Cromwell, who was organizing the army of the Eastern Association. Thus on October 7, 1643, Freeborn John returned to the war as a Major of infantry in the regiment of the Presbyterian Colonel King, and he spent a disturbing winter stationed in Lincolnshire.

Major Lilburne's disquiet during the winter of 1643–44 came from the discovery that his commanding officer was a corrupt Parliamentary field commander. The Colonel not only seemed too interested in collecting Royalist property and wealth for himself, but he also was apparently bent on forcing Presbyterianism on his troopers. To Lilburne, the issues of the war were clear. They were fighting to overthrow a tyrannical government that had no respect for property rights, civil liberties, or individual religious preference. Now, it seemed, the faults of the King's government had spread to the Parliament and its army. Incensed by what he saw, Freeborn John filed charges against Colonel King with the Commons, but before any action was taken the campaigning season of 1644 opened and the disillusioned Major had to concentrate on his military duties.

The season was a busy one for Lilburne. In March, he experienced another of Prince Rupert's surprise attacks and barely escaped capture. Two months later, he was wounded in the arm during a skirmish. Finally, on July 2, 1644, Freeborn John took part in a battle that, because of its strategic results, was one of the key events of the war: the battle of Marston Moor. It marked the rise to prominence in the army of Eastern Association troops under Oliver Cromwell, and it was the first time that a Royalist army was routed in a pitched battle. Thus Marston Moor foreshadowed the decline of King Charles's military fortunes. In this clash Lilburne, who had been promoted to Lieutenant Colonel, got his chance to even the score with the King's men for his previous humiliations, for he was stationed on the extreme left of Cromwell's troopers. According to contemporaries, Freeborn John bore an "eminent" share of responsibility for the victory. Briefly elated by the sight of Rupert's men dead, captured, or fleeing for their lives, Lilburne's elation was soon replaced by disillusionment with the leadership of the Parliament's forces.

Barely eight days after the triumph at Marston Moor, what came to be called the Tickhill Castle affair started Freeborn John on the road toward as fierce an opposition to the Parliament as he had shown toward the King. Lilburne learned that the Earl of Manchester, who was the Parliamentary commander-in-chief, was unwilling to accept the proffered surrender of the castle by its Royalist garrison. Indeed, the Earl was not only reluctant to accept the surrender of Tickhill Castle, but he was also unwilling to prosecute the war vigorously enough to bring about the total defeat of the King's forces. Manchester's attitude infuriated Freeborn John, but the importance of the affair scarcely lay in the fact that it aroused the indignation of a young Lieutenant Colonel.

Most dramatically, the Tickhill Castle episode demonstrated a fundamental split in the Parliamentary opposition to the ruler. One group, generally Presbyterian, did not want to defeat the King in the field. They preferred to negotiate a settlement with him that would center on establishing a Presbyterian state church in England. This faction was powerful in the Commons, and the Earl of Manchester was its most important representative in the army. The other group was composed principally of religious Independents, and it aimed at imposing total military defeat on the King and winning unqualified guarantees of individual liberty and freedom of conscience. In the Commons this faction was inferior in number to the Presbyterians, but in the army it was strongly represented by troopers of the Eastern Association and had a powerful ally in Lieutenant General Oliver Cromwell. Freeborn John was, of course, an Independent, and when he told Cromwell of the Tickhill Castle affair it precipitated important developments both for his own future and the course of the war.

Cromwell seized upon Lilburne's news, combined it with other damning evidence against Manchester, and on November 25, 1644, he accused the Earl of being dilatory in prosecuting the war, incompetent militarily, and guilty of generally betraying the Parliamentary cause. One of the chief witnesses called to prove Cromwell's charges was Freeborn John, who explained the Tickhill Castle affair and left no doubt about his opinion of Manchester's fitness for command. The Earl was relieved of his duties, and General Cromwell took his first major step to advance the cause of Independency and to elevate himself to political leadership. Manchester's fall meant little to Lieutenant Colonel Lilburne, however, for he was too disturbed by one of the requirements for holding a commission in the New Model Army to appreciate Cromwell's victory. Specifically, he was troubled by the demand of the Presbyterian-dominated Commons that all officers sign the Scottish Covenant as a prerequisite for holding their commissions. Freeborn John agonized over the issue of the Covenant for several weeks, and despite the fact that Cromwell and others urged him to sign it, Lilburne finally decided that it was a matter of principle and refused. On April 30, 1645, Lieutenant Colonel Lilburne resigned his commission and left the army. From that point on, thanks to his stubborness and convictions, he became one of the most noteworthy governmental critics in England.

The crucial year both for the first civil war and the career of John Lilburne proved to be 1645. For the war, it marked the domination of the House of Commons by the Presbyterians, the formation of the New Model Army, the decisive defeat of the Royalists at Naseby, and the growing influence of Oliver Cromwell. For Freeborn John 1645 was a period of disillusion, anger, and political creativity. His disillusion grew from a realization that the Presbyterians in the lower house were replacing the autocracy of Charles Stuart with their own oligarchy, and this infuriated Lilburne. From his anger came the activity that made him a feared and hated enemy of the Presbyterians and also the creator of a political movement that expressed itself through a unique party: the Levellers.

Upon termination of his military career, Freeborn John began attacking the leaders in the Commons who had, in his estimation, betrayed the original aims of the Parliament. He was promptly arrested and brought before the Committee of Examinations, which had substantially taken the place of the old prerogative courts of Star Chamber and High Commission. Since John's criticisms were principally directed at the religious policies of the Commons and entailed no overtly illegal activity, he was eventually freed after a number of angry exchanges with members of the committee. In July 1645, however, he was arrested again and taken before the committee, this time for slandering the Speaker of the Commons. His writing of the time reflected both an intensification of his opposition to the Commons and an expansion of his interests beyond the realm of religion and politics. In one of his pamphlets he indicated considerable interest in socioeconomic equality, and that disturbed the Commons at least as much as his tracts on religion and politics. The combination of slander and radical pamphleteering apparently was more than the committee was willing to permit, for this time they ordered him imprisoned in Newgate Jail. A few days later the order was confirmed by the lower house, and Freeborn John remained confined until October, when he was released after pleading that no formal charge had been filed against him. Thus in six short months, the man who had been a martyr to Stuart autocracy and who fought hard and well for the Parliament's army was dangerously close to becoming a victim of the Presbyterian oligarchy.

Martyrdom was always a satisfying role for Freeborn John, and he knew how to play it for the greatest effect, but it was not the most important of his activities in the autumn of 1645. Much greater in consequence was his writing of a pamphlet resoundingly entitled "England's Birthright Justified," which outlined in rough form Lilburne's belief in what the goals of Parliament should be. As a forward-looking political program it was extraordinary, for it claimed rights for the subject and condemned abuses by government both royal and parliamentary that were far more extreme than anything made public to that time. In a short time "England's Birthright" had attracted the interest of numerous Londoners, and it soon became the manifesto for the radical Leveller party. Centered on London, with Lilburne as its leader and several able organizers and propagandists as his lieutenants, the party soon enlisted thousands in its ranks and became for a time one of the most dynamic forces in the English Civil War.

During the first months of 1646 Freeborn John directed most of his criticism at the Presbyterians in control of Parliament. He was careful to keep his attacks subtle enough so that he was not arrested in the first half of the year. But in June, he accused the Earl of Manchester of complicity in the treason of Lilburne's old adversary, Colonel King, and the House of Lords ordered Freeborn John arrested for slandering one of their members. Once again Lilburne was clapped in Newgate Jail and, when brought before the Lords on the charge, he promptly denied the right of the upper House to try him for any crime. He argued logically from his knowledge of Magna Carta and the Common Law that since he was a commoner he was entitled to a trial by a jury of his peers. The Lords, therefore, had no right to try him. He appealed to the Commons for justice and was returned to Newgate to await a decision. As he expected, the Presbyterian-dominated Commons ignored his appeal, and on July 11, 1646, he was brought to trial before the upper house. Despite his refusal to recognize the court and his staunch denial of its right to try him, he was found guilty as charged. The sentence was so similar to that of the Star Chamber nearly a decade earlier that it is not difficult to understand why Freeborn John became more radical and bitter in his opposition to Parliament. He was fined £2000 and imprisoned in the Tower under close confinement during the pleasure of the Lords. Angered rather than cowed by the sentence, Lilburne soon became an even more dangerous and implacable enemy to the victorious rebels than he had been to the defeated Stuart King.

By 1646 the First Civil War was over, for the King had been beaten and had surrendered to the Scottish army rather than to Parliamentary forces. The Presbyterians at Westminster had extended their control to include the City of London, and to Freeborn John it looked as though Cromwell's comment that "New Presbyter is but old priest writ large" had become a reality. John's distress at this turn of events spurred him to greater activity, and he stepped up the output of his pamphleteering as the most promising technique of calling attention to what he thought was an unjust settlement to the war. Most of his barbs in the fall and winter of 1646 were aimed at the Presbyterians controlling the City, but he also criticized both houses of Parliament generally as well as individual politicians. This flood of criticism naturally irritated its victims, not only because of Lilburne's charges but also because he was supposed to be a close prisoner and unable to write pamphlets or have them printed.

In February 1647, Lilburne pushed his enemies too far in a pamphlet attacking oppression, and he was once again called before the Committee of Examinations to answer a charge of "sedition." Freeborn John was by then a seasoned veteran in dealing with interrogators, and the ease with which he frustrated and embarrassed the committee members was soon the talk of the capital. Yet, despite his humiliation of the Parliamentary committee, the year was going badly for Freeborn John. His friends were being arrested and held incommunicado, the printing presses that made it possible for him and the other Levellers to take their case to the public were being shut down with alarming regularity, and the party's funds were nearly exhausted.

It was under these circumstances that Freeborn John made a crucial decision that easily might have changed the outcome of the civil war. Between March and May of 1647, the Parliament rejected out of hand three Leveller petitions for redress of grievances and the release of Lilburne. With that, John gave up hope of coming to any terms with the Presbyterians at Westminster and resolved to take his case to the nation as a whole and the army in particular. The result was the famous army "revolt" that nearly succeeded in the spring and summer of 1647. In this rebellion the single most striking feature was the influence of Freeborn John Lilburne, who, despite his captivity in the Tower, gave both program and direction to the discontented troopers. Moreover, the revolt and the reforms it implied rallied to the Leveller party all of the loosely organized radical sentiment that opposed the Presbyterian Parliament. For the next three years the Levellers were one of the most important political forces in England.

The difficulties between Army and Parliament were precipitated by the question of the future of the troopers now that the war was won. Dominating Parliament, the Presbyterians wanted to remain in power and dictate a settlement to the King that entailed a diminution of his powers and the foundation of a state church modeled on the Kirk of Scotland. The Army was also in favor of reducing the King's powers, as were the Levellers, but since many of the soldiers were Independents rather than Presbyterians, they had no desire to see Anglican intolerance replaced by a narrow Presbyterianism. In addition, the Parliament gave no indication of producing money for the arrears in pay owed to the soldiers. Indeed, there were plans at Westminster to disband most of the New Model Army and send what was kept under arms to quell the uprising that had broken out in Ireland. It was the intent of Freeborn John and the Levellers to exploit these differences between factions of the Parliamentary side to their own ends, which they claimed were a reaffirmation of the original libertarian goals of the rebellion. To accomplish this, Lilburne developed a superb intelligence system that, through the periodic visits of radical soldiers, kept him in close touch with the malcontents in the army. Through these troopers Lilburne not only received news, but also sent out advice and propaganda to fuel the discontent. When the unhappy soldiers of the various regiments elected "agitators" to represent them in the newly organized Army Council, the army revolt began in earnest.

Coincidentally with the increase of Leveller activity in the army, Oliver Cromwell came out on what seemed to be the side of Parliament by urging the troops to disband before petitioning for their arrears of pay. The Lieutenant General's motives for this recommendation may well have been innocent, but they immediately aroused the suspicion of Freeborn John. He viewed Cromwell's advice to the soldiers as just one more betrayal of the cause, and he began treating his erstwhile friend like an enemy. A deterioration began in their relationship that soon turned to hatred on both sides, and Freeborn John Lilburne added one more powerful element to the growing camp of his dedicated foes.

Any doubt about the course of the Army-Leveller coalition was resolved in May 1647, when the insurgents learned of a Presbyterian conspiracy to remove the King to Scotland and to use Scottish troops to disband the New Model Army regiments by force. As soon as they heard the news the agitators acted, and on May 29, 1647, the artillery train at Oxford was secured by 1,000 reliable men. Four days later, 500 troopers seized King Charles and transported him to Newmarket, where the entire army was assembling to decide a course of action in the crisis. For two months the soldiers debated their next move and negotiated with the Parliamentary representatives, but by August they decided that it was necessary to act. On August 6, 1647, the army entered Westminster to resolve the dispute with violence if necessary, and two weeks later they accomplished at least part of their goal; the Commons purged itself of the leading Presbyterians, leaving the Independents in control, and the English Civil Wars changed course once again.

The events of August were, in many ways, the watershed of the rebellion against the Stuart monarchy, for they entailed the first direct participation by the Army in politics. The process that had brought the Army to the capital was begun in March by the work of Freeborn John and the Levellers, and it led the imprisoned radical leaders to expect an immediate release from confinement, for they had, after all, played a major part in the evolution of political awareness in the New Model Army. But Lilburne and his friends were not released from prison by the Army, and after the purge of August 20 they understood why, for the Civil Wars were about to take another turn. Shortly after the purge, the Levellers and their imprisoned leaders saw a gulf widen with alarming speed between their allies, the agitators, and the officers of the army, whom they dubbed the "Grandees." The continued confinement of Lilburne and his associates was the principal symptom of this rift in the army, and the Levellers feared with considerable justification that another betrayal of the original Parliamentary cause was in the offing.

Evidence supporting the Leveller's fears was presented dramatically in September 1647, when Cromwell inspected the ordnance in the Tower and paid what was made to appear a causal visit to Freeborn John. In the course of their conversation a fundamental disagreement became evident, for Lilburne attacked the tyranny of the Parliament, claiming that it was worse than the King's, and Cromwell defended it and tried to persuade his former friend to moderate his accusations and demands. It quickly became obvious that the two could not agree, for Lilburne was determined to maintain his conception of the original aims of the Parliamentary cause, and Cromwell seemed principally concerned with preserving order.

Early in November, Lilburne was suddenly granted permission to leave the Tower during the day to prepare for his trial before Parliament. Two days after his release, on November 11, 1647, the King escaped from Hampton Court and fled to the Isle of Wight, thus setting in motion a chain of events that in a matter of months precipitated the second Civil War. The King's flight compelled Freeborn John and the other Levellers to ask themselves what their position really was in the midst of such rapidly changing circumstances, and their answer was constitutional and legal in nature. In essence, the Leveller leaders decided that the basic position of their party centered on the much-debated but undefined "fundamental laws of the realm," so they determined to define these laws and express them in a written constitution. The result was a document called "The Agreement of the People," which was both the most original part of their program and a vital contribution to the evolution of English political thought.

The "Agreement" of the Levellers called for four basic reforms which would, they claimed, finally resolve the issues of the war. First, Parliament was to rule the country, and all England and Wales were to be divided into equal electoral districts with manhood suffrage; only women, servants, and beggars were to be excluded from the franchise. Next, the existing Parliament, which by no means could be called representative of the country, was to be dissolved. Third, all future Parliaments were to be elected biennially. Finally, unrestricted freedom in certain spheres of action, most notably religion, was to be preserved from change by any Parliament and guaranteed by the constitution. In the 17th century these reforms were revolutionary. When they were discussed by the Army from October 28 to November 11, 1647, they proved to be the foremost obstacle to unity among the Parliamentary forces, for they reduced the issues of the war to the barest essentials of a question of rights: those of each individual against those of each property holder.

At the Army debates the final and most fundamental division of Englishmen to result from the war developed. In the Council of the Army two distinct factions arose and each coalesced around a dynamic leader. Perhaps the most forceful of these men was Commissary General Henry

Ireton, Cromwell's son-in-law and a very able politician. He spoke for the party that Freeborn John had derisively labeled the "Grandees." To Ireton and his friends, political democracy as outlined in the "Agreement" would surrender the government of England to the broad mass of common men, who would undoubtedly use their power to legislate confiscatory taxes and hence attack directly the rights of property owners. According to the "Grandees," the war had been fought to protect property rights and establish religious toleration, so they found the Leveller's "Agreement" equally as repulsive as the abuses of the Stuart monarchy. The opposition party, propounding the "Agreement," was led by Colonel Rainsborough, who argued that the present government was no less despotic than that of the captive monarch had been. He went on to claim that if the "Agreement" were not the basis for settling the war, then most of the men who had fought to secure what they thought were their liberties would be badly cheated. The Ireton and Rainsborough factions soon reached an impasse in the debates, and the result was a final division of the triumphant Parliamentary Army into two camps, one championing the rights of the individual and the other the rights of the property owner.

After days of futile discussion, the Army Council decided to reject the "Agreement of the People" as a summary of its war aims. This was an especially bitter blow to the Levellers, for they had worked closely with the Army in the past. Despite the officers' rejection, Freeborn John Lilburne determined to continue to press his case for the "Agreement," and he turned away from the Army to the nation as a last resort. In January 1648, he produced the "Smithfield Petition," a succinct statement of the platform detailed in the "Agreement." The Levellers circulated this document throughout the southern counties, and their efforts were initially successful. Thousands signed the petition in the first few weeks of circulation, but this attempt to circumvent the Army Council was soon halted by the "Grandees" before it could gather momentum. On February 20, 1648, Freeborn John's bail was rescinded by order of Parliament and he was sent back to the Tower to be held as a close prisoner once again. To his previous charges were added those of treasonable and seditious practices stemming from the petition, and his absence deprived the Levellers of the leadership necessary to forge a powerful weapon out of the Smithfield document. Ultimately, it failed as completely as had the Leveller efforts at the Army debates.

From February until August 1648, Lilburne fumed in the Tower, but events finally came to his rescue. On May 1, 1648, the second Civil War broke out in Wales, and this served to bring the quarreling parties of the Parliamentary side together again to face the danger of a Royalist onslaught. In three months the need for unity was so apparent that the House of Commons released Freeborn John so that Parliament could be assured of Leveller support against the King. The fine levied against the Leveller leader in 1646 was remitted, and for the first time in two years he was a free man so far as the law was concerned. Lilburne had, of course, no illusions about why the Parliament was suddenly treating him so generously, but he still appreciated his freedom. So much of his adult life had been spent in confinement that two of his three children had been born while he was a prisoner, and one of them was even named "Tower" in honor of his latest residence.

It was probably the desire to remain free at least temporarily that persuaded Freeborn John to take no part in the second Civil War. He gave his moral support to the Parliamentary Army, and wrote a letter to Cromwell wishing him well in his campaigns, but Lilburne made no attempt to secure a commission. The most compelling explanation for his behavior is that he deeply distrusted both the Parliament and the Army, and knowing that both were determined to squelch the Leveller movement, he decided to take no part in strengthening their positions. Instead, he concentrated his efforts on trying to collect some of the compensation voted to him by Parliament for his suffering at the hands of Star Chamber. He involved himself in politics only occasionally, most notably when he argued with Ireton about the goals of the war, but he soon tired of that because of the polarization of their two positions. Ireton's attitude only deepened Freeborn John's suspicions of the "Grandees," and he virtually retired from politics, tending to his family and staying away from Westminster for weeks at a time.

Neither the final defeat nor the capture of the King and his transportation to London as a prisoner in 1648 were sufficient to bring Lilburne back into politics. His lieutenants held the party organization together, but Freeborn John declined to resume leadership even when King Charles was tried, found guilty, and executed. The furthest that Lilburne would go politically was to state that it was not only a strategic mistake to permit the "Grandees" to dispose of the monarch, and thus remove a counterbalance to a military despotism, but also wrong to deny the monarch his rights under the law. Friends and associates of the Leveller leader urged him to come out once again in defense of the rights of all Englishmen, but Lilburne refused on the grounds that he had neglected his family too long. Events in the weeks following King Charles's execution, however, soon led him to change his mind.

On February 13, 1649, the victorious army established a Republic, headed by a Council of State composed of many of the "Grandees" who had debated the Levellers in 1647. Both the monarchy and the House of Lords were abolished, and it now appeared that the real victors in the hard-fought wars were an oligarchy of propertied officers and politicians answerable only to the twice-purged House of Commons.

This settlement, repulsive to every other faction in the island ranging from Levellers to Royalists, was more than Lilburne could bear. He emerged from his self-imposed retirement on February 26, 1649, with a pamphlet pugnaciously entitled "England's New Chains," which was brutally critical of the army officers, the Council of State, and the perpetuation of martial law. As before, Lilburne began to work among the rank and file of the army to fashion a weapon to destroy what he viewed as an incredibly corrupt and unacceptable settlement of the war.

In the army the work of Freeborn John and the Levellers bore fruit almost immediately, for the troopers were no happier about being denied their arrears in pay by the Council than they had been when the Presbyterian Parliament had denied them. The most striking expression of the soldier's discontent was a pamphlet with the bitterly amusing title, "The Hunting of the Foxes from Newmarket and Triploe Heath to Whitehall, by Five Small Beagles," which was at least in part written by Lilburne. This document recounted the common soldiers's treatment by their officers from the formation of the Council of the Army to the construction of the Council of State, and its theme was one of continual betrayal of the troopers. The pamphlet's significance, however, did not rest on its illustration of strife in the army. It summarized the tortuous course of the entire war by asking the question that Freeborn John had been posing for some time. "We were before ruled by King, Lords, and Commons; now by a General, a Court Martial, and House of Commons; and we pray you what is the difference?" Buried in a Leveller-Army pamphlet of March 1649, this question was the basic one of the civil war, and its answer eventually returned the Stuart monarchy to the English throne a decade after the question was asked.

Lilburne would have been much better advised to have stayed in retirement, for the "Grandees" reacted swiftly and harshly to the sentiments expressed in "England's New Chains" and "The Hunting of the Foxes." They determined to remove the menace of Freeborn John Lilburne permanently. On March 28, 1649, the Leveller leader was taken prisoner along with several of his associates. The radical group was brought before the entire Council of State in Whitehall for a hearing, and Lilburne spoke for all of the prisoners when he denied the right of the Council to arrest, try, or imprison them on the grounds that the Councillors had no authority founded on the laws and customs of England. During a recess of the hearing, Freeborn John overheard the Council members discussing their decision concerning the Levellers, and he heard Cromwell beat his fist on the table and shout in a fury that the Council must break the Levellers or they would destroy the Council. When the hearings resumed, the Leveller chief showed only resignation at the Council's decision. Freeborn John was ordered confined once again in the Tower of London as a close prisoner, and this time the charge was not sedition or slander; it was high treason, a capital crime.

From March until October, John was kept in the Tower awaiting trial. It seemed for a while that the Council would be content simply to hold him in custody, but events in the summer of 1649 forced them to act. The Levellers still at large continued their agitation, and the Council was alarmed to learn that an army mutiny was again threatening. By October the situation was so serious that the "Grandees" determined to bring Freeborn John to trial immediately and in the process get rid of both Lilburne and the Leveller agitation at one stroke. Accordingly, Freeborn John was tried in the London Guildhall in October 1649, charged with violations of the treason statutes passed by the Rump Parliament in May and July of that year. Throughout the trial, the Guildhall was filled to capacity with Freeborn John's supporters, and the Leveller propagandist took care to see that their time was not wasted. He argued his indictment point by point with the judges, discredited the state's main witnesses, and put on an altogether brilliant display of legal learning, debating skill, and courtroom dramatics. The result was the exact opposite of what the "Grandees" had expected. Lilburne was found not guilty by the jury. It was the apex of Freeborn John's career, for at the same time he frustrated the government and vindicated the causes of civil rights and sanctity of the law so dear to the Levellers. It was Lilburne's greatest opportunity to play the martyr, propagandist, and defender of the rights of every English subject. Yet, he refused to exploit the victory for the benefit of the Leveller movement.

Upon release from the Tower, he returned to his family and again retired from politics. This second self-imposed retirement proved disastrous for his party, but despite its importance there is no satisfactory explanation for Lilburne's action. For 18 months he lived quietly, for a while in Southwark and then in the City of London, working as a soap boiler and giving no evidence of hostility toward the government. There were no pamphlets, harangues or petitions, and by 1651 both Freeborn John's friends and his enemies concluded that he really intended to stay out of England's many political quarrels. Indeed, he probably would have remained in retirement until his death if he had not agreed to give legal advice to his uncle in Durham. That decision, innocent enough in itself, propelled Freeborn John inexorably back into contention with the Commonwealth government in the last act of a stormy career.

The autumn of 1651 saw the vestiges of the old Freeborn John in action when he agreed to argue his family's case in a dispute over the disposition of sequestered Royalist property in Durham. When the case was referred to the principal Committee of Sequestrations sitting in the Haberdasher's Hall in London, Lilburne presented his uncle's claim so poorly that the committee ruled against him. Unwilling to accept the rebuff, Lilburne fell back on his old tactics of pamphleteering and petitioning, violently attacking the committee in his first writing in nearly two years and sending his first petition to the Rump Parliament. The reaction of the Parliament was harsh and immediate. It declared both pamphlet and petition libelous and passed a savage sentence on the amateur barrister. He was fined £7,000 and banished from the realm on pain of death. The "Grandees" and their allies had not forgotten the defeat handed to them by Lilburne in 1649, and the extent of their thirst for vengeance stunned the former Leveller leader. Apparently he was unable to understand how his enemies could hate and fear him so deeply that they would pass a sentence against him so disproportionate to the trivial nature of the offense.

What Freeborn John overlooked was the fact that, while the Leveller party had largely died because of government suppression and lack of leadership, the troubled Commonwealth was still sensitive to attack. The dead King's son had recently stirred a rebellion in Scotland that threatened the government, and complaints against high taxes as well as the constant hatching of plots gave no rest to England's governors. The last thing that the Commonwealth needed was Freeborn John Lilburne stirring up popular discontent as he had in the past, so when the chance arose to exile him his enemies seized it without hesitation. As a result, the first day of 1652 found John Lilburne in Holland, expelled from his country, and while there he suffered worse torments than he had ever experienced in an English jail. The Royalists in the Netherlands viewed him as a Cromwellian spy, while in England the "Grandees" accused him of plotting with the fugitive King's followers to overthrow the Commonwealth government. Under those circumstances, Holland became as repulsive to Lilburne as England was attractive, so, his impatience growing daily, he waited for some development in England that would enable him to return.

What seemed to be Freeborn John's only hope to go back to England occurred on April 20, 1653, when Oliver Cromwell dissolved the Rump Parliament. Since it was the Rump that had sentenced him, Freeborn John grasped at the hope that its dissolution would invalidate his exile. He wrote immediately to Cromwell requesting a pass to reenter the country, and moved to Calais in anticipation of the permit. For nearly a month he waited for the reply that Cromwell did not send, and finally on June 14, 1653, he took his greatest risk. He crossed the Channel without a pass to enter England, and rode to London hoping to persuade Cromwell that he would cause no more trouble. Arrested when he reached the capital, Lilburne was charged with violating a Parliamentary sentence of exile, and he was taken to his old familiar residence, Newgate Jail, to await trial.

On July 13, 1653, Freeborn John was tried in the Old Bailey on a capital charge, and a huge crowd turned out to support the man who for over 15 years had personified the hopes and despair of many of the people of London. The crowd was in a much uglier mood during this trial than in any of his previous ones, and it made no secret of the fact that there would be violence if he were sentenced to death. The trial itself was anticlimactic compared with the treason trial of 1649. There were the usual disputes and haggling that had come to characterize a Lilburne trial, and there was even a postponement until August, but Freeborn John's guile and courtroom antics could not persuade the jury that he had not reentered England in defiance of a Parliamentary order. Lilburne was found guilty, but the jury did not demand his death. Their unusual verict of "John Lilburne is not guilty of any crime worthy of death" left the final disposition of the case up to Cromwell and his associates, who had little inclination to be merciful to the man who had caused them so much trouble for so many years.

Soon after his trial, the government declared John Lilburne to be a danger to the state and sentenced him to be held prisoner indefinitely. Until the spring of 1654 he was kept in the Tower, but then he was transferred to the island of Jersey to make certain that he could not communicate with his friends or effect an escape. For 18 months Freeborn John was imprisoned on the windswept Channel island, until Cromwell finally yielded to the pleas of Lilburne's wife and allowed him to return to England. John Lilburne was still a prisoner when he landed at Portsmouth in October 1655, but he obviously posed no threat to the government of the Protectorate. His interests were no longer political but rather religious, for he had given all of his attention to the doctrines of a relatively new denomination, the Society of Friends. The last months of Freeborn John Lilburne's life were thus spent in contemplating the beliefs and practices of Quakerism and in visiting his family. On August 29, 1657, he died at Eltham in Kent, still a prisoner of the Cromwellian military government and a declared danger to the state. One year later the Lord Protector himself, Oliver Cromwell, died, and with his death the long and intricate convulsion that was the English Civil Wars ended. By 1661 the son of the executed Stuart King sat on the throne in Whitehall as King Charles II, and a new, predominantly Royalist, Parliament met at Westminster. A reaction had set in that made the 20 years of struggle and sacrifice of the civil wars seem a vain exercise.

The wars were not, however, fought in vain, for the reaction that accompanied the Stuart restoration did not produce an absolute monarchy in England. On the contrary, monarchical power was restricted, and in the following years the legal extent of governmental power over the individual, too, was limited. Freedom from arbitrary arrest and imprisonment, for instance, was guaranteed to the English subject by the

Habeas Corpus Act of 1679, and ten years later the Bill of Rights secured by inference many of the other individual liberties that were so fundamental to Freeborn John's program. As an identifiable party, the Levellers ceased to exist well before the restoration of Charles II, but radical agitation and demand for reform continued with regularity throughout the remainder of the 17th and on into the 18th centuries. As a result, the Levellers reinforced one of the most vital features of the British political system, the capacity for change without violence. In the mid-19th century the Leveller party was, in a sense, reincarnated when the backers of the Great Charter appeared with a program and tactics similar to that of their forbears of the Stuart era, but by then England had changed so much that the Chartists did not consciously identify with Freeborn John and his followers. Yet, the Chartists and most other reformers since 1660 owed a debt to Lilburne and the Levellers, for they laid an important part of the foundation for the radical reform tradition that has been one of the most dynamic forces in the shaping of modern England.

SUGGESTED READINGS

The English Civil Wars have been the subject of intensive investigation by historians for the past 200 years, and there is no other single development in British history that has received so much attention. Consequently, the Leveller party and John Lilburne have been the subjects of some high quality historical scholarship. Most recently, Howard Shaw, *The Levellers* (London: Longmans, 1968) has briefly but systematically and thoughtfully analyzed the Leveller movement. An earlier but similar treatment of the Levellers that emphasizes their religious concerns is D. B. Robertson, *The Religious Foundations of Leveller Democracy* (New York: King's Crown Press, 1951). Less broad in their scope are two works that concentrate on the career of John Lilburne. One is the excellent biography by Pauline Gregg, *Free-born John* (London: Harrap, 1961). A somewhat older, but still very valuable account of the Leveller leader is Mildred A. Gibb, *John Lilburne* (London: Lindsay Drummond, 1947). Perhaps the best collection of Leveller political propaganda has been compiled by William Haller and Godfrey Davies, *The Leveller Tracts, 1647–1653* (New York: Columbia University Press, 1944).

From a drawing by Christine Lombardi Andrus

Chapter 8

ROBERT HOOKE:
The Growth of
Modern Science

As the only salaried research scientist of the Royal Society during the first 40 years of its existence, and as a brilliant inventor, competent architect, and lucid author, Robert Hooke held a critical position that shaped the development of Restoration science. His unique abilities brought to English science, already stimulated by Puritan benevolence and educational reform during the Interregnum, the enthusiasm, wide range of interests, and technical skill necessary to help make the last 40 years of the 17th century one of the greatest periods in scientific history. When combined with the accomplishments of Isaac Newton, Robert Boyle, Edmund Halley, and many others, Hooke's contributions brought about the final phase in the lengthy, complex process that has been dubbed the Scientific Revolution.

The roots of this revolution have been traced as far back as the 15th century, but for English science its sources were relatively close chronologically to the Restoration. In practical terms, the work of William Gilbert on magnetism and William Harvey on the circulation of the blood served to stimulate interest in science and encourage wider and deeper investigations of all natural occurrences. So, too, did the founding of Gresham College in 1597, where, despite the avowed practical purpose of the college, of teaching mathematics and astronomy to facilitate navigation and increase trade, interest in pure science and research was encouraged nearly as much as teaching. In a less practical but hardly less significant way, two 17th-century philosophers, Francis Bacon and René Descartes, played a key role in England's scientific progress. In his book *Novum Organum*, published in 1620, Bacon argued persuasively that the correct procedure for scientific investigation was an inductive method rather than a deductive one, whereby the collection and evaluation of data should be used to determine axioms pertaining to natural phenomena. Bacon's influence was such that throughout Robert Hooke's long career, every scientist of consequence almost religiously claimed to be a Baconian, even though many of them clearly were not. In the 20 years following the publication of *Novum Organum*, Bacon's views were supported and amplified by Descartes, an equally brilliant Frenchman, whose principal addition to Baconian theory was an insistence on the importance of mathematics to the experimental method. Together these men convinced most scientific thinkers of their own and subsequent centuries that the Aristotelian approach to science, overwhelmingly deductive in nature, was substantially an exercise in futility. In the process, Bacon and Descartes engineered the philosophical revolution that was a prerequisite for the far-reaching accomplishments of Restoration science.

In the years between the accession of Charles II in 1660 and the death of Sir Isaac Newton in 1727, English scientists made discoveries and observations, formulated laws, and invented instruments that became so fundamental to every aspect of modern life that their importance is nearly incalculable. Sir Isaac Newton, the mightiest scientist of his own and possibly any era, not only synthesized the work of John Kepler, Tycho Brahe, and Galileo Galilei on planetary and terrestrial motion in the *Philosophiae naturalis principia mathematica*, but he also discovered the calculus separately and simultaneously with Leibnitz and formulated the basic laws of optics, along with producing a host of other achievements. His contribution was so great that science was, until the 20th century, classified as Newtonian or Pre-Newtonian. Two lesser astronomers, but men of great talent, were contemporaries of Sir Isaac: Edmund Halley and Sir Christopher Wren. Halley's most noteworthy feat was predicting the periodic reappearance of the comet that bears his name, and Wren was Savilian Professor of Astronomy at Oxford until he decided, to the great benefit of London, to devote himself to architecture.

English science was not limited to the studies of physics and astronomy, even though those disciplines were of paramount interest. Some major discoveries were made in chemistry by Robert Boyle, who formulated Boyle's law of gases and established a basic chemical principle by distinguishing between elements and compounds. All of these men, through their research and writing, helped to lay a firm foundation for modern science, and each has been rightly credited with being an important figure in European intellectual life. But Robert Hooke, who was considered a great scientific virtuoso by his contemporaries, was virtually forgotten for over two centuries, largely because he quarreled bitterly and extensively with Newton. Hooke's reputation and abilities were, as a result, buried by the horde of Newtonian hero-worshippers, and it was not until recent years that Robert Hooke was recognized as a giant figure of the Pre-Newtonian science upon which the edifice of Newtonian science was built.

For a man who was to rise to great public prominence and associate with such figures as Charles II, Boyle, Wren, Hobbes, and Newton, Hooke's origins were notably without distinction. Born in 1635, Robert was the second son of the Reverend John Hooke, whose parish was on the Isle of Wight, and the Hooke family doubted seriously that Robert would survive his birth by more than a few weeks. Small in stature, sallow in complexion, and very frail, Robert Hooke seemed a good bet to succumb to the myriad diseases that then gave Europe such a high infant mortality rate. Yet, the youngest Hooke proved far sturdier than either his father or elder brother John; for despite the phlegms, agues, dizziness, and assorted aches and pains that plagued him throughout his life, he not only survived but grew into an unusually energetic individual. Robert Hooke's seemingly chronic ailments combined with his father's financial circumstances to compel the Reverend Hooke to follow the haphazard but effective path of educating his younger son at home. By modern standards, Hooke's education was very irregular, ranging sporadically from lessons in mathematics, which he enjoyed, to classical languages, which he barely tolerated. His only discernible interest seems to have been a natural enough one for a child, making and playing with toys. But the toys of young Robert Hooke were very uncommon ones, for they were sundials, clocks, model ships, and various machines that would fly: objects that foreshadowed his interest in and talent for scientific inquiry.

With the death of his father in 1648, when Robert Hooke was 13 years old, he was left pretty much to his own devices, so he took his inheritance of £100 and made his way to London. In order to prepare himself for a career, young Hooke at first tried painting, studying with Sir Peter Lely, one of England's foremost portrait painters. Hooke showed little skill at painting, however, so he left Lely's studio and entered Westminster School to complete his education. Westminster was then, as now, one of the finest schools in the British Isles, and Hooke apparently responded with enthusiasm to what it had to offer. He was especially captivated by mathematics, and it was in that discipline that he soon gained a reputation as a promising student by mastering the first six books of Euclid in a week. He further impressed the masters by devising in his spare time 30 separate theoretical ways to fly. These and other feats were viewed as evidence of a mind that deserved further cultivation; so after five years at Westminster Hooke went up to Oxford as a servitor, combining the roles of servant and student, in Christ Church College.

Hooke's tenure at Oxford led directly to his scientific career, for when he went there as a student the university was employing a number of men who were confronting many of the basic research problems of natural science. Under the influence of Bacon and Descartes, men like Bishop John Wilkins of Chester, William Petty, Thomas Willis, Seth Ward, Robert Boyle, and Christopher Wren were grappling with the fundamental questions of mathematics, physics, astronomy, and chemistry. It was through his associations with these individuals that Robert Hooke's gifts were discovered and developed. Willis, for example, first noticed Hooke's talent in 1655 and engaged him as an assistant in a series of chemical experiments. Impressed with his aide's performance, Willis introduced Hooke to nearly every important scientist at Oxford. These meetings resulted in the student's both sharpening his skills and making numerous important contacts. Seth Ward interested him in astronomy, while Christopher Wren taught him astronomy as well as the principles of architecture. Bishop Wilkins and William Petty encouraged his study of mathematics, and the prelate was constantly urging Hooke on in his periodic attempts to invent a machine that would enable man to fly.

These scientific relationships that Hooke developed in the 1650s also frequently developed into close personal friendships. Although they were a full generation older, both Wilkins and Petty became two of Robert Hooke's closest personal friends. Indeed, Wilkins's death in 1672 distressed Hooke so greatly that, as he wrote in his diary, he could do nothing but grieve for "my Lord of Chester" for over a week. Christopher Wren, who was approximately Hooke's age, became his closest friend, and their personal association proved eventually to be the foundation for a lucrative business relationship. Robert Boyle was another lifelong comrade, and Hooke's connection with him was probably the most immediately significant one of his Oxford days; it effectively launched his career and made his reputation as a promising young scientist.

In the last few years of the 1650s, Boyle was experimenting with the nature and quality of the air. His research was restricted, however, because he was unable to fashion a pump that would either create a vacuum or compress the air satisfactorily. When the chemist learned of Robert Hooke's flair for invention he explained his dilemma and asked for the student's opinion. The result made scientific history. Hooke designed and constructed a successful air pump for Boyle, and the pioneer chemist then used it to complete his experiments. These studies led directly to Boyle's gas laws, which form part of the foundation for modern chemistry. Moreover, Hooke's pump proved valuable in fields beside chemistry, for it became one of the ancestors of the pumps of Savery and Newcomen and through them of the steam engine.

The invention of the air pump made Robert Hooke's reputation at Oxford as a scientist and inventor, and his relationship with Boyle soon turned from one of research assistant to that of scientific associate. Through Boyle, Robert Hooke met a group of men who proved to be the largest bloc in what was to become the Royal Society, one of the most prestigious scientific associations in the world. Oddly enough, the Royal Society was not founded by an Englishman, but rather by a German immigrant, Theodore Haak, who started the organization in 1645 by suggesting that a group of London scientists meet at Gresham College to discuss their work. In 1648, part of the group went to Oxford and the rest disbanded. By 1660, however, the Oxford scientists returned to London, and the original club was reconstituted. Within two years the group was chartered by King Charles II as the Royal Society.

Robert Boyle was one of the most important of the Oxford men to return to London, and he persuaded Robert Hooke to accompany him. With Boyle's help, Hooke soon came to know all of the members of the scientific circle quite well, and he impressed them especially with his mechanical skills. When the Royal Society was formally chartered, Boyle suggested that Hooke's talents be made permanently available to the group by offering him an official position. The Society took up Boyle's suggestion and tendered Hooke the newly created post of Curator of

Experiments with an annual salary of £80. Hooke readily accepted the Society's offer, and began almost immediately to prepare the "considerable experiments" he was required to present to the membership every week. For two years he worked diligently and successfully at his experiments, frequently astonishing his colleagues with his knack for defining and solving complex research problems. In 1664, they demonstrated their appreciation for his work by combining their influence and resources to see that he was appointed both Cutlerian Lecturer in Mechanics and Gresham Professor of Geometry at Gresham College. The Cutlerian position carried a salary of £50 a year, which Hooke found impossible to collect from the miserly Sir John Cutler. The Gresham Professorship gave Hooke something much more valuable to a scientist than money: full use of the College's facilities and a suite of rooms in Gresham College on Bishopsgate Street where the Royal Society had established itself. Thus from 1664 until his death in 1703, Robert Hooke was comfortably situated in the capital with an adequate salary and doing what he preferred above all else for a living. A childhood hobby had been developed into a satisfying adult livelihood.

Hooke's natural gifts, cultivated by his affiliation with the Royal Society and his residence at Gresham College, made him in a relatively short time one of England's premier scientists. His remarkable mind, most striking in the wide range of his interests, carried his attention from one scientific subject to another almost constantly, and insights occurred to him so rapidly that he frequently could not find the time to pursue them. Similarly, many of his ideas were so far advanced that his age lacked the technical means of confirming his intuitions. For example, he postulated that a substance in the air, which Hooke called *menstruum*, supported combustion. Over one hundred years later, Antoine Lavoisier, a French chemist, proved that Hooke's hypothesis was correct and that his *menstruum* was oxygen. Hooke's breadth of interests and acute observations coincided perfectly with the concerns of the Royal Society, which investigated practical matters such as navigation, land transportation, cartography, ballistics and mechanics, medicine, and microscopy. In one way or another, and frequently with dramatic effect, Robert Hooke's talents encompassed all of these fields and more. By utilizing the Royal Society as a sounding board for his ideas, presenting his discoveries to its members, soliciting their advice, and in many instances incorporating their suggestions, he made a number of vitally important contributions to scientific research.

In 1665, shortly after Hooke's appointment to Gresham College, he produced *Micrographia*, a book which was an extraordinary demonstration of the quality and intensity of his mind. It consisted of 246 pages of microscopical descriptions, but its methodology and conclusions were revolutionary. In its planning, explanations, and illustrations, Hooke set a new methodological standard that made all preceding experimental demonstrations seem clumsy and unconvincing. By the use of clear, concise proofs to support his conclusions, and drawings, many of which were used in biology books as late as the mid-19th century, Hooke outlined graphically how experimental science should be approached. Moreover, *Micrographia's* conclusions contained at least six major and specific contributions to science. In its format of 60 observations of objects viewed through the microscope, proceeding from inorganic to living matter, the book also shows how carefully and yet unpretentiously Hooke could present some of his more significant discoveries. First, he dealt with optics in a tightly organized account of the colors of thin plates observed principally in pieces of mother-of-pearl. Almost as an afterthought, he discussed the phenomenon of diffraction, where white light is divided into its elemental colors by the bending of its rays through a prism. Hooke's theory of primary colors as stated in the book has since been proven incorrect, but his work was read carefully by Isaac Newton, then cloistering himself at Cambridge, and Newton later acknowledged that the *Micrographia* influenced his formulation of the laws of optics. In a letter to Hooke, somewhat patronizing in tone, Newton wrote that if he had achieved anything of consequence in dealing with light it was because he had stood on the shoulders of "giants," Descartes and Hooke.

The subject of optics was only one small part of the book. Hooke also explained his theory of combustion with admirable simplicity and clarity, stating that a flame did not exist as a separate entity, but rather was the product of air, a combustible substance, and heat. Hooke even devised an ingenious experiment to test his hypothesis. He put charcoal in a closed container, covered it with sand, and then placed it in an intensely hot oven. Noting that the charcoal did not burn, regardless of the amount of heat applied, until it was exposed to the air, Hooke concluded that air was a necessary part of the combustion process. Lacking a grasp of the composition of air, he was unable to complete the experiment by isolating the element that supported combustion.

From combustion Hooke moved naturally to work on respiration, and again theorized correctly that respiration was a form of combustion. He even experimented on himself in a chamber with one quarter of the atmosphere removed, and noted that the experience temporarily deafened him and gave him earaches as well as headaches. As a sideline to his respiration work, Hooke also carried out some important research on artificial respiration by opening a dog's thorax and keeping the beast alive with an air pump. The experiment was performed only twice, however, for Hooke found the work too cruel to pursue at the cost of further suffering.

One of the most valuable sections of *Micrographia* dealt with a microscopical subject of the greatest significance to the advance of biology. This was the observation, description, and explanation of the cellular structure of plants. Using very thin slices of cork, Hooke observed that cork appeared to be constructed of innumerable tiny packets that he determined were the basic structural item of the plant. There is no mistaking his excitement at the discovery, as he calculated that there were one and one quarter billion of these packets in a cubic inch of cork, "a thing most incredible, did not our Microscope assure us of it by ocular demonstration." Hooke called these packets "cells," and thus gave to science the term that is still used to describe the basic unit of all protoplasm. Additionally, Hooke opened up a whole new branch of science, cytology, or the study of cells.

Almost inadvertently included with his primary discussions of optics, combustion, and cells were Hooke's less compelling interests. One was a careful description of the structure of feathers, their relation to flight, and the optical properties of both feathers and insect wings. The first complete viewing and illustration of the metamorphosis of a water gnat was another achievement, but even though Hooke was awed by witnessing the process, he grossly underrated its importance. A third was a painstaking and elaborate description of the compound eye of "a Grey drone-fly and of several other creatures," which he included in *Micrographia* so offhandedly that it seemed an afterthought. Finally, Hooke discussed the structure of the muscles and joints of insects and speculated on how these formations enabled insects to generate such surprising lifting power. These secondary accounts alone would have given Hooke a claim to greatness as a scientist, but the book contained still more in the form of intuitive speculation that further proved the power of Robert Hooke's mind.

First, he theorized that sponges were animals rather than plants, or more precisely that they were at best a combination of plants and animals, and that too many scientists overemphasized their physical similarity to vegetation in concluding that they were plants. The absence of a comprehensive differentiation between animals and plants made it impossible for him to prove his theory to the satisfaction of his peers, but modern science has vindicated him. Next, and particularly interesting, was Hooke's speculation that the "vales" of the moon were not really bombardment craters but instead were the result of volcanic action. He went to great lengths to prove this theory, which incidentally was also held by a number of other contemporary scientists who lacked Hooke's ability in contriving experimental demonstrations. In the first of two experiments, he prepared a mud composed of pipe clay and water and then dropped bullets on it to simulate the moon's surface. As Hooke suspected, the "vales" produced by his bullets looked nothing like the lunar surface, so he stated emphatically that the craters of the moon could not "proceed from any cause analogous to this." His second experiment, in contrast, assured him that the "vales" resulted from the moon's volcanic action, for in it he observed the cooling of a heated pot of alabaster and noted that it was "covered with small pits, exactly shaped like those of the moon." The question of the origin of the "vales" is still unresolved in the 1970s, despite extensive lunar surface testing, but the available evidence indicates that Robert Hooke was probably correct once again. Finally, in his account of the composition of silk fiber, he suggested that it should be relatively easy with the proper machinery to manufacture artificial silk. The modern synthetic fiber industry has proven the truth of that surmise.

Considering together all of the observations and speculations of Hooke's *Micrographia*, it must be concluded that this large and carefully illustrated book ranks second only to Newton's *Principia* as a pillar of Restoration science. The volume was well-received by the scientific community and the general reading public, and served both to establish Hooke's reputation as a truly seminal thinker and to make him a familiar public figure in London. Samuel Pepys, the inveterate diarist, read *Micrographia* avidly, and stayed up most of the night to finish it. In a typical burst of Pepysian enthusiasm, he proclaimed it the "most ingenious book" he had ever read. Isaac Newton also read it with great care and took copious notes on the items that particularly interested him. The positive reception of his book gratified Hooke immensely, and the fame that accompanied it had the virtue of bringing him to the attention of powerful men in government and society. This renown made it possible for Hooke to pursue his scientific studies while making a fortune at two of his avocations: architecture and civil engineering.

One year after the publication of *Micrographia*, London was almost completely destroyed by the worst fire in her history. Most Englishmen viewed the fire as a catastrophe, several Puritans claiming that it was God's punishment for the King's many and varied sins, but Robert Hooke and his friend Christopher Wren took a more positive position. They looked upon the fire as a glorious opportunity to rebuild London along symmetrical and aesthetically pleasing lines. Accordingly, each of them and John Evelyn, the diarist and historian, produced a plan for the reconstruction and submitted it to the King. Evelyn's plan was largely a rehash of medieval London, but Hooke's and Wren's were radical in that they aimed at anticipating the needs of the capital in future years rather than simply rebuilding a London where Edward III would have felt at home. Wren's model called for an urban configuration with streets laid out to form the spokes of wheels that centered on St. Paul's Cathedral and the Royal Exchange. Hooke's plan, in contrast, was conceived as a gridiron of streets, the familiar form of many modern American cities. None of the plans were accepted by King Charles, but he did establish a commission late in 1666 to oversee the rebuilding of his capital, and the most notable royal appointment to the commission was Christopher Wren. London's municipal governors also appointed Robert Hooke to the commission on the strength of his original model.

By 1669 Wren and Hooke had become the dominating figures on the commission, with Wren fully in control of reconstruction and Hooke assisting him and supporting his building plans. As an ally, Hooke was vital to Wren, for the *Micrographia's* author had been given the lucrative post of Surveyor of the City of London as compensation for the rejection of his original plan, and had he opposed Wren the London that arose out of the ashes might have looked very different indeed. As City Surveyor, Hooke's duties were primarily those of an engineer, and his mathematical training and mechanical skills proved invaluable in solving the many technical problems that he faced. While Wren thought out and drafted the plans for most of the new buildings, Hooke surveyed their foundations and marked off the boundaries of the streets where they would be located. He also spent a good deal of time checking the quality of building materials, advising Wren on the internal constructions best suited to support his more massive structures, and adjudicated disputes over property boundaries and the prices of stone, brick, and timber. Hooke's task was simplified by his power to enforce new building codes that limited construction to largely nonflammable materials. At the same time, his engineering skills enabled him to plan and then supervise most of the new work on canals, bridges, quays, and sewers that was done in the City after the fire. Since most of London was rebuilt between 1668 and 1674, excepting only the City churches, Wren and Hooke together were principally responsible for the new metropolis.

Along with being a competent surveyor, Robert Hooke was also a capable, if not brilliant, architect, and he planned and built several famous London buildings. His first commission came from the Royal College of Physicians, whose members approached him in 1670 about designing their new residence in Warwick Lane, and by 1671 he had completed the plans and was supervising work on the structure. It took eight years to finish, and it survived until the 19th century. Perhaps the greatest tribute to Hooke's architectural skill resulted from his design of the Physician's College, for until the publication of Hooke's diaries it was admired as a classic designed and built by Wren. Another Hooke building was Bedlam Hospital, a London landmark and scene of perverse amusement where sane people paid to watch the insane suffer. A huge stone building with a facade 540 feet long, Bedlam combined the merits of being both graceful in design and functional. Separate rooms were provided for each patient, and the grounds were carefully landscaped to provide a relaxing atmosphere. There was, however, no doubt about the building's purpose, for dominating the attractive gateway were two statues depicting raving madness and melancholy madness.

Hooke was also responsible for a number of other public buildings, but some of his best efforts were devoted to constructing private homes. One of the earliest of these was the mansion he built for Ralph Montagu who, after bilking the mad Duchess of Albermarle out of her fortune, used part of the money to erect Montagu House on the present site of the British Museum. Palatial in size and splendid in decor, Montagu House was one of Hooke's finest buildings. It was also his least enduring one, for it burned down six years after it was finished through a maid's carelessness. Another private house begun by Hooke was Ragley Hall, a country mansion built in Warwickshire for Lord Conway. It still stands today and is one of Britain's better-known stately houses. The present building is Hooke's only in general outline, however, for the death of Lord Conway and financial shortages interrupted construction so frequently that it took over 50 years to complete the structure.

Over a 20-year period, from 1670 to 1690, Robert Hooke designed and built a number of public and private structures, but only one survives today that can be attributed to him alone, the Monument to the Great Fire of 1666. Christopher Wren is still credited with the design, but as with the Royal College of Physicians, Hooke's diaries leave no doubt about who conceived and built it. The "piller" as Hooke called the Monument, located on Fish Street Hill parallel to Pudding Lane where the conflagration started, was begun in 1673 and completed in 1676. It is a white, fluted, Doric column 202 feet tall with steps giving access to a platform at the top. Today, it is rivaled only by the General Post Office Tower and the dome of St. Paul's as a unique feature of the London skyline, and in Hooke's time it was one of Europe's great architectural curiosities. Intended principally as an adornment to the capital, the Monument was also utilitarian. Hooke and other scientists frequently used it to compare atmospheric pressure at its top and bottom, and lovers met there so often that jokes were plentiful about its peculiar attraction as a trysting place. On a more grim note, it attracted numerous people bent on suicide, and a railing eventually had to be erected to thwart their intentions. Compared to Bedlam, Montagu House, and other Hooke designs, the Monument is perhaps the least of his architectural efforts, but it does survive, dominating the City and commemorating Robert Hooke's talent for planning and construction as well as the Great Fire that made possible the display of his talent.

During what can be called his architectural period, from 1666 to about 1680, Robert Hooke was a very busy man. His job as City Surveyor and his commissions for buildings consumed great amounts of his time, but they were really only a small part of his overall activity. Most of his time was devoted to science and recreational interests and while the former gives him historical significance, the latter reveals him as a fascinating and complex personality. His domestic life, for instance, was so hectic and his personal behavior so unorthodox that, in contrast to his cool and almost mechanical scientific objectivity, he appears as virtually a dual personality.

Emotional, neurotic, and committed to a life style that can best be described as unconventional, Robert Hooke had a fair claim to being Britain's original "boffin," a brilliant scientist who behaved strangely. He was a very wealthy man, who left a large, locked case full of money when he died; yet he lived a very modest, if not Spartan, life in his suite at Gresham College. He spent his money freely for scientific books and instruments, of which he was a dedicated collector. His only vanity seems to have been clothes; he thought nothing of spending an exorbitant sum for a velvet suit. Preferring to walk, or perhaps trot is more accurate, wherever he went on business or pleasure, he saw no need to maintain a coach and was firmly convinced that travelling on foot was good both for his health and purse.

Hooke's relationships with members of his household seem unusually charged with emotion, and they often provide insights into the complexity of his personality. In 1675, for example, he took in his young cousin Tom Gyles to educate him for a career in the navy, and then he fussed and fumed constantly at Tom when he slept during lessons and showed what Hooke thought were signs of laziness. The scientist seemed perpetually irritated by the boy, but when Tom died of measles in 1677, Hooke described the progression of his illness in one of the most moving passages in his diaries. The women in Robert Hooke's life cast in even greater relief his innermost drives and reactions. A confirmed bachelor, Hooke took several mistresses over the years, most notably a housemaid named Nell Young and his niece, Grace Hooke. The scientist could not, however, leave uncomplicated what began as casual affairs. He soon turned a sexual attraction into an emotional dependence, and whatever pleasure was derived from his relationships was negated by jealousy, suspicion, possessiveness, and quarreling. Most of his lovers escaped by finding employment elsewhere, but Nell Young and Grace Hooke were unable to free themselves. Nell remained his mistress for fully 20 years after her marriage, seeing him once a week until early in the 1690s, and his affair with Grace, by any standard a stormy one, was ended only by her death.

In some ways, Robert Hooke's public personality was obscured by the more peculiar features of his private life, and over a period of three decades his enemies, supporters either of Henry Oldenburg or Isaac Newton, used many of the aberrations in his behavior against him with devastating effect. Taking, as a case in point, Hooke's depressions caused by his unhappy love affairs as serious character defects, they portrayed him as a moody, crabby, and thoroughly unpleasant old recluse. The result was the construction of a reputation for Hooke as being a social misfit. In reality, he was one of the more gregarious men of his unusually social era. A frequent visitor of coffee houses and pubs, a dinner guest at innumerable parties in fashionable society, and an affable host in his rooms in Gresham College, Hooke was an entertaining conversationalist who combined the virtues of being a good talker and a good listener. He also had a positive mania about clubs, joining them at the hint of an invitation and founding nearly as many as he joined. In 1675, for instance, he organized a club devoted to natural philosophy with Christopher Wren and Wren's brother-in-law. The next year this club foundered, so he engineered the Decimal Society, enrolling Wren, Jonas More, and Boyle as the most prominent charter members. Moreover, he was one of the first members of the selective and semiofficial Royal Society Club, which he viewed as the social Valhalla of England's scientific elite.

Despite the drain on his time and energy caused by his various building projects and personal involvements, the decade of the 1670s was perhaps Hooke's most productive scientific period. Although his attention was divided among a number of different subjects, his most immediately fruitful work was in the field of mechanics, where his accomplishments ranged from the invention of valuable tools and instruments to theoretical and practical horology, the science of watch and clock-making. During the first six years of the decade he devoted most of his attention to horological problems, and his motivation as well as the difficulties he experienced in his research is revealing of both the interests and characteristics of European scientists at the time.

Hooke's involvement in horology came about partly because of long-standing interest but largely because of the national need to develop an extremely accurate timepiece. By 1670, enough was known about astronomy to hold out the promise that useful practical results might be derived from the observation of celestial events. Specifically, many Englishmen, including King Charles, suspected that astronomical data could be used to solve the thorniest of all navigational problems, the finding of the longitude. In fact, Charles II founded Greenwich Observatory with the longitudinal problem foremost in his mind, and the brass plaque at Greenwich indicating the location of zero degrees longitude is a tribute to the third Stuart King's farsightedness. The men concerned about the relationship between astronomy and navigation were, however, frustrated by the fact that the most promising path to uncovering the longitude lay in timing the differences between selected astronomical events. Since that required a timepiece that would lose a second or less a month and thus achieve chronometer precision, there was no hope of measuring the longitude satisfactorily without first concluding some basic research in horology.

Hooke's horological difficulties were twofold. First, he determined that he would have to replace the undependable verge escapement of contemporary clocks, the device that controlled the speed and regularity of the balance wheel, with something much more accurate. Then, he would have to find a means of negating the effects of gravity on his new clock. The initial problem he solved by imposing on the verge escapement the isochrony, or equality of time length, of a free pendulum. It was Hooke's good fortune to know a great deal about pendulums before he even began his serious work in horology, for in 1664 he and Lord Brouncker, one of the Royal Society's early presidents, had measured at precisely 39 inches the length of the pendulum that vibrates seconds. That length had to be reduced for Hooke's purposes, however, so he replaced the verge escapement with a much more sophisticated apparatus, the anchor escapement. Fundamental in modern clocks, the anchor escapement was a supremely accurate detaining catch that controlled the speed of a balance wheel or pendulum, and by inventing it Hooke made an important breakthrough in horology. He attacked the effect of gravity with equal success, inventing the spiral balance spring to reduce the influence of gravity on his watches. Despite Hooke's inability to produce an instrument of chronometer accuracy, either of these inventions would give him a reasonable claim to being the founder of modern horology, for they were the two essential discoveries that eventually led to the production of the chronometer.

His status as sole inventor of both items has been disputed, however, and the controversy over the balance-spring watch led to some of the most vicious in-fighting ever to occur in the Royal Society. The dispute over who created the anchor escapement was by far the milder of the two controversies, since it centered on the issue of whether Hooke or a clockmaker named William Clement produced it. The available evidence indicates that Hooke's claim should be given priority, largely because he demonstrated the mechanism to the Royal Society in May and October of 1669, but there were several Clement supporters who found this evidence unconvincing for one reason or another. In contrast, the issue of the spiral balance-spring watch divided the Royal Society into two warring camps that bickered and struggled for nearly two years. The quarrel began in 1675 when Henry Oldenburg, one of the Society's two secretaries, published an account in the *Philosophical Transactions* of the Society explaining how Christian Huygens, a Dutch scientist, applied a spiral spring to a watch balance. Oldenburg, who had persuaded Huygens to grant him the English patent to the device, claimed that the Dutchman's invention was original, and this infuriated Robert Hooke, who insisted that he had invented such a mechanism fully 17 years earlier. He even produced documentation to prove his claim in the form of letters proposing the formation of a company to exploit the invention, but his adversary remained intractable. Oldenburg sought support among the members of the Society, as did Hooke, and the two men and their allies ruined several meetings of the organization with their bitter recriminations. After a year of struggle, Oldenburg technically won the battle, for the Council of the Royal Society published a statement supporting him and disavowing Hooke; but King Charles refused to grant either of them a patent for the mechanism. Hooke felt that in the end he was vindicated, albeit indirectly, for when Oldenburg died in 1677 the Council appointed Hooke to his secretarial position, in effect apologizing to him for their stance in the quarrel.

Although the argument disturbed Hooke deeply and produced some of the more emotional entries in his diary, it did have a positive result. It motivated him to carry out a number of important experiments on springs, which resulted in the publication of his law of the spring, still taught in all elementary physics classes. From 1675 to 1678, Hooke experimented with various sizes of springs and evaluated their responses to different weights. His studies led him to conclude that there was a natural law governing the action of springs: "the power of any spring is in the same proportion with the tension thereof." At approximately the same time, Robert Hooke demonstrated his versatility by inventing three useful devices which were entirely unrelated to each other. One was the universal joint, so necessary for modern automobiles, which Hooke first described fully in 1676 as a means "for communicating a round motion through any irregularly bent way." In France this joint is referred to as a Cardan joint, after Jerome Cardan, the 16th-century Italian inventor and mathematician; but since Cardan's gimbal joint allowed free rotation only on perpendicular axes, it was not a true universal joint in the sense that Hooke's invention was. Another Hooke creation was the weather clock, begun in 1673 and finished in 1679. Powered by a pendulum clock, this ingenious instrument recorded every 15 minutes on a rotating cylinder of paper the barometric pressure, temperature, humidity, direction and velocity of the wind, and the rainfall. Finally, there was a mechanical marvel, the iris diaphragm. Originally, Hooke intended it for use in regulating the amount of light entering the lenses of his telescopes used in astronomy, but modern photography, by incorporating it as a principal feature of most cameras, has considerably extended its usefulness.

All of Hooke's research work in the 1670s appeared in published form, either in the *Transactions* of the Royal Society or as *Cutlerian Lectures*, and while his inventions gave him the reputation as the foremost mechanical scientist of his age, they were really secondary to his principal interest, astronomy. Throughout the 1660s, Robert Hooke made one noteworthy astronomical discovery after another. His drawings of Mars aided scientists two centuries later in determining the rotation rate of that planet, and he was the first to infer that the planet Jupiter rotated by observing the movement of a spot that he noted on its surface. Moreover, he discovered the fifth star in the Orion trapezium, made the first observation of a star by daylight, and reported variations in the fixed star Gamma Draconis that ultimately led to the discovery of the phenomenon of aberration.[1] Since the questions of planetary rotation rates, the apparent movement of fixed stars, and the relations of celestial bodies to the earth were particular aspects of a general scientific problem, planetary unity, Hooke finally summarized these bits and pieces of research in a prescient essay. Entitled "An Attempt to Prove the Motion of the Earth by Observation," the essay appeared in 1674 as a *Cutlerian Lecture,* and in it Hooke sketched the broad outline along which Newton proceeded so successfully. It was, of course, Newton and not Hooke who solved the problem of planetary unity in the *Principia,* but Hooke's essay deserves some attention. It shows, in 21 drawings and 28 pages of text, Hooke's originality, the critical faculty of his mind, and the careful methodology that characterized his work. It is, perhaps, the best evidence of his importance to the evolution of science.

At first glance, the "Attempt" was unprepossessing, for it was brief, the drawings were simple and the demonstrations clear, and the conclusions stated with almost mechanical terseness. Yet, in the 17th century it was as pregnant with scientific implications as any early treatise on astronomy could be. Hooke began by examining critically all previous attempts to prove the earth's motion, and soon concluded that other investigators erred both in equipment and method. Their equipment he found to be too primitive and inaccurate, and their methods too haphazard and ill-conceived. He then explained at some length how he approached the question, and the result was a profile of a determined scientist willing to sacrifice personal comfort to arrive at the truth. First, he fashioned a large telescope, 36 feet long, and took pains to see that it was attached with the greatest precision to a complex device that would indicate astral movements in fractions of seconds in angular measurement. Next, he applied all that the available technology could provide to make his instruments impervious to the effects of temperature and moisture. Finally, he hacked a sizable hole in the roof and floor of his suite at Gresham College so that he could make his observations. Choosing as his aiming point "the bright star in the head of the Dragon," he began his experiment, measuring seeming alterations in the position of the star in relation to the zenith of Gresham College in December,

---

[1] In astronomy, aberration is the small apparent change in the position of a celestial body caused by the motion of the earth and the effect of light.

March, June, and September. By utilizing what astronomers know as parallax,[2] Hooke then proved to his own satisfaction that the earth did in fact move, since a fixed star by its definition could not move. This led him inevitably to some startling conclusions, or in Hooke's word, "suppositions."

His first conclusion was that all celestial bodies have an attraction or gravitating power toward their own centers. This, he claimed, not only kept them from flying apart into space, but also gave them the power to attract all other bodies that lay in the range of their gravitation. From that, Hooke concluded further that any body that was put into motion would move in a straight line unless it was deflected by some power and forced into a circular or elliptical motion. Finally, he concluded that the attractive power of bodies was greatest at their centers and diminished in relation to distance from their centers. Stripped of their complex mathematical proofs, these conclusions anticipated those that Newton reached in his explanation of the phenomenon of universal gravitation. Robert Hooke made no claim, however, in the "Attempt" to have solved the problem of planetary unity, for he had neither the time nor the mathematical genius for that accomplishment. Isaac Newton did, but there is no doubt that he owed Hooke a debt, and he grudgingly acknowledged it with as little grace as possible in the first book of the *Principia*. It was the final quarrel in a series of three unhappy encounters between two of England's foremost scientists, and it cost Hooke his reputation and his rightful place in scientific history.

The first confrontation between Hooke and Newton occurred in 1672. It began as a professional disagreement over a paper on light which Newton sent to the Royal Society, but the quarrel rapidly disintegrated into a personal vendetta. Hooke started the fight by criticizing Newton's theory of light, and then added insult to injury by claiming that Newton had not properly credited Hooke's *Micrographia* as one of his sources. Thin-skinned, Newton responded angrily to Hooke's remarks, and he was encouraged by Oldenburg who, envying Hooke's success, thought it a marvelous idea to set Hooke and Newton at each other's throats, apparently in hopes of profiting in some way from the struggle. After simmering for five years, the dispute finally ended when Newton satisfied Hooke's claim to recognition in a letter. The quarrel erupted again two years later, however when Hooke was impolitic enough to correct a minor error Newton made in a paper describing the line of a falling body. In reality, the author of the "Attempt" was enthralled by Newton's work on gravitation, and was merely trying to be helpful, but Newton was deeply offended and accused Hooke of pettiness. From that point

---

[2] Parallax is the apparent difference in the position of a heavenly body in relation to a given point on the earth's surface and some other point, and is expressed as a triangle.

on, the two were bitter enemies, and whatever hope there might have been for a reconciliation vanished in 1687 when Edmund Halley persuaded Newton to publish the *Principia*. Hooke immediately claimed that his work in the field should be acknowledged by Newton, and Newton threatened to suppress the most important part of the work, the entire third book, rather than give Hooke any credit. Fortunately, Halley smoothed Newton's ruffled feathers and somehow convinced him to mention Hooke's research briefly, but from then on Newton and Hooke stayed well clear of each other. In fact, their hatred was such that despite Newton's standing as the greatest scientist of his generation, he felt that he could not accept the Presidency of the Royal Society as long as Hooke was its Secretary.

Because of his inventions, discoveries, and versatility, Robert Hooke deserves a place of respect not only in English science, but in that of the Western world generally. His brilliantly penetrating mind moved with ease from one subject to another until, well before middle age, he had made important contributions in a wide variety of areas. Yet, except for some attention from specialists in the history of science, he received virtually no recognition for nearly three centuries. Today, for instance, scarcely one person in 100 turns on an electric light without knowing that Thomas Edison made it possible by inventing the bulb, but of the innumerable photographers all over the world only the most zealous collectors of esoterica know that Robert Hooke invented the iris diaphragm. Hooke's obscurity raises a fundamental question in the study of history: how are individuals who are preeminent in their own era lost to succeeding generations? In Hooke's case, as in most, the answer is a complex one.

On an elementary level, Hooke's fate can be explained as the logical outcome of his temperament and life style. His quarrel with Newton, apparently professional in origin, was at least as much personal as it was scientific. Seven years Newton's senior, Hooke expected a deference, respect, and professional acknowledgment commensurate with his status as a charter member of the Royal Society. Instead, Newton met Hooke's expectations with suspicion and hostility, and the clash of their personalities made them appear as caricatures of scientists in their pettiness and bickering. Isaac Newton's increasing fame only made matters worse, for Hooke's jealousy of his younger colleague became progressively more obvious and his critics tended increasingly to ascribe most of Robert Hooke's critical professional opinions to envy of Newton. Moreover, Hooke's private life contributed in part to his temporary disappearance from the history of British science. Many of his contemporaries, usually those who thought him unduly jealous of Newton, also accused him of greed; but their most effective criticism was the assertion that Hooke was not "strictly virtuous" in his relationships with women. This claim, especially in the Victorian era, did more than anything else to deny Hooke his proper place as a noteworthy British scientist. Indeed, his diary was not published until 1935 because many of the passages were considered offensive to public morality and hence unprintable.

On a complex level, Hooke's obscurity was the result of historic forces that make his personal quirks and his quarrel with Newton seem inconsequential. Newton's achievements gave rise among his followers to the revival of a belief derived from Platonism that theory was superior to experiment. Although Newton himself was, with his famous motto *Hypotheses Non Fingo*, as much a Baconian as Robert Hooke, the Baconian insistence on experiment which inspired most of Hooke's triumphs withered in proportion to the glorification of Platonic theory. Somehow, generations subsequent to Hooke's and Newton's misinterpreted the scientific method and philosophy of these two men. Newton, the Baconian who added new dimensions of mathematics to his science, was, because of the old Platonic belief in the superiority of mathematics over experiment, viewed not as a Baconian at all but rather as the paragon of Platonic "mind." Robert Hooke, an able but not brilliant mathematician, and master of the experimental method as well as a mechanic without peer, was by these same scientific generations perceived as little more than a common craftsman. Perversely, as Francis Bacon's appreciation in scientific circles has risen and fallen, so has Robert Hooke's, while Sir Isaac Newton, never really identified with Bacon, has been consistently hailed as one of the world's greatest scientists.

In more practical, scientific terms Hooke also suffered a diminution in his reputation because of the wide range of his interest. Thoroughly Baconian, Hooke seems to have accepted without question the universalism that Bacon urged on scientists, and this produced many difficulties for him. Foremost was his flair for rarely finishing an experimental project, which seems inherent in his attempt to deal with all fields of scientific inquiry. Additionally, his ranging over the entire scientific landscape irritated specialists in narrowly delineated fields once scientific specialism became fashionable, and they were quick to criticize any errors he committed while working in their fields. In the process, the specialists concentrated so much on his shortcomings that they failed to appreciate his unique abilities. His stature as a scientist was in their opinion diminished accordingly.

Robert Hooke was, in short, the archetype of a Pre-Newtonian scientist, who cherished the Renaissance ideal of diverse interests, and as such he had the misfortune to become obsolete in his own lifetime. He had, to be sure, a genuine talent for integrating experiment and hypothesis, and the range of his research was impressive. Yet, these most outstanding features of his ability worked against him historically, for the values of Newtonian science, most notably a dominance of abstract disciplines, a rigidity of methodology, and a stringent demand for disciplinary specialism, made Hooke appear to be an intellectual gadfly worthy of nothing more than passing notice. In effect, Hooke and his science suffered from having been innovative and obsolete all in a few decades, with Newton doing to Hooke what Einstein later did to Newton. The only variation in the progression lies in the fact that Sir Isaac Newton is still a titan of modern science while Robert Hooke remains largely a nonentity.

Hooke has, however, his own unique place in the evolution of modern science. His mechanical discoveries and inventions contributed much of the foundation for the triumphs of modern technology, and his speculations in abstract fields lacked only a deeper understanding of mathematics to make him a rival of Newton. The evolution of chemistry and biology would have been delayed for decades without him, and the architectural face of London would have been less attractive without his talent. But, the most intriguing questions that Robert Hooke poses for the study of history are only peripherally related to his achievements. How much does his career tell us about connections between personality and interpersonal relations and scientific prominence? Or, how heavily and how critically should a historian depend upon the comments of an individual's contemporaries in arriving at general conclusions about the nature and impact of a person's life and career? Neither question lends itself readily to a definitive answer, but the fate of Robert Hooke certainly raises some of the issues that are central to current historical methodology.

SUGGESTED READINGS

Considering the extent of his contribution to science, surprisingly little has been written about Robert Hooke. Margaret 'Espinasse, *Robert Hooke* (Berkeley: University of California Press, 1956) is the only major modern biography. The chapter on Hooke in James G. Crowther, *Founders of British Science* (London: Cresset, 1960) is also informative. Basil Willey, *The Seventeenth Century Background* (London: Chatto & Windus, 1934), while not dealing directly with Hooke, is valuable for understanding the philosophical foundation of Pre-Newtonian science. Hooke's great contemporary and foe, Sir Isaac Newton, has been the subject of extensive research, and two works are especially useful in outlining the relationship between Newton and Hooke: Louis T. More, *Isaac Newton: A Biography* (New York: Scribner's, 1934), and Frank E. Manuel, *A Portrait of Isaac Newton* (Cambridge: Belknap Press, 1968).

Perhaps the best way to understand Hooke and his science is to read two of his better-known works, which have been made available to American libraries through the Short Title Catalog and Wing project of University Microfilms, Ann Arbor, Michigan: *Micrographia*, Wing No. 2620, Reel No. 188 and *Lectiones Cutlerianae*, Wing No. 2617, Reel No. 107.

Chapter 9

ROBERT CLIVE:
Impetus toward Empire

For almost two centuries after 1750 Great Britain ruled over millions of square miles of land and hundreds of millions of non-European peoples throughout the world. The exercise of worldwide authority and influence permeated the British experience and nourished the proud belief that, although the British Isles were smaller in size and population than the major continental European countries, Britain nevertheless was the greatest power in the world. Ultimately there evolved an ethnocentric imperial mystique to justify British control over non-Europeans; British dominion, it was asserted, meant service, for the great European nation was guiding its overseas subjects into the light of civilization.

At the core of the perception that Britons had of themselves as an imperial people lay their rule in India. The result of commercial enterprise, the Indian Empire came to represent the most characteristic expression of benevolent imperial guidance, as generations of civil servants in India implemented the self-imposed civilizing mission. Yet, such professions of disinterested service would have sounded strangely out of place at the inception of the Indian Empire, for initially the British sought only to serve themselves in India. Their rule was the product of self-interest, trickery, luck, and the driving personal ambition of one man.

The foundation for two centuries of British rule over an empire in India was laid by Robert Clive. Of all Englishmen in the mid-18th century, only he worked steadfastly and ruthlessly toward the goal of safeguarding Britain's interests there. His effectiveness determined the context in which men after him had to operate and defined the necessities and opportunities that delimited their activities. Before Robert Clive, it was not at all inevitable that England would come to rule the Asian subcontinent. Because of what he did, British territorial empire in India became almost a certainty.

Born on September 29, 1725, Clive was, like so many major figures in English and imperial history, from the lesser gentry. The Clive family, strongly Puritan in background, had a tradition of public service. One of Robert's ancestors, Sir George Clyve, served as Queen Elizabeth's Chancellor of the Exchequer in Ireland and another, Clive's great-great grandfather Robert, fought as a Colonel under Cromwell and later sat in the Barebones Parliament. Richard Clive, Robert's father, was a barrister-at-law and a country gentleman in Shropshire, but he possessed neither the wealth nor the connections that would give him the prominence and importance that he desired. All biographers of Robert Clive agree that, because of a tyrannical and harsh bent on the part of the father and a tempestuous and independent temperament on the part of the son, Robert's early years were unusually difficult.

As the number of his younger sisters and brothers increased, he was sent to live with his maternal aunt and uncle at Hope Hall, Manchester. Childless, they lavished affection on their nephew while withholding discipline from him and he became wild and uncontrollable. Climbing a local steeple earned him the leadership of a gang of boys whom he led in destructive pranks and in exacting tribute from neighboring shop-keepers. Letters from uncle Daniel Bayley to Richard Clive lamented the "wildness," "fierceness," "imperiousness," and the "desire to domi-nate" of "this little Caesar." But on occasion, too, they expressed gratifica-tion at his "exceeding Patience" and "meekness."

Robert Clive seems to have been more than a normally headstrong boy. His powerful and dominating will and his mischievous tricks re-flected more than just high spirits. So, also, did his periods of submission and meekness indicate more than simple filial obedience. A child of extremes, he would, perhaps, have been classified as a manic-depressive by later generations. Whatever the case, Clive as a mature man seemed to possess unusually compelling drive and to feel emotions intensely.

His reputation for recklessness and turbulence was strengthened by further exploits which included heavy drinking at a boarding school in London, where he failed utterly to please the schoolmasters. His father echoed the general sentiment when he wrote that his son was "that idiot," "not only bad . . . but stupid," and "making progress [only] in evil." Despairing of his eldest son's learning a profession, or of his being a suitable heir for the family estate of Stych Hall, he decided to "send [him] off to make a worthwhile man of [himself] or die of [his]evildoing." In March of 1743, when Robert was just 17 years old, he boarded a ship for the long voyage to India. No one came to the East India Docks to bid him farewell.

Young Clive was employed at a salary of £5 a year as writer, or clerk, by the Honourable Company of Merchants of London Trading into the East Indies. The East India Company had been chartered almost a century and a half before, and it had built up a thriving trade with England and China from the Indian ports of Madras, Bombay, and Calcutta. Clive arrived at Madras in May of 1744, after an unusually long voyage of 15 months and a shipwreck on the Brazilian coast which cost him his luggage and much of his small capital. Madras, the head-quarters of English commerce on the southeastern coast, had a popula-tion of 25,000, of whom less than 400 were European; these were Com-pany employees and soldiers. English activity centered at a fortified factory, or trading post, named Fort St. George, that had been erected 100 years before. Around it spread what the English inelegantly called "Black Town," which exceeded in squalor any slum Clive had seen at home.

A Company writer worked at the chief factor's countinghouse in the fort. His working day began at six A.M., and he sat on a high stool at his desk, copying letters, keeping accounts and, when a ship was in, checking cargo. At noon came dinner, followed by a rest and then a return to the countinghouse in the late afternoon. His meals were communal and free, and he was given a room in the writer's barracks, once a Muslim College and now infested with rats and cockroaches. To pay for his servants, candles, laundry and other necessities, he received an extra allowance of £3 10s.

Clive did not like India, his job, his superiors, or his colleagues. Still, he felt that he could not return to England defeated and penniless. With the other Europeans he was haughty, quarrelsome, and quick to take offense. On one famous occasion the Governor forced him to apologize to his supervisor for an insult. Afterward, when the factor asked him to dinner Clive remarked: "the Governor ordered me to apologize, but he did not command me to dine with you." It is important to note that Clive did follow the Governor's orders and apologize in the first place. However proud, he was always an obedient subordinate to men in positions of power over him.

In the evenings he succumbed to the erotic temptations of Black Town. He also fell foul of a Company regulation of 1661 which required, in certain cases, that young men be circumcised to safeguard their health. One recent biographer has suggested that the psychological and physical consequences of the operation became driving forces in Clive's life. Although this contention is incapable of proof, it is probable that Clive's "mutilation," as he first called it, did assist him in his later dealings with Muslim rulers in India who despised men who were not, as they called it, purified. Later, Clive bragged: "I am proud of bearing the marks of an empire [the Moghul Empire] which we may one day rule ourselves."

At times he was desolate and filled with self-pity. Opium pills were little help and twice, when he was 19, he attempted suicide. Tradition has it that when the pistol misfired he concluded that "fate must have something great in store for me." Thereafter he started to learn Hindu and Persian languages, which would bring him a £30 yearly bonus, and in September of 1746 his life changed suddenly when a French fleet approached Madras. His years of riches, glory, and power were about to begin.

The ancient land of India, with its advanced civilization and fabulous wealth, had always attracted would-be conquerors, from Alexander the Great through Genghis Khan to, finally, the French and the British. In the early 16th century Muslim invaders from the north had established the Moghul Empire over the predominantly Hindu people of India. Decline had begun early in the 18th century and was completed in 1739 by a military defeat at the hands of the Persians, who carried off the jeweled Peacock Throne and the Koh-i-Nur (Mountain of Light) diamond from the imperial capital at Delhi.

Europeans had first come to India at a time when the Moghul hold over the subcontinent had not yet loosened. When the Portuguese, Dutch, French, and English traders acquired permission to establish factories, they had been definitely in an inferior position. Small enclaves of alien traders, little more advanced technologically than the Indians, the Europeans were very conscious that their continued presence and their commercial activities depended on the good will of the Emperor at Delhi. It was, on the whole, a mutually profitable arrangement. Europe received the indigo, spices, calico, silk, and saltpeter it desired, and Indian rulers were enriched by the increasing commerce with Europe and the extensive trade that British merchants also developed with China. As the emperors and their local governors, or *nawabs,* amassed great treasure, so also did individual English and Indian traders. The wealth of the English nabobs, a British corruption of *nawabs,* came not from their salaries, however, which were extraordinarily low, but from the perquisites they enjoyed as Company employees in India. From governor to sea captain to chaplain, all, except the apprentice writer, had the right to carry on trade privately. This was why Englishmen went to India: to make fortunes as quickly as possible and return to England as nabobs. This is what Clive hoped to do, and did.

Throughout the first decades of the 18th century the Indian trade became more and more important to Great Britain. In 1740 England's imports from India were valued at £1,795,000, which was 20 percent of her total imports and equivalent to just over 10 percent of the national revenue. Additionally, Englishmen at home depended on the industries that supplied shipping and provisions for the eastern trade. The prosperity of the East India Company and the moneymaking opportunities of its servants depended not only on the cooperation of Indian rulers but also on their competence. When Moghul power declined, their viceroys, as Macaulay noted in his essay on Clive, became sovereigns. Bribery and corruption were already a way of life in India as, indeed, in England, but now petty princes increased their exactions and no appeal to the Emperor could restrain them. Individual princes might maintain law and order internally very well, but their efficacy tended to be diminished by constant palace intrigues and plots. Above all, with the waning of Moghul power, the separate parts of the Empire began fighting among themselves, and robber warriors from the Maratha state inaugurated a long career of banditry and pillage.

As the position of British traders seemed likely to become more and more insecure because of Indian conditions, the merchants faced a threat of total annihilation from another quarter. Not far from the English factories at Calcutta and Madras the French East India Company had established posts at Chandernagore and Pondicherry, and in the 1740s the French and English commercial establishments in India were drawn into the "second hundred years' war" between the two European nations.

Like the campaigns in North America, the battles in India indicated a shift in emphasis in the traditional Anglo-French rivalry from a European to a worldwide context. In the War of the Austrian Succession the extra-European fighting in many ways outweighed in importance the struggle in Europe itself, and India became one of the major arenas of conflict. Reflecting the new priorities, the French Governor of Pondicherry developed a strategy aimed at destroying the English presence in India entirely.

Joseph-François, Marquis de Dupleix, immersed himself totally in the tortuous and perfidious world of Indian politics. His policy included more than present-giving and bribery to gain favor; he dipped into local plots, took sides in cases of disputed successions, and allied himself with one or another of the quarreling Indian successor states. In the process he introduced a new element into the Indian military scene: the sepoy. Named after the Persian word for soldier, *sipahi*, sepoys were Indian troops trained and armed in the European manner. As such, they were infinitely superior to the undisciplined and poorly armed soldiery of the Indian rulers. The rapid volley firing of sepoy muskets, together with improved artillery, enabled the sepoys to withstand a cavalry charge, the favorite tactic of Muslim commanders.

This combination of political maneuvering and military power threatened to make the French the dominant power in India. The states they protected against internal and external foes tended to become permanent dependencies, and their rulers were expected to take measures against English trade. Should Dupleix have had continuing success, British well-being would have been jeopardized. Clive's great contribution to the Company that employed him was to prevent this from happening by copying the French strategy and successfully turning it against them.

When the French attacked Madras in 1746 they were victorious, partly because the British were unprepared and partly because a French shell opened access to the fort's liquor supply. As the men deserted their guns for the bottles the defense disintegrated. Disguised as an Indian, Clive escaped south to Fort St. David at Cuddalore and arranged for a transfer to the Company's army. His gallantry later in an unsuccessful siege of Pondicherry, as well as in other small engagements, attracted the attention of his commander, Major Stringer Lawrence, a veteran of Fontenoy and Culloden, who led the Company's troops. With the coming of peace Clive returned to civilian life, where his friend Major Lawrence secured for him a post as steward at Fort St. David, Cuddalore. As steward he bought provisions for the garrison and settlement and, in times of war, supplied the armies in the field. In India as in England, great opportunities for personal gain accompanied this position and, like army contractors in Britain, Clive made the most of them.

When hostilities reopened, for example, he made a 50 percent profit on each man he provisioned. Shortly, he had accumulated £40,000.

Although France and Britain had signed the Peace of Aix-la-Chapelle in 1748, ending the War of the Austrian Succession in Europe, Dupleix continued implementing his plan to build up a French Empire in India. Bringing French power into play in disputed successions to the thrones of the two southern states of the Carnatic and the Deccan, his French and sepoy troops defeated all enemies and established pro-French rulers. Early in 1751 a new Governor of the British Company, Thomas Saunders, agreed to support Muhammed Ali Khan in his bid for the throne of the Carnatic. Clive understood that the outnumbered British forces stood little chance of victory in a direct encounter with the French. To draw the French troops away from Trichinopoly, where they were besieging Muhammed Ali and a Company detachment, he persuaded Governor Saunders to authorize an attack on Arcot, capital of Dupleix's puppet Nawab of the Carnatic.

Enrolled in the Company's military arm again as a Captain, Clive led 200 European soldiers and 300 sepoys, with 3 howitzers, to Arcot. Amazingly, the fact that his troops marched through a drenching thunderstorm seems to have persuaded the 1,000-man garrison at Arcot to decamp. Resistance against such men who defied the fury of Allah's wrath would, they feared, be useless. The 25-year-old Clive marched in unopposed and took possession of the citadel. Wealthy citizens of Arcot, following the traditional Indian custom of generosity to conquerors, lavished precious gifts on their new ruler. Clive, in turn, restrained his soldiers from pillaging, and the grateful populace refused to help his enemies, even when he was besieged later in the fort.

The master plan of creating a diversion worked. More than 4,000 Indian and French troops left the walls of Trichinopoly and moved in to dislodge the presumptuous English from Arcot. With reinforcements the host soon totaled 10,000 men; 250 were French. The siege of Arcot lasted 50 days. Clive's soldiers were put on half rations and fell sick until he had only 320 men to face the 10,000 outside the walls. Clive had little military training, but he did have common sense, dash, and luck. He also had the inspiring quality of leadership which stirred his troops, European and Indian alike, to extraordinary feats of valor and endurance. Sorties from the fort kept the enemy disconcerted and convinced them of the fighting spirit of the defenders. After a relief expedition from Cuddalore failed, Clive requested aid from a Maratha chief who was plundering in the area. When the besiegers spied the Maratha horsemen reconnoitering their camp, they tried to bribe Clive to surrender. That failing, they launched a final all-out attack. When that, too, failed, largely because their elephants were maddened by the steady and accurate shooting from the fort, they retired. Some 600 sepoys deserted to Clive.

Shortly thereafter Stringer Lawrence relieved Trichinopoly and Muhammed Ali was enthroned as Nawab of the Carnatic. The French had been checkmated. The English Company had suddenly become a major force in Indian political affairs. It was now *Kampení Jehán Behádur,* "the bravest company in the world"; Europeans thereafter were to call it simply "John Company."

As Arcot was a watershed for the Company, so also was it a turning point for Clive, for it gave him his reputation. It was not that English soldiers acclaimed him; British army officers never accepted him as a first-rate commander. But among the Indians, especially the rulers, who had good reason to hold military success in the highest esteem, the psychological effect of Arcot was overwhelming. Thereafter Indians knew Robert Clive as *Sábit Jang Behádur,* "the greatly daring in war," a name applied to him by Muhammed Ali, whose rule of the Carnatic Clive had made possible. It was the reputation that Sabit Jang earned at Arcot that provided the foundation for the rest of his triumphs.

The struggle continued, as the French and English fought each other in India as they soon were to do in North America, long before the governments in Europe finally declared war formally again. In minor campaigns Clive enhanced his image as a military commander, so much so that on occasion sepoys refused to serve under anyone else. Almost incidentally he acquired a 16-year-old wife, the sister of one of his associates. In March of 1753 the newlyweds left for England; the penniless boy of nine years before took home a fortune of £50,000.

In England, Clive conformed to the pattern set by nabobs before him: He entered London society, became a man about town, and spent recklessly. Shrewder than many military heroes, he capitalized fully on his fame: "a Man is not the farther from Preferment by paying a Visit to his Native Country," he wrote his brother-in-law in India. He courted the members of John Company's Board of Directors and, having no more scruples than English politicians, he bought a seat in the House of Commons. In this, however, he chose the wrong patron, and opposing factions succeeded in having his election declared void. Like everyone else, his family lionized him and his father declared that he was not so much of a "boob" after all. His family was also a drain on his purse, and soon it was empty.

The day after he lost his seat in the House of Commons Clive called on the Company Board of Directors, and at the end of April 1755 he sailed again for India. He had been appointed Lieutenant Colonel, Governor of Fort St. David at Cuddalore, and Deputy-Governor of Madras. En route, he was to put down some pirates who were troubling the Company factory at Bombay. He did, receiving £5,000 as his share of the booty, and in June of 1756 he arrived to govern Fort St. David. He was not yet 31 and he had been in the Company service for only 14 years.

Shortly after his arrival events drew him to Bengal, where he made his enduring mark on history. The northeastern province of Bengal was the wealthiest of the Moghul's domains, paying easily an annual levy of nearly £2,000,000 to the Muslim emperor. It produced cotton goods, rice, sugar, silk, spices, and saltpeter in abundance, and the channels of the Ganges River delta were major roads of European and Asian commerce. On the westernmost tributary of the Ganges, the Hughli River, the British and French had built factories at Fort William in Calcutta, and at Chandernagore. To the north on the Hughli, not far from the junction with the Ganges proper, lay the Nawab's capital, Murshidebad. Nawab Alivardi Khan had seized power in 1740; he had kept the Marathas at bay by buying them off and he had kept tensions between his Muslim and Hindu subjects to a minimum. On his death in 1756 he was succeeded by his favorite grandson, 27-year-old Siraj-ud-duala.

Siraj seems to have developed all the vices that Western imperial rulers have liked to ascribe to the non-European despots they displaced. He was cruel, corrupt, perverted, self-indulgent, and a liar, characteristics which were not balanced by a strength, or an ability to govern, that might have kept him on his throne. When, in 1756, the British and French began repairing the fortifications around their factories in preparation for the coming Seven Years' War, he ordered them to stop. When the French obeyed and the British did not, he concluded incorrectly that they intended to attack him; he also believed incorrectly that they were supporting a rival to his throne. In June, 50,000 men of Siraj's army laid siege to Calcutta. Foolishly, the British had in fact done little to improve their defenses, and in a few days the commander of the 520-man garrison and the Governor of the settlement cravenly led the flight to the ships in the Hughli and safety. After only four days, Siraj entered Fort William in triumph. Estimates of the number of English prisoners he took vary from 64 to 146, but their fate became legendary. Confined on a hot June night in the Black Hole, a room measuring 18 feet by 14 feet, 10 inches, only 21, or possibly 23, emerged alive. The incident of the Black Hole of Calcutta resulted from the incompetence of the Bengali army rather than any calculated cruelty on the part of Siraj, but the British later were to make of it a full-blown atrocity story.

It made a strong impression at that time to the south at Madras, where, fortuitously, reinforcements had come from England for the expected war with France. The blow at British prestige was dangerous enough in a land where reputation meant everything. It was especially worrisome, too, because everyone believed that open war between France and Britain was imminent, and the loss of Calcutta weakened the British position among Indian rulers, to the benefit of the French. Dupleix had been recalled in 1754, but the very able Marquis de Bussy was carrying out his policies in the South with considerable success. Status aside, however, the British were still primarily interested in trade in India, and the loss of Calcutta meant a sharp decrease in profit. In the campaign that followed, they did not plan for territorial gain; much less did they profess any high intentions of ridding Siraj's subjects of a cruel and merciless ruler. Their prime motivation was, simply, commercial profit.

Fortunately for Clive, the three men senior to him at Madras all were incapacitated in one way or another, so he was given command of the expedition. With a force of 900 Europeans and 1,500 sepoys he sailed for Calcutta in October of 1756. After an inconclusive battle in January 1757 the Nawab's army unaccountably withdrew from Fort William. The evacuation was discovered by a drunken sailor who wandered into the fort, found it almost empty, called his companions, and captured it. The young Nawab called for a truce, a treaty was signed in February, and the British traders returned to their countinghouses in Calcutta.

The treaty included an alliance, for Siraj feared an attack from the Afghans who had just reached Delhi. In signing the treaty Clive was doing as Dupleix had done, associating the Company with an Indian state to ensure that its government would be friendly to English interests. In return for help against the Afghans, Siraj permitted the English to pursue actively in his territories the now openly declared war against the French. In March Chandernagore fell to Clive's forces.

The Afghan invasion of Bengal did not materialize, and soon Siraj became resentful and frightened of the increasing power of the English in his state. Frantically, he tried to build up a French counterpoise against them. He harbored and armed French refugees from Chandernagore and opened negotiations with de Bussy in the South. Siraj was not acting as a reliable puppet should. At this point the intricacies of Bengali politics presented an opportunity for the English to rid themselves of their untrustworthy ally.

In addition to Siraj and Clive, two men figured prominently in the complex and amoral maneuvering that took place. Mir Jafar Khan was Siraj's granduncle, one of his foremost military commanders and skilled in the politics of deviousness and betrayal. Omichand Mahajan was a Hindu from the Punjab who had lived in Calcutta for 40 years. A banker and trader, he had enriched himself through his dealings with the Company, and lived luxuriously in the European section of the town. His greed and lack of scruples were unsurpassed.

The motives of the actors in the drama were all straightforward: Mir Jafar wanted his grandnephew's throne; Siraj wanted to keep his throne and to assert himself against the growing English influence in his state; Omichand wanted money; Clive worked to safeguard, beyond all danger, the Company's interests in Bengal, to make money, and to gain fame.

Siraj's failure as nawab had diminished his stature as a ruler and encouraged plots against him. As early as April 1757 the conspirators solicited English aid, promising in return land, money, and preferential treatment for the Company. On May 1 the Governor and Council of Fort William agreed that the deposition of Siraj would be "for the interest of the Company" and in the following days an extensive correspondence developed among all the principals. Siraj and Clive alternately assured each other of eternal friendship and threatened each other with removal of favor and support; Mir Jafar played the loyal granduncle and then the righteous conspirator, while Omichand constantly demanded more money. Clive entered into the game, as he called it, of mutual dissimulation with an energy and an expertise that far outshone all the others. Compromising messages were written in lemon juice which became legible only when heated, and were carried hidden in slippers or in intimate parts of the body. Soon Mir Jafar agreed to turn a large portion of the Bengal Treasury over to the English and to support them against the French, provided the English would back him with 5,000 Company soldiers.

Up to this point it was a routine conspiracy, the kind the French had regularly engaged in, but then Omichand and Clive gave it a new duplicitous turn. Unless, the Hindu wrote, he received all of Siraj's jewels and five percent, estimated at £2,000,000, of the Bengal Treasury, he would reveal all to the Nawab. Clive then did something that provoked the calumny of his enemies and has embarrassed patriotic English historians of India ever since. He prepared two secret treaties for the conspirators to sign. One, on pink paper, spelled out the terms of the general agreement and acceded to Omichand's blackmail. The other treaty, on white paper, omitted reference to Omichand entirely; it was the one Clive planned to honor. Admiral Charles Watson, commander of the King's ships in the Hughli, declined to be a part of the "villainous deceit" and refused to sign the pink treaty. Watson's scruples, however, did allow him to permit Clive to have his name forged to the pink treaty. The actual forgery was committed by Henry Lushington, the courier who carried the papers from one conspirator to another. As a survivor of the Black Hole of Calcutta, he was quite willing to return evil for evil. Clive never denied being an accessory to forgery and asserted that he would do it again a hundred times. To him, as to many Europeans overseas, morality was a matter of geography, and it was no crime to turn the immorality of Indian politics against greedy Indian malefactors.

By June 11, 1757, the treaties bore the signatures, forged or not, of all the plotters. Two days later, leaving only skeleton garrisons in

Fort William and Chandernagore, Clive led the army that was to institute Britain's Indian Empire north through the early monsoon rains toward Murshidebad. He had 1,022 European soldiers, including a battalion of royal troops, and 2,100 sepoys. There was no cavalry and his ordnance consisted of eight 6-pounders and two small howitzers. Siraj had 50,000 infantrymen, 20,000 cavalrymen and 53 heavy-caliber guns manned by Frenchmen. The Nawab's army was encamped on the Hughli at Plassey, 20 miles south of his capital and 120 miles north of Calcutta.

The risk Clive was taking was great. Should his luck fail and his army be defeated, the English undoubtedly would be pushed out of the wealthy province of Bengal entirely. Sabit Jang relied on 10,000 troops under Mir Jafar to shorten the odds somewhat, but he had seen no sign of them. His messages to the aspiring nawab became more and more desperate and Mir Jafar's replies were increasingly opaque. Perhaps, Clive feared, the conspiracy had collapsed.

He had been under a severe nervous strain since he had committed himself and the Company to the plot. Now he broke under the pressure. His self-confidence gone, he wrote anxiously to the council at Calcutta, complaining of Mir Jafar's unreliability, pointing to the terrible consequences of defeat, promising not to endanger his army, and asking humbly for advice. Then he heard a report that more French troops, only three days' march away, were approaching to support Siraj. Depressed and nervous, he called a meeting of his officers, one of the few councils of war he ever held. Should the English force, he asked, fight at once, or should it maintain its position until after the monsoon season had passed and see what turned up then? Seven officers voted to fight immediately and ten voted to wait. Accounts vary, and Clive understandably denied it later, but it seems that initially he voted with the ten officers who advised delay. After brooding for an hour in a mango grove, he strode back to camp and announced that they would proceed, after all, with the attack. What convinced him to change his mind in that hour is not known. It is probable, though, that he preferred the risk of battle because he realized that delay might well be interpreted as an admission that Sabit Jang, the hero of Arcot, had blundered badly. The consequent loss of prestige both for him and for the Company would be disastrous. At sunrise on June 22, 1757, his army crossed the Hughli and by midnight it had completed a 15-mile march in heavy rain to Plassey.

Compared to its overwhelming political significance, Plassey was not much of a battle. At eight o'clock in the morning of June 23, an artillery duel began and just before noon an hour-long rain ended hostilities temporarily. Siraj's artillerymen did not cover their guns and powder, but Clive's men did. Assuming that the English cannons were out of action as his were, Siraj ordered a cavalry charge, supported by elephants, after the rain stopped. Encountering the full fire of the English 6-pounders and muskets, the elephants were frenzied by the shot and the charge disintegrated. Then the English infantry advanced. When their attack succeeded, Siraj begged Mir Jafar, who had remained aloof from the battle, to send his troops against the English. Mir Jafar remained vague and the terror-stricken young Nawab rode for his capital on a fast camel.

When Siraj's soldiers learned of their leader's defection they, too, fled north. By five o'clock in the afternoon the Company army held the Nawab's camp. The English had suffered 100 casualties; Siraj had lost 500 men.

Siraj had also lost his throne. In disguise, and carrying a casket of jewels, he ran to the north where he was identified by a man whose nose and ears he had ordered cut off a year earlier, and was captured. He was returned to Murshidebad in chains and later murdered in prison.

The morning after the battle Mir Jafar hesitantly approached Clive's camp. The honor guard did not shoot him, as he feared they would, and Clive greeted him as Nawab. The Englishman who was to have been merely a paid accomplice in the conspiracy had become the king-maker of Bengal.

Elated by triumph, and his attack of nerves behind him, Clive turned to exploit the consequences of victory for his employer and for himself. A treaty with Mir Jafar secured the Company's position, assigned to the Company all the French possessions in Bengal, and specified full compensation for the losses incurred when Siraj had taken Calcutta. Private merchants were indemnified too, and the soldiers and sailors were rewarded. Hundreds of ships sailed down the Hughli loaded with gold, silver, and jewels, visual evidence to everyone that the Black Hole had been avenged. Mir Jafar gave £234,000 to Clive alone as a personal gift. In addition, the new Nawab extended to the goods of private English merchants the immunity from internal customs duties that Company goods enjoyed. This gave them an immense advantage over Bengali traders, and in its results, was to be one of the major causes of Clive's third and last tour of duty in India.

When Omichand appeared to collect his share of the spoils, he was shown the pink and white treaties and fainted. As if to compensate him for the deception, he was later given a contract to supply saltpeter, at very favorable terms, to the Company. At his death he left a large part of his fortune to the Foundling Hospital and a reformatory for prostitutes in London.

Now, after Plassey, it looked as if all of John Company's, and Clive's, problems had been solved. Sabit Jang was at the apex of his career. Wealthy beyond his dreams, he dominated the Company officers, dictated to the ruler of Bengal and, the first of a long line of English

Sahibs, received from the Indians the flattery and obeisance due to a conqueror in that ancient land. His status was truly imperial, for only an emperor gave orders to a nawab. Son of a poor country squire, first a bookkeeper and then a soldier, Clive had become the arbiter of a rich and populous country. His pride and arrogance grew proportionately; surely it was only appropriate that everyone, white and brown, should bow before the wishes of the mighty Sabit Jang.

He was appointed Governor General of Bengal and remained until February of 1760. He hoped that the Bengali problem had been solved: according to his view of the future, Mir Jafar would be titular ruler and his officials would still conduct the government, but power at the court of Murshidebad would really be held by a British resident agent. Mir Jafar struggled against this tutelage, however, constantly working up new plots and constantly having to be kept in check. In public, Clive treated the Nawab with great ceremonial respect, but the Indians were not deceived; they knew that the real power in Bengal lay in the fort at Calcutta and not in the palace at Murshidebad. The result was a loss of respect for the Nawab's authority and the beginning of the disintegration of the Muslim state. As this happened the administration of Mir Jafar became a less and less reliable vehicle for the protection of British interests in Bengal.

Clive did not take part personally in the war against the French. The glory of the capture of Pondicherry went to Colonel Eyre Coote, and the Governor was playing cards when another officer fought off a futile Dutch invasion. Only when the son of the Moghul emperor himself independently took the field to capture Bengal did Clive fight, and win, again. After this victory Mir Jafar rewarded the Englishman who had made him Nawab and now had saved his realm. Clive had been appointed *Tumandar*, "Holder of Ten Thousand Horse," by the Emperor and now Mir Jafar gave to him a *jagir* to support his eminence as a nobleman of the Moghul Empire. Mischievously, the *jagir* comprised the quitrent paid by the East India Company to the Nawab for its landholdings in Calcutta. Thereafter the Company was to pay to its employee the £30,000 annual rent it formerly had paid to the Nawab of Bengal. Clive thus became a kind of feudal superior of John Company, his employer. At first the Board of Directors felt that they would rather have an Englishmen over them than a "rascally Moor," but as the payment came due, year after year, the *jagir* became a major point at issue between Clive and the Company.

For other reasons relations between Clive and the Board had already become strained. A new chairman, Francis Sulivan, deplored the expenses that the Company was incurring in its political and military ventures and called for a return to the pre-Dupleix days of restricting the Company activities to trade. But Clive by now had become a conscious imperialist. Not yet apprised of Sulivan's views, he wrote to the chairman, recommending that the Company assume territorial jurisdiction over all Bengal, and pointing out how easily British arms could accomplish the conquest. He also made a similar proposal to William Pitt, the Elder, suggesting that the British Crown, rather than the Company, should take over Bengal directly. Pitt was tempted but stated prophetically that, while the conquest might be easy, maintaining it might not be. Sulivan on the other hand was violently opposed, and so Clive began provoking opposition in the Company itself that was to plague him the rest of his life.

Clive was only 35 and a national hero when he returned to England for the second time in 1760. Having an income of £45,000 a year, he provided large dowries for his spinster sisters, gave generous annuities to friends, including Stringer Lawrence, and paid his father's debts. For over a year he was seriously ill, suffering from nervous prostration, fever and hallucinations; "no excellent soul is exempt from a mixture of madness," he told Samuel Johnson, who visited his sickbed. In 1761 he was elected as a Whig to the House of Commons. He also secured seats for his father, a brother, a cousin, a friend, and his secretary, at a cost of £2,000 an election. King George III invested him with the Order of the Bath and wearing the coveted red ribbon of the Order, he was painted by Thomas Gainsborough. The King also granted him an Irish peerage. He purchased an estate in County Clare which he renamed Plassey but never visited. Sabit Jang, Holder of Ten Thousand Horse, became Baron of Plassey.

Irish peers could sit in the House of Commons, and there he joined the faction headed by Pitt and the Duke of Newcastle, a miscalculation because the new King and his ministers liked neither. Voting against the treaty that ended the Seven Years' War, he earned the enmity of the King's increasingly powerful Court party.

Meanwhile the hostility of Sulivan threatened to cost him the major part of his income, the *jagir*. Citing the technicality that the Moghul Emperor had not ratified the original grant, Sulivan moved to stop payment. Thereupon Clive tried to oust Sulivan from his chairmanship and, in effect, take over the Company and direct its policies according to his imperial ideas. Clive tried to gain control of a majority of the Company stock and enlisted the parliamentary aid of the Duke of Newcastle. But Newcastle was not in power and the Administration, which had not forgiven Clive for his vote on the 1763 treaty, dispensed funds to support Sulivan. Sulivan won and stopped the *jagir,* an act of gross ingratitude, Clive felt, in return for the services he had rendered his Company and nation.

Still Clive's luck held. In Bengal his successors were less adept at Indian politics than he. Mir Jafar proving troublesome, they substituted his son-in-law Mir Kasim as Nawab, profiting handsomely through the change in rulers. Then Mir Kasim turned out to be even more tiresome about British abuses of their immunity from internal tariffs, practices that were in fact impoverishing his state. Open war broke out in 1763 and the British finally prevailed a year later. Before the news of victory reached London, however, news of atrocity did. On October 5, 1763, Mir Kasim had first mistreated and then slaughtered 170 English men, women, and children at Patna. Among them had been Henry Lushington, survivor of the Black Hole and forger of Admiral Watson's signature.

Everyone knew that only the victor at Plassey could make things right again. Removing Sulivan from the chairmanship, the Directors swallowed their pride and asked Clive to save Bengal. Striking as hard a bargain as they could, they agreed that Clive could keep his *jagir* for ten years but ordered him to enforce new regulations against private trade and taking presents. Pointedly, the Directors were informing the world that these practices, the very ones through which Clive had gained eminence, were major evils in Bengal. So Clive, too, had to swallow his pride and on June 4, 1764, he left England to vindicate his triumph at Plassey. He must demonstrate again that political involvement and, if necessary, war were prerequisites of commercial advantage in India.

After another long voyage of 11 months he arrived the next May; he was not yet 40 years old. The military challenge had been met before he arrived and so the major reason for his appointment no longer existed. He turned immediately to make what he planned to be a final settlement of John Company's, England's, and his affairs in Bengal. The English, he wrote to a friend on the Board of Directors, must become nawabs themselves. Mir Kasim had died of venereal disease in a male house of prostitution of Delhi, and the new young Nawab, Najm-ud-daula, 16-year-old son of Mir Jafar, was deprived of his army and given an annual allowance of £600,000. Instead of protesting, Najm was grateful: "Thank God! I shall now have as many dancing girls as I please." This attitude effectively put an end to the autonomy of the once-proud rulers of Bengal. Clive proceeded 600 miles up the Ganges to Allahabad where he met with the virtually powerless Moghul Emperor, Shah Alam. There he accepted the *dewani,* or control of Bengali taxes, from the impotent emperor, who, having received no revenues at all from Bengal for years, had long been willing to assign the *dewani* to John Company. In effect, this meant that for every three rupees of tax the Company collected, one would be divided between the Emperor and the Nawab and two would go into Company coffers.

The acceptance of the *dewani* was probably the most important thing that Clive did in India. The right to tax is a large part of the right to govern. True, Clive expected the Nawab's officials to continue as revenue-collectors, but the proceeds would be controlled by the Company. Additionally, as he wrote the Board of Directors, "no future Nawab will either have power or riches sufficient to attempt your overthrow, by means either of force or corruption." Whether the Sulivan faction liked it or not, Clive was transforming the Company into a government.

One of the circumstances that had brought about the crisis in Bengal had been the emptying of the Nawab's treasury through constant present-giving to Company officers. Mir Jafar's original gift to Clive had started the avalanche and thereafter all Company employees solicited and accepted gifts as a matter of course. When they returned to England, their *nouveau riche* display provoked bitter criticism of the practice. Clive always felt that his case was different for he, after all, had been a conqueror and kingmaker at Plassey and took only what was due a conqueror. He was, he told the House of Commons later, "astonished at [his] own moderation" in accepting so little, when all the wealthy men of Bengal had been laying rubies, gold, and silver at his feet. His successors had done nothing to earn their gifts, as he had. Righteously, he compelled all employees to sign new covenants eschewing gifts, and he enforced the prohibition rigorously. As if to set an example, Clive, by now one of the richest subjects of George III, displayed a new-found probity and refused all presents himself.

The other means Company employees had used to supplement their small salaries and enrich themselves had been private trade. When Mir Jafar had removed the internal customs duties on their goods, their expanded and unscrupulous activities had impoverished the Bengali merchant class, the peasantry, and the Nawab's treasury. They had also neglected their duties to carry on and advance the Company's commerce. With a few exceptions, Clive abolished all private trading. To raise the salaries to a reasonable level, he assigned the proceeds from the salt monopoly to Company servants by rank. The justification for private trade had been removed.

Imperiously he overrode all opposition to his policies. He reorganized the army, and when the officers mutinied against the loss of their perquisites he arrested them with sepoy troops. He cared little, in reality, for the welfare of the Englishmen or, for that matter, the Indians, in Bengal. His concern was for the effect his measures would have in England and how they might secure his reputation and position once and for all when he returned.

After the army mutiny he again had a nervous breakdown. For two months he suffered fits of hysterical weeping and came near madness. Recovered, he sailed for England in January 1767. In only 18 months he had laid the administrative foundations for Empire.

He reached England in July of 1767. Feeling that once again he had performed an invaluable service for his country, he expected praise, respect, and honors. While in Bengal he had purchased a great deal of Company stock which, he knew, would appreciate in value when news of the *dewani* reached London. Now he sold it and bought land. He was, after all, not really a merchant, or a professional soldier; he was a member of the landed gentry. Surely his success indicated that he should become one of the great aristocratic forces in English life. Soon, he felt, an English peerage would come and the Clive family would be elevated to membership in the great noble ruling class of the nation.

At first, adulation was forthcoming. The prosperous Directors placed a statue of Sabit Jang in East India House and confirmed his *jagir*. King George III received him in private audience and was generous with praise. Soon, however, fortune turned against the "Great Nabob." His nerves became more unreliable, his liver weakened, and he was subject to agonizing pain from gallstones. He spent months taking the waters at Bath, but only increasingly large doses of opium deadened his pain. Still in his 40s, he appeared to be 20 years older than he was.

Then his settlement in Bengal began to crumble when a combination of maladministration in London and in Calcutta and a famine in Bengal itself brought John Company into financial trouble. Clive, in many ways the representative nabob, was made the scapegoat, as Sulivan and all the men Clive had alienated while he was governor launched a campaign of scurrilous public abuse against him. He had enriched himself at the expense of the Bengali administration and the shareholders, they charged, and, it was hinted darkly, he was guilty of excessive and perverse dissipations. In the summer of 1772 the now-bankrupt Company asked for a government subsidy, and two House of Commons committees met to investigate the causes of its troubles. Here, the anti-Clive forces, led by Colonel (later General) John Burgoyne, introduced a resolution that pilloried him for using his position as agent of a chartered company for private gain. With his last stores of nervous energy Clive came brilliantly to his own defense. Like the conquistador that he in reality was, he emphasized that without him Bengal would have been lost. He defended his methods by insisting that in the East dishonesty had to be met with dishonesty, and asserted that his wealth was a just recompense for the great benefits he had brought to the nation. Finally, in 1773 a saving amendment was added to the charge, referring to the "great and meritorious services" he had performed, but the entire resolution passed.

Clive kept his wealth. But he lost something more precious to him, his good name. He was not an acknowledged national hero any longer, he was not even respected as a private citizen. His enemies had destroyed him. There remained only death, and on November 22, 1774, in his mansion at 45 Berkeley Square he slashed his throat with a penknife and died. He was 49 years old.

As in life, so in death, Clive has remained a controversial figure. How he has been judged has depended on how men have assessed the relative importance of means and ends and what they have thought of Clive's accomplishments themselves. A law unto himself, he refuses to be fitted into the standard patterns for heroes and villains. Certainly, he was one of those rare men who dominate events, who impose their wills and characters on their times and surroundings. Plassey, the *jagir*, and the *dewani* gave form to ensuing Indian history. Lord North's Regulatory Act of 1773 and Pitt's Government of India Act 11 years later stemmed directly from Clive's destruction of an Indian state and the pillage by Company servants that followed. The first Act initiated, and the second effected, the assumption of responsibility by the British Government for Indian affairs.

Such responsibility came to entail more and more direct administration in India itself. After 1772 Englishmen replaced Bengalis as tax collectors and before the end of the century the powerless and useless Nawab himself was deposed and the British assumed control of the law courts. Clive's abolition of gift-taking and private trade was implemented, and the Company's employees were reorganized into salaried commercial and political branches; thus, an efficient and honest British civil service was being created for India. Governors after Clive, too, were bound by his solution to the problem of preserving British interests. To protect the territory they governed, frontier provinces had to be controlled or annexed. The problem of security led to a continuous expansion of British dominion until, in a few years, all of India was under British rule. That authority, inaugurated by Clive, endured, for good or ill, until 1947.

Even before Clive died Sulivan removed his statue from India House and ordered it to be broken up. No other memorial, of any sort, was raised to him in England or in India until the 20th century.

SUGGESTED READINGS

No biography captures fully the elusive character of Baron Clive. Most successful are the recent work by Mark Bence-Jones, *Clive of India* (London: Constable, 1974), and the older book by A. Mervyn Davies, *Clive of Plassey* (New York: Charles Scribner's Sons, 1939). Allen Edwardes, *The Rape of India: a Biography of Robert Clive and a Sexual History of Hindustan* (New York: The Julian Press, Inc., 1966) is a frequently outrageous psychosexual study that relies heavily on Indian and suspect English sources. The short and sympathetic essay by Thomas Babington Macaulay in *Critical and Historical Essays* (3 vols.; London: Methuen, 1903), vol. 2, can still be read with profit and pleasure. Henry Dodwell, *Dupleix and Clive: The Beginning of Empire* (London: Methuen & Co., Ltd., 1920) is a thorough, but heavy, study. Of the thousands of books on India, R. C. Majumdar, *An Advanced*

History of India (London: Macmillan & Co., Ltd., 1953) is excellent, while Percival Spear, *India: a Modern History* (Ann Arbor: The University of Michigan Press, 1961) is more analytical. Philip Mason (pseud. Philip Woodruff), *The Men Who Ruled India: The Founders* (London: Jonathan Cape, 1953), and Percival Spear, *The Nabobs: A Study of the Social Life of the English in Eighteenth-Century India* (rev. ed.; Gloucester, Mass.: Peter Smith, 1971) fill in the social background, while the East India Company is covered well in Brian Gardner, *The East India Company* (London: Rupert Hart-Davis, 1971) and Lucy S. Sutherland, *The East India Company in Eighteenth-Century Politics* (Oxford: Clarendon Press, 1952).

Chapter 10

JOSIAH WEDGWOOD:
Industrialism and Technology

I N the course of 30 years, Josiah Wedgwood, master potter, "converted a rude and inconsiderable manufacture into an elegant art and an important part of national commerce." So reads the epitaph on his tomb in the porchway of the parish church in Stoke. At the time of his birth in 1730 the best earthenware in England was imported from the factories of Holland, France, Saxony and China. North Staffordshire, later the largest center of pottery manufacture in the world, had just over 50 potters, producing mostly a coarse, crude ware valued at less than £15,000 a year. By 1785, ten years before Wedgwood's death, there were 200 firms, employing 20,000 workers, making high quality earthenware for English and foreign markets that was worth almost £100,000. The man primarily responsible for this growth was Josiah Wedgwood, a scientific potter, an enterprising businessman, and a man of taste and artistic talent. Wedgwood was a seminal figure during the early years of England's industrial revolution, and his life illustrates the nature of the transformation that altered the basic economic and social fabric of the English nation.

In the early 20th century Josiah Wedgwood's great-grandson, a Fabian Socialist and Member of Parliament, traced his family to 1299, when they were tenant farmers on a manor in west central England. In the following centuries the family remained obscure, neither amassing great wealth nor playing an important part in national or provincial affairs. The Wedgwoods were prolific, however, and at the beginning of the 1700s there were six families of Wedgwoods in the small village of Burslem, North Staffordshire, alone. Most of them were potters; Josiah himself was the son, grandson, and great-grandson of a potter.

Potters needed two components to manufacture earthenware, clay and fuel. Clay is found in abundance throughout England, and as long as firewood was plentiful pottery-making was a local industry throughout the country. With the increasing scarcity of wood in the late 17th century, however, a new source of fuel was needed, and in Staffordshire, seams of coal lay side by side with what was called coal measure clay. At least five times more coal than clay was required to make earthenware, and the abundance of coal in North Staffordshire enabled the potters to take advantage of the new opportunities presented to the industry in the 18th century.

Despite some recent improvements in manufacture, pottery-making in Staffordshire was still a small, localized peasant occupation when Josiah Wedgwood was born in 1730. Once mined, the hard clay was spread on the ground to weather for two to three years. Softened by sun, wind, and rain, it was thrown into a pit lined with flagstones and mixed with water. Then it was "blunged," or stirred, by a man wielding a long paddle with crosspieces on the handle. The stones and gravel were allowed to sink to the bottom and the fluid clay was ladled off and strained into a shallow tank, or sun-kiln. Again it was weathered until it was dry enough to be cut into blocks. After it had aged for a few months in a damp cellar it was ready for use.

The potter then either pressed the clay into a mold or shaped it on a potter's wheel. The resulting mugs, jugs, and pitchers were decorated, dried, glazed, and then fired in a kiln. Potters in Burslem produced either lead-glazed or salt-glazed ware. They secured galena, lead sulfide, from a mine six miles from Burslem, pounded it into a coarse powder, and dusted it over the clay vessels before placing them in the firing oven. They produced salt-glazed ware by casting salt into the kiln while the clay was being fired.

The kilns were cylindrical in form, 8 to 14 feet high and 6 to 7 feet in diameter. They were constructed of brick and were heated by six to eight fireplaces built into the base. Workmen placed the clay vessels in saggars, or clay boxes, and then into the kiln, where the temperature reached about 1,050 degrees Centigrade. They fired the kilns on Fridays, stoked them for the last time on Sunday mornings, and opened them on Mondays.

In 1730 there were 42 potters in Burslem, most of them firing only one oven. Typical of the small scale of most industry before the industrial revolution, a master potter employed five to seven apprentices and journeymen, and each man performed all the tasks involved in making the finished ware, from blunging to modeling to firing. With rare exceptions the products were crude and clumsy in conception and execution. Traveling peddlers sold the wares at neighboring marketplaces and fairs.

A peasant industry, Staffordshire pottery served peasants. Well-to-do Englishmen used silver or pewter, or porcelain from China and the factories at Meissen and Sevres. They also used Delft, a tin-enameled ware, from the Netherlands and potteries near London. Yet, the increasing prosperity of the middle classes, the general improvement of manners, a new reluctance to use wooden trenchers as plates, and the rising popularity of hot tea and coffee created a market for high quality earthenware. Porcelain was very expensive and metal tea and coffee sets were impractical. It was this new demand that Josiah Wedgwood met and exploited.

The date of his birth was not recorded, but he was baptized at St. John's Church, Burslem, in July 1730, the 13th and youngest child of Thomas and Mary Wedgwood. His father, a mediocre potter, was the master of Churchyard Works and his mother was the daughter of a unitarian minister. Their house was small, constructed of mortar and timber, and thatched; close behind it were the workshops and the kiln.

Burslem in 1730 was a small village of thatched cottages. The surrounding moors, rich in clay but infertile, could support only a small part of the population who kept dairy cattle, so most of the villagers were connected in one way or another with the "pot banks," as the potteries were called. Burslem, then, was not an ordinary rural village. The marks of early industrialization were prominent; clay and coal pits and piles of broken pottery lay everywhere, even by the village maypole and near the small parish church. On Fridays when the kilns were fired up the sky over the village became so black, it was said, that day was almost turned into night.

The few winding streets of the village were narrow, rutted, and unpaved. Roads leading from Burslem were little better than the lanes of the village itself. Narrow "hollow ways," or paths beaten below the surface of the surrounding fields, they were dusty and holed when dry, and virtually impassable quagmires when wet. As late as 1768 the writer Arthur Young measured a hole two feet deep in what he described as the "infernal" and "dreadful" North Staffordshire bridle paths. Carts could not run on the roadways, so pack horses or mules, carrying baskets, supplied the needs of Burslem.

When Josiah was six years old he attended the Burslem dame school, a kind of kindergarten taught by a local woman in her own house. Then for two years, until he was nine, he walked the seven miles, there and back, to a school in neighboring Newcastle-under-Lyme where he learned reading, penmanship, and arithmetic.

Upon the death of his father in 1739 his eldest brother, Thomas, removed him from school and employed him in the Churchyard Works. Early experience in the pottery trade was considered essential so that the developing muscles of young boys could be trained to the potter's wheel. Josiah became skilled at "throwing," or modeling on the potter's wheel. When he was 11, however, he suffered an especially virulent attack of smallpox. The disease affected his right knee permanently and, since the potter's wheel was turned by a kicking motion, it debarred him from steady work on the thrower's bench. The knee troubled him regularly until 1768, when his right leg was amputated; he was to have his own children inoculated against smallpox in 1767, the year vaccination was introduced into England by Lady Mary Wortley Montagu. The long childhood illness and the afflicted knee probably forced him to become particularly adept at other branches of the industry. He perfected his skills in decorating and in making and fitting handles and spouts. Soon he excelled in the more exacting and artistic aspects of potting. In dedicating a statue to Wedgwood 120 years later, W. E. Gladstone suggested that the injury constituted a major source of Wedgwood's success. Since he could no longer be a whole and active workman, he meditated, Gladstone surmised, on "the laws and secrets of his art" and so reached an unrivaled "perception and grasp" of the potentialities of earthenware.

As was customary in the pottery trade, young Wedgwood entered in 1744 a five-year period of apprenticeship, in his case under his eldest brother. Unable to throw, he molded such articles as plates, knife-handles, and snuff boxes. He also began the experiments with the body and glaze of earthenware that he continued until his death. Thomas Wedgwood, as indifferent a craftsman as his father, was unsympathetic to his younger brother's experiments, and declined Josiah's suggestion that they form a partnership. For two years after the termination of the apprenticeship Wedgwood worked as a journeyman for his brother. Then, in 1752 he put his savings and, although there is some doubt that he ever received it, possibly a £20 legacy from his father into a partnership with John Harrison, a businessman from Newcastle-under-Lyme. After a disagreement with Harrison, he formed another partnership in 1754 with Thomas Wheildon, the best potter in Staffordshire. The arrangement was very profitable for both men. For the first time Wedgwood worked with a first-class potter who shared his enthusiasm for excellence and who was interested in new ways of improving his product. Wheildon also had wide-ranging business connections and Wedgwood gained experience in marketing. At Wheildon's pot bank, all the latest methods were being exploited: coal-firing had replaced the old method of sun-drying the clay, and workmen were using lathes to produce more even and regular pots. The senior partner, in turn, benefited from the improvements young Wedgwood made in manufacture and from his continuing experiments. The partners agreed that any discoveries Wedgwood made would be utilized for the advantage of the firm, but Wedgwood could keep his new methods and formulas secret. During these years the young man began keeping his *Experiment Book.*

While he was associated with Wheildon, Wedgwood invented a new "agate" body, a multicolored mixture produced by working together different colored clays; he also made significant improvements in the currently popular green and yellow glazes. Plates in the form of leaves and teapots modeled after pineapples and cauliflowers found buyers as distant as York and London. Among the apprentices was Josiah Spode, who later became a leading manufacturer of chinaware.

In five years Wedgwood had enough capital to forego partnerships and to establish himself as an independent potter. The arrangement with Wheildon was terminated in 1757 and Josiah rented the Ivy House Works in Burslem for £10 a year from two of his uncles who were retiring. The works included a cottage, workshops, sheds, and two kilns. To assist him he employed as a journeyman a cousin, another Thomas Wedgwood, who had experience at the new china works at Worcester. Thomas soon became his principal assistant and, after 1766, his partner.

At Ivy House the 29-year-old master potter participated in all aspects of the business. He was the most skilled craftsman and designer, he prepared special mixtures of clays and supervised the firing, and at times he even acted as his own clerk and warehouseman. The high quality of Ivy House ware soon earned for the young potter a reputation for excellence. At first he produced mainly agate and green and yellow glazed jugs, plates, sauceboats and tea sets. They were finer and more practical than any ever produced in England before. The plates stacked, the handles stayed on, the lids fit, the spouts poured smoothly, and the molded decoration and the gilding were handsome and appropriate to the lines of the wares. He accepted difficult commissions to reproduce broken dishes from sets of Chinese porcelain. As the business prospered he rented in 1763 the larger Brick House pottery, usually called the Bell Works, because he called his men to work with a bell rather than by sounding the customary horn. Appropriately, the Wedgwood Institute was opened on the site of Bell Works in 1863.

During the years at Ivy House and, later, the Bell Works, Josiah Wedgwood became England's finest potter and the most dynamic businessman in North Staffordshire. He made a superior product, led in changing industrial organization, stood forth as a major promoter of canals and turnpikes, and became a colleague of England's foremost scientists and engineers.

In the eyes of the English middle and upper classes, heavy colored earthenware never lost its association with the peasantry. Black was acceptable, for black teapots showed to advantage the white hands of fashionable ladies, and all the Staffordshire potters made what they called Egyptian Black teapots. White and translucent porcelain, or china, however, was the expensive ideal. Whether it came from China, Saxony, or France, or one of England's few new factories, it was costly and very fragile. Delft and salt-glazed stoneware had the whiteness of china, but otherwise were unsatisfactory substitutes. The dishes were heavy, the glazes were uneven and, when the pieces were chipped, the cheap darker earthenware body was revealed only too clearly. The salt-glazed ware also tended to crack when hot liquids were poured into it. When Wedgwood rented Ivy House some lighter-colored earthenware was already being produced in Staffordshire, but it was still far from perfect. The body contained ground flint and white clays that came from outside the county, and it was light throughout. The vessels were fired twice: first to what was called the "biscuit," or unglazed and porous, condition; then they were dipped into a liquid mixture of flint and lead and fired again to fuse the glaze to the body. From this base, Wedgwood developed the cream ware which was to be the mainstay of his firm for more than two centuries. His recipe, which has remained unchanged, improved both the body and the glaze. The result was an inexpensive, versatile, durable, and beautiful product. Cream ware could be formed easily into a great variety of articles, the glaze did not become checked, and it withstood heat well. It surpassed anything produced in England to that time. Other English potters were quick to copy it, and cream

ware became the basis of a prosperous export trade. Soon potters in
France and the Germanies also were imitating it, thus acknowledging
that the creative stimulus in European pottery-making was shifting from
Meissen and Sevres to Staffordshire.

Wedgwood's improvements went beyond the practical chemistry of
earthenware. He was a superb designer and had a keen eye for the
utility of his products. He was the first English potter to originate forms
that were perfect for their purposes, forms that also could be duplicated
with precision in large numbers. His ware was attractive; cream pitchers,
coffee pots, and teapots designed by Wedgwood were produced for
more than 200 years. But above all his products were functional. Cream
ware could be made into almost anything; Ivy House and Bell Works
turned out bulb pots, statues, busts, fish slicers, cameos and much else,
all designed by Wedgwood.

Unlike contemporary china, which was ornately decorated, much of
the cream ware was plain or bore little more than simple hand-painted
classical or naturalistic borders that Wedgwood created. Further embel-
lishment came to be applied by transfer-printing, a method which placed
decoration of pottery on a mass-production basis. In this process a design
from a copper plate was printed on a paper and pressed onto the unfired
glaze; then the pattern was fixed on the piece by firing in a so-called
muffle oven. Beginning in 1761 Wedgwood sent his wares to Liverpool
to be printed by the men who had developed the process, and in 1763
he purchased the right to do the printing at his own works. The ware
was either decorated entirely by transfer, or outlines of a design were
printed by transfer and enamelers colored them later. Thus, Wedgwood
supplemented, and in some cases replaced, the slow and expensive process of decorating by hand.

Improvements in method extended to the modeling of the clay itself.
In 1763 Wedgwood introduced engine-turning, the use of a more sophisticated lathe, into his works. The lathe is, in essence, a potter's wheel
turned on its side, the potter's hand being replaced by a cutting tool.
Wedgwood first encountered engine-turning in a metal workshop in
nearby Birmingham, and he purchased and had translated a French
book describing new refinements in moving the cutting tool. Initially
he used the new machine tool to incise simple patterns on the edges
of plates and bowls; later he was to employ engine-turning to impress
intricate and delicate patterns on his finest ornamental ware.

Technological innovations, improved quality, and increased demand
produced greater efficiency of manufacture at Ivy House and the Bell
Works. Wedgwood's employees were forced to become specialists and
production was divided precisely into separate compartments. Blungers
mixed the clay, block cutters cut it, modelers formed it, and warehouse-
men shipped it. Thus Wedgwood superseded the informal ways of the

past, as his workmen became less and less potters and more and more distinctly firemen, throwers, modelers, and the like. Responding to charges that he sacrificed the creativity of the individual workmen, Wedgwood maintained that instead of destroying skills, he limited, refined, and developed them.

His superior goods found ready markets and in the 1760s Wedgwood was exporting his pottery to North America and the West Indies through Liverpool. To meet the growing demand for his earthenware he rented a warehouse in London and established a workshop at Chelsea where enamelers decorated his ware. Late in the decade he employed more than 150 persons.

On a business trip to Liverpool in 1762 his horse shied and Wedgwood struck his knee against the bank of the hollow way. Incapacitated, he spent several days recovering in Liverpool. There he met Thomas Bentley, who was to become his business partner, his closest friend, and the most important personal influence on his life. Bentley was a widower and six months older than the master potter. Though of yeoman stock like Wedgwood, he had a classical education and had toured France and Italy. He was an excellent businessman and accountant and managed his own wool and cotton wholesale warehouse in Liverpool. Polished and cultured, he was active in public affairs, helping to found a library and nonconformist academy in Liverpool. Through Wedgwood's friendship with Bentley, the country potter was introduced to the world of English society, letters, and fashion. From their meeting in 1762 until Bentley's death in 1780 the two men corresponded regularly. Wedgwood's letters survive, and they reveal the deep mutual affection between the two men and Wedgwood's reliance on his friend's commercial and artistic judgment.

In January 1764 Wedgwood married his third cousin, Sarah Wedgwood, daughter and heiress of a cheese merchant. Like Bentley she came from a social and economic background somewhat higher than her husband's. She was a cultivated and intelligent woman and frequently acted as Josiah's secretary. By all accounts the marriage was a happy one; they had five children, and the eldest was to become the mother of Charles Darwin.

As the premier manufacturer in Burslem, Wedgwood played an increasingly important part in public projects that would benefit his industry. A clear-sighted businessman, he realized that a major obstacle to economical operation of the potteries was the primitive means of transportation serving the area. Carriage by pack horse was slow and expensive; the cost of flint and imported clays was correspondingly high. Carriage on the rivers was also expensive, and goods on the barges were especially subject to pilferage.

In the mid-18th century the solution to this problem lay in turnpikes and canals, as new road and canal engineers were revolutionizing transportation just as Wedgwood was transforming the manufacture of pottery. In most cases turnpikes and canals required authorization from Parliament. Wedgwood turned first to roads, but proposals for turnpikes connecting Burslem directly with major markets and sources of supply encountered fierce opposition, primarily from innkeepers along the old routes who feared for their livelihood. Consequently, although a Parliamentary Act of 1763 permitted some construction, the turnpikes that were built only partially served the interests of Burslem. Carts began to replace pack horses, but the cost of transport was still high.

Although well-traveled Englishmen knew of the canals that had been built in France in the previous century, it was not until the 1750s that construction began on a large scale in England. The most influential new canal was built by Francis, the third and last Duke of Bridgewater, between Manchester and his mines at Worsley. It opened in 1761 and turned a profit immediately. The Duke then began a second canal to join Manchester to the port of Liverpool. It was not yet completed in the spring of 1765 when promoters advanced a proposal to connect the Trent and Mersey Rivers. No area stood to gain more from this scheme than the potteries, for such a waterway would link them efficiently to both Liverpool to the northwest and the port of Hull on the eastern coast of England. Thus, clay and flint could be carried in, and the finished ware sent to market, more safely, rapidly, and cheaply.

Such a route had been surveyed in the late 1750s by the Duke of Bridgewater's canal builder, James Brindley, the leading engineer of the time. Sixteen years Josiah Wedgwood's senior, Brindley had rented a millwright shop in Burslem from one of Wedgwood's many relatives and in 1756 had erected a small mill to crush flint. Wedgwood knew Brindley well, and it was undoubtedly his friendship with the engineer that convinced him of the practicality and the value of the canal.

Wedgwood became the leading advocate of what came to be called the Grand Trunk Canal. The first step was to petition Parliament to approve the scheme. He traveled the countryside securing the support of prominent men and signatures for petitions and he persuaded Bentley to write a pamphlet advertising the canal. He spent a day with the Duke of Bridgewater, arranging to join the two canals near Liverpool, traveling the nine miles of the Worsley canal with the Duke in his gondola and, incidentally, taking an order for a set of dinnerware.

Opposition came from wagon masters, turnpike owners, rivermen, other canal promoters, and landowners who refused to sell rights of way, but all objections were overborne or bypassed. Wedgwood convinced doubters that the rivers would not be drained, that springs would not run dry, and that the mills would not be stopped by a shortage of water. He subscribed £100 to finance the preliminary work and early in 1766 the matter reached Parliament. It cost £431 for entertainment and gifts to push the measure through the legislature, and both Wedgwood and Bentley spent much of January, February, March, and April testifying before a Parliamentary committee and impressing the legislators with the value of the canal. On May 14, 1766, the project received the royal assent.

Wedgwood was appointed Treasurer of the new joint-stock canal company and on July 26 the town of Burslem celebrated with ceremonies, roast sheep, ale, and fireworks in front of Bell Works. Wedgwood turned the first sod for the canal and James Brindley wheeled it away. Work was begun the next day and in six years all but the tunnel under Harecastle Ridge, north of Burslem, was completed; the tunnel was finished five years later. Measuring 93 miles long and 4½ feet deep, with 75 locks, 5 tunnels, and aqueducts over 3 rivers the canal was one of the great engineering feats of the day. The Harecastle tunnel, completed in 1777, ran one and one half miles. Here there was no tow path and until motors were introduced in 1914 men propelled the barges through by lying on their backs and "legging," or kicking against the sides and roof of the tunnel; the trip took two and one half hours. The canal reduced freight costs to 1¼ pence a ton per mile, one seventh of the previous rate. In 30 years the shares of the stockholders had tripled in value. More than two centuries later, the Wedgwood firm still found it most economical to ship some of its products by canal.

Wedgwood's work on the canal brought him into touch with the world of English science and engineering. In the spring of 1765 on a promotion trip to Lichfield, south of Burslem, he had met Dr. Erasmus Darwin, prominent physician, poet, and amateur scientist. A clumsy and ugly, but charming and witty, man of fifty, Darwin had just married a beautiful rich widow 30 years his junior, and was to become one of Wedgwood's closest friends. Darwin was a member of the Lunar Society of Birmingham, a group of 14 men who met regularly on the afternoon of the Monday nearest the full moon. They discussed science and its practical applications, advised each other, occasionally financed the ventures of fellow members, and wrote each other extensively. Aside from Darwin and Wedgwood, the most important and influential members were: Joseph Priestly, a Presbyterian minister and radical political philosopher who isolated the element oxygen; Matthew Boulton, engineer and manufacturer at Soho, just outside Birmingham; and Boulton's partner, James Watt, the inventor of the first steam engine with condenser and rotary motion. The Lunar Society provided a forum for the ideas that launched England's industrial revolution. Through his association with its members, Josiah Wedgwood was in touch with the most creative and practical minds of his time. Their examples also inspired him to make his own experiments more scientific and professional.

The mid-1760s were formative and crucial years for Wedgwood in other ways. In 1765, through the agency of a Staffordshire lady at Court, he received an order from Queen Charlotte for a tea service. Usually special orders were a great deal of trouble and not very profitable, and Wedgwood later remarked that he accepted this one because no one else would take it. It is more likely, however, that he took it because he saw in the tea service an opportunity to gain publicity and marketing advantage. He conferred with the Queen several times, worked on the set personally and, after it was delivered, Charlotte appointed him "Her Majesty's Potter." To distinguish the cream ware Bell Works was making from all other cream ware he named his product "Queensware," in effect giving it a brand name; thus "Queensware" became one of the earliest known examples of branding. Wedgwood also cultivated connections with Sir William Meredith, M.P., who sent him Dresden china "to pattern from," allowed him to use his frank, or right to free postage, and even took orders for Queensware. In 1766, Wedgwood opened his first showroom in London; he already had a thriving export trade.

Wedgwood's increasing acquaintance outside Burslem introduced him to the new fashion for antiquity that was becoming popular in aristocratic and artistic circles. Visiting the Duke of Bridgewater, he viewed the marbles His Grace had purchased in Rome. Lobbying in London for the canal, he inspected the ancient gems and vases at the mansion of the Duke of Bedford and the collections at the British Museum. He knew every important new book on antiquities, most notably the works of the Comte de Caylus, James "Athenian" Stuart, and Sir William Hamilton. Hamilton, the British minister to the King of Naples, became notorious in later life as the complaisant elderly husband of Lord Nelson's mistress, but at that time he was respected as the leading British antiquarian. He excavated the Roman ruins at Herculaneum and, even before the results were published in 1766–77, Wedgwood received copies of the illustrations. Wedgwood lived, then, at the time of a major classical revival, during the years that great noble collections of Greek and Roman artifacts were started and the "antique" was the height of fashion. He was the first potter to capitalize on the new movement. As early as 1763 he was making antique vases in cream ware, in 1767 he modeled them in an improved Egyptian Black body, and in 1769 he patented an "encaustic" method, copied from ancient potters, for decorating them with red figures.

The new demand for his "ornamental" ware and the steadily expanding market for the "useful ware" was rapidly outgrowing the limited resources of Bell Works. In July 1766, after Parliament had approved the canal, he paid £3,000 for the 350 acres of Ridgehouse estate two miles south of Burslem and bordering on the proposed waterway. He also reorganized his enterprise. In 1766 his cousin Thomas became a partner, receiving one seventh of the profits in the production of useful ware. The next year Thomas Bentley agreed to form another partnership, capitalized at £1,441, to share equally in manufacturing and selling ornamental ware.

Until the factory finally closed in 1950, "Etruria," as Wedgwood called his new estate after the contemporary designation of classical works as "Etruscan," was inextricably linked with the name Wedgwood. In Etruria, Josiah Wedgwood conceived a model 18th-century industrial community. The factory itself covered six acres of the estate. Facing the canal, which was widened at the works, was the brick Georgian front of the main building, topped by a belfry to call the labor force to work. Behind it on a spur of the canal were the workshops and the kilns, some of which were in use more than a century and a half later. The layout was orderly, systematic, and rational. The clay, flint, and coal were unloaded at one end of the plant, moved logically through it, and the finished earthenware was placed on barges at the other end. The whole was divided into two large parts: White Bank Square for Queensware, and Ornamental Works. In each were five sections for the major stages of manufacture, an arrangement which became a pattern for all future potteries. Waste was disposed of frequently; everything was always neat and clean. On a long street adjacent to the factory Wedgwood built houses for his workers. They had earth floors, but they were of brick, with glass windows and front door steps of iron. Wells were sunk, and for two farthings a loaf villagers could bake their bread in the village ovens.

At a distance across the canal from the works, Wedgwood built Etruria Hall, a 34-room brick mansion for himself, and a house for Bentley; however, to the potter's regret, his partner was too busy in London ever to use it. Wedgwood consulted Bentley and the members of the Lunar Society continuously about the placement of the buildings, the decoration and furnishings of the Hall, and the development of the barren moor surrounding the Hall into a park. Ultimately, Capability Brown, England's leading landscape architect, was employed to plant groves of trees, make hills and valleys, and to construct a lake.

Etruria was a vast improvement over the thatched cottages and cluttered pot banks of Burslem; it was an efficient and beautiful industrial park. On July 13, 1769, while Thomas Bentley turned the wheel, Wedgwood threw six Egyptian Black antique vases to commemorate the opening of the factory. They were painted with "encaustic" red classical figures and bore the inscription *Artes Etruriae Renascuntur*, The Arts of Etruria are Reborn. Production of ornamental ware began immediately. His family moved into the Hall in September 1770, and two years later the manufacture of useful ware was transferred from Burslem.

With the building of Etruria, Josiah Wedgwood entered the fullest and richest period of his life. Through the Lunar Society he was intimately involved with the scientific and engineering advances of the time, and he himself made important discoveries in ceramic chemistry. He developed his ornamental ware to a perfection never before achieved by an English potter, and he was successful in persuading the government to advance and protect the well-being of the pottery industry. He planned and supervised the education of his children at Etruria Hall and rejoiced in the increasingly close friendships of Thomas Bentley and Erasmus Darwin.

Initially Etruria produced ornamental ware mostly in the Egyptian Black body, which Wedgwood refined and hardened and, in 1773, named basalt. So great was the "rage," as he called it, for antique busts, medallions, statues and vases, that other potters rapidly imitated his products. To ensure the distinctiveness of his pieces he imprinted them after 1771 with the names Wedgwood and Bentley, a new departure in the industry.

In the late 1760s Wedgwood had begun experiments aimed at fabricating a new body for ornamental ware. He called upon Darwin, Priestley, Brindley, and Bentley to send him sample clays and minerals, enjoining them to secrecy lest the direction of his research become known. After 10,000 experimental firings he had produced, by 1775, the first major advance in ceramics in 1,000 years. A dense, powdery-finished, slightly translucent stoneware, Wedgwood's new material resembled the texture of the semi-precious stone, jasper, after which he named it. Jasperware was cheaper than marble, its finish could be polished or left flat, it took colors easily, and could be formed into objects varying from the smallest cameos to large vases, statues, and plaques. It was the crowning ceramic achievement of the master potter of Etruria.

Wedgwood commissioned designs from the best artists of the day and so, as his Victorian admirers were fond of saying later, combined art with industry. Most important was the talented sculptor John Flaxman, who was supported principally by Wedgwood's commissions between 1774 and 1787. Flaxman created designs especially for Wedgwood's striking classical bas reliefs that were executed in the pale translucent beauty of jasper. In addition to the sculptor's work for Wedgwood in England, Flaxman also went to Rome for seven years after 1787 with a subsidy from Wedgwood; he regularly sent back to his patron drawings, models, and casts inspired by the classical art he saw in Italy.

Wedgwood also blended art with a highly developed business acumen. He understood that the mass production of Etruria required forceful marketing, and his letters to Bentley show the same keen interest and enthusiasm for methods of selling that Wedgwood felt for the processes of artistic creation and manufacture. When he had persuaded Bentley to become his partner he had promised that their enterprise would unite beauty with profit, and profit was always an important concern. The business in London was managed by Bentley until he died in 1780. Initially this included showrooms in Charles Street and later St. Martin's Lane, and the enamelers at Chelsea; after 1774 the showroom and shop were combined in an establishment in Greek Street, Soho, which included two floors of display rooms and a workshop housing 28 enamelers and a muffle kiln to fire the decorated pieces.

Snob appeal was the basis of Wedgwood and Bentley's marketing policy. Every ceramic innovation he made, even by 1786 the jasper, was copied and sold more cheaply. So, Wedgwood relied on a reputation for quality and distinction. His prices were always quoted in guineas, somehow held to be more elegant than pounds, shillings, and pence. They were also very high, always two times, and frequently three times, those of his competitors. Stories were told of how he smashed defective vases with his cane at Etruria, stating: "This will not do for Josiah Wedgwood." This action was usually attributed to his insistence on beauty, but it was just as indicative of his business policy; poor quality was bad advertising for a firm that based its sales on prestige. His patronage of sculptors like Flaxman gave him the imprimatur of the artistic set; painters willingly placed antique Wedgwood vases in the backgrounds of noble portraits. His successful cultivation of royalty and the aristocracy made his goods fashionable. As he wrote to Bentley, if the partners could "capture the world of fashion," if they had the custom of the aristocracy, then all the world would want to buy from them.

Part of the appeal of Wedgwood's goods, of course, lay in his exploitation of the fad for antiquities, but his success also followed upon a shrewd assessment of the foibles of the buying public. The establishment on Greek Street opened with a display of the famous 952-piece Queensware dinner service made for Catherine the Great of Russia and valued at £2,200. Each piece of the Russian service bore a separate view of an English mansion or county scene, and it filled five rooms of the building. For two months all of fashionable London crowded in to see it. There were also seasonal shows at Greek Street, to be viewed by ticket only. Common folk were excluded, the showrooms were made especially pleasant for ladies, and important personages were given previews and their advice was heeded attentively. Basalt vases were shown to best advantage in alcoves papered in yellow. Dinner services were set out on tables as if ready for use and pattern books were at hand for immediate order. Buyers could even watch their own dinnerware being decorated in the workshops behind the showrooms.

Wedgwood solicited orders from royalty and accepted special orders from the nobility. These rarely produced much profit, the Russian service did not, but all went on display at Greek Street as testimonies to the prestige of Wedgwood and Bentley. New designs were named after royal or noble houses; images of public figures were printed on plates and on pots. A series of busts of great men of the present and past was brought out amidst great publicity. The partners inspired articles in the newssheets and occasionally placed decorous and refined advertisements.

In all of this Bentley had an essential part. The two men possessed complementary qualities. Where Wedgwood was the industrial leader and innovator, Bentley had the knowledge of markets and the entrée into important social circles. He was an expert on tastes and demands, English and foreign, and quickly transmitted every new fashion to Etruria. It was he, for example, who persuaded Wedgwood to cease gilding his vases, because gilding was now considered vulgar; he suggested that Wedgwood drape most male classical figures because they were "too warm." Bentley was a man of fashion himself, he was at ease with the aristocratic clientele and could extol the beauties of a new ornamental piece in sentences interlarded with French and Italian phrases. Wedgwood always deferred to him in matters of taste and fashion and accepted his assessment of what policies would advance the image the company wished to project. Each man had a good business sense, but as an entrepreneur of taste, Bentley educated Wedgwood as to the best marketing of his wares.

Wedgwood and Bentley wanted more than the patronage of fashionable London; they wanted to sell to the world. To retail excess stock of seconds and lower quality goods, which were usually sent to North America, the partners occasionally held a kind of pottery supermarket sale where, as Wedgwood suggested to his partner, customers could "serve themselves." They opened showrooms in Bath, Dublin, and Liverpool. Three traveling salesmen, among the first ever seen in Britain, toured the provinces. They had the Wedgwood and Bentley catalog translated into French, German, Italian, Dutch, and Russian; they created special designs for overseas buyers; at Greek street, they employed clerks who spoke foreign languages; and they opened warehouses abroad. Even His Majesty's ambassadors patriotically acted as salesmen for the outstanding new earthenware that the English firm of Wedgwood and Bentley was producing. Lord Cathcart, for example, arranged for the Russian service, and Sir William Hamilton regularly sent in orders from Naples.

Bentley set the prices for their goods, and he set them as high as he thought the market would bear. During a brief recession in 1772, however, Wedgwood himself worked out a method of cost accounting that did not become a normal practice among British manufacturers until more than a century later. In August 1772 he composed a "price book," listing all his expenses from the clay to the sales counter, including rent, depreciation, and loss from breakage. At first his figures would not balance, but when an embezzling head clerk was found out, they did. Such close figuring of expenses did not become an integral part of the business, because thereafter market conditions always made high pricing possible, but later Wedgwood did cost the Russian service, the expenses of new processes and new clays, and he made new additions to his price book as late as 1789. Although he used cost accounting only intermittently, he learned some of the major lessons it taught, and he always strove to increase sales and production to reduce the overhead per unit.

Prominent among the fixed costs was labor. In June 1790, Wedgwood employed almost 300 workers at Etruria alone. He encountered, then, the same problem that faced every factory owner in the early years of the factory system, that of maintaining and disciplining a large labor force. Large-scale industrial enterprises were, after all, quite new, and workers, accustomed to the more personal and informal circumstances of the smaller shops, resisted the rules that were necessary for successful operation of modern industry. The problem was especially difficult because no tradition of a managerial or foreman class had yet evolved. When Wedgwood was at Etruria he maintained order through force of personality, but when he was absent, overseers in each department found it difficult to keep the potters from erratic, wasteful, and careless habits. Like all industrialists, Wedgwood believed that punctuality, regularity, and prevention of waste were the foundations of efficient production, so in 1789 he prepared instructions for his overseers to enforce.

Six mornings a week the bell summoned the workers, at 6:30 between March and November, and at 7:30 during the winter months. A clerk greeted each worker and praised him if he was punctual and criticized him if he was late. Each laborer dropped a ticket in a box on arrival, a kind of primitive clocking-in system. Workers were allowed half an hour for breakfast, one hour for dinner, and left the works at 6:00 P.M., or 4:00 on Saturdays. The clerk kept individual wage sheets and levied heavy fines for gambling and drinking on the job and for leaving fires and scraps. In the molding room a clerk measured out clay by weight to ensure uniformity and to avoid waste.

It was difficult to find and to keep skilled workers who met Wedgwood's standards. Older potters objected to the regimentation and few younger ones already had adequate skills and experience, especially in decorating. So, Wedgwood sought to develop talented young men and women into skilled artisans. It cost between 30 and 40 pounds to train each apprentice, and competitors always tried to lure them away in order to learn Wedgwood's secrets and processes. Many workers, too, were tempted to emigrate, and Wedgwood tried unsuccessfully to secure parliamentary legislation to stop them.

Wedgwood was justly proud that he had doubled the wages of his potters, replaced mud and wattle huts with brick cottages, provided a free library, and started a sick fund, but he demanded submission, hard work, and regularity from his workers. Patriarchal and autocratic, he did not doubt that the restraints he attempted to impose on his employees benefited them as much as they promoted his business.

He had the same clear view of means and ends concerning the education of his children that he had about industrial production. With some justice, he had little respect for the existing secondary schools. Dr. Darwin agreed with him, on the grounds that their sons were destined for trade and the professions and so stood to gain little from the classical curriculum of the public schools. Together, Darwin and Wedgwood carefully planned the education of their children, and in the 1770s and 1780s Etruria Hall became a school, frequently for Darwin's children as well as for the young Wedgwoods. The scholars had a French tutor, a paroled prisoner captured in the war with the North American Colonies, and, in addition to the fundamentals, they heard frequent lectures on chemistry, electricity, and geology. Thus Wedgwood trained his sons, who otherwise were surrounded by all the trappings of the landed gentry, to follow the profession of their father.

Wedgwood continued his scientific experiments until his death in 1795. He created two additional varieties of earthenware and several new glazes. He invented a pyrometer, a device for measuring the temperature inside a kiln, that was used for more than a century. He provided ceramic laboratory utensils for Priestley and made a new body for mortars and pestles that was still in use almost two hundred years later. He experimented with clays and minerals from all the Western world and kept his notes and more than 7,000 specimens carefully cataloged at Etruria. Presaging the 20th century, he proposed, without result, that the Staffordshire potters form a ceramic research organization for the benefit of the entire industry.

In 1783 he was elected a Fellow of the Royal Society, and contributed five papers to the *Transactions*. He had an extensive chemistry library, proposed a color method for distinguishing chemical symbols, experimented with improving glass, and with freezing, and was an amateur geologist. He subscribed to a pension to support Priestley's experiments and offered him asylum at Etruria Hall after his home and laboratory were destroyed in the Birmingham riots of 1791.

As a rising industrialist, Josiah Wedgwood was always searching for any improvement that he might put to use at Etruria. Darwin designed for him a horizontal windmill to grind flint, which was erected in 1779. Wedgwood also sponsored the steam engine, the new source of power which made possible the rapid mechanization and expansion of industry. He advanced £5,000 to Matthew Boulton during the experimental stages of the manufacture of the Watt-Boulton steam engine and was one of the first major factory owners to make use of the new invention. One of the first Watt-Boulton engines was installed at Etruria in 1782 and a second was added in 1784, fully three years before the engines were introduced in the Lancashire cotton industry. Yet a third engine that Wedgwood ordered in 1793 was still in working condition when it was scrapped in 1912.

Frequently the interests of Etruria and the other Staffordshire potteries drew him into public life. He led a successful campaign against the holder of a monopoly on the china clay of Cornwall, an essential component of cream ware. In 1783 he lobbied on behalf of Staffordshire concerning the commercial treaty being negotiated between Britain and the United States of America. Again representing the potters, he was the most active member of a new General Chamber of Manufacturers of Great Britain between 1785 and 1787. He opposed successfully a proposed trade agreement with Ireland, to the detriment of his sales there, and secured free trade for English pottery in the French trade treaty of 1787.

Wedgwood was descended from a strong dissenting and radical tradition, which was reinforced in later life by his association with Bentley and the members of the Lunar Society. He was an autocrat at Etruria Works, but in any matter and did not bear on the well-being of the potteries as he conceived it he championed the cause of liberty. Supporting the rebellion of the American colonists, Wedgwood corresponded with Benjamin Franklin, and reproduced cameos and busts of both Franklin and George Washington. He "rejoiced," he wrote Darwin in 1789, in "the glorious revolution" that occurred in France. A prominent member of the Anti-Slavery Society, he welcomed William Wilberforce to Etruria Hall and gave financial support to the investigations of Thomas Clarkson into conditions in the slave trade. The Etruria Works produced one of its most famous cameos, picturing a black man in chains and inscribed, "Am I not a man and a brother?", which he distributed free.

His closest friend, Thomas Bentley, was one of the founders of the "Society for the Spread of Constitutional Information" that was formed during the John Wilkes agitation. In his letters Wedgwood indicated his sympathy with the ideology of the Society which, with its program of universal manhood suffrage, annual parliaments, equal electoral districts, secret ballot, and payment of members of parliament, harked back to the Levellers and looked forward to the Chartists. Above all, Wedgwood advocated universal suffrage and annual parliaments. When mobs destroyed spinning machines in October 1779, he was sympathetic and opposed military intervention. The mob, after all, was a part of the vast unrepresented majority of Englishmen, and violence was the most forceful way they had of making their will known. His ideas modi-

fied, however. When workers at Etruria hijacked a provisions barge
during a food shortage in 1780 he asked for support from the militia;
two men were arrested and one was hanged. Liberty could not, certainly,
mean license to riot and steal.

In reality, politics were never very important to Wedgwood, compared
to the fascination that potting and business held for him. He might
write Darwin criticizing violently the administration of William Pitt
the Younger and the reactionary philosophy of Edmund Burke, but
he did not consciously seek any fundamental alteration in the English
constitution. All men should have votes, there should be yearly elections,
but he believed that these reforms would only bring about more justice
and efficiency in government. His experiences with the governing English
aristocracy generally had earned them his respect, and as far as the
pottery industry was concerned, the government was responsive and
helpful. A busy industrialist and researcher, he seems not to have thought
a great deal about political ideologies and merely reflected the dissenting
and radical milieu of the late eighteenth century.

In 1790 Wedgwood completed his last major ceramic piece, a perfect
copy in jasper of the ancient Portland Vase. Since Bentley's death in
1780 he had managed the firm without any close associate, and in 1790
he began laying the groundwork for his retirement. He took two of
his sons, and a nephew Thomas Byerley, into partnership. The sons,
preferring to live as landed gentlemen rather than to pursue the trade
their father had carefully educated them for, withdrew from the business,
and Byerley steadily assumed the sole responsibility for Wedgwood,
Sons, and Byerley. Late in 1794 Josiah Wedgwood became ill, and he
died at Etruria early in January 1795 of gangrene of the mouth and
throat. He was not yet 65 years old.

Since his death writers have attributed too much, perhaps, to Wedgwood as an innovator in the industrial revolution. Division of labor
had already developed quite extensively in the potteries and in other
industries before he rented Ivy House, and he copied a great deal from
Matthew Boulton's metal works at Soho. He was not the first man to
promote canals and turnpikes, and his chemical discoveries were not
of fundamental importance. Even in ceramics, aside from inventing
jasper and the pyrometer, his primary contribution lay in improving
the work of others and in imposing regularity and discipline on the
product and the potter. Yet, he was the catalyst for the industrial revolution in the potteries, was responsible for major developments in marketing and accounting techniques, pioneered in the industrial use of the
Watt-Boulton engine, and personally created objects of enduring utility
and beauty.

He developed a peasant occupation into a great national industry
exporting its products to the entire Western world. Of yeoman stock,

with only three years of formal schooling, he came to move with grace among England's aristocracy and royalty and became an important contributing member in leading scientific circles. Moreover, throughout, he retained a kind of youthful simplicity and enthusiasm. His letters to Bentley and Darwin reveal an open, affectionate, and generous man, with an engaging zest for experiments, for Etruria, and for artistic and business challenges.

Josiah Wedgwood saw only the best of the industrial revolution. Surveying Etruria Works, village and Hall, he could see everywhere improvement over the pot banks of his youth. He and his associates did not doubt that the transformation accompanying industrial change was all to the good. Etruria was an efficient industrial garden which drew admiring visitors from all of Europe, and it represented a means of escaping the dirt, ignorance, and backwardness of the past. It was a working vision of the better future that the industrial revolution seemed to be bringing to England.

His sons chose not to live in Etruria Hall and their descendants found it unpleasant to do so, for soon industrialization blighted Etruria. In the 19th century the potteries expanded, the coal deposits drew a gas works, the iron ore attracted a great steel company, and a railway was constructed in front of the mansion itself. The great smokestacks of the steel mill appeared behind the Hall and their effluvia killed the grove Capability Brown had planted. The park became an industrial wasteland and great mountains of slag, towering over the Hall, replaced the trees. Josiah Wedgwood's house became the offices of the Shelton Iron, Steel and Coal Company. Digging for coal undermined the foundations of Etruria Works and the buildings began to sink. By the end of the Second World War the level of the factory floor was 12 feet below Brindley's canal. In 1950 the kilns were fired for the last time and Josiah Wedgwood and Sons, Ltd., moved to a new model factory on a 380-acre estate at Barlaston. As forward-looking as Josiah Wedgwood had been 180 years before, the firm built a modern all-electric works and a garden village for the employees.

SUGGESTED READINGS

Though written more than a century ago, Eliza Meteyard, *The Life of Josiah Wedgwood* (2 vols.; London: Hurst and Blackett, 1865–66) has not been superseded; it was reprinted by the Cornmarket Press, London, in 1970. Excellent insights into Wedgwood's life and personality may be found in Ann Finer and George Savage, eds., *The Selected Letters of Josiah Wedgwood* (London: Cory, Adams & MacKay, 1965), and the memoir by Wedgwood's great-granddaughter, Julia Wedgwood, *The Personal Life of Josiah Wedgwood the Potter* (London: Macmillan, 1915). Among the articles by Neil McKendrick, those in *The Economic History Review* vol. 12, no. 3 (April 1960), pp. 408–33; vol. 23, no. 1 (April 1970), pp. 54–67; and *The Historical Journal,* vol. 4 (1961), pp. 30–55, reflect the best recent scholarship. Of the many books describing Wedgwood's earthenware, the one by master potter William Burton, *Josiah Wedgwood and His Pottery* (London: Cassell and Company, Ltd., 1922) remains the best. Lorna Weatherill, *The Pottery Trade and North Staffordshire 1660–1760* (Manchester: Manchester University Press, 1971) and Robert E. Scholfield, *The Lunar Society of Birmingham* (Oxford: Clarendon Press, 1963) provide excellent background material.

Chapter 11

MARY SHELLEY:
The Romantic Rebellion

MARY Shelley was born at the end of the 18th century of a union between England's pioneer feminist and the nation's most prominent radical political philosopher. When she was 16, she eloped with a leading romantic poet and before she was 20 she had published *Frankenstein*, the first science-fiction novel. Growing up in the milieu of the rationalist reform movement of the late 1700s, she was inculcated with the libertarian philosophy of her father. Yet, as a child she heard Samuel Taylor Coleridge read his *Ancient Mariner* in her father's parlor, and her lover introduced her to the romantic movement of the early 1800s. Her heritage, her associations, and her own literary work, are representative of the paradoxical intellectual currents of late 18th-century England.

Her father, William Godwin, was 40 years old when he became the lover of Mary Wollstonecraft. The son and grandson of dissenting preachers, he was born in Cambridgeshire on March 3, 1756, and educated for the ministry. William seems to have been an earnest and precocious boy, and at the age of 11 he proceeded from ordinary Calvinism to become a disciple of Robert Sandeman. Later, Godwin described the rigors of the Sandeman doctrine which, "after Calvin had damned ninety-nine in a hundred of mankind, had contrived a scheme of damning ninety-nine in a hundred of the followers of Calvin." Although Godwin later became apostate, Sandeman's insistence on following the dictates of severe logic to their conclusions, along with his teachings of economic communalism, became fundamental to his philosophical outlook. Godwin attended a nonconformist college, began preaching, and published a modest volume of sermons. While he was in the 20s he succumbed to the temptation of doubt and was unable to find anyone who could confute to his satisfaction the logical arguments he raised against the faith. Abandoning not only his Sandemanian Calvinism but also Christianity itself, he moved to London in 1783 at the age of 27 to embark on a literary career. There he read extensively in the philosophes, published a tedious *Life of Chatham* and supported himself through hack writing. From time to time Thomas Wedgwood, radical son of the great Josiah, helped him financially; on one occasion Godwin visited Etruria Hall. Godwin also became acquainted with the nature of British political life, which accorded neither with the teachings of God, nor Voltaire, nor Rousseau. Lord North and Charles James Fox had just formed their brief unholy alliance in February 1783. Their successor, William Pitt the Younger, was frequently to be seen in a drunken sleep on the Prime Minister's seat in the House of Commons, and political corruption was an accepted tradition of government. Such was the condition of British political life when Godwin learned of the revolution in France in 1789.

While some Englishmen tended to be self-congratulatory on seeing the French supposedly move toward the British model of government, and while others soon subscribed to Edmund Burke's conservative con-

demnation of revolutionary excesses, Godwin and other English radicals
were exalted by the French example and set out to activate in England
the principles of the revolution. Although they differed as to what these
principles might include—Natural Rights, Social Contract, Return to
Nature—all agreed that the revolution would bring the triumph of Reason. Godwin, nothing if not a disciple of reason, immersed himself in
the revitalized radical movement in England, and in February 1793,
he published his most important work, *Enquiry concerning the Principles
of Political Justice*. A trenchant rebuttal of Edmund Burke's organic
conservatism, it was a synthesis of all the major doctrines of enlightenment thought. Well-argued, orderly, occasionally eloquent, it elevated
Godwin into prominence as the premier radical political philosopher of
the period.

Men, Godwin declared, are motivated by reason and, as John Locke
wrote, they develop according to the impressions made upon them by
their environments. If forces influencing men were made consonant with
the principles of reason, men, and all of human society, could be perfected. The purpose of society is to serve the interests of individual
men and to guarantee personal liberties; good actions are those which,
reason indicates, work for the benefit of men in society. Coercion is
never legitimate, because force violates individual liberty; and governments which make and impose unjust laws are illegitimate, for they
are fundamentally irrational. Private property, too, is unjustifiable, for
each man should have a fair share of the world's goods. Marriage is
wrong because it constitutes a monopoly, and so violates the freedom
of the individual.

Godwin's thought reflected in its fundamentals the outlook on man
and the world set forth by most of the leading men of the 18th-century
Enlightenment. He shared their optimistic view that the mysteries of
the universe, including the nature of man, were potentially comprehensible. They believed that the key which would reveal the secrets was
within man himself, in the rational processes of his mind. All problems
concerning man and nature could be resolved by man if he subjected
them to the rigorous test of logic. Through reason man could win the way
to truth; through reason man could master himself and the universe. Such
faith in reason did not convert all men of the Enlightenment to radical
political beliefs, but when melded with Godwin's Sandemanian background, it produced in his thought an emphasis on liberty and equality.

Godwin's treatise attracted widespread attention and became an inspiration and manifesto for England's reformers and young literary
rebels, especially Samuel Coleridge and William Wordsworth. Recognized now as a major thinker and teacher, Godwin left off hack
writing and devoted the remaining 40 years of his life to philosophy
and literature.

He had met Mary Wollstonecraft late in 1791, but they had parted, he wrote later, "mutually displeased with each other." Just over three years later their acquaintance resumed. Mary Wollstonecraft was born in 1759 in London into an impoverished family with pretensions of gentility. Her father, a silk weaver who had inherited some tenements from his father, was a bully, a drunkard, and a spendthrift. He moved with his wife and six children from London to try farming in various places, but with no success. Mary's mother was a weak and sickly woman, and the young girl did her best to interpose herself between the brutal tyranny of her father and the rest of his family. Frequent clashes with her father made her life unbearable and when she was 19 she left to make her own way in the world.

It was, all too clearly, a world designed primarily for the convenience and benefit of men. Married women could not hold, inherit, or bequeath property; these rights, as well as any wages they might earn belonged to their husbands. In addition, married women could not sue in court in their own names, were required to prove more grounds than men in divorce cases, and could not obtain custody of their children. Some of the legal inhibitions could be bypassed, but the social sanctions were more restrictive. The mores of the time dictated that women find their places in life through a dependent relationship with men in marriage. Since they always were to be protected by men and were to play distinctly inferior roles, social pressures and whatever education they received were directed towards those ends. In this male dominated society opportunities for a respectable single woman were severely limited. The professions were, of course, closed to her. She might become a governess, teach in a girl's school, or act as a companion; otherwise she had to remain dependent on her family.

Initially, Mary became the companion of a rich, bad-tempered, old woman in Bath. Then, she successively lived with a beloved woman friend, ran a girl's school, and served as a governess in Ireland. She wrote bad novels and a treatise on the education of girls, and in the late 1780s began working as a translator in London for a publisher who introduced her into left-wing political circles. Like Godwin, she was exhilarated by the hopes and opportunities represented by the French Revolution, and in 1791 she wrote the first answer to Edmund Burke, *A Vindication of the Rights of Men;* it was also one of the first serious political tracts composed by a woman. The following year she published her masterpiece, *A Vindication of the Rights of Women.* Not, like Godwin's *Political Justice,* derivative of enlightenment thought, *Vindication* was the first public literary challenge to the traditional image of women as inferior beings created only to serve men and renew humanity. Why, she asked, should the libertarian ideals of the revolution apply only to men? Women, she asserted, were not mere creatures of instinct, but possessed as much intellectual potential as men and commanded as much right as men to have opportunities for intellectual development. As for "female follies," they were the self-protective consequences of "the tyranny of man." Even though women's functions differed from those of men, especially in their primary maternal responsibilities, they still merited individual freedom, she argued, and deserved equal political, legal, and social rights.

Vindication brought recognition and prestige, and in December of 1792 the now famous Miss Wollstonecraft traveled to Paris to report on the revolution. There, she fell deeply and disastrously in love. Although she was 33 and had experienced several intense platonic relationships with both men and women, physical reluctance rather than any moral scruples had restrained her from expressing her emotions fully. The barrier was overcome by Gilbert Imlay, an American agent and adventurer who became her lover in the summer of 1792. The affair lasted two years, until Gilbert deserted Mary and their young daughter Fanny in August 1794. Mary finally realized that he was a cad, but she clung to him, even agreeing that he might take another mistress. She followed him to London, undertook a business trip to Scandinavia on his behalf, wrote humble, passionate, and despairing love letters to him, and twice attempted suicide. By the beginning of 1796, she finally admitted to herself that she could not regain Imlay's affections and unhappily began rebuilding her life without him.

As Godwin later put it in his memoir of his wife, a "friendship" begun in April between him and Mary had, by August, "melt[ed] into love." She was 37; he was 40. They shared common ideals, both had become targets of criticism from the Tory reaction to the excesses of the French Revolution, and both set the highest value on individual freedom and privacy. Perhaps above all, Mary, disillusioned by her experience with Imlay, was grateful to find in Godwin a man who recognized her worth as an individual, not merely as a female. They established separate residences a few doors from each other so that they could have privacy to continue their literary work, and communicated regularly by note. In March 1797, William abandoned his principles for the sake of the child that Mary was carrying and they were married. The discarded mistress of Imlay and mother of the American's illegitimate daughter, author of *Vindication* or not, ardently desired the marriage. Their child was born on August 30, 1797, and ten days later Mary Wollstonecraft Godwin died of childbed fever.

The widowed philosopher was left with two children. Four years after his wife's death he married his neighbor, Mrs. Mary Jane Clairmont, a widow with two children; a year later she gave birth to a son. Godwin became a publisher, producing Charles Lamb's *Tales from Shakespeare,*

Walter Scott's *Scottish Tales and Ballads,* and a series of children's books. His house became a mecca for major literary, political, and philosophical figures, including the equivocal American Vice President, Aaron Burr. Despite its excellent list of writers, the publishing house foundered, for neither Godwin nor his second wife were good at business. For the rest of his life, the philosopher experienced frequent financial crises, was always short of money, and was usually in debt.

The daughter of Mary Wollstonecraft and William Godwin grew up in a household which included her mother's first child by Imlay, her stepmother's son and daughter, and her father's son by his second wife. She was educated at home, where a portrait of the first Mrs. Godwin hung prominently over the parlor mantelpiece. Apparently she felt that, as a child of extraordinary parents, she was an exceptional person, so she barely tolerated her prosaic and rather narrow-minded stepmother. She was passionately devoted to her father.

While Mary was on a visit to Scotland early in 1814, Percy Bysshe Shelley and his wife Harriet became frequent visitors at the Godwin's. Bysshe, as he was called, was the heir to a baronetcy which had been enriched by his grandfather's succession of wealthy elopements and marriages. In 1814 he was 22 years old. He had attended Eton and had been "sent down" from Oxford for writing a pamphlet entitled *The Necessity of Atheism.* He had also written some Gothic romances, several political tirades and one major poem, "Queen Mab," which essentially presented the ideas of Godwin's *Political Justice* in verse. A convinced radical reformer, he regarded himself as a disciple of William Godwin; he also espoused the cause of Irish freedom. Most of all, he wanted to convert mankind to the rational libertarian ideas of *Political Justice* and the French Revolution through the inspiration of his romantic poetry. Like his grandfather he, too, had eloped, but with the 16-year-old daughter of a tavern keeper, rather than with an heiress. He and Harriet had one son, and in 1814 she was pregnant again. Shelley was estranged from his father, Sir Timothy, a rather stolid Sussex squire, and already had begun selling "post obits," that is, raising loans at ruinous rates on his future inheritance.

Although Shelley was drawn to Godwin by the fact that the two men shared many of the same beliefs, he had based his conclusions on different sources, arrived at them through different means, and possessed, in reality, a fundamentally dissimilar outlook. Instead of Calvin and Sandeman, Bysshe had read Platonic philosophy, Gothic romances, and sentimental poetry, and they guided his thinking to an entirely diametric set of suppositions. For him, the intellectual arbiter was not reason but a mixture of emotion and revelation. Rather than develop answers to questions logically, he somehow perceived them intuitively.

Instead of Reason, he exalted such Platonic concepts as Beauty, Love, Truth, Equality, and Freedom. In his outlook he was just as representative of the Romantic movement of the early 19th century as Godwin's philosophic system mirrored the Enlightenment of the 18th century. Godwin was flattered by the admiration of the aristocratic young poet, however, and gratified that Shelley was willing to pay his debts; Shelley agreed with what Godwin had written in *Political Justice*, that wealth should be distributed according to need.

With curly golden hair, a childlike oval face, vivacious, and earnest, Shelley was very attractive to women. When 16-year old Mary Godwin met him, she was captivated by the radical young aristocrat. To avoid the disapproval of her stepmother she had developed the custom of reading by her mother's grave in the St. Pancras churchyard, and there, in the presence of the spirit of Mary Wollstonecraft, she and Bysshe met, arranged rendezvous, and came to love. On June 26 Mary declared her love and he responded; on June 27 they became intimate and in July she was pregnant. They revealed their love to Godwin, but the author of *Political Justice* and the lover of Mary Wollstonecraft was furious, probably fearing what people would say about him and possibly, it has been charged, because he loved his daughter too well. Bysshe suggested to Harriet that all three live together, Harriet as his sister and Mary as his wife, but she, as furious as Godwin, also refused.

Young Shelley did establish a *ménage à trois*, but without his wife Harriet. When he and Mary eloped on the night of July 28, 1814, Claire Clairmont, also 16 and daughter of Mrs. Godwin by her first marriage, fled with them to the continent. The lives of the three were to be intertwined until the death of Shelley eight years later. Mrs. Godwin followed them to Calais in an attempt to retrieve her errant daughter, but Claire would not return to London. Shelley wrote Harriet, asking her to join them, but she again refused. The trio traveled through France, mostly on foot, for Shelley had almost no money, moving toward Switzerland through the same countryside over which Napoleon had fought a desperate campaign only six months before, attempting to keep Russian invaders from Paris. Once they stayed at the same inn and slept in the same beds that Napoleon and his staff had used. Carefree and high-spirited, the truants returned to London on September 13, 1814.

In England the young lovers and their companion were brought face to face with harsh reality. Shelley was penniless and found that Harriet spitefully had withdrawn all his money from the bank. His father refused to allow him more unless he acknowledged the Christian God, ceased writing subversive and immoral pamphlets and poems, and stopped living an irregular life. Harried by creditors and stalked by bailiffs who threatened debtor's prison, Bysshe apparently never considered seeking ordinary employment; he was, after all, a poet and the son of a baronet. Instead, he set about arranging for more post obits. But until he could do so, he and Mary parted and he became a fugitive. Godwin refused to see the daughter who was living according to the precepts he and her mother had set forth and acted upon, and he wrote Mary that he would communicate with her only through a solicitor. On the day she received the letter she ruefully reread part of *Political Justice*. Godwin complicated the situation further by shamelessly demanding more money from his daughter's seducer, despite a rumor that he had sold Mary and Claire to Shelley for a total of £1,500. Meanwhile, Bysshe became the father of a daughter by Mary and a son by Harriet, and his best friend, Thomas Jefferson Hogg, who earlier had fallen in love with Harriet, now began paying court to Mary. Mary, the true daughter of her mother, believed that sexual monopoly was wrong and apparently entertained Hogg's suit seriously, with Bysshe's consent. As Shelley was to write later to justify his own actions:

> I never was attached to that great sect
> Whose doctrine is that each one should select
> Out of the world a mistress or a friend,
> And all the rest, though fair and wise, commend
> To cold oblivion . . . .

Initially Mary's pregnancy interfered with consummation, and then she decided that she was not, after all, physically attracted to Hogg.

Finally in March of 1815, Bysshe's father guaranteed him £1,000 a year, and the post obits were redeemed. Mary's first child died and soon she bore a second, a boy named after her father. She and Bysshe developed a routine that they were to follow the remainder of their years together. Mary, like Bysshe, wanted to become a writer. She believed that she had inherited literary talent from her parents, and one of the few possessions she had taken on the elopement was a box containing her early writings. They were convinced of their potential for greatness, and each encouraged and assisted the other. They read widely, discussed themes, ideas, problems, and techniques, and criticized each other's work. They felt that they were in almost total communion, passionately in love and dedicated to achieving the same goals. In 1815, Mary was composing *History of a Six Weeks' Tour*, an account of their travels in 1814 which was published anonymously in 1817. In the spring of 1816 they left again for the Continent, planning to visit Italy. Claire persuaded them to go to Geneva instead.

Mrs. Godwin's daughter was without artistic talent, and she undoubtedly felt inferior to, as well as attracted by, the brilliant company she was keeping. She was possessive of Bysshe, jealous of Mary, and frequently the two girls quarreled. Competitively, she determined to capture a poet of her own.

Charles Gordon, Lord Byron, was a peer, not merely the heir to a baronetcy. He was the handsomest man in Europe, the height of fashion, a notorious rake, and already much admired as a poet. Claire wrote him, soliciting an interview; twice he failed to keep appointments, but she was persistent. He had just left his wife and was bored and restless, and sometime early in 1816 she became his mistress. Late in April Byron left for Geneva and Claire was pregnant.

In persuading Bysshe and Mary to go to Geneva, Claire Clairmont arranged an encounter that was to influence both Shelley and Byron profoundly and to inspire Mary Shelley's most enduring work. Byron was accompanied by his physician, Dr. John Polidori, and at this time was writing the third canto of *Childe Harold*. He leased a villa, where John Milton once had stayed, near Shelley's cottage. The two parties were constantly together, sailing on the lake and conversing in the evenings. Quickly rumors spread in England that Shelley, Byron, Claire, and Mary were living together in an orgy of free love. Actually, they spent most of their evenings telling ghost stories. In this atmosphere Mary conceived *Frankenstein,* the story of a man-made monster. Published two years later and with a preface by Bysshe, it soon became a bestseller and remained more popular and well known than anything Bysshe ever wrote. Thereafter, a signature "by the author of *Frankenstein*" on a title page ensured a ready market for all of Mary Shelley's writings.

Frankenstein is more than just a gripping horror story. It reflects a romantic reaction to the orderly philosophy of the enlightenment. In that it exalts passion and emotion, the novel denies everything that the Age of Reason and perhaps, William Godwin as well, had stood for. Like the philosophes, Dr. Frankenstein believed that man could understand and conquer everything, and his fate stands as a warning to those who, moved by intellectual arrogance, would tamper with the mysteries of the universe.

Yet, at the same time, Mary Shelley goes beyond the contemporary aversion to the rational construct. Her novel is subtitled *The Modern Prometheus,* and it closes with a quotation from *Paradise Lost*. As Prometheus had stolen fire from the Gods and as Milton's Satan had challenged the Judeo-Christian God, so also Dr. Frankenstein had presumptuously taken to himself the perquisites of the divine. One can find examples of enlightenment thought in the novel: the monster, neither good nor bad when animated, is, as Locke suggested, made to do evil by his environment; the manufacture of the monster has scientific underpinnings and was, indeed, inspired by an experiment of Dr. Erasmus Darwin; Dr. Frankenstein, like Faust, tries logic before he resorts to the supernatural. On the whole, however, Frankenstein's frame of reference is emotion rather than thought. Its text is feeling, suffering and overweening ambition. When the monster educates himself, he reads Goethe, not Montesquieu, and he craves companionship rather than knowledge. In *Frankenstein* wisdom is found not in the mind but in the heart. By writing the novel, Mary Shelley demonstrated that she was as much of the new century as her father was of the old.

Whatever hopes Claire Clairmont might have entertained for a reconciliation with Byron were not fulfilled. The poet remained cold and uninterested, and other circumstances drew the party back to England. Fanny Imlay, hoping to become a teacher at a school run by her mother's sisters in Ireland, wrote a despairing letter, and Godwin's finances were again in a critical state. Early in September 1816, Mary and Bysshe, accompanied by a Clair now obviously pregnant, established themselves in Bath. Although the couple tried to concentrate on writing—Mary was composing *Frankenstein*—mundane problems and the tribulations of others distracted them constantly. Godwin's finances, and Bysshe's own, took Shelley frequently to London. Claire was querulous in pregnancy and worried about what provision Byron would make for their child; she bore him a daughter in June 1817. Fanny Imlay was rejected by her aunts on the grounds that Mary's reputation would jeopardize their school; probably Fanny also believed that they had refused to employ her because of her own illegitimacy. Despondent, she committed suicide. Harriet Shelley who, gossips hinted, had consoled herself with other men after Shelley had abandoned her, was found floating in the Serpentine River, dead and far advanced in pregnancy. Bysshe, after a long court suit, failed to gain custody of his two children by Harriet because, the court determined, his immoral principles and conduct rendered him unfit to rear them.

Mary seems to have blamed herself partially for these tragedies, and they constituted the first major threat to the idyll she and Bysshe were living. Perhaps, it seemed to her, the principles of individual liberty on which she and Bysshe had acted possessed limits which they had transcended; perhaps true love did not justify everything. Perhaps she and Bysshe had been not so much carefree as feckless, unheeding of the shattering consequences that their actions might bring to others. Only 19, she began to make the same move toward respectability that her mother had made, a move that threatened the spiritual communion between her and Bysshe.

Nineteen days after Harriet's death, Mary and Bysshe were married. Mr. and Mrs. Godwin attended the ceremony; at last Mary was reconciled to her beloved father.

In the spring of 1817, Bysshe leased a house near London; Mary finished *Frankenstein* and gave birth to her third child, a daughter. Bysshe began a close friendship with Leigh Hunt, editor of the *Examiner*, whose columns were filled with slashing attacks on the oppressive post-war Tory regime. Bysshe also wrote *The Revolt of Islam*, an obscure and heavily symbolic poem about the French Revolution, and other poems about earthly and spiritual love. Harriet's creditors were harrassing him, he was arrested for debt, his health began to deteriorate, and in May of 1818 Mary and Bysshe again left England, he for the last time.

For four years they roamed from hotel to villa to spa in Italy, attracted by the compelling fascination that the peninsula exercised for Englishmen in the early 19th century. They were not drawn just by the antiquities of Rome, Pompeii, and Herculaneum, nor the Renaissance beauties of Florence, Venice, and Milan. Nor was it the warmer climate, which contrasted sharply with Britain's damp and cold, or the general belief that living expenses were lower in Italy that lured them. To many Englishmen, Italy stood for romance and, unaccountably, given the repressive governments in the peninsula after 1815, it represented, somehow, freedom. English expatriates did not have to worry about their reputations in Italy, for very few who lived there had any left to lose. Italy was a refuge for cashiered army officers, for remittance men, and above all, for adulterous couples whose relationships were not countenanced by their associates in England. Even Lord Byron came to Italy to escape the scorn he encountered when his incestuous relationship with his half-sister was revealed; he settled down to a hectic domesticity "in the strictest adultery," he wrote, with an Italian countess. It was in this raffish community, enlivened by an occasional Greek or Italian nationalist, at least one damsel in distress, and thieving and blackmailing servants, that the Shelleys moved. Their main goals were creative. Bysshe was to inspire reactionary and phlegmatic England with his poems and plays, and Mary was to continue the career as novelist she had launched with *Frankenstein.*

Yet, personal problems and tragedies constantly intervened. Byron proved difficult about his daughter Allegra, refusing to support her unless Claire relinquished the child to his care in Venice. Claire finally gave up her daughter, persuaded that Allegra would benefit from an aristocratic English upbringing. But she grieved for Allegra, importuned Bysshe to help her, and a sympathetic and warm-hearted Shelley acted as intermediary with Byron. He traveled alone from Leghorn to Venice and persuaded Byron to permit his discarded, and now despised, mistress to visit their daughter. Unfortunately, his efforts brought death to his own child. His daughter, Clara, was ill when Bysshe wrote summoning Mary and Claire from Leghorn to Venice and, weakened by four hot days of travel, she died shortly after they arrived. A few months thereafter their three-year-old son William died of fever in Rome. Mary bore another son, Percy Florence, in November 1819, but she was heartbroken by the loss of her other children.

Byron, it turned out, was not providing Allegra with an aristocratic English education, but had placed her in an Italian convent. Claire pined for her daughter and pleaded with Bysshe incessantly to intercede again with Byron and persuade him to return the girl to her mother. Frantically, she even proposed that they spirit Allegra away from the convent. By now Byron loathed Claire and continued to refuse, writing that he disapproved of the Shelleys' vegetarian diet and their gypsylike mode of life, and noting cruelly that the Shelleys could not even keep their own children alive: "Have they even reared one?" he asked sarcastically. Then Allegra, too, died of typhus in the convent.

Thus, before Mary was 22 years old she had lost three children and experienced the suicides of her half-sister and her husband's discarded wife. Her association with Bysshe seemed to be at the root of these tragedies, and their cumulative effect placed a strain on their relationship that it could not bear. They had always rejoiced in what they felt was a total harmony of mood and interest, but now the union of spirits was broken, as Mary became cold, distant, and apathetic. Although they continued together, they never recovered the early rapture of their love. Their crumbling relationship was clearly reflected in Shelley's poems. In *Epipsychidion* Shelley tells how at first Mary enthralled him with her intellectual light, but then her light "was quenched" and he discovered that they would not always be in complete sympathy.

Philosophically and temperamentally a free spirit, Bysshe continued to search for a worldly embodiment of spiritual and intellectual beauty and truth. He believed he found it at least twice, only to be disillusioned again. He became the romantic champion of Teresa Viviani, an Italian girl immured in a convent awaiting an arranged marriage; she finally did marry the man her father chose and then wrote asking Shelley for money. Then, he worshipped Jane Williams, common-law wife of Ned Williams, a half-pay Lieutenant in the army of the East India Company. The Shelleys and the Williamses shared lodgings and traveled together in 1821 and 1822, but Jane turned out to be intellectually a disappointment. Although apparently neither of these loves found physical expression, Mary felt betrayed for she knew that to Bysshe, spiritual affinity was paramount.

In the spring of 1822 Mary was testy and short-tempered, and Bysshe complained that she was unfeeling and lacked understanding. In July she almost died after a miscarriage at Casa Magni on the Gulf of Spezia. Four days later Shelley and Ned Williams sailed their boat, the *Don Juan,* to visit Byron and Leigh Hunt concerning a plan to establish a newspaper. On July 5 they began the return journey and their ship foundered in a storm. A week later their bodies were recovered.

In August 1822, Byron, Hunt, and Edward Trelawny, a Cornish adventurer who was visiting at Casa Magni, cremated the poet's body on the beach and his ashes were buried in Rome next to those of his son William. Trelawny, who was to be interred next to Shelley 60 years later, recovered Bysshe's heart from the furnace; Mary kept it until she died.

In July of 1823, almost a year after Shelley drowned and a week after Byron left Italy to go to his death in Greece, Mary Shelley returned to England. Twenty-five years old, she was widowed and penniless. Contemporaries described her as slender, with a high forehead, gray eyes, and long golden hair. Even after smallpox marred her complexion in 1828 she was accounted beautiful. In 1823 half of her life lay before her, and she had a past that she could treasure, for she had, as she wrote in her journal, "communicated, with unlimited freedom," for eight years with a man whom she considered a genius and the best poet of the age. She also had his son, Percy Florence, not yet four years old. In addition, she had a promising literary reputation upon which she could build; she had published two books, one of which was already famous, and a third novel, *Valperga,* was in press. A new phase of her life, consisting of three themes, Bysshe's memory, their son, and her own literary career, was about to begin.

She soon found, however, that she was not to be entirely her own mistress. For the next 21 years her activities were to be inhibited by the demands and prejudices of Sir Timothy Shelley, her father-in-law. After Harriet's son died in 1824, Sir Timothy grudgingly set a small allowance for his new heir Percy Florence, but he did so only after repeated letters from Mary, and he demanded that in exchange she not sully the Shelley name further. She was not to sign her own books or write a biography of his black-sheep son. He held rigidly to the stipulations. When the author of *Frankenstein* published *The Last Man* in 1826 the reviewers mentioned that she was Mrs. Shelley, and the allowance, then at £200, was interrupted. Sir Timothy was 71 when he began paying the annuity and laid the proscription. No one expected him to live very long, but he did not die until 1844, after he had restricted Mary Shelley's freedom for more than two decades.

With his grandfather's allowance and the proceeds from his mother's writings, Percy Florence entered Harrow and Mary went to live near him. A good and loving son, Percy was nevertheless a disappointment to his mother. Descended from Mary Wollstonecraft, William Godwin, and Percy Bysshe, he seemed to have inherited none of their fire, verve and brilliance; he lacked, Mary complained, "sensibility." He went to Cambridge and shortly after graduating entered politics briefly and then retired to live as a country gentleman on the estate he inherited from his grandfather.

Although Mary could find little of Bysshe in their stolid son, she cherished his father's poetry and memory. Sir Timothy had forbidden a biography, but in 1839 she prepared an edition of Shelley's work containing extensive illustrative and biographical notes. In her novels the heroes were thinly veiled copies of her adored husband. As much as the strictures of Sir Timothy permitted, she worked to achieve recognition and appreciation of Shelley's poetic genius.

She did not struggle, however, for the victory of the ideals that she had shared with Bysshe for eight years. Although she had been as enthusiastic as he on behalf of liberty, radical political reform, and the rights of women, and although she had supported Italian, Spanish, and Greek revolutionaries and even championed Queen Caroline, she dared not speak out in the confining shadow of Sir Timothy. Moreover, she considered herself to be not so much a radical activist as a woman of letters. While she might still have subscribed to Shelley's ideals in the abstract, she did not believe that it was up to her to work constantly to implement them. Above all, she was the mother of an heir to a baronetcy, and she would not risk the prospects of her son for the sake of distant ideals. Perhaps she felt that she had seen already the terrible effect that unpopular actions in the name of a libertarian cause could exert on those she loved. Even the teachings of her revered mother were denied when the daughter of Mary Wollstonecraft refused to associate herself publicly with the feminist movement.

Nor would Mary be a priestess at the center of a continuing Shelley circle. Leigh Hunt blamed her for withdrawing from Shelley during the last months of his life. Byron, who had promised to help Mary financially, finally decided that he did not really like her and even refused to honor a £1,000 bet he had with Shelley. Trelawny went to Greece with Byron and returned to England in the late 1820s. Mary helped him find a publisher for his book, *The Adventures of a Younger Son*, but refused to give him material for a biography of Shelley. When he proposed marriage she made it painfully clear that she preferred to be the widow of Shelley to being the wife of one of his satellites, and he went on his travels. Like Trelawny, all the men who paid court to the famous and handsome young widow, including even Prosper Merrimeé, seemed to pale before the shining brilliance of Percy Bysshe.

Only with Jane Williams was Mary willing to risk again the total commitment she had shared with Bysshe. In 1824 the two widows lived together, treasuring their memories and consoling each other. "I love Jane better than any other human being," wrote Mary in her journal, but Jane's affection was less profound and exclusive. When Jane had returned to England before Mary she had carried Mary's letter of introduction to Thomas Jefferson Hogg, Bysshe's school friend and suitor of both Harriet and Mary, and soon it became obvious that Jane was not as willing as Mary to live emotionally in the memories of the past. She became Hogg's mistress shortly after they met and in the summer of 1827 she went to live with him as his wife.

Initially, Mary was pleased that Jane found happiness with Shelley's old friend, but soon Jane began boasting of her place in Shelley's affections and poetry and criticizing Mary's treatment of her husband. Mary reacted violently, partly because she was aware that she had indeed failed Bysshe during the last few months of his life, but mostly because she believed that her relationship with him had, on the whole, been a happy and a good one. She knew that she had acted as a stimulus to his writing and feared that Jane was destroying her place in history as Shelley's helpmate. Jane's treachery was especially crushing, too, because Mary had been in love with her. As she told Trelawny later, "I was so ready to give myself away, and being afraid of men, I was apt to get *tousy-mousy* for women."

After Jane Williams' betrayal, Mary banked the emotional fires that had enriched her years with Bysshe. No longer was she open-hearted; no longer did she trustingly give her affection. For her that aspect of life was finished, and her capacity for love focused narrowly on Percy Florence. For recognition, friendship, and companionship she looked to the more respectable and established elements of English society. The wife of Shelley was also the author of *Frankenstein*. Her writing not only could augment Sir Timothy's meager allowance and ensure Percy Florence's education as a gentleman, it could also, she hoped, win for her an acknowledged and respected position as a leading woman of letters.

Five more novels appeared from her pen in the 1820s and 1830s. Ranging in subject matter from the Italian Renaissance through Perkin Warbeck to the death of humanity at the end of the 21st century, none of them gained the immediate popularity or possessed the lasting fascination of *Frankenstein*. They did not win her a high reputation at the time, and since then have served primarily as grist for the mill of literary historians who have identified in their characters the qualities of Shelley, Byron, Godwin, Trelawny, and Wollstonecraft. Of much better quality were essays on Italian, French, and Spanish writers that she contributed to Lardner's *Cabinet Cyclopedia*. Mary was a thorough researcher and a perceptive critic and could write with economy and clarity. As she did in her commentary on Bysshe's poetry, she placed the work of her subjects securely in their historical backgrounds. Yet, like the novels, this work, too, was transient, for although Mary had the potential to become an excellent literary historian she was untrained and her judgments were questionable.

Although Mary rejected the more disreputable elements of the Shelley circle, and even though she designed her novels to appeal to early 19th-century evangelical sensibilities, she never achieved the recognition she felt she deserved. In reality, living as she had on the artistic and radical fringes of English life, her yearnings were based on ignorance. However she had tamed herself, it was unlikely that she would have won acceptance from the dominant groups in English society. It was even more unlikely that the daughter of Mary Wollstonecraft and William Godwin and the widow of Shelley would have been content amid either the shallow frivolity of post-regency aristocratic high society or the philistinism of the upper middle classes. Nevertheless, the self-deception embittered her later years.

Shelley's disciples accepted and perpetuated the myth that she had always been an unworthy helpmeet to their dead master and condemned as a betrayal her refusal to support radical causes. Aside from Percy Florence she had few associates or close friends. Deprived of the support of sympathetic human intercourse, frequently she was lonely, and the theme of loneliness appeared repeatedly in her writings.

Her stepmother continued to stand between Mary and her father. Mary had stayed briefly with the Godwins on her return to England after Shelley's death, but she left as soon as she could and her association with the Godwin household was never close. William Godwin continued to mishandle his finances and Mary assigned to him the profits of one of her novels. Her love for him was not diminished by his egotism, vanity, and lack of sympathy, or his readiness to act contrary to the principles of *Political Justice.* She also came to realize that their relationship had, perhaps, been too intense in the first place, that possibly he had been attracted to her as the reincarnation of Mary Wollstonecraft and that she, in turn, had felt too romantic and passionate an attachment for him. She and Shelley had explored this awful possibility, and Shelley had written *The Cenci,* a play about a Renaissance count who had raped his daughter. Still, Mary's admiration of the Godwin of *Political Justice* was undiminished, and she used what influence she possessed with Sir Timothy to secure for him a sinecure as Yeoman Usher of the Exchequer which provided him with a house and an income of £200 a year. She was with him during his last hours in April of 1836 and buried him next to Mary Wollstonecraft as he had wished. Emotionally atrophied, she felt no great shock at his death. He had asked her to publish his final condemnation of religion, *The Genius of Christianity Unveiled,* but she refused to chance the opprobrium that it would arouse. Sir Timothy was still alive, and she would not sacrifice the prospects of the living Percy Florence to the wishes of her dead philosopher father.

In 1840 and again in 1842 and 1843, Mary, accompanied by Percy Florence, toured the continent. She returned to Geneva where she had developed the concept of *Frankenstein* and revisited old friends in Italy. While staying with Claire in Paris, something of the young Mary flared up briefly. Forty-five years old, she became infatuated with a handsome and glib young Italian nationalist. She wrote some foolish letters to him and dedicated the proceeds for her last book, *Rambles in Germany and Italy,* to him. Fickle and devious, he threatened blackmail, but the Paris police forestalled him.

After Sir Timothy's death in 1844 Percy Florence had an income of £2,000 a year. He had matured into a solid and unimaginative young man, but he was a loyal and loving son. With him Mary found comfort, protection, and shelter. Early in 1848 she met Jane St. John, a well-to-do widow. The two women were immediately drawn to each other and Percy obligingly married Jane on June 22, 1848. They lived alternately in London and in Field Place, the Shelley family home in Sussex, in an affectionate tranquillity that was marred only by one or two hysterical visits from Claire Clairmont. "She has been," Mary confided to Jane, "the bane of my life ever since I was two."

Late in 1850 Mary's health began to fail; a visit to Nice did not bring improvement. She became paralyzed on one side and died on February 1, 1851, not yet 54 years old, attended by her son and daughter-in-law. She was buried, as she had wished, between her mother and father.

Percy Florence, who had served briefly as a Conservative Member of Parliament, retired from politics to live in the country. In abilities and in outlook he became a model English squire. Only in a proficiency for drawing, a passion for amateur theatricals, and, perhaps, his attachment to boating, did he resemble his adventuring and artistic parents. He was a kindly and decent Sir Timothy, representing the antithesis of the romantic idealism of his father and mother. Lady Jane devoted her life to collecting materials about Mary and Percy Bysshe. The couple died childless, and the baronetcy passed to Bysshe's younger brother. The vitality and genius of Mary Wollstonecraft and Mary Godwin Shelley have no direct inheritors. Only through Harriet's daughter Ianthe does Percy Bysshe have descendants. Claire Clairmont lived on, increasingly neurotic and vicious, until she died in Florence in 1879 at the age of 81.

Posterity has not awarded either Bysshe or Mary the kind of recognition each sought. True, scholars have ranked Shelley among the premier romantic poets but, except at times when political radicalism has been popular, few men have looked to him for the libertarian inspiration he set out to offer. Mary has been remembered as the mistress and wife of a great poet, but her own novels have not stood comparison with those of Elliot, Thackeray, Scott, Trollope, or Dickens. Her invention, Frankenstein's monster, has entered popular culture, but few persons identify the tortured creature with its originator or appreciate the deeper meanings of the novel.

Perhaps only in the way that Mary and Bysshe lived and by virtue of the circles in which they moved did they make a lasting impression on England. They broke convention in the name of individual liberty and lived contrary to the tenets of Judeo-Christian morality. Promiscuity and adultery such as theirs and Byron's certainly was not new in artistic, or in any, circles, but they were the first to excuse it philosophically on the grounds that it was justified by a transcendent principle. Their higher morality was closely connected with the radical philosophy of the French Revolution, and more conservative persons could point only too easily to the disintegrative and disruptive effects of applying these principles. Obviously, following the ideal of individual freedom meant that wives were abandoned, 16-year-old girls were seduced, fathers were disobeyed, decency was flouted, and debts were not honored. The political radicalism Mary and Bysshe espoused entailed not only a sharp departure in governmental practice; it threatened the very foundations, it seemed, of organized society.

The lives of Shelley's circle also erected a new barrier between a large part of the English public and English artists and intellectuals. The new evangelical movement, with its insistence on orthodox morality, came to be antipathetic to artists and literary men, their creations, and their ideas. So appeared the belief that society and true artists were in opposition, that freedom of expression was necessarily accompanied by behavior that was unacceptable in orderly society. In the future, conventional persons tended to associate creativity with promiscuity and a lack of respect for established values, whereas aspiring artists tended to assume that creativity and sexual freedom were inseparable, that artists should not be bound by the strictures that governed the lives of ordinary men.

Paradoxically, these complementary myths have constituted Mary Shelley's most important legacy to the nature of English life.

SUGGESTED READINGS

For the general reader the best of several excellent studies of Mary Shelley is Muriel Spark, *Child of Light* (Hadleigh, Essex:Tower Bridge Publications, Ltd., 1951). More specialized and highly interpretive are R. Glynn Grylls, *Mary Shelley* (London: Oxford University Press, 1938) and Elizabeth Nitchie, *Mary Shelley* (New Brunswick, N.J.: Rutgers University Press, 1953). Newman Ivey White relates Shelley's poetry to his relationship with Mary in his very readable *Portrait of Shelley* (New York: Alfred A. Knopf, 1945). *Shelley and His Circle* (4 vols.; Cambridge, Mass.: Harvard University Press, 1961, 1970), edited by Kenneth Neill Cameron, reflects the most recent scholarship. Information about Mary's parents may be found in: Eleanor Flexner, *Mary Wollstonecraft* (New York: Coward, McCann & Geoghegan, Inc., 1972) and Ford K. Brown, *The Life of William Godwin* (London: J. M. Dent & Sons, Ltd., 1926). Guy Bolton's *The Olympians* (Cleveland, Ohio: The World Publishing Company, 1961) is a sentimental novel about Mary and Bysshe. Bysshe, Mary, Lord Byron, Frankenstein, and his monster all appear in a superior novel by Brian W. Aldiss, *Frankenstein Unbound* (London: Jonathan Cape, 1973).

Courtesy of the Government of South Australia

Chapter 12

EDWARD JOHN EYRE:
Race, Democracy,
and Empire

O N an October Saturday during 1865 in the vestry court at Morant Bay, Jamaica, James Geoghagan angrily shouted a protest against the fine assessed one of his friends who had been convicted of assault. Geoghagan, as one police-sergeant complained ruefully, always came to "cheek" him in the court, but this bit of "cheek" did more than just unsettle a colonial policeman.

Geoghagan's contempt of court set in motion a chain of events which brought rebellion and savagery to one of Britain's oldest colonies. It ruined the career of a promising colonial governor, Edward John Eyre, who was accused of the wholesale slaughter of hundreds of his subjects and was finally retired from government service while still in his fifties. It provoked a sharp reaction in colonial policy, as institutions of representative government were abolished in Britain's Caribbean colonies. It raised grave constitutional questions about martial law, individual rights, the authority of the state, and the responsibility of state officials. It elicited painful soul-searching among English men of letters and produced sharp divisions in England's literary community as British writers chose sides for and against Governor Eyre. Above all, it evoked fundamental questions about race, democracy, and empire: it asked if whites in England and blacks in the colonies had the same rights under the same law; it pointed out a potential contradiction between an England becoming increasingly democratic and her possession of an empire governed by authoritarian methods; and it inquired into the basic nature of Britain's imperial role.

Jamaica, the island setting for the drama of Morant Bay, had been captured for Cromwell's Britain by Admiral William Penn, the father of the founder of Pennsylvania. One of the largest and richest of the Caribbean islands, it became a major producer of sugar and other tropical products for the mercantile British Empire. Black slaves were introduced from West Africa and soon made up a majority of the population. Jamaica held an important position in the North Atlantic System, sending sugar and molasses to Old and New England and receiving food, manufactures, and slaves from the mid-Atlantic colonies, England, and Africa. For more than a century Jamaica was one of the most valuable places in the world, and Britain sent her finest admirals and ships to guard the island and her sister colonies in the Caribbean.

After 1800 a combination of factors brought decline and neglect. Humanitarianism in England brought an end to the slave trade in 1807 and slavery itself in 1833. The free trade economics of Adam Smith deprived Jamaican sugar of its favored position in the British market when the sugar duties and, hence, the tariff preferences for colonial sugar were abolished in the late 1840s. Concurrently, new and frequently more efficient producers of both cane and beet sugar threatened the primacy of British West Indian sugar in the world market.

As the economic importance of Jamaica and the rest of the British

West Indies diminished, they became the slums of the British Empire. Everywhere, the white population declined, both in numbers and in vigor, as men of ability, ambition, and vision saw no future in the British West Indies. Plantations were taken out of production and, in the descriptive Jamaican term, fell "ruinate." Because of special circumstances in one or two of the colonies, sugar production throughout the whole British Caribbean remained at a high level for several years, but profits were low and the future was not hopeful.

As the islands lost their value to Englishmen, they were left to shift for themselves. Eventually, a new West Indian culture was to emerge, but in the 19th century English visitors like the historian J. A. Froude and the novelist Anthony Trollope saw just stagnation and a reversion to barbarism. Only missionaries and, occasionally, a Colonial Office administrator paid much constructive attention to the colonies. Most men believed that nothing could or should be done; in the laissez faire atmosphere of the 19th century, the colonies faced the world alone.

In Jamaica the default of creative white leadership meant that the black freedmen had to make the painful adjustments to their new liberty virtually without aid and guidance. Moreover, these adjustments were made especially difficult by economic depression, straitened colonial finances, and absentee ownership of many of the fertile lowland plantations. Yet, of all the West Indian islands, Jamaica offered the best opportunities for building a new and genuinely West Indian society. It was comparatively large, and, unlike estates in colonies such as Barbados and Antigua where land was at a premium, Jamaican estates had always contained provision grounds, that is, plots of land where the slaves had grown yams, ackees, and breadfruit for their own sustenance. Even in the 18th century slaves had been permitted to sell their surpluses at weekly markets. Jamaican freedmen, then, could be largely self-sustaining, and plantation labor was not their only source of livelihood. This was the major reason why sugar plantations were falling "ruinate" in Jamaica. To a man, the ex-slaves disliked labor in cane fields and regarded it as a shameful badge of slavery. After the planters' power of coercion was abolished in 1833, there existed no correspondingly strong economic pressure to force the freedmen to perform the tasks which they considered suitable only for slaves. Furthermore, unlike planters in Trinidad and British Guiana, the planters in Jamaica would not agree to the British government's terms for the importation of indentured labor from India. Accordingly, they needed the labor of their ex-chattels more than the freed blacks needed the menial jobs the estates provided.

This situation also explained the reputation for laziness that Jamaican blacks gained in England. Disgruntled planters reported that the blacks would not willingly plant, hoe, and cut cane; ergo, they would not work, but preferred to take their ease and enjoy the fruits of a rich tropical island while the cane rotted in the fields. Nor had Jamaican blacks learned the work ethic from their ex-masters; if half a day's toil would support life, that was enough, for there was more to living than drudgery in the fields. Of course Jamaican freedmen would work, but they labored for themselves, and they saw no reason to work more than necessary or to perform tasks reminiscent of their degrading past on the old slave plantations.

The independence of Jamaican blacks accounts for yet another factor which poisoned the colonial atmosphere. Although many freedmen left the plantations after Emancipation to start new farms and communities on vacant land in the foothills of the Blue Mountains, others preferred to continue to work the provision grounds, which they now claimed to be theirs by custom. The planters, however, maintained their rights of ownership and charged rent, sometimes quite high rent. In this way they endeavored to force the blacks to earn money by working for the white proprietors. It was a stratagem much used in the whole British empire, then and later. The situation became particularly tense when estates were abandoned, black squatters moved in, and new owners attempted to assert their property rights. The court at Morant Bay was called upon especially often to adjudicate such land disputes. Staffed by men reflecting the planter interest, the court regularly upheld the property rights of owners and new purchasers against black squatters.

On newly cleared small farms in the Blue Mountains, on abandoned estates in the lowlands, and among Jamaicans of mixed blood who lived mostly in the towns, many of the characteristics of a new Jamaican society were slowly appearing. The freedmen received little assistance or guidance from the white culture that had brought their ancestors from Africa. The Jamaican planters were interested in them only as a labor force, and the British government had offered merely temporary judicial help through a system of special magistrates. Only church groups ran counter to the prevailing indifference, and missionary societies, especially Baptist groups, worked actively among the freedmen. Although a few missionaries helped to start new free villages, most were concerned primarily with the freedmen's conditions in the next world rather than in this one. Nevertheless, their teaching found receptive ears among the blacks. Conversions multiplied and congregations increased.

But in religion, as in other matters, the freedmen were jealous of their new independence. They refused to be bound by white Christian doctrines, practices, or pastors. Untutored blacks founded their own churches, uniquely African ceremonies infiltrated the purity of English Christian practice, and African religious beliefs frequently went hand in hand with the worship of the Nazarene. It was an especially African version of Christianity that prevailed among the freedmen of Jamaica.

English Baptists persisted in their ministrations, however, and the investigations and writings of one of them, Edward Bean Underhill, contributed substantially to the background of the Morant Bay riots and the reaction to them in England. In his book, *The West Indies*, and in a letter to Colonial Secretary Edward Cardwell in 1865, Underhill criticized the Jamaican government sharply, charging it with taxing the blacks unfairly, foisting unfair courts on them, and denying them political rights. When published, Underhill's criticisms served as rallying cries to the disaffected in Jamaica and gave new fire to English humanitarian sentiment.

Underhill was right. The government that he castigated was ill-suited for the troubled colony of Jamaica. Established in the 1660s, the Jamaican constitution resembled those of the 13 North American colonies. It provided for an elected assembly of 47 members, a council, and a governor. Granted before cabinet government had evolved in England, the constitution had the defects of the 17th-century English constitution, where the executive was dependent on the elected legislature for money, but not answerable to the legislators for its policies and actions. In the 1840s an attempt had been made to introduce cabinet government in Jamaica, in the form of an "Executive Committee," but the Committee had failed to bridge the gap between Governor and Assembly. Quarrels between the executive and the legislature continued to be endemic in Jamaica, and were to be particularly bitter during Edward John Eyre's tenure as Governor.

The Jamaican Assembly might have been elective, but the Jamaican oligarchy of planters and merchants had seen to it that it was not democratic. After Emancipation in 1833, succeeding legislatures had so restricted the franchise that in the 1864 elections only 1,903 Jamaicans of a total population of 400,000 were qualified to vote. It was not simply a question of white ruling black. Many men of mixed blood, called "coloreds" in Jamaica to distinguish them from the pure blacks, had become large landholders and successful business and professional men, and had joined the local oligarchy. Men of color could, and did, govern as selfishly in their own interests as did whites. Complicating the situation were bitterly antagonistic "Town" and "Country" parties and socioracial barriers. Jamaican whites arrogantly maintained themselves far above the majority of the population who, in their blackness, bore more clearly the shameful marks of past servitude.

In 1862 Edward John Eyre was commissioned to administer the colony of Jamaica temporarily as Acting Governor. The Colonial Office thought well of Eyre, and his record seemed to indicate that he was an excellent choice to govern the polyglot and unhappy island. Son of a Yorkshire clergyman, Eyre had emigrated to New South Wales, Australia, at the age of 17. In the 1830s he had become a successful sheep farmer, had served as magistrate, and had pioneered an overland cattle and sheep route between New South Wales and the new colony of South Australia. Exploring expeditions he had led into the interior gave his name to a lake and a peninsula. The resourcefulness and determination he had displayed in overcoming severe privations and dangers in that inhospitable land had earned for him the status of an Australian hero. As magistrate, and in a book he wrote describing his exploring expeditions, young Eyre put himself forward as a champion of the nomadic Australian aborigines, who were being forced into the barren interior by predatory white settlers. In 1845, when he was only 30 years old, Eyre returned to England with two aborigine boys. When the heroic explorer and author was presented to Queen Victoria and Prince Albert, he took the boys with him to Buckingham Palace. Eyre's presentation at Court brought him to the attention of the Colonial Office. Here was a young man, a hero to white settlers, yet at the same time concerned for the welfare of nonwhites in the world, who might be quite useful in an empire troubled by friction between colonists and darker indigenous races. In 1846 Eyre returned to the South Pacific as Lieutenant Governor of the six-year-old colony of New Zealand.

In New Zealand Eyre served under the able and colorful Governor Sir George Grey. In a colony where English settlers encountered native Maori, he added further distinction to his reputation. He returned to England in 1853 where Grey, then Secretary of State for the Colonies, appointed him Lieutenant Governor of St. Vincent in the eastern Caribbean. He served briefly as Acting Governor of the Leeward Islands and early in 1862 a confident and approving Colonial Office sent him to Jamaica.

The Governorship of Jamaica was a senior position paying £6,000 a year, and even though the appointment was temporary, it was definitely a plum for a man still in his forties. After serving as second-in-command for 15 years, Eyre was now given his chance to prove himself worthy of entering the top ranks of the colonial service.

The fact that Eyre was only Acting Governor produced difficulties with the fractious Assembly, and he soon added a personal ingredient to the troublesome Jamaican situation. Indeed, it became obvious almost immediately that the new Governor could not fill the office adequately. Eyre could lead small bands of men into the unknown against almost insurmountable odds, he could serve ably as an adjutant, but he could not by himself govern successfully a West Indian colony. The new Governor was deceived by a persuasive but corrupt colonial engineer about a highly suspect tramway contract. He upheld the engineer despite overwhelming evidence of his professional misconduct, even to the point of writing misleading reports to his superiors in the Colonial Office. The advisers and friends he chose were unpopular with many leading men of the colony. Unwisely he did not remain scrupulously above party politics, but fraternized primarily with men whom he probably saw as the Jamaican counterpart of the English ruling classes, the white planter rural gentry members of the "Country" party. Notable among his cronies was Baron von Ketelhodt, German husband of an English-woman who owned property near Morant Bay. To the disappointment of convivial Jamaicans, he did not entertain as frequently and lavishly at Government House as colonists liked their governors to do.

Soon, not only the Assembly but even his own Council was against him. The Jamaican press pilloried him as weak, vacillating, and undigni-fied. The Assembly refused to pass a money bill, Eyre dissolved it, and both sides appealed to the Colonial Secretary. The Colonial Office upheld its favorite and Eyre, to his credit, soon agreed to prosecute the embezzling engineer, but he was not chastened by his experience.

Basically, Eyre just did not possess abilities equal to his assigned post and, like many men who find themselves in positions beyond their capa-bilities, he became touchy, assertive, and jealous of his prerogatives. Undoubtedly the fact that he was only Acting Governor hampered him, but undeniably, he also found it awkward to mingle socially with Jamai-can men of color. Continuing friction with the Assembly had produced a movement for his recall by 1864 but, largely because Eyre had a staunch personal supporter in Permanent Undersecretary of State for the Colonies Frederic Rogers, his appointment as Governor was made permanent instead.

Eyre further alienated the oligarchy and also the population at large by virtue of his religious convictions and his views about sexual conduct. The son of a country parson, he was rigidly Anglican in outlook. He entertained a typical Church of England dislike of Baptists and other dissenters and soon made known his shocked disapproval of the very unorthodox forms that dissent had taken among Jamaican blacks. Rigidly puritanical, he was horrified also by the easy-going attitude that all Jamaicans, high and low, white and nonwhite, exhibited toward sex. Accordingly, to the plaudits of the missionaries, but to the dismay of nearly everyone else on the island, he issued a "morality proclamation" in which he announced that all holders of public office must prove that they were honest, sober, and moral. Such an ill-judged proclamation would give offense in any society, but in Jamaica, where the illegitimacy rate was well over 70 percent and concubinage was the norm, it was particularly odious.

The morality proclamation sheds a clear and hard light on the makeup and deficiencies of the Governor. It reveals his political naïveté, of course; but more than that, it shows the tragedy of Eyre's character and position. Undoubtedly he was a good man and was genuinely con-cerned about the welfare of the indigenous peoples whom Englishmen encountered in their world empire. He would protect them from white invaders, but as a good father, he would also dictate to them, insist that they behave according to his concept of propriety, lead them to the one and only Anglican God, and expect that they gratefully acknowledge their inferiority in the face of his beneficent authority. But Jamaica was not Australia, or East Africa. For better or for worse, Jamaicans had been in touch with Western culture for two centuries and the well-meant, condescending, and paternalistic tutelage that might possibly have been suitable for Australian aborigines was not at all appropriate for them. Instead of arousing grateful love and loyalty, Eyre provoked only resentment.

This resentment found its strongest expression in the figure of George William Gordon. Just as Eyre came to be regarded by many men as the villain of the Morant Bay affair, so Gordon was its hero. He was the colored illegitimate son of a Scottish overseer and a slave. Born a slave, he, as well as his mother, her sister, and his six brothers and sisters, had been freed by his father. Gordon was a man of ability and drive. He had educated himself, had become a merchant in Kingston and, largely because of his father's association with sugar estates, had become well-to-do. Eventually his father had fallen on hard times and ultimately Gordon supported not only him but also his legitimate white children. Although Jamaican custom dictated that Gordon's white half-sisters and half-brothers not recognize him socially, he had married Jane Shannon, white daughter of a Kingston schoolmistress. Gordon was generous with his money, but he was also reckless with it. He speculated wildly in land and, in the 1860s, he owed more than £30,000 to a London firm that held mortgages on his property. He seems to have been a compulsive joiner and, even though he was a member of the United Church of Scotland, he saw no conflict in serving also as a Native Baptist preacher.

Because Gordon owned an estate near Morant Bay, he acted as a magistrate there until Governor Eyre removed him for interfering with the operation of the parish jail. Eyre did this on the advice of Baron von Ketelhodt, also a magistrate at Morant Bay, and his action inaugurated a personal vendetta between the Governor and the ex-slave. No longer a magistrate, Gordon lost his seat on the Anglican vestry, which was also the local governing body of the parish. He sought reelection and won, but was not readmitted because the authorities took the position that Gordon, as a member of one Native Baptist congregation and a major figure in another, could not in good conscience become an Anglican churchwarden.

Gordon was also a member of the Assembly, where he stood forth eloquently as the champion of Jamaican blacks. One of the first colored West Indians to identify himself with the well-being of his blacker brothers, he soon won a large personal following among the freedmen. He was also vain, litigious, and a braggart. Just as Eyre came to stand as the model of the misguided and authoritarian colonial governor, so Gordon was the prototype of the nationalist demagogues that British rulers were to face everywhere in their empire during and after the Second World War. Prickly, somewhat equivocal, motivated by a mixture of self-interest and a genuine concern for the welfare of Jamaican freedmen, he certainly would not accord to Eyre the humble gratitude an uncivilized savage owed his Governor for the paternalistic supervision of the British evangelical. In the Assembly, Gordon came to be one of Eyre's hottest critics, until Eyre came to ignore Gordon just as habitually as Gordon damned Eyre.

In 1865 the freedmen of Jamaica were in a state of fevered excitement. Underhill's letter to Colonial Secretary Cardwell calling attention to the political and economic grievances of the freedmen had just been published, along with Eyre's refutation of the charges. The fact that the freedmen had found an advocate in England and that the Governor seemed to be thwarting him gave rise to "Underhill meetings" all over the island. The meetings, where Gordon played a prominent part, produced resolutions and petitions to the Queen. Popular feeling was raised to an even higher pitch by an enthusiastic Native Baptist religious revival.

The petitions drew from the Colonial Office staff a stern Calvinist response in the form of the so-called Queen's Reply. In essence the freedmen were advised that if they would work industriously and regularly on the plantations, their problems, and Jamaica's problems, would be solved. Loyal freedmen concluded that the Queen could not have been so hard-hearted as to approve such a document and chose instead to believe, incorrectly, that the Governor himself had written the "Reply." Moreover, unscrupulous agitators claimed that a phrase in the "Reply" about working "steadily and continuously" in reality meant that the Governor was planning to reintroduce slavery.

Gordon made the most of the furor. He traveled constantly through the island, speaking, and issuing broadsides, which the Governor promptly suppressed. In his speeches and writings he seemed to be genuinely revolutionary, referring to the near future when all white men would be gone from Jamaica, and admonishing the freedmen to "do what Haiti does." To his friends he said that he was only talking, that he had no intention of fomenting a rebellion, and that he meant only to "make a demonstration of it."

But the Governor and the Jamaican oligarchy could not know of Gordon's intentions, and they also realized that while Gordon might understand the distinction between a rebellion and a "demonstration of it," his less sophisticated audiences might not. White men in the

West Indies were always nervously conscious that they were a small, pale island in a sea of black. There had been a slave rebellion in Jamaica as recently as 1831, and the specter of revolts and massacres in the nearby black Republic of Haiti was always before them. In fact, Haiti was at that moment undergoing another of its bloody civil wars. Additionally, the Indian Mutiny, which engendered racial suspicion and distrust throughout the empire, was only seven years in the past. If the black majority of the island was being excited in racial terms, it was only natural that the whites should respond in kind.

It was in this atmosphere that James Geoghagan shouted his objection in the court of Petty Sessions at Morant Bay on Saturday, October 7, 1865. Saturday was market day and the court was full. Geoghagan was cited for contempt, resisted arrest, and was rescued from two constables by bystanders led by Paul Bogle. Bogle was a Native Baptist deacon, and a close associate of George William Gordon, who soon was to show that he did not grasp the difference between rebellion and a demonstration of it. The triumphant mob retired five miles away to Bogle's new chapel at Stony Gut. Three days later they overpowered eight black policemen who had been sent to apprehend Geoghagan and Bogle; they persuaded the policemen to "cleave to the black," and to stop doing the white man's dirty work.

The Custos, or senior Justice of the Peace, at Morant Bay was Baron von Ketelhodt, and he was warned that Bogle planned to bring several hundred men to town the next day. Von Ketelhodt ordered out the volunteers and called upon his friend, the Governor, for help. Eyre dispatched 100 troops on board H.M.S. *Wolverine* to Morant Bay.

On Wednesday, October 11, Bogle and 400 men arrived at Morant Bay, raided the police station for arms, and threw stones at the 27 ill-trained black and colored members of the Volunteers who were arrayed before the courthouse. Amid a thickening hail of projectiles von Ketelhodt read the Riot Act and the unnerved militia opened fire, killing seven rioters. But the Volunteers fired all at once, and while they were reloading, Bogle's men overpowered them. The courthouse was besieged and finally burned; its occupants were either clubbed, hacked, or burned to death. Bogle killed von Ketelhodt personally. Thereafter Bogle and his men freed the 51 prisoners in the jail and retired to Stony Gut, where the militant deacon held a service of Thanksgiving to celebrate his success.

The next day, with an enlarged following, Bogle began raiding throughout the eastern part of the colony, and refugees carried harrowing tales of ferocity, murder, and destruction to Kingston and the colonial capital at Spanish Town. Governor Eyre's response was neither weak nor vacillating. He acted promptly and decisively according to the information at his disposal. Considering the uneasy atmosphere of the island, he feared that a savage race war was erupting, so he declared martial law over the whole county of Surrey, sent all available troops to the area and went to Morant Bay himself. His quick and firm actions were appropriate and very commendable, if in fact a full-scale rebellion were in the offing.

The soldiers were joined by Maroons, descendants of runaway Spanish slaves who lived independently in the fastnesses of the Blue Mountains. They all seemed to regard the suppression as a sporting event, and any black they encountered was flogged, hanged, or shot. In all, 439 "rebels" were killed, either in skirmishes or by execution, 600 were flogged, and 1,000 dwellings were burned. Bogle was caught, court-martialed, and hanged.

Then Governor Eyre apprehended Gordon, whom he considered to be the "chief instigator" of the rebellion. Ill from bronchitis and dysentery, Gordon was in Kingston, quietly issuing propaganda leaflets. He surrendered voluntarily and was taken from Kingston, where martial law was not in effect, to Morant Bay, where it was. There he was court-martialed, and hanged from a yardarm of H.M.S. *Wolverine*. The Governor was determined that Jamaica should not be another Haiti.

Both in Jamaica and Whitehall the brief fury at Morant Bay was interpreted as proof of the failure of Jamaica's colonial institutions, and the rising produced a sharp break in British policy toward all of her Caribbean colonies. Earlier, in the midst of his conflict with the Assembly, Governor Eyre had suggested to his superiors that the troublesome and inefficient representative constitution be revoked. As befitted an executive agency of the British government, however, the Colonial Office had regarded the colonial legislature with the respect due to its two centuries of existence, and had declined the Governor's proposal. But after Morant Bay, the Colonial Office concluded that West Indian government must be taken out of the control of creole planters and merchants, whose selfish policies had provoked a rebellion in Jamaica. The West Indian legislatures could not be mended; they must be ended.

This new attitude coincided with a frightened desire on the part of the Jamaican ruling class itself for strong government, and a sense that only England could solve Jamaica's problems and save her from the dangers posed by popular demagogues. Governor Eyre had now become the hero of the Jamaican oligarchy, who saw him as the savior of the colony. At his suggestion, the Assembly abolished Jamaica's 200-year-old constitution and asked the Queen to provide a new government for the colony. Soon the Colonial Office instructed other West Indian governors to follow the example of Governor Eyre. Within ten years the oligarchies in all but two British West Indian islands had relinquished their representative institutions, and, with them, local control over colonial affairs.

Morant Bay marked a critical divergence on the part of the West Indian colonies from the course followed in the newer English settlement colonies in Canada, Australasia, and South Africa. There, the settlers were gaining more and more control over local government as, one after another, the colonies attained cabinet government. But the West Indian colonies became Crown Colonies, where governors ruled with the assistance of appointed councils. There were no longer any elected legislatures. Once established, the pattern remained fixed in its essentials for more than 70 years.

The policies and purposes of the new Crown Colony governments were not exactly what the West Indian oligarchies had desired. True, they and their interests were to be protected, but the well-being of the freedmen, well-being that had been so callously ignored, was to be protected too. The new policy was trusteeship, for all segments of the community, white and nonwhite, rich and poor. On the whole, the new governments worked very well for several decades, and they constituted a pattern and a philosophy which could be applied to other nonwhite areas, in Africa, at the end of the century.

Initially Colonial Secretary Cardwell praised Governor Eyre for his success in dealing with the rebellion. Other Englishmen saw the matter differently, however, and soon they were in full cry after the allegedly brutal and tyrannical Jamaican Governor. The first news to reach England in November emphasized not the 28 men, women, and children killed by Bogle's followers, but rather the ferocious repression of the rebels. As one newspaper headlined, there were "eight miles of dead bodies." By December huge delegations were overwhelming the Colonial Office with demands, not for an impartial investigation, but for the head of Governor Eyre. He was damned as a wholesale murderer who must be dismissed and punished. This pressure came from a group called "Exeter Hall," so named after their headquarters near the Strand in London.

Exeter Hall was one significant part of the more general humanitarian movement which imprinted its goals deeply on all facets of 19th-century English society. English humanitarianism itself was rooted in the evangelical revival of the late 18th century, and took its inspiration from Christ's injunction that each man be his brother's keeper. The fraternal solicitude of the humanitarians had done much already to ameliorate brutality and suffering in English society. They had been the major force behind the reform of England's prisons and laws in the 1820s and the passage of the Factory Acts of the 1830s and 1840s.

Exeter Hall, more particularly, was composed of non-Anglican religious sects and various philanthropic and missionary societies. The groups were bound together by their concern for the welfare, as they understood it, of the nonwhite peoples of the empire. Monuments to their successes in the past were the abolition of the slave trade and

Emancipation itself, and the sons of men who had achieved those gains were still active in the movement. Exeter Hall had infiltrated the Colonial Office in the 1840s and had left a strong impression on British policies in New Zealand and South Africa, and its members, especially the Baptists among them, felt a particular concern for black Christians in Jamaica.

Before the year 1865 was out, a "Jamaica Committee" had been formed to unite for action all men who opposed Governor Eyre. The first chairman of the Committee was Charles Buxton, Member of Parliament, and son of Thomas Fowell Buxton, the famous antislavery leader. The Committee included 18 other M.P.'s. Foremost among these was John Bright, leader of the Anti-Corn Law League of the 1840s and the major advocate of democracy in the 1860s. England's leading philosopher and civil libertarian, John Stuart Mill, had just won a seat in July on a platform calling for universal manhood suffrage. Another democrat and new M.P. was Thomas Hughes, author of *Tom Brown's School Days*, who was also interested in trade unionism and Christian Socialism. Other M.P.'s were carpet manufacturers, hosiers, and contractors, all closely involved with humanitarian and missionary movements of the time. Thirty-two members of the Committee were nonconformist clergymen, some were journalists, and others were university dons. Most of the original 300 members of the Committee came from the developing industrial north and hence were representative of the new urban England of business and manufacturing rather than of the old England whose strength was derived from agriculture.

Responding to their pressure, the Colonial Office began an investigation into the Morant Bay disturbance. Royal Commissioners took evidence in Jamaica from late January through late March of 1866. The several volumes of their Report, including the testimony of 730 witnesses, were published in June. On the whole, the Commissioners seemed to exculpate the Governor. They praised the "skill, promptitude and vigour" with which he had acted against what they concluded was a genuine danger to the colony. Had the initial rising been more successful, they believed, the insurrection undoubtedly would have spread throughout the whole island. The Report, however, condemned rigorously the savage repression of the disturbance and stated that martial law had been in effect too long. In reality, this constituted a reprimand of Eyre. His career was severely damaged, if not ended.

The more extreme members of the Jamaica Committee were not satisfied, and they launched a campaign of vengeance against Eyre. They now determined to bring the criminal Governor to trial for murder. The campaign was fought in Parliament against the new Tory ministry of Lord Derby and in the streets of Britain's cities. Soon it was joined closely with the growing movement for parliamentary reform. Leading exponents of broadening the suffrage, like Bright, Mill, and Hughes, again roused to action the English workingmen, who had been quiescent politically since the Chartist agitation of the 1840s. They would wield the threat of revolution to persuade England's oligarchy to accept a further installment on democracy. It was to be 1832 all over again. Monster gatherings assembled in Trafalgar Square, presented themselves before Tory houses and clubs shouting impolite and threatening jibes at Tory ministers. Finally, on July 23, 1866, a mob broke through the railings and gates of Hyde Park to hold a meeting that had been prohibited. The police reacted strongly, and many workingmen had to be hospitalized. They, and their reform leaders, saw only too clearly the similarity between police truncheons at home and Governor Eyre's guns, nooses, and whips in Jamaica.

Other sections of English society also drew the analogy, but from a different standpoint. To them, a black rabble killing local officials in the colony of Jamaica, and a lower class mob defying constituted authority in the imperial capital itself, seemed to be very much the same thing. Each threatened the very foundations of the established order. They saw, too, the similarity betweeen Hyde Park, Morant Bay, some extremely violent trade union activity occurring in the Midlands, and the outrages being committed by Fenians in their fight to liberate neighboring Ireland from British rule.

Governor Eyre, then, was not without his champions. Relieved of his post, he left the colony on the day following the Hyde Park riot, carrying with him an address of support and sympathy signed by 1,200 Jamaicans. On his arrival at Southampton in mid-August 1866, he was presented with yet another memorial address and invited to a dinner to be held in his honor. One hundred men dined with the disgraced Governor, including the Earl of Cardigan, commander of the Light Brigade in the Crimea who had a reputation as a flogger of troops. During the proceedings anti-Eyre forces demonstrated outside the hall against the "Banquet of Death."

The Southampton banquet roused radical newspapers and workingmen to new heights of vituperation and action. Eyre, now identified in the popular mind with Tory authoritarianism, was burned in effigy by incensed workingmen. This moved his sympathizers to respond, and by the end of August an Eyre Defence Committee was soliciting money for the Governor should he be prosecuted. Thomas Carlyle, historian and celebrator of the Hero in history, presided at the first meeting, and John Ruskin, England's most famous art and literary critic, became the first chairman of the Committee. Eventually, more than 30.000 persons contributed to the Eyre Defence Fund. Among them were 71 peers, 6 bishops, 20 M.P.'s, 40 generals, 26 admirals, and several hundred Church of England clergymen. The Eyre Defence Committee was as much the voice of the old landed conservative England as the Jamaica

Committee, which claimed 800 members by the end of 1867, was the spokesman for the new urban and business-oriented England.

All over the country, Englishmen addressed themselves earnestly to the moral issues of the case. The nation's men of letters and scientists split badly over Governor Eyre and Jamaica. Carlyle, Ruskin, Charles Dickens, Charles Kingsley, and John Tyndall, a science popularizer, endorsed Eyre. To them he stood as an heroic guardian of civilized order who had baffled the powers of barbarism and chaos. Mill, Hughes, Charles Darwin, and his disciple Thomas Huxley, the geologist Charles Lyell, and the historian Goldwin Smith supported the Jamaica Committee's charge that Eyre had arrogantly and callously murdered 439 Jamaican blacks.

In 1867 the "Jamaica Prosecutions" began. First, two military officers, and then the Governor himself were accused by the Jamaica Committee. Leading in the preparation of the cases for the Committee was James Fitzjames Stephen, grandson of an antislavery campaigner and son of a Colonial Office undersecretary who had been notable for his concern about fair treatment of blacks in the empire. Paralleling the trials were new Fenian outrages and further street demonstrations for parliamentary reform. Early in 1867 Colonel A. A. Nelson and Lieutenant Herbert Brand were brought before a London Grand Jury but were not indicted. Governor Eyre was living near Wales in Shropshire, where law was still dispensed by Justices of the Peace. Attempts to persuade these landed gentlemen to bring in an indictment against the Governor failed, even though two of them had disqualified themselves because they had contributed to the Eyre Defence Fund. Eyre's lawyer in this instance was Hardinge Stanley Giffard, later Lord Chancellor and, as Lord Halsbury, the leader of the "die-hard" faction in the House of Lords constitutional crisis in 1910.

Eyre had been persuaded not to go to London to testify in defense of Nelson and Brand. In 1868, however, he moved from the rural conservatism of Shropshire to London, pointedly announcing his arrival to the Jamaica Committee. The Committee brought a charge of High Crimes and Misdemeanors before the Grand Jury of Queen's Bench, but again the court failed to bring in an indictment. The Jamaica Committee had lost.

Throughout the excitement, Eyre conducted himself with the dignity and self-possession befitting a Victorian gentleman and servant of the Crown. In Jamaica he had refrained from joining in the unseemly crowing over the retribution meted out to the freedmen. At the Southampton banquet, where the Earl of Cardigan had permitted himself to indulge in extremes of abuse, Eyre had been calm and reasonable. During the prosecutions he was a controlled and cooperative defendant. But he, too, had lost, for his career was over and his good name destroyed.

In the eyes of many of his fellow countrymen, he stood condemned as a man of cruelty and blood.

After the Liberal Party victory in the election of 1868, at least four members of the Jamaica Committee found places in the new administration. This put an end to any hope that Eyre might have had of receiving another colonial appointment. Although some £16,000 had been raised on his behalf, the government did finally agree to pay the legal expenses of their ex-servant, and in 1874 a new Conservative administration awarded him a pension. Thereafter, Edward John Eyre, for three years at the storm center of English public life, withdrew into seclusion. He lived on for 30 years, unemployed and in complete retirement, until he died in 1901 during another major colonial disturbance, the Boer War.

Aside from a small flurry of rhetoric over the question of Eyre's trial expenses in 1872, the excitement of the Eyre case died down after 1868. Yet the case of Edward John Eyre had raised fundamental questions about the nature of the British polity and Britain's stance in the world.

It elicited a landmark opinion on martial law. Eyre, it will be remembered, had declared martial law over the county of Surrey, excepting Kingston; it had remained in effect for the full statutory 30 days, that is, for two weeks after the rebellion clearly was over. In England the issue focused on two officers who sat on the Morant Bay court martials, Colonel Nelson and Lieutenant Brand, who were charged with murder. On this point the Jamaica Committee was firmly in the English tradition of civil liberties. They held that rebels must risk being killed while fighting, but if captured, they must be tried according to civil law, not in military courts. Citing the Petition of Right and Bill of Rights of the 17th century, they held that, in the English legal system, martial law could never apply to civilians in peacetime. They insisted that even in the colonies England's free institutions should not be liable to suspension by a governor. Further, raising the same question that was to pervade the Nuremberg and My Lai trials in the next century, they held that officers serving on such illegal courts were personally responsible for their crimes. They could not justify themselves by pleading that they were merely following orders. They were still murderers, and so also were the men who ordered them to conduct the illegal trials. British rule in a colony should be the rule of law, they maintained, as British rule was in England itself, and no man, whatever his color, should be subject to indefinite powers claimed by the executive. The Morant Bay court martials were an especially dangerous precedent, for there men had been killed not because they were guilty of crimes, but in order to discourage others. This amounted to administrative terrorism. No ruler is ever justified in exercising such power over another man. If such proceedings were judged permissible in the colonies at present, they might be allowed in Ireland next, and in England herself thereafter.

These arguments were unanswerable, or so concluded the Lord Chief Justice of England, Sir Alexander Cockburn. Cockburn was a flamboyant man in a conservative profession and soon was to be famous for his temper tantrums in the *Alabama* arbitration court and for delivering a charge that lasted 18 days and filled 1,800 printed pages. An able constitutional lawyer, he upheld the Jamaica Committee's position fully in his charge to the grand jury.

A large segment of the British public, however, particularly the propertied classes, declined to see any relationship between court martials of black freedmen in Jamaica and the rights of white Englishmen at home. Instead, they felt that the Jamaican authorities were upholding British law and the constitution before the attacks of threatening savage mobs. Besides, many men asked, how could Britain keep order in the colonies, and in Ireland, if her agents were hampered and restrained by Cockburn's interpretation of martial law? Reflecting this point of view, the jury refused to indict the two officers. Actions were permissible in a colony, apparently, that were not acceptable in England.

The Eyre case obliged men to examine their first political principles. For some, like Carlyle, who had been examining his all his life, this was easy, but others, like Alfred Tennyson, arrived at conclusions about Governor Eyre and what he represented only with great difficulty. The Eyre case also caused men to reveal their intellectual inconsistencies. Social Darwinists, apostles of the survival of the fittest, ranged themselves on the side that would protect the weak, while many supposedly sentimental poets and writers took the side that would exalt might over right. Moreover, running through the entire Eyre controversy was a dualism which stood out plainly in the arguments advanced by his critics and his advocates.

The arguments of the anti-Eyre contingent were quite straightforward. They were based on the concept of the unquestioned primacy of law, the equality of all men before law, and the belief that there must be no division between private and public morality. Mill insisted that the principle of government by law must never be sacrificed to arbitrary power, whatever the circumstances. Goldwin Smith pleaded that no excuse of necessity could ever justify the destruction of morality by force. Huxley maintained that colonial governors had no more right to kill than anyone else had. These men insisted, in essence, that the principles of Western Christian law were universals and that Englishmen, wherever they were and whatever the circumstances must always be accountable to them. The question was, as Buxton put it in the House of Commons: do Englishmen, does the English government, approve atrocities, or not?

Many members of the Jamaica Commitee were opposed to the very existence of the empire on the grounds that it was an unprofitable burden on England. Undoubtedly this attitude influenced their views of any colonial governor. Not all men who condemned Eyre were anti-imperial, however. Buxton, for example, stated that one could keep a colony without continuing to be cruel after putting down a rebellion. Others, men like E. G. Wakefield, colonial reformer and founder of the colony of New Zealand, took the position that the best way to keep an empire was to establish a reputation for just and fair rule. Justice for nonwhites in the colonies was in the best interest of maintaining the empire.

In Thomas Carlyle, Governor Eyre had Britain's leading philosopher on his side. Carlyle's thought was based on a gospel of inequality, power and order. Reared a Scottish Presbyterian, he believed deeply in the doctrine of work, and somehow managed to transform the Calvinist concept of the elect into worship of the Hero, the strong man who would crush anarchy and maintain order in a tumultuous, selfish, and violent world. Carlyle also felt a profound contempt for all nonwhite peoples. His views were buttressed by John Ruskin's contention that the major villains in England were not arbitrary colonial governors, but British capitalists who, for their own selfish profit, had brought a new slavery to English workingmen. It was, he maintained, hypocritical of them to oppress Englishmen and to oppose Factory Acts at home while condemning an English governor for keeping the peace abroad.

Other defenders of Eyre were more specific. They chastised philanthropists who, from the comfort and safety of their armchairs, dared to sit in judgment of their compatriots who were risking health and life working for England in dangerous conditions abroad. It was argued that it was proper to kill in order to protect one's possessions, in this case, a colony. Tennyson believed that the needs of empire must outweigh humanitarian considerations. The scientist John Tyndall contended that firm action saves more lives than it takes, that if Eyre had not acted sternly, even more lives would have been lost. "Philanthropists can unconsciously become shedders of blood," he noted ironically. Very practically, Under Secretary of State for the Colonies Charles Adderley warned the House of Commons that if Eyre were punished it would be virtually impossible to recruit men to undertake the "fearful responsibility" of governing the colonies.

Above all, Eyre's champions spoke for order over anarchy. Most of the English governing classes had always been very suspicious of their own countrymen. The English lower classes were regarded as undisciplined, lazy, and profligate. They were not naturally bad, but they somehow had been debased over the centuries. Like potentially destructive children they needed to be kept in order by force if necessary, whether it be in St. Peter's Fields in 1819 or in Hyde Park in 1866. The English upper and middle classes were surrounded, it seemed, by threats of anarchy in the 1860s. Most of them knew that the Irish were even more unreliable than the English lower orders, and the Indian Mutiny, countless colonial wars, current fighting against the Maori in New Zealand, and now Morant Bay convinced them that nonwhite peoples were the most untrustworthy and savage of all. It was the duty of England to use her authority and her might to stem the tide of chaos.

Lastly, Eyre's defenders utilized a simple personal appeal. Charging the grand jury in Eyre's hearing on the charge of High Crimes and Misdemeanors, Mr. Justice Colin Blackburn asked the jurors to imagine themselves in Eyre's position. As head of the colony of Jamaica his prime obligation was to maintain law and order; this was the first obligation of any government. It was his responsibility both as steward for the English Crown and nation, and as a ruler entrusted with the care and government of the colonial population itself. The volatile and gullible people of the island were in an uneasy ferment, crediting lying rumors and attending mass protest meetings. They were heeding a false prophet, George William Gordon, who was setting black against white. Local officials, his closest friend among them, had been defied and then brutally murdered. A body of armed men attacked the militia and burned a courthouse. All of the evidence before him seemed to point to the outbreak of a fearsome racial war of thousands of blacks against a handful of whites. Undoubtedly, personal considerations entered in, too. Earlier, the press had condemned him for being vacillating. He had already made one error in judgment which might now be retrieved. His friend was involved. In this situation what was his duty as Governor of the Colony?

Perhaps more than anyone else, Thomas Huxley understood what was involved in Eyre's action, and the fundamental implications and significance of the entire Eyre case. In November of 1866 he wrote his friend Charles Kingsley that concern about Eyre could cause "a great many people to find out what their deepest political beliefs are." Huxley was a member of the Jamaica Committee, but a great many good men, men of conscience, were on the other side. Charles Kingsley contributed to the Eyre Defence Fund. Each man who committed himself to the Eyre controversy, no matter which side he supported, was forced to inquire into what his deepest political beliefs were.

SUGGESTED READINGS

Twentieth-century writers have differed sharply in their assessments of Governor Eyre and Morant Bay. Geoffrey Dutton is generally sympathetic to Eyre in *The Hero as Murderer* (London: Collins, 1967). The Fabian ex-Governor of Jamaica, Lord Olivier, pleads the cause of the Jamaica Committee in *The Myth of Governor Eyre* (London: Hogarth Press, 1933), while

William Law Mathieson assumes a Carlylean stance in *The Sugar Colonies and Governor Eyre, 1849–1866* (London: Longmans, 1936). In *Two Jamaicas* (Cambridge, Mass.: Harvard University Press, 1955) Philip Curtin is less critical of the Governor than Olivier, but his work is still anti-Eyre. The most balanced account may be found in Bernard Semmel's *The Governor Eyre Controversy* (London: MacGibbon & Kee, 1962); this book also contains the most complete discussion of the controversy in England. Contemporary accounts are highly partisan. A. H. Hume's *The Life of Edward John Eyre, late Governor of Jamaica* (London: R. Bentley, 1867) and W. F. Finlason's *The History of the Jamaica Case* (London: Chapman & Hall, 1869) are hagiographic. George Price's *Jamaica and the Colonial Office: Who Caused the Crisis?* (London: The author, 1866) is damning.

Courtesy of Sir Geoffrey Harmsworth

Chapter 13

NORTHCLIFFE:
Fleet Street and
the New Democracy

Aᴀғᴛᴇʀ the Reform Act of 1867 had doubled the number of voters in Britain, Robert Lowe, leader of the Whig opposition, observed sourly that the nation now must at least educate "our future masters." The Whig's challenge was accepted by W. E. Gladstone's first ministry, which sponsored W. E. Forster's Education Act in 1870. By 1891 schooling in Britain was compulsory and free for children from their 5th through their 13th years. The male illiteracy rate, which had stood at more than 20 percent in 1870, had been lowered to less than 2 percent in 1900.

No one had inquired, however, what the new schooled public would read. Largely urban, working in factories, in domestic service, clerking in stores and offices, and running households, their experiences and interests differed sharply from those of persons who had been educated at Harrow, Winchester, or even Wesleyan Sunday Schools. Until Alfred Harmsworth, later Viscount Northcliffe, entered publishing, British journalism had, with the exception of religious and self-help pamphlets and sensational "penny dreadfuls," failed to tap the new market extensively. It was the genius of Harmsworth that he sensed the potential of the new mass market and created for it the popular British press. Before the development of radio and television, the press was the major medium for informing, entertaining, and influencing the new mass man of the 20th century. With such a wide audience at his command, Viscount Northcliffe also represented a new kind of political force in Britain. The mass media might be utilized in an attempt to manipulate the minds of British citizens, and this possibility raised novel and critical questions about the nature and workings of 20th-century democracy.

Although Alfred Harmsworth was perhaps intellectually and temperamentally akin to the people who were to buy his papers, his background was somewhat different. When Alfred's father was in his cups, a not infrequent occurrence, he liked to boast that he was descended from kings, the royalty in question being Frederick, Duke of York and son of George III. Supposedly the Hanoverian prince was the sire of Hannah Carter, Alfred's grandmother, who married Charles Harmsworth. The connection was never established and probably had never existed. Charles and Hannah Harmsworth started a shop selling vegetables and then coal in northern London, and their eldest son, Alfred, was Northcliffe's father. He became a schoolteacher and encountered his future wife while he was teaching in a military school in Dublin. Although Northcliffe later was frequently to refer to his Celtic Irish blood, his mother, Geraldine Maffet, came from a staunch Presbyterian Scotch-Irish background. Her father was a well-to-do land agent, or estate manager, and the Maffets were superior socially to Geraldine's handsome young English suitor.

The new Mrs. Harmsworth had a forceful and dominating personality and persuaded her rather easygoing husband to study for the bar. Two years after their first child, Alfred, was born in 1865, the young family moved to London. There, more children appeared rapidly, until they totaled eight boys and three girls, while Alfred Senior worked desultorily and without profit at the law. Having been reared among many servants, Geraldine was a poor housekeeper, her husband was not a good provider, and the household existed perilously on the brink of poverty.

They lived in north London, a part of the metropolitan area that was rapidly changing under the joint pressures of increasing population and urbanization. Everywhere, the small villages, market towns, and fields that had ringed the capital were giving way to housing developments. Mostly ill-planned, hastily and poorly built, the new row houses and two-family dwellings represented an early indication of the suburban man of the next century. Clerking in the city, the product of recently introduced mass education, these new men of the lower middle classes traveled to and from work on the new subways and street railways. Northcliffe was to create something for them to read while they were commuting.

Alfred, descended from kings, and Geraldine, reared a gentlewoman, managed to maintain a precarious status above the clerks and manual laborers. Their sons were sent to cheap private schools nearby, but it was made clear to them that a rudimentary education was the only start in life that the hard-pressed parents could provide. Consonant with the high Victorian individualist ethic, the Harmsworths led their sons to expect nothing from the world save what they could earn through initiative, hard work, and self-help. In the case of the Harmsworth offspring, following these tenets produced extraordinary results. By the early 1920s the two eldest brothers had become Viscounts, another was a baron, and two others were baronets; their assets totaled at least £30 million.

Alfred, the eldest Harmsworth son, grew up to resemble in appearance a blond Nordic God. Of medium height, well-formed, with a square head, regular features, a fresh complexion and a lock of golden hair hanging over his forehead, he had naturally assumed positions of leadership in playroom and in school. He did not distinguish himself at his studies and was always troubled by arithmetic, but he read widely, could play the piano, excelled at sports, and started a school magazine.

Sixteen and one half years old when he left school, with no certain career before him, young Alfred dallied with the family parlor maid and soon she was pregnant. Providentially, a young clergyman advertised for a secretary-companion to accompany him on a Continental tour, and Alfred secured the job. The parlor maid bore a son, Alfred Benjamin, in November 1882.

After his return from the Continent in the fall of 1882, Alfred became independent, for his mother refused to allow her errant son to live at home. He took lodgings first with Herbert Ward, who later went with

Stanley to the Congo, and then with Max Pemberton, who became a lifelong friend. He set out to become a journalist and, by the time he was 18, he was earning £3 a week from free-lance writing. He also composed a waltz named after the actress Ellen Terry, served briefly as editor of a boy's paper, and became an enthusiastic bicyclist, making long cross-country endurance runs on the popular new vehicle.

Much as the automobile was to do later, the bicycle was beginning to modify radically the patterns and mores of English life. Invention of the "diamond" frame and the chain drive made possible the development of the "safety" bicycle which possessed wheels of equal size, and at the end of the 1880s pneumatic tires were to become common. As *The Times* noted prophetically, the new vehicle "augments at least threefold the locomotive power of an ordinary man." Urban young people, especially, who could not afford horses and who appreciated the convenience of a handy means of transportation that did not need to be fed, groomed, or stabled, found the bicycle a fascinating new machine. Cycling clubs, meets, and runs developed everywhere and, incidentally, gave new freedom to young women.

The center of the cycling industry was Coventry, whose population was almost doubled by the cycling boom. It was also the center of cycling literature: of catalogs, technical papers, and magazines which fed upon the new cult. Alfred had written some articles for cycling papers, and in April 1886, not yet 21, he became the editor of *Bicycling News*. With what soon became known as the Harmsworth touch, he revived the faltering circulation by brightening the articles and sparking controversy. The magazine thrived, but Coventry was dull, and within a year Alfred had returned to London. With some partners, including a barrister friend of his father, Edward Markwick, he launched a shoe-string publishing enterprise distributing self-help pamphlets, a professional magazine for private schoolmasters, and an American sporting magazine. Solvent, if not prospering, on April 11, 1888, he married Mary Milner, the daughter of a sugar importer; the ceremony was performed by the reverend Mr. Powys, the clergyman who had taken a disgraced Alfred to the Continent seven years before; Edward Markwick was best man.

Young Harmsworth had continued sending articles and features to journals, and determined to found his own. The field he wished to enter was dominated by vigorous, but tradition-bound patterns. All the major London and provincial daily newspapers of the 1880s were modeled on *The Times*. Costing a penny, they were formal and restrained in appearance and were directed at an audience that was primarily male and of the upper and middle classes. Most of the papers were family owned, and although they reported some business, sporting, and religious news, and even an occasional scandalous court case, they were primarily oriented toward politics. Each tended to champion the point of view of one political grouping or another and devoted column after column to speeches of the nation's leaders. The debates of Parliament were reported at length, verbatim. In format the papers made few concessions to catch the attention of the readers; the paragraphs were long and the headlines were few and stilted. In effect, the press delivered the news raw and undigested. Ordinarily, editors did not rewrite reports in order to emphasize and clarify salient points or to condense less important details. The proprietors of the papers held and advanced definite beliefs, but they prided themselves on exerting their influence responsibly and honestly. They set forth their opinions only in the leading articles, or editorials, and restricted the news articles to factual reporting. With the exception of a few cheap and sensational publications, the magazines were just as staid and formal as the daily press. Even the scandal-mongering of W. T. Stead did not disturb very much the dignified format of the *Pall Mall Gazette;* nor did he direct his exposés of prostitution toward the masses rather than the establishment.

The new reading public found little in the columns of the staid journals of the time to engage their attention and interest. To the extent that they read at all, they bought literature of the penny-dreadful variety, which contained lurid accounts of pirates, highwaymen, and murderers; or after 1880, they purchased a weekly paper, *Tit-Bits.* George Newness, a former traveling salesman and owner of a vegetarian restaurant, had started *Tit-Bits* as a hobby. It was essentially a scrapbook of short human-interest items. The words were simple, the sentences and paragraphs were short, and almost everything was presented as a story. It found a wide audience among the new readers whose horizons were narrow and who could follow print only with some effort. Newness also introduced the techniques of enticing readers with prize competitions and free insurance to increase the sales of his paper.

Alfred had met Newness in 1885 and had contributed some features to *Tit-Bits.* In 1888 he found a financial backer for his own venture in Alexander Beaumont, a retired Captain of the Royal Welsh Fusiliers who had married money, and *Answers To Correspondents,* later simply *Answers,* appeared. The initial format was roughed out over a copy of *Tit-Bits* and included some items clipped from the model. The stated purpose of *Answers* was to supply the responses of specialists to questions from readers, and its publisher stressed the presentation of what were described on the masthead as "Interesting," "Extraordinary," "Amusing" facts. Selling for one penny and printed on cream-colored paper, the first issue of June 2, 1888, told the public about such things as "What the Queen Eats," "How Madmen Write," "How to Cure Freckles," and "Horseflesh as Food."

Answers was, of course, supposed to be useful; an early issue promised:

We are a sort of Universal Information provider. Anybody who reads our paper for a year will be able to converse on many subjects on which he was entirely ignorant. He will have a good stock of anecdotes and jokes and will indeed be a pleasant companion.

Primarily, however, it aimed at providing entertainment for the superficially educated masses.

New publishing ventures appeared and failed quickly in the last two decades of the 19th century; some 200 came out in 1888 alone. For the first eight months Answers limped along. Circulation dropped from an initial 12,000 to 8,000, and then began to rise only slowly toward 20,000. Even though Alfred wrote or collected all the articles and jokes for the first issues himself, unpaid printer's bills mounted. His solution was publicity. Answers was given a glaring orange cover, it solicited orders for colored reproductions of famous works of art, it offered free insurance for persons killed in railway accidents with copies of Answers in their possession, it advertised Answers puzzles and Answers pens, and men with sandwich boards acclaiming the paper patrolled the streets.

Circulation began to climb, but very gradually, and then Alfred hit upon the idea that securely established the future of Answers and launched him on the way to wealth and power. Characteristic of the new journalism he was creating, his idea had nothing to do with the quality of the product, but dealt rather with the methods of promoting it. In the course of a conversation with a tramp on the Thames Embankment, he heard the derelict observe that if he had one pound each week for the rest of his life he would be happy. A man could live on that sum at the end of the 19th century, and Harmsworth immediately sensed its popular appeal. The next issue of Answers offered a pound a week for life to the person who came closest to guessing the exact amount of gold coinage in the banking department of the Bank of England at the conclusion of business on December 4, 1889.

Where Harmsworth had expected perhaps 5,000–6,000 entries, as many as previous contests had drawn, the Answers office was overwhelmed with more than 700,000 responses, seeking the free security offered by a pound a week for life. Ultimately 20 temporary clerks were hired to deal with the entries. Since each entry had to be countersigned by five witnesses, Harmsworth had publicized Answers to more than four million people. It had cost him only £1,100, the expense of an annuity paying one pound every week. The issue announcing the winner, a soldier who died eight years later of tuberculosis, sold 205,000 copies. Answers was a success.

Meanwhile, Alfred, the first prosperous Harmsworth, became in effect head of the family. He had a strong sense of familial responsibility and even while he had been in Coventry he had sent money to his brothers. His father sunk slowly into dipsomania and died of cirrhosis of the liver at age 52 in July of 1889. Alfred's brothers abandoned their jobs and sought their futures in association with him. Leicester resigned from the Internal Revenue Department and began organizing the sale of *Answers* in the north of England, Hildebrand joined the staff immediately after leaving school, and Cecil finished at Trinity College, Dublin, and then associated himself with his brother's enterprise. Most important was Harold, who was good at arithmetic. He left a secure job in the Civil Service to become Alfred's business manager. Ruthlessly cutting costs, he provided the necessary financial acumen that Alfred lacked. Indeed it was he, perhaps more than Alfred, who embodied the new commercial age of British journalism that was dawning. While Alfred always remained primarily a newspaperman, Harold was basically a financier and saw journalism mostly as a means of making money. As Lord Rothermere, he was to dominate the English press between the two world wars.

Alfred's mother, Geraldine, remained a dominant figure in his life. It was apparently part of his conception to himself that he was a loving and dutiful son, and he worked on building this image until it seemed almost an obsession. Perhaps he was trying in part to atone for his youthful escapade with the parlor maid. Naturally when the money started coming in he established Geraldine in surroundings of comfort and luxury she had not known even as the daughter of an Irish land agent. But more, he was in a continuous, frequently daily, communication with her throughout his life. His notes and telegrams were couched in embarrassingly adoring, even fawning tones; often he signed them "Your Firstborn." He consulted his mother on matters of taste and morality in his papers and on one occasion, at least, her views influenced the political stand of the entire Northcliffe press. During the controversy over Home Rule for Ireland before the First World War she insisted that she would "not have Ulster coerced," and her ultimatum brought Alfred's wavering papers solidly to the support of the Unionist party. It appears that Harmsworth continuously hungered after his mother's approbation. The matter of fact, dictatorial, and even cold and distant nature of her replies suggests that she never freely gave him the emotional security he was seeking so desperately. Indomitable and restrained, demanding yet impervious, the Harmsworth matriarch outlived her firstborn by three years.

From the profits of *Answers*, Harmsworth began building his press empire. Alfred and Harold formed a new publishing company and entered the field of the early illustrated comic papers. In the spring of 1890, in close succession, the Harmsworths introduced *Comic Cuts* and *Illustrated Chips*. Each sold for a half penny, in contrast to the penny price of their rivals. They were constituted mostly of jokes and puns, and *Chips* had crude line drawings. Although certainly not on an elevated intellectual level, they did not pander brutality, crime, and vice as most of the penny dreadfuls did. Immediately popular and profitable, they were, as Alfred stated on the masthead of *Chips,* "Amusing without Being Vulgar."

Harmsworth saw his publishing ventures as reinforcing each other. "Puffs," or free publicity, for *Chips* appeared in *Answers,* and *Chips* asked its readers to buy *Comic Cuts.* Further, Harmsworth, like entrepreneurs after him, saw no reason why he should not hold both first and second places. *Comic Cuts* and *Chips* were designed to forestall competition and to monopolize the field. They appealed not only to juveniles but also to adults who were not accustomed to reading. Harmsworth divined their interests and limitations intuitively. Line drawings became a series of pictures telling a story with a minimum of words and, in *Chips,* the comic strip was born.

Unlike *Answers,* both *Comic Cuts* and *Chips* sold well immediately and even penetrated to Westminster, where the Deputy Speaker of the House of Commons was spied one day reading *Comic Cuts* concealed in the "Orders of the Day" for the House. Beginning a story in one issue and continuing it to the next, an innovation for this kind of paper, ensured a continuing loyal readership. Soon both papers passed *Answers* in circulation; *Comic Cuts* was to be published for 60 years.

Steadily, the creation of new magazines built up the Harmsworth empire. A women's journal, *Forget-Me-Not,* appeared in November 1891, the illustrated *Funny Wonder* in July 1892, and *Home, Sweet Home,* a fiction magazine, in December 1892. *Halfpenny Marvel, Union Jack, Pluck Library,* and *Boy's Home Journal* enjoined English boys to be patriotic, adventurous, and physically fit, and *The Sunday Companion* purveyed uplifting reading for religious homes. Soon more than 13 periodicals bore the Harmsworth imprint. In 1894 the combined circulation of each issue of only nine of them reached almost two million copies.

After some difficulty and hard feelings, and some fast dealing on the part of Harold, Captain Beaumont was bought out, receiving an annuity of £2,400 a year for an original investment of only £2,000. Thereafter the profits were kept in the family. As early as 1893, when he was 28, Alfred had more than £100,000; workmen of the time reared families on less than fifty pounds a year. "Why, they're only boys!" remarked one shareholder at the annual meeting of Harmsworth Brothers.

Prosperity made possible a place in the country and travel to the Continent and to the United States. The responsibilities of his papers also tended to overtax Alfred's health. Despite his hale and rugged appearance, his constitution was frail and frequently he was ill. A case of rheumatic fever consequent on a bicycle run in cold rainy weather in the early 80s probably had damaged his heart permanently. His concern for his health developed into severe hypochondria, and often provided a convenient excuse for avoiding unpleasantness. Soon he became an absentee proprietor, staying away from his offices for days and weeks. He preferred to remain at Elmwood, a small country estate he and Mary purchased on the seacoast in 1890. There, surrounded by telephones, he slept late, rested on a sofa, read his periodicals, and dispatched detailed orders to his staff.

His wife Mary, however, hungered after the brilliance of high society, a house in London, and a country mansion. These he provided, but he was always a reluctant partner in her highly successful social ventures. They were childless, and already by the mid-1890s each was seeking companionship elsewhere.

Looking for new worlds to conquer, he entered politics in 1895 as a Unionist candidate for Portsmouth. He campaigned tirelessly, bought a local newspaper to advance his candidacy, and ran a serial story on the siege of Portsmouth in a modern war, but he tallied only third in the polls.

Before his defeat at Portsmouth he had entered a field that was to garner him more influence, power, and prestige than any member of Parliament from Portsmouth ever possessed. In August 1894 he and Harold purchased for £25,000 the *Evening News and Post,* a failing Conservative daily newspaper. Like the rest of the English press, *The Evening News* had not been affected by the new journalism being popularized in the United States by Joseph Pulitzer and William Randolph Hearst, but immediately the Harmsworth touch remodeled the stolid paper and transformed the £100 weekly deficit into a profit. Alfred introduced new type, a daily short story, a women's column that soon became a women's page, and contests; the solid makeup of the pages was broken with heavier headlines and shorter paragraphs. Within three years the new owners had recovered the purchase price from the paper's earnings.

The *Evening News* was a training and proving ground for the *Daily Mail,* the first modern British newspaper and the foundation of Harmsworth's enduring reputation as an innovative journalist and entrepreneur. Three months of intensive preparation went into the new paper. News and cable services were established; presses with a new paper-folding device were purchased. The most modern linotype machines were installed, of French and American make, because, as Alfred noted unhappily, they were superior to the British models. Beginning in February 1896 a staff began printing what finally totaled 65 experimental editions. Subeditors were trained to cut, rewrite, and enliven news dispatches. At length, after a barrage of publicity, the *Daily Mail* rolled off the presses on May 4, 1896, with accounts of war in Africa, assassination in the Middle East, concentration camps in Cuba, and the beginning of a serial, "Beauregard's Shadow." Alfred autographed the first copy and a messenger delivered it to his mother.

Eighty, or even 40, years later, readers accustomed to the excesses of the "yellow press" would find nothing in the first issues of the *Daily Mail* that was much different from the most prestigious and respectable dailies of their own decades. In 1896, however, its short paragraphs, its features, and its sprightly articles were revolutionary. Although Lord Salisbury scoffed that it was written by office boys for office boys, his sneer was not justified. Harmsworth designed the *Daily Mail* not just to entertain but also, even primarily, to instruct. Like *Answers*, it attracted the new readers who had never been persuaded to read much before, and it presented to them accounts of national and world affairs that they were not receiving from any other source. Harmsworth was the first publicist who succeeded in informing the new mass democracy of England daily about important events, issues, and problems of the world around them. He began finally the education of England's "future masters" to their role as citizens voting on problems of national import.

Perhaps the greatest transformation, however, embodied a change in the nature of the news that was presented. When subeditors predigested accounts for the readers, they could not help but distort them. As they followed Harmsworth's orders to "explain, simplify, clarify," and as they attempted to make the news interesting, they tended to emphasize the sensational rather than the pithy, and to highlight color more than content. Murders received more coverage than parliamentary debates, and fires and railway accidents were alloted more space than international issues. But this was one of the ingredients that made the *Daily Mail* such a success, for this was what caught the attention of the new readers most effectively. As one of Harmsworth's editors commented, it was unlikely that the English taste for public hangings and whippings had been erased by the "cheap schooling of a single generation."

Most significantly, as information became entertainment, point of view and opinion appeared in news articles as well as in the leading articles. The *Daily Mail* might serve the news to millions of new readers, but it did not necessarily purvey honestly all the facts that were necessary for mature and considered judgment on issues. At its birth, modern English journalism denied its readers the opportunity to arrive at rational decisions derived from neutral facts.

In contrast to most papers, the *Daily Mail* cost not a penny but a halfpenny. The first issue sold almost 400,000 copies, nearly as much as all the other penny papers combined. Steadily and surely the circulation reached and surpassed the million mark in only a few years. In newspapers, as in other enterprises, a high volume of sales indicated success.

Emphasis on high circulation, however, also endangered the freedom of newspaper proprietors, as it threatened to make them dependent on the wishes of the businessmen who sold their goods through the papers. With his usual keen insight, Harmsworth sensed the threat early, and the first issues of the *Daily Mail* promised its audience that their reading and entertainment would not be hampered by "the usual puzzling maze of advertisements." Yet, from the beginning, the Harmsworth periodicals had all publicized each other; *Answers* had sold pens, puzzles, and pictures; and notices selling tea, meat extract, soap, and patent medicines appeared in all the Harmsworth periodicals. Accordingly, Harmsworth sought always to increase the circulation of his papers; he publicized the number of copies sold, not the number printed, and insisted that other journals also announce honest "net sales." Nevertheless, his attitude toward advertising was always ambiguous. Advertising was in its infancy, but it, too, was to be a new powerful force in the 20th century, and while Harmsworth actively sought their money, he feared the potential power of advertisers. He knew that while he was building his press empire on high circulation and advertising revenues, he was making its well-being reliant on them. To the end of his life he fought with his business departments, trying to keep advertising in its place. His successors, including his brother Harold, tended to see the press first of all as a means of making money; having fewer scruples, they placed the English press in the thrall of the advertisers.

Proprietorship of the *Daily Mail* elevated Harmsworth to a position of national prestige and influence. By 1901 his annual income was nearly £150,000 and his net capital worth exceeded £900,000. He had been invited to join the most exclusive West End clubs, he knew Sir Arthur Sullivan, Sarah Bernhardt, and the Dukes of Edinburgh and Abercorn, and he entertained the Asquiths, Austen Chamberlain, and the future Lord Curzon. His house in Berkeley Square, not far from the mansion Robert Clive had leased 150 years earlier, adjoined the house of Lord Rosebery and occasionally the peer and the newspaperman took morning walks together. He began patronizing writers and poets such as A. Conan Doyle, W. E. Henley, Max Beerbohm, and Rudyard Kipling. In June 1897, a Paris restaurateur and his staff were hired to prepare a dinner honoring the Colonial Premiers who were attending a conference during the celebration of Queen Victoria's Diamond Jubilee. On that occasion, Paderewski played the piano and Dame Nellie Melba sang before Members of Parliament, foreign princesses, and the cream of London Society. Someone commented that Harmsworth's nose was "just like Napoleon's" and he might have been conscious of a parallel to the French Emperor. He began collecting Napoleonic engravings, busts, and books and, once on trying on Napoleon's hat at Fontainebleau, exclaimed, "It fits!"

Harmsworth's power arose, naturally, out of his new wealth but, as was generally believed, it stemmed mostly from the fact that his publications were the only ones that millions of Englishmen read. It was assumed that, since he had awakened and was continually nourishing popular interest in public affairs, his press could mold that concern to any ends he desired. As W. L. George commented in his biographical novel about Northcliffe, the new public lived in suburban houses that were all alike and had gardens that were all alike; therefore, their tastes and desires must be all alike: it was "a monstrous sort of public with staring eyes and a great, loose mouth, and no brain . . . that could be pleased . . . that would crow like babies if only you shook the right rattle."

He held, it seemed, an awesome power, one which was manifested first at the very end of the century. Northcliffe understood clearly that interesting and exciting news produced sales, and sensed just as distinctly that war and imperialism were two subjects that were particularly thrilling. The South African War, beginning in 1899, contained just the right ingredients for popular exploitation. *Daily Mail* correspondents in the Transvaal cabled sensational accounts of the campaigns, the paper blossomed with maps, pictures, and black headlines, and special *Daily Mail* "war trains" carried editions to the north of Britain. A new printing press and office was established at Manchester, connected with London by telephone lines. By 1900, through inciting and manipulating the demand for war news, the *Daily Mail* had become Britain's first genuinely national newspaper and was read simultaneously in Southampton and in Edinburgh. It could help form and represent, for the first time, a truly national public opinion. Throughout Britain, the *Daily Mail* drummed up interest in and support for the government's war policy, support which helped to produce the Conservative Party victory at the polls in 1900.

Rapidly, he extended and consolidated his holdings. Provincial newspapers fell into Harmsworth's hands; he started the *Mirror*, an illustrated paper which became the first of the tabloids; he purchased the prestigious *Observer*; in 1905 he brought out a Paris edition of the *Daily Mail*; and all his periodicals were incorporated into The Amalgamated Press. The new company was capitalized at £1,600,000 and earned profits of £255,000 in its first year. The Harmsworth presses produced a children's encyclopedia, a series of self-education pamphlets, and booklets commemorating royal deaths, marriages, and coronations. He purchased thousands of acres of forest in Newfoundland and erected a pulp mill to provide his presses with abundant cheap newsprint. Young aspiring politicians like Winston Churchill asked that the *Daily Mail* award favorable coverage to their speeches, society hostesses requested that the *Daily Mail* support their favorite charities, and cabinet members conferred with the new press magnate. Grateful and apprehensive governments named Harmsworth Baronet, then elevated him to the peerage as Baron and, finally, Viscount Northcliffe.

Nevertheless, Northcliffe really did not want to wield political power directly. He was principally a journalist and he wanted principally to make his papers the best in the world. He was able to do just that because the wellsprings of his character were really more similar to those of the English masses than of the governing classes. His interests and prejudices were essentially the same as the interests and prejudices of the readers he sought to beguile, and he had an almost uncanny sense of what would catch the popular fancy, for what was the "coming thing." His press provided entertainment; and news, even news of war and threats of war, did not have enough entertainment. Accordingly, his papers presented serial stories, women's sections, and prize competitions. The *Daily Mail* sponsored a polar expedition, offered prizes for long-distance airplane flights, publicized and popularized the game of golf, and stirred up controversies in its columns about women's beach wear and dancing clergymen. His papers were undignified, but they informed, entertained, and sold.

The best newspaper in England, however, was *The Times*. With a long tradition of responsible reporting and comment, it instructed and advised the business and governing classes about their world. It had not adopted the new journalistic techniques that Northcliffe employed and, while it was everywhere respected, it was not widely purchased and was losing money. In 1908, when Northcliffe, the purveyor of comic strips and dancing curates, purchased a controlling interest in *The Times*, conservative England reacted with shock and dismay. Yet, Northcliffe regarded his new possession with the same respect and near awe as they did, and his proprietorship of *The Times* showed another side of his character. Realistically, he understood that national institutions such as the monarchy, or Westminster Abbey, or *The Times* could survive only if they were supported. Carefully, with sensitivity and finesse, he set about ushering the venerable journal into the 20th century. Bit by bit, overcoming opposition that argued from decades of tradition, he introduced typewriters, installed new presses, improved the wire services, and shortened the articles. Gradually, the modifications took effect and in a few years *The Times* turned a profit. It was still the best, most responsible, and informative newspaper in Britain, and Northcliffe had ensured its future by enabling it to support itself financially. He was justifiably proud of his achievement and regarded himself as a steward of *The Times* on behalf of the people of Britain. This was reflected in a will which he dictated before the Great War, which bequeathed his share of *The Times* to the nation and proposed a board of trustees which would include the Archbishop of Canterbury, the Speaker of the House of Commons, and the Lord Chancellor.

Although Northcliffe moved among the most important men in Britain in the years before the war, his tastes remained simple. He enjoyed the power and the convenience that money provided, but he made no attempt to ape the life of the English aristocracy. At the wish of Lady Northcliffe he leased Sutton Place, a Tudor country estate later owned by the American oil millionaire J. Paul Getty, and he occasionally entertained there, but he preferred their first country home, the more modest Elmwood. There, sunken in the garden, was a lifeboat from the Arctic expedition he had sponsored, and in the hall stood a stuffed polar bear. Once, when Mary redecorated the house, he commanded that everything be changed back to what it had been in 1890 when they purchased it.

In many ways he retained what several of his biographers have described as a boyish quality: he was interested in everything and jumped from one enthusiasm to another; he liked tricks and practical jokes, even if they were a bit cruel; he fancied new mechanical things, such as airplanes and Rolls-Royces. Like his readers, he did not have an extensive formal education; he did not know Latin or Greek, any modern foreign language, or much history. Undoubtedly it was the partly adolescent quality of his mind, and the wide, if superficial, range of his interests that made him such a successful newspaperman. He had the same kind of intellectual interests and limitations as the crowd which purchased his papers.

Although he insisted that nothing of questionable taste appear in any of his journals, both he and Lady Northcliffe seem to have shared the sexual mores of a society headed by King Edward VII. Most of the time they lived apart and pursued their own inclinations. He had at least one mistress of long standing, a mysterious Mrs. Wrohan, and three more illegitimate children appeared; his son by his mother's parlor maid worked briefly for his papers and died finally of alcoholism in an Australian insane asylum.

Northcliffe's interest in the "coming thing" placed him in the vanguard of social forces that were transforming Britain. From the beginning he employed women in positions of responsibility in his offices. He endorsed women's suffrage, and his newspapers, with their large women's sections, drew women for the first time into the newspaper audience. He paid high wages, encouraged professional journalist's organizations, and, after the First World War, placed all his workers on a five-day week. His newspapers also created new appetites among the English working classes. Bombarded with advertisements for desirable goods, they were made aware constantly of the existence of a better material life. By contributing to the build-up of such pressures and discontents, Northcliffe inadvertently helped to bring about far-reaching changes in the distribution of wealth of Britain.

On the eve of the Great War, Northcliffe's Amalgamated Press published one half of all the newspapers and periodicals sold in the British Isles. Later in the century, such communications networks were to be used as media of propaganda to advance and sustain political movements and parties, and at the time politicians and political commentators feared Northcliffe's power. Yet, Northcliffe neither sought to rule the United Kingdom himself nor to champion any single party platform, political philosophy, or national leader. Moreover, what political beliefs he held derived not from extensive study or wide reading, but from emotion and instinct. At the very base of his outlook lay a fundamentalist British patriotism, and in this he was one with most of his readers. He judged issues by the simplest criteria: did he feel that a given policy, or a given politician, boded good or ill for Britain? Protective tariffs to him meant dear food; therefore he was a free trader. Attacks on the Empire weakened Britain; therefore he was an imperialist. The German navy jeopardized the nation's mastery of the seas; therefore he supported a strong navy. The policies of Wilhelmine Germany menaced Britain's interests and well-being; therefore, he was anti-German. To the extent that his press had a political platform, it advanced these views. They happened to coincide with deep-seated and inarticulate fears and desires of millions of his fellow countrymen. By day-to-day warnings and exhortations, his papers helped to form a public opinion that defeated Tariff Reform, supported the Boer War, demanded an accelerated naval construction program, and distrusted Germany. To the very great degree that his papers fathomed and gave voice to popular sentiment, Northcliffe helped to create the atmosphere in which the United Kingdom went to war in 1914.

He felt, however, that the information and influence did not pass in just one direction, that he was intimately in touch with the sentiments of his readers. Since he had started *Answers,* he had believed in the importance of correspondence columns in his papers. These constituted, he wrote Lord Milner in 1918, his "barometer of public feeling." Through them he was, he maintained, more closely and immediately in touch with the popular will than any political party or politician could be. The people, in effect, spoke through him. Although he neither understood the ideology nor knew, probably, the phrase, he seems to have come finally to regard himself as an embodiment of Rousseau's General Will. Politically, he saw his function as being that of a popular advocate representing the true wishes of the people before the self-interested and frequently incompetent and wrong-headed politicians. He would not become a cabinet minister himself, for such a formal association with government would limit his freedom of action. But, as the people's ombudsman, as the repository of the popular will, he could play upon the politician's fear of his press to force them to make the right decisions and undertake the correct policies.

It was as such a self-appointed guardian of popular welfare that Northcliffe saw his role in the First World War. Because many politicians believed in his power, he was remarkably effective in imposing his wishes. He railed against censorship on the grounds that only an informed people could fight a war effectively, and forced the government to release more information about the campaigns. He exposed the critical munitions shortage and Lord Kitchener's mishandling of the war effort, and helped bring about the appointment of David Lloyd George as Minister of Munitions. Further press attacks criticizing the casual way in which the cabinet appeared to be managing the war helped to cause Asquith's downfall and the elevation of Lloyd George to the Prime Ministership. Generals praised by his papers gained command, and virulent anti-German propaganda maintained and intensified the popular willingness to make sacrifices for the war effort.

To Germans he became an arch-villain. They created a "Medal of Hate," featuring a caricature of Northcliffe, and German destroyers singled out Elmwood for their shells. Englishmen, too, were intimidated by the tremendous power he seemed to exercise. Politicians might leak secrets to him and curry his favor, but they resented the influence which, apprehensively, they permitted him to exert. To many acute observers, it seemed that the authority he held was, in the last analysis, subversive of democratic representative government itself, as the nation's rulers held themselves answerable not to their constituents or their consciences, but to a Press Lord. To counter him they bought papers of their own, and they tried to control him by offering him a seat in the cabinet, but he declined.

Ultimately Lloyd George appealed to his patriotism and his increasing megalomania by persuading him to head the British War Mission in the United States. The task of the Mission was to purchase vast amounts of supplies and float huge loans. Before Northcliffe's arrival on June 12, 1917, it had done its job about as well as Asquith had run the war before he was replaced. Tactfully bypassing an antagonistic and resentful British Ambassador in Washington, Northcliffe worked from the American commercial and financial center, New York, and soon brought order and efficiency to the handling of Britain's affairs, spending in the process some £2,000,000 a day. He was open in his liking for Americans and became incidentally an effective ambassador of good will, countering much of the traditional American fear and jealousy of British imperial power.

Returning to England in November 1917, he plunged into the storm center of wartime politics. Although two of his brothers had accepted government posts and he himself became Director of Propaganda in Enemy Countries, he retained his freedom to "say what I think" of the War Cabinet and its actions. What he thought was usually uncomplimentary, for he had concluded that the War Cabinet, like Asquith, was conducting the war ineptly. His papers also reflected the weariness, the frustrations, and the tensions of almost four years of war. They detected disloyalty and German spies everywhere and demanded stringent action against anyone suspected of being sympathetic to the enemy. Northcliffe even began spying on his own staff.

Nevertheless, after his return from the United States, Northcliffe's fortunes began to decline. His hypochondria came to be justified when a lump appeared in his neck, and he underwent a difficult thyroid operation. His recovery was slow and painful. He seemed generally, too, slowly to be losing his grip on reality. He had always been prankish: At one time years before he had lined up the men in the press room according to height and promoted the tallest; at another he had appointed a doorman to be chief censor. Now he became increasingly erratic and his pranks became malevolent and vindictive, as he berated editors viciously in the presence of their subordinates and insisted that impossible tasks be performed immediately.

One biographer has suggested that he was suffering from the tertiary stage of syphilis, which affected his brain. The evidence is largely circumstantial and the hypothesis cannot be demonstrated conclusively. Northcliffe might have feared he had contracted syphilis but a Wasserman test administered before his death proved negative. According to his physicians he died, ultimately, of septo-endocarditis, a kind of blood poisoning which eventually produces delusions. Whatever the origins, the consequences were the same: a gradual failing of Northcliffe's reason and intellectual powers.

The diminution of Northcliffe's political power followed upon a long-overdue reaction against him in Westminster and Downing Street. Conservative politicians, especially, detested him and they led attacks in the House of Commons on his overweening ambition and irresponsible use of his position. They were seconded by Conservative periodicals, most notably *The Spectator*. Prime Minister Lloyd George himself swelled the chorus of abuse in the House of Commons, ridiculing Northcliffe's suggestions for the peace settlement, tapping his head and scornfully assailing Northcliffe's "diseased vanity."

Lloyd George spoke in April 1919, after he had freed his administration from vassalage to Northcliffe and destroyed the myth of press power which British politicians had anxiously acknowledged for more than a decade. Aside from the usual politician's desire to rid himself of as many restrictions and commitments as he can, Lloyd George was probably convinced by several other factors that he could challenge the Press Lord successfully: Northcliffe's manifest unpopularity in political circles; a conviction that Lloyd George's own popularity and power were greater, and that the British public would realize that he represented more legitimate authority in a democratic society; a suspicion, perhaps, of Northcliffe's declining abilities and a realization that Northcliffe, not a political revolutionary, would accept the people's decision; and the advice of Max Aitken, Lord Beaverbrook, a Canadian millionaire and British Press Lord and politician, who had engineered Lloyd George's rise to power in 1916.

According to Beaverbrook, although his report cannot be confirmed, Northcliffe finally did bid for concrete political power in the summer of 1918. Supposedly he proposed that the Prime Minister appoint him Lord President of the Council in a new Northcliffe-Lloyd George cabinet, indicating that such an administration would have the full support of the Northcliffe press. Lloyd George refused, foreseeing that Northcliffe would attempt to dictate policy by threatening his colleagues with blackmail by newspaper. Whether or not Northcliffe made such a request, his press did condemn the government's conduct of the war with increasing harshness after August, and it began advancing a peace program based on the complete humiliation of Germany. Again in October 1918, Northcliffe indicated to Lloyd George that he would support a new cabinet only if he had approved its membership beforehand; Lloyd George once more refused.

As Ludendorff's armies disintegrated, Northcliffe, who felt that he had been the veritable spirit of Britain at war, determined to perform essentially the same function at the peace table. He suggested to Lloyd George that Northcliffe's propaganda department shift to Versailles and conduct publicity during the conference for the right kind of peace settlement. The most Lloyd George would allow was that Northcliffe rent a house near Versailles so that the Premier might confer with him if he wished. Balked, Northcliffe fielded his last great press campaign, an intense, vengeful chant of hate against the defeated enemy. Articles accused Lloyd George and the Cabinet of contemplating easy peace terms so that Germany could counter the Bolshevik threat from the east, and demanded that Germany instead be punished drastically. Vindictive and unrelenting, the Northcliffe press insisted that Lloyd George commit himself to demanding a postwar trial of the Kaiser and, above all, a high war indemnity. "He Has Not Said It," and "They will cheat you yet, those Junkers," cried the Northcliffe papers and, for the last time, Northcliffe touched a responsive chord among the war-weary English people. Under popular pressure, incited and led by Northcliffe, the Prime Minister capitulated and in the election of December 1918 promised that he would mete out stringent punishment at Versailles to the defeated enemy.

Northcliffe had asserted his power, but he had alienated Lloyd George completely and permanently. Whatever the chances that the British Prime Minister would consult with him at the Conference might have been, there was no likelihood now. Northcliffe did rent a house, and his press representatives occupied it, but he was not there to dictate to the British peace delegation and keep it up to the mark.

Once a major voice in British public affairs, Northcliffe suddenly found himself not only damned but ignored. He did travel to the Continent, to Fontainebleau, and the Riviera. His papers continued sniping at Lloyd George, demanding that Germany be trodden into the ground, but to little effect. Politicians no longer courted him; they no longer leaked secrets to him; they no longer curried favors from him. He tended to his newspapers, replacing the editor of *The Times*, and fending off labor troubles. But his only impact on public affairs occurred when he persuaded Melba to sing on the new radio, and the two pilots first to fly the Atlantic collected a *Daily Mail* prize. Even his newspaper stunts fizzled, as a promotion for a supposedly sensible, but still very peculiar, "*Daily Mail* hat" failed to persuade Englishmen to discard their bowlers, toppers, and caps. The circulation of the *Daily Mail* stood at 1,350,000 in 1920, the largest in the world, and Northcliffe still issued instructions to his editors. But he was obsessed with his health and recovered only slowly from his thyroid operation, and Beaverbrook's *Daily Express*, modeled on the *Daily Mail*, was presenting the first serious challenge to Northcliffe's journalistic supremacy. Moreover, it was clear to everyone that, as politicians no longer accepted his instructions, he was drifting toward the periphery of world and national affairs.

On May 1, 1921, 7,000 persons applauded him in Olympia Hall at the celebration of the *Daily Mail's* 25th anniversary, and on July 16, the day after his 56th birthday and the 32d anniversary of his father's death, he sailed on the *Aquitania* on the first lap of a world tour. Along with a huge well-stocked medicine chest, he took a devotional book, *Daily Light on the Daily Path*. It was a gift from his mother; they had agreed to read the same passages at the same times each day he was away.

His diary indicates that he kept his pledge and his daily messages to Geraldine from Canada, the Philippines, India, and Jerusalem, were adoring. His cables to his papers, however, were erratic, frequently irrelevant, and often insulting. His return to London in the spring of 1922 was brief and he soon left again for the Continent. He carried a .32 Colt revolver and 200 cartridges, for he was convinced that someone was trying to shoot him. He visited Germany and began writing a series of garbled and vicious articles which, mercifully, were not printed. He became seriously ill, having been sold, he maintained, poisoned ice cream by the Germans. Soon his moments of rationality were only intermittent and very fleeting.

The family closed in and moved him to London. Doctors diagnosed septo-endocarditis, but they could not cure. He attacked a male nurse with a poker and only rarely was he rational. "Tell mother she is the only one," he pleaded in one of his moments of clarity, and he begged visitors to deliver him from captivity. On August 14, 1922, he died. His memorial service was held in Westminster Abbey.

Controversy has surrounded Northcliffe in death as it did in life. He left several wills and a hotly contested lawsuit resulted. His associates published uncomplimentary memoirs and biographies, and gossips asserted that he died syphilitic and mad. His policies towards *The Times* were maligned and a book by an ex-mistress tarnished his reputation further. Above all, he was portrayed as the prototype for a new dangerous kind of 20th-century villain, the unrestrained and irresponsible Press Lord who attempted to mold the will of the people and determine public policy according to his merest whims.

The charge, in fact, suited later Press Lords very well, but as the first Press Lord, Northcliffe and his reputation have paid for the sins of his successors. True, his papers were designed to entertain and they contained a great deal of foolishness, but they always aimed just as much at informing the British public about world and national affairs The Northcliffe press never descended to the depths of later tabloids which proffered only scandal, sex, and sports. Northcliffe's papers were good papers, and his management of *The Times* probably saved that august paper from extinction or, at the very least, a radical and destructive change in its character.

As to the menace of irresponsible press power, for which he has been made the representative, that too has been overrated. The power of the press, like the later power of television, has been limited in the open British society by the very popular sentiment upon which it is based. When the views expressed in the newspapers have coincided with public opinion, or when they have divined an underlying popular sentiment, the press has served to refine and focus these attitudes. When, however, the stand of the press has not coincided with public feeling, it has not been able to impose its will on matters of fundamental importance. Lord Beaverbrook discovered this in the 20s when he tried to convert England to Empire Free Trade, and Lord Rothermere rediscovered it when his newspapers endeavored to persuade the English people to call for the restoration of the King of Hungary.

Northcliffe's campaigns usually were successful; having essentially the same attitudes and options as the English public, he sensed their will intuitively. A master of crowd psychology, he worked hand-in-hand with the public to bring about ends which he believed to be, and which usually were, beneficial to the nation. When, however, Lloyd George defied him successfully, he learned that power in England is limited by the popular will.

SUGGESTED READINGS

No one biography of Northcliffe is really satisfactory. The best of the lot are: Reginald Pound's and Geoffrey Harmsworth's, respectful and encyclopedic *Northcliffe* (London: Cassell and Company, Ltd., 1959); Paul Ferris's disrespectful and sketchy *The House of Northcliffe* (London: Weidenfeld and Nicolson, 1971); and Hamilton Fyfe's older and readable *Northcliffe* (New York: The Macmillan Company, 1930). The memoirs of a nephew, Cecil H. King's *Strictly Personal* (London: Weidenfeld and Nicolson, 1969) lays bare the family skeletons. Northcliffe's impact on the British press is covered well in: Edward Francis-Williams, *Dangerous Estate: The Anatomy of Newspapers* (London: Longmans, Green, 1957) and Wickham Steed, *The Press* (Harmondsworth, Middlesex, England: Penguin Books, 1938). Steed was one of Northcliffe's editors of *The Times*. W. L. George's *Caliban* (New York: Harper & Brothers, 1920) is a clever and cruel biographical novel.

Chapter 14

JAMES RAMSAY MacDONALD:
The Voice of Labour

A founder of the British Labour Party and Prime Minister of the first two Labour Governments, James Ramsay MacDonald has virtually been forgotten by his nation and either dishonored or ignored by his party. In the years before the First World War he guided the infant party to a recognized place in the political spectrum and he worked successfully to harmonize its frequently antagonistic, yet always complementary, theoretical socialist and labor union wings. He charmed the movement away from the siren call of international revolutionary socialism and guided its exertions into constitutional channels. In the 1920s he demonstrated that a socialist party was capable of governing the nation. Yet, MacDonald himself always held that the national interest transcended loyalty to class, and twice his conception of that interest drove him to act counter to Labour policy. On the first occasion, he condemned Britain's participation in the First World War, only to emerge after a decade as leader of the first Labour cabinet. The second time, when he became head of the National Government in 1931, the party rejected him on the grounds that he was a traitor to the cause. From this action his reputation has never recovered, and the party he did so much to form has consistently denied its creator.

Unlike so many other British leaders MacDonald came not from the gentry, but from the Scottish peasantry. The future Prime Minister was the illegitimate son of Anne Ramsay, housekeeper on a farm in the Scottish lowlands, and John MacDonald, a plowman from the Scottish highlands. To bear her child, Anne Ramsay returned to her mother who lived in Lossiemouth, a village of poor fishermen and farmers in Morayshire on the coast of northern Scotland. James Ramsay MacDonald was born in his grandmother's two-room thatched cottage on October 12, 1866. Reared by two women, he never met his father. His grandfather had abandoned his family years before, and James's grandmother had reared four children alone. Left penniless, she had supported her family through farm labor, helping the fishermen, and needlework. In these activities she was now joined by her daughter Anne. By virtue of ceaseless work they lived, but not well.

The village was poor, but the Ramsay women understood fully the value of education. At considerable sacrifice, MacDonald's mother and grandmother sent him to schools operated by the Free Church of Scotland, so that he might receive the proper religious training, and by the Church of England so that he might learn from the best teachers in the area. Jamie, as he was called, walked four miles each day to the Anglican school, and his education took eightpence a month from the meager purse of the Ramsay household, but his grandmother and mother were convinced that Jamie was special, and they knew that education provided the only avenue of escape from the grinding poverty of Lossiemouth. Responding eagerly to the opportunity, young MacDonald became a brilliant scholar. He mastered Latin and Greek, read

intensively in English literature, and developed a strong interest in biological studies. He was educated far above the station in life that the
illegitimate son of Scottish peasants might hope to attain.

In 1884, when he was 18, MacDonald followed the many Scots before
him who had left the poverty of Scotland to seek their fortune in England. He went first to Bristol. His job, working with a church boys'
club, did not go well, but he made intellectual contacts that were to
form the future direction of his life. His first venture to the south coincided with the rebirth of socialism in England, and Bristol was the
only major city outside London to harbor a socialist group. This was
a branch of the Marxist Social Democratic Federation. At Lossiemouth
MacDonald had already read some socialist literature, including Henry
George's *Progress and Poverty*, and he joined the Bristol socialists. The
branch was given mostly to street-corner speeches and distributing socialist literature, and it was probably the young MacDonald's association
with it that cost him his job with the boy's club. After only a year
in Bristol he returned, a failure, to Lossiemouth.

A few months later in the spring of 1885 he went south again, this
time to London. For several months he lived in a poverty exceeding
that of Lossiemouth, sustained only by parcels of oatmeal from home,
which he scrupulously paid for, and hot water which, he asserted, tasted
as good as coffee when one became accustomed to it. He finally found
a job addressing envelopes for the Cyclist Touring Club at a time when
Alfred Harmsworth had just become editor of *Bicycling News* in Coventry. Then, for 15 shillings a week he clerked in a warehouse. He pursued
his interest in biology and began studying for a science scholarship
at the South Kensington Museum; he overworked, his health broke,
and again he returned to Lossiemouth.

Once more, in 1888, he went back to London and, after more temporary jobs, he became private secretary to Thomas Lough, a Liberal
Member of Parliament. Through this position MacDonald was introduced to the arena of national politics and to another world, that of
the prosperous, reform-oriented, middle classes. MacDonald's new
friends, well-educated, well-mannered, financially secure and expressing
a concern for improving the lot of the poor, represented a continuation
of the reform tradition that had nourished British society since the 16th
century. In endeavoring to correct the ills they saw about them these
bourgeois reformers constituted a contemporary manifestation of the
ability of British society to change from within and adjust itself peace-
ably to new circumstances. They drew inspiration from differing sources:
Christian humanitarianism, Marxian Socialism, and the writings of
Robert Owen, Auguste Comte, Henry George, and John Ruskin. Their
ideologies varied; some professed socialism and others merely wanted
to do good. They, or their children, worked in the new settlement houses

in the slums of the East End, they managed private charities assisting the poor, and they subscribed to funds to succor families of striking London dock workers. Usually they voted Liberal, supporting the radical wing of the party, and they were in sympathy with Keir Hardie, who became an avowed Labour Member of Parliament in 1892.

Among the socialists MacDonald encountered were George Bernard Shaw, H. G. Wells, and Sidney and Beatrice Webb. The Webbs were to be the self-appointed consciences of Britain for half a century and Sidney was to serve in both of MacDonald's cabinets. They were members of the Fabian Society, a lobbying organization working to bring socialism gradually to the United Kingdom.

Although the young MacDonald was not attuned to the very practical orientation of the Fabian Society, which was inclined to address itself to the hard and complex details of immediate legislation, he did join. He also joined a branch of the Social Democratic Federation, the Swedenborgian Fellowship of the New Life and, even, the Scottish Home Rule Association. He was temperamentally suited to be a valuable member of any organization, for he was willing to perform the pedestrian tasks of taking notes, keeping records and accounts, and writing the general correspondence that have always been the mainstay of any successful club. Accordingly, he soon became secretary to most of them. The experience he gained was valuable training for his later work in maintaining the new Labour Party. His experience with these disparate groups also tended to make him impatient with what Shaw called "revolutionary heroics" and with men whom MacDonald himself termed "phraseologists." True, like the Marxian Social Democrats, he maintained that his socialism was scientific and demonstrated by the principles of Charles Darwin, but MacDonald emphasized not the struggle and violence, but rather the evolutionary aspect of the new biology. To him, a successful change would be accomplished not suddenly, by fighting the forces of the age, but rather by harnessing them and directing them gradually along collectivist lines.

MacDonald's socialism as it developed in the nineties was evolutionary and parliamentary, and it was essentially doctrineless. It was not, above all, couched in economic terms, a grave deficiency when his cabinets later faced critical economic problems. Further, MacDonald, who was himself rising from poverty through hard work, felt that governments should do nothing that would undermine the self-reliance of Britain's poor.

The Fabians hoped to accomplish the socialist millenium through permeating established political parties, but in 1893 there appeared the Independent Labour Party, evolutionary like the Fabians, but aiming at establishing a distinctively socialist party government. The Independent Labour Party was closely associated with the new unions of unskilled workers and its ideology was vague. Its leader, Keir Hardie, announced that, Marx notwithstanding, socialism "is not a system of economics." This suited MacDonald perfectly, and in 1894 he joined the new party. In 1895 he stood for Parliament and was defeated at Southampton. The association with the Independent Labour Party was to be at the center of MacDonald's political life for almost 40 years.

MacDonald felt immediately at home in the comfortable drawing rooms of his new friends, and the world he found in London welcomed him. Although he made no effort to repudiate Lossiemouth, no one thought on first meeting him that he was a member of Britain's proletariat. He might, some thought initially, be an army officer. Tall and slender, with dark curly hair that later turned white, a handsome face and a luxuriant mustache, he carried himself well and spoke in a cultivated accent with a slight and intriguing Scottish burr. His demeanor and bearing seemed to indicate gentle breeding and he was acknowledged to be one of the best-looking men in London.

To Margaret Gladstone he became "*My*[sic.] him, my sir, my knight." Daughter of Dr. John Hall Gladstone, Fellow of the Royal Society, she was archetypical of the circles in which MacDonald now was moving. Her father, a famous chemist, had been one of the founders of the YMCA, and Margaret taught Sunday School and did social work. The Gladstones employed seven indoor servants at their house in Pembridge Square. Margaret and Ramsay, as he now called himself, met at meetings of various societies, became engaged on the steps of the British Museum, where MacDonald often worked, and were married in November 1896. He was 30; she was 27.

By virtue of this marriage the illegitimate son of a Scottish housekeeper and a plowman became a member of the English middle classes. It was a very happy marriage until Margaret's death in 1911. The couple had five surviving children; their eldest son, Malcolm, became a leading politician. Like the union of Mary and Bysshe Shelley, it incorporated a conjunction of intellect and vocation as well as emotion. Though not wealthy, Margaret had a small income, and this freed the couple to devote themselves entirely to socialist and humanitarian causes. Their apartment, 3 Lincoln's Inn Fields, and their cottage in the country, soon became the centers for socialist and labor politics in Britain.

The MacDonald's private means also enabled them to travel widely: to the United States and Canada, to South Africa, to India, and to socialist meetings across the Channel. MacDonald met leaders of continental socialist parties and became the most knowledgeable man in the British labor movement about international affairs.

His major concern, however, was to bring socialism to the United Kingdom, and in 1899 he and Keir Hardie composed a resolution which made possible the formation of a strong labor party. The resolution, written in the offices of Hardie's newspaper, the *Labour Leader,* and adopted at a meeting of the Trades Union Congress in 1899, reversed the previous decisions of the Trades Union Congress against participating directly in politics. From it came in 1900 the Labour Representation Committee, composed of delegates from Trades Unions, the Independent Labour Party, and socialist societies, including the Fabians; in 1906 it became the Labour Party. In its constitution nothing was said about socialism, but 5 of the 12 members of the Executive Committee were from the socialist societies, even though they represented only 70,000 members as compared to 500,000 trade unionists.

The new Labour Representation Committee elected MacDonald to be its secretary. Financially independent, devoted to the cause and good at paper work, MacDonald was ideally suited to the position. When the Committee became the Parliamentary Labour Party in 1906 he was elected M.P. from Leicester and soon became the party's leader.

In the years before the First World War MacDonald worked untiringly for the movement. He believed that Labour could not hope to win a parliamentary majority for decades to come and maintained that, until then, Labour's major task was to educate and to persuade. He became the major persuader, as he worked to develop and propound a theory of socialism that was particularly British and one that would be appropriate to the special characteristics of the British people and their unique history. Of Marx, he read only the *Communist Manifesto;* otherwise, MacDonald studied the writings of his friend, the radical economist John A. Hobson, and secondhand accounts of the philosophies of St. Simon, John Stuart Mill, August Comte, Robert Owen, and John Ruskin. From these sources he developed a socialism that he described as specifically British, a program that could not be condemned as a foreign importation, but one which based itself on the British experience.

In books, articles, and speeches, MacDonald asserted that socialism would be a natural outcome of the industrial revolution, as the technology which had produced the great advances in the production of goods would next be applied to the problems of distribution. The result would be "social control" of the productive apparatus. What technical form this would take, or the specific steps by which it might be accomplished, he did not indicate. Nor did he suggest that "social control" would necessitate any significant change or expansion in the machinery of government, for MacDonald, like most Britons of the time, feared and opposed big bureaucratic establishments. He argued, anyway, that institutional change alone would not bring true socialism. Rather, he felt, socialism had to be built into men's minds.

Nor was it inevitable that socialism would come to Britain. A necessary precondition was a change in attitude. So the major duty of socialists in MacDonald's time was, as he wrote in 1909, to educate, to improve "public intelligence," and to organize "moral forces." Even in the political field, propaganda comprised the major function of socialists, not legislation and administration. He wrote little of immediate concrete legislative programs. Education came first, and until the nation was genuinely converted to socialism the people had to be content to wait. MacDonald's safe and sane, yet promising, arguments found a wide appeal among young reformers, who came to regard him as the intellectual prophet of a more perfect and a more just Britain. His socialism also became, in essence, Britain's socialism in the first four decades of its existence, and its strengths and weaknesses were those of the British Labour Party.

After the 1906 election returned a solid group of party members to the House of Commons, MacDonald guided them, supporting the Liberal cabinet's measures which brought the dawn of socialism nearer, yet insisting that the small Labour Party guard its independence and not be captured by the Liberal giant. In this he was assisted by Philip Snowden and Arthur Henderson, men who approached him in ability and training. Many of the new M.P.'s, however, had come up from the ranks of the unions and gave their primary allegience to them rather than to the party. These members, whether they liked it or not, had to be educated to accept a broader political responsibility. In the process of teaching them, MacDonald became an excellent parliamentarian and party leader.

The party also had to counteract the persuasiveness of the international Marxist and syndicalist programs of direct and violent action through strikes, riots, and revolts. It had to prove that it was not necessary to attack or overthrow the established system, but that 19th-century Britain could be brought to adjust to changing conditions and respond to new needs through constitutional means. The existing Liberal administration seemed obviously to be demonstrating this adaptability as, with Labour votes, it enacted legislation beneficial specifically to the working classes.

Indeed, the legislation of the Liberal parliaments before the Great War seemed to indicate clearly that Britain was going to become a collectivist society. This made it possible for MacDonald, the leader of the Labour Party, to view the difference between his party and the others not as one of ideology or means but one primarily of pace. Above all, any change must be legal and gradual. As he lectured the Independent Labour Party in 1909,

> We can cut off King's heads after a few battles; we can change a Monarchy into a Republic; we can deprive people of their titles and we can make similar superficial alterations by force; but nobody who understands the power of habit and of customs in human conduct . . . who understands the delicate and intricate complexity of production and exchange which keeps modern society going, will dream

for a single moment of changing it by an act of violence. As soon as that act is committed, every vital force in society will tend to re-establish the relationships which we have been trying to end, and . . . will conquer us in the form of violent reaction . . . .

When the violence which MacDonald disavowed as a political instrument erupted between the nations of Europe in August 1914, he refused to sanction it. Britain's entry into the First World War was, he told the House of Commons, unjustified, and he rejected the Government's plea to close political ranks on behalf of the war effort. Other members of the party, like Snowden and Hardie, also opposed the war, but while they based their stand on a pacifist ideology, MacDonald did not. He assumed the more ambiguous stance that Britain must win the war, even though her entry into the conflict had been mistaken. Meanwhile, he asserted, the heat of battle should not seduce the nation into a vindictive militarism. Rather, men must strive to keep alive the spirit of rational moderation so that peace when it came would be a genuine and permanent peace, based on justice and not on revenge. His position was characterized by more subtleties and less clarity than is indicated here, and in explaining it he frequently became obtuse. Some fogginess and fence-straddling earned him the jeers of many of his erstwhile colleagues, but the masses of the British public, caught in the black and white simplicity of wartime emotion, concluded that he was a dangerous enemy of the nation. In their eyes MacDonald, in reality a moderate, became a symbol of the most extreme pacifism, socialism, and treachery.

The labor unions and the vast majority of the Labour Party supported the war. MacDonald resigned the chairmanship of the party in 1914, although he remained treasurer, and his successor, Arthur Henderson, joined the wartime cabinets. At the very opening of the war MacDonald encountered a vicious personal antagonism which intensified during the years of conflict. In December 1914 he traveled toward Belgium to serve in an ambulance unit, and British military authorities at Dunkirk arrested him on the grounds that his presence near the front would endanger the war effort. He was released immediately; an embarrassed Lord Kitchener gave him a pass to visit the front at any time, and he did return on one occasion. Nevertheless, the commander at Dunkirk reflected the general attitude toward MacDonald more closely than Kitchener.

In opposing the war, MacDonald worked with men who were far to the left in the political spectrum. Many, although not all, supported the Marxian view that the masses constituted a world brotherhood, and asserted that the workers properly owed their loyalties to an international proletariat rather than to capitalist nations at war. Many were syndicalists and believed that the workers could best attain their goals through violent industrial action rather than through constitutional instruments, while many others were primarily pacifist and civil libertarian in their views.

In association with these disparate elements on the fringes of British politics MacDonald fórmed organizations such as the National Council for the Protection of Civil Liberties and the Union of Democratic Control, which alerted the nation to violations of individual rights and called for parliamentary control over foreign policy. MacDonald's speeches and writings, frequently reported out of context by the pro-war press, were never censored, and they made him the most unpopular subject in the United Kingdom. Police raided the offices of the UDC and the Independent Labour Party, and at every meeting he encountered boos and insults; public halls were closed to him, he was accused of being in the pay of the Germans, and the Lossiemouth Golf Club expelled him. Perhaps worst of all, Horatio Bottomley, chauvinist editor of *John Bull*, published a copy of his birth certificate, exposing his bastardy to the world.

Before the war British socialists, especially the well-traveled MacDonald, had always maintained ties with the socialists on the Continent. The socialist societies were affiliated with the International Socialist Bureau, or Second International. Even though members from allied and neutral countries had held a conference in London in 1915, they were suspect because of their prewar relationship with German and Austrian socialists. The Russian revolutions of 1917, then, both brought an intensification of the attacks of MacDonald and posed new critical questions for the socialist movement and the Labour Party in Britain. Three months after the Russians overthrew the Tsarist autocracy in March 1917 and attempted to establish a moderate constitutional regime, the Independent Labour Party and British socialists held a conference in Leeds. There the enthusiastic meeting "hail[ed] the Russian Revolution" and resolved that the British people should "follow Russia." MacDonald was one of the organizers of the conference and had introduced the resolution hailing the revolution, an action which was to haunt him and British socialism after the second, more radical, Marxist-Leninist, revolt in the fall. The Leeds meeting had been held in an atmosphere of increasing dissatisfaction with the progress of the war, and it named MacDonald as a member of a delegation of the Labour Party to an International Socialist Peace Conference at Stockholm which had been organized by the Second International. British seamen refused to work any ship carrying the delegates, and the British government declined to issue passports. In protest, Arthur Henderson resigned from the cabinet. He and MacDonald, recently divided over the war, now found a common cause and the Labour Party was strengthened and unified as the two leaders combined forces. The restored unity was sealed when the party adopted a statement of war aims drafted by MacDonald, a manifesto that was similar to President Woodrow Wilson's Fourteen Points.

The party was consolidated further in 1918 when MacDonald, Henderson, and Sidney Webb hammered out a new constitution which broadened its base. Where hitherto the party had been a federation of trades unions, socialists societies, and the ILP, now membership was opened to individuals, whether they were members of the original constituent bodies or not. Thus it became an ordinary political party and could rest on a broad and heterogeneous popular base.

Although the breach between MacDonald and the party had been healed he still fought the 1918 election with the reputation of being a pacifist and traitor who had called on the British workers to "follow Russia." For MacDonald it was a dirty and hard-fought contest, and he met a crushing defeat. Beaten again in a by-election in 1921, he did not regain a parliamentary seat until the general election of 1922.

With the victory of the Lloyd George coalition in the 1918 election, the Labour Party, risen from 42 to 59 M.P.'s, became the official opposition. Since both MacDonald and Henderson had lost the election, however, the parliamentary leadership of the party was weak. And it faced a time of severe trial. Many Englishmen were discouraged by the fact that the movement seemed to have achieved so little as yet through parliamentary methods and they were tempted by calls to other means of bringing socialism to England. The syndicalist influence emerged strong in the dislocation following the war and some unions launched a series of crippling strikes. In addition, many British socialists were attracted by the revolutionary propaganda now issuing from Bolshevik Russia. In July 1920 a British Communist Party was formed and made the first of many requests for membership in the Labour Party.

During the four years after 1918, MacDonald, although not in the Commons, acted as a moderating and unifying influence in the movement. He was especially active in the ILP, keeping it from affiliating with Lenin's Third International. He persuaded the Labour party to reject all official association with British Communists. More speeches, articles, and books exercised a restraining pressure and kept before the movement the ideals of a socialism that was peaceful and British, not alien and violent.

After the voters returned 142 Labour M.P.'s to the House of Commons in 1922, the party reelected MacDonald, a new member from the mining constituency of Aberavon, as its leader. No one else in the party could match his credentials. He was Labour's leading theoretician, a superb speaker, and was recognized as one of the very few good parliamentarians in the party. Above all, his opposition to the war now paid political dividends. Not only was he acceptable to the radicals who had worked with him during the war, but many other Englishmen also had come to believe that he had been right all along after 1914.

As the conflict between the ex-Prime Ministers, H. H. Asquith and David Lloyd George, cast the Liberal Party into increasing disarray, and Conservative Prime Minister Stanley Baldwin miscalculated concerning the electorate's willingness to accept protective tariffs, the Labour Party got its chance to govern. The election of 1923, which brought 259 Conservatives, 191 Labourites, and 159 Liberals to the Commons, was a milestone in the rise of Labour to the position of second major political party. MacDonald, who had written only five years before that nothing would "be more damaging to Labour than . . . to be presented with political power by the masses who vote for it because other parties are for the time being unpopular," had not foreseen the outcome of the balloting. Not until after the polls had closed was he faced with the dilemma of forming, or not forming, a minority Labour Government.

Firebrands in the party suggested that they take office, introduce radical socialist measures immediately, and go down to defeat before a combined Conservative-Liberal vote, with their socialist principles intact and their red flags flying. MacDonald rejected such a quixotic gesture as "phraseology." He was, of course, attracted by the temptation of office, but he also saw two immediate gains that could be achieved from forming a minority government: experience and respectability. A period of apprenticeship would provide training that would be of value in later Labour administrations, and a Labour government could, by its moderation, persuade many Englishmen, who feared that a Bolshevik mob would soon be in the streets, that Labour could rule responsibly and well.

On January 22, 1924, Ramsay MacDonald, illegitimate son of a Scottish plowman, kissed hands as the first Labour Prime Minister of the United Kingdom, while King George V mused in his diary about what "dear Grandmama . . . would have thought of a Labour Government." Although the party had campaigned on a program of public works, reform in unemployment insurance, raising the school-leaving age, and a capital levy, the platform had actually been, in the MacDonald way, mostly educational. The new administration had few concrete ideas as to how they might accomplish such a program. Without a majority, it was also, of course, dependent on votes from the Liberals.

The new cabinet officers were inexperienced, in a great number of instances they were not very able, and they spent much of their time learning their jobs; soon many became creatures of the conservative permanent civil servants. Many, too, took what their constituents judged to be entirely too much pleasure in the trappings of office. Aside from launching a successful housing scheme, the Labour administration did little to solve the many problems of the nation. The budget, prepared by the strict Gladstonian, Philip Snowden, was conservative. Nothing was heard about a capital levy, or even any increase in taxes on the rich, for both Snowden and MacDonald believed that the welfare of Britain's people depended on a prosperous economy. Flourishing industries, unhampered by high taxes or government regulation, would create wealth for the entire nation and jobs for the workers. Back-bench radical Labourites could see little difference between this outlook and that of the capitalist parties. Frustrated because the Government did not seem even to be attempting in any socialist way to make a better Britain, they began sniping regularly at the administration.

As for MacDonald, it appeared as though he had been smothered willingly in an aristocratic embrace. Erect, white-haired, and still very handsome at 57, he looked every inch a peer of the realm while he chatted affably with the sovereign. As if to the manner born, he moved through the salons of noble London hostesses, providing tangible evidence that they were not to be murdered in their beds by Bolsheviks. He was a particular favorite of Lady Londonderry, owner of the mines in Aberavon whose workers had sent MacDonald to Parliament. MacDonald accepted a free limousine from a biscuit manufacturer who was an old friend and who had just received a peerage. As a character in Howard Spring's biographical novel about MacDonald observed cruelly, he might have sprung from the working classes, but "he took care to spring a good long way from 'em." His new life might have served, as has been charged, as a personal apotheosis for the illegitimate son of Scottish peasants who now finally had found genuine acceptance. True or not, his obvious relish for his new surroundings and acquaintances tended to vitiate the party's reforming zeal. Critics began questioning his commitment to help the workers, asserting that he should spend less energy in mollifying frightened aristocrats, and devote more attention to getting on with the task of socializing Britain.

MacDonald was Foreign Secretary as well as Prime Minister; after all, he had specialized in diplomacy since 1900. As such he paid much less attention to domestic affairs than to foreign relations, and at the Foreign Office he was an unqualified success. He moved among world leaders with the same ease and grace as he conversed with society hostesses, and in the foreign arena, unlike the domestic, he seemed to possess a clear vision of what could and should be accomplished. There were, he believed, no conflicting interests that could not be harmonized through moderation and conciliation. He perceived Britain's, and his, role as being that of a pacific mediator, assuring all nations of Britain's good will and sympathy, facilitating negotiations, and suggesting how grievances might be resolved. In this spirit he persuaded the French to withdraw their troops from the German industrial district of the Ruhr; he sponsored the Dawes plan, a successful compromise of the reparations issue; and he promoted the Geneva Protocol, which called for arbitration, disarmament, and for mutual support in cases of aggression. Mac-Donald's only failure concerned relations with Soviet Russia. His Government extended formal recognition, but failed to conclude a settlement of the debts of the Tsarist regime or a trade treaty.

It was because of Soviet Russia, ultimately, that the first Labour Government fell, on a vote of censure against the cabinet's interference in the prosecution of an editor who had urged British soldiers never to shoot their Russian communist brothers. In the ensuing election campaign, envenomed by the publication of the forged Zinoviev letter which seemed to prove that the entire Labour Party took orders from Russia, Labour's representation fell 40 seats and the Liberals continued their decline. It was a defeat for Labour, but they still held more seats than after the election of 1922, and considering the advancing disintegration of the Liberals, were still further along the way to being the second major party.

Under MacDonald's leadership, Labour had proved that it could govern: if not well, at least no more badly than the other parties. Few men blamed MacDonald for the electoral defeat; yet there were some recriminations, and among the party leaders there was an attempt to depose him. Their action, combined with the troubles he had experienced with the radical wing of the movement during the period of office, tended to estrange MacDonald from the party. Aloof by nature, especially since his wife's death in 1911, he really did not like any of his colleagues and resented the fact that they, and much of the party, had given him more criticism than assistance while he was leader of the government. Thereafter, although his speeches continued to thrill large audiences at party meetings, he consulted rarely, and then only formally, with his colleagues in the leadership of the movement.

Humanly, the party blamed the poor record it had made in 1924 on external considerations: the fact that they had been a minority government, and the wickedness of the opposition. Having explained away their inadequacies, they failed to remedy the lack of preparation which really accounted for most of their poor showing in office. To MacDonald, of course, this was unimportant, for he still interpreted the party's mission as being mainly propagandistic. There was no point in altering institutions until men's minds had been changed, and the minority opposition held by Labour in the Commons was proof that the conversion had not yet occurred. He failed to see that, if British voters were to be persuaded to vote Labour, surely the next Labour government must be prepared to give concrete demonstration of its superior ability to deal with the nation's critical problems of unemployment and industrial and commercial torpor. Therefore, under MacDonald's leadership, the glowing manifestos continued to be framed after 1924, but immediate practical planning was still lacking. Although Ernest Bevin secured the passage of a party resolution never again to form a minority government, and although some segments of the party moved toward the left after 1924, MacDonald kept it resolutely on a middle and primarily propagandistic course. Even during the emergency of the General Strike of 1926 he took little part, except to counsel moderation.

When MacDonald again became Prime Minister on June 5, 1929, his party was just as unprepared to introduce practical legislation to deal with basic problems in British society as it had been in 1924. Certainly it had not equipped itself to master the financial emergency that it encountered 24 months later. Again, holding only 288 seats to the Conservative's 260 and the Liberal's 59, Labour was a minority government, but initially all went well. The nation was reasonably prosperous when the party assumed power. The government continued public housing subsidies and established new regulations concerning the coal mines, agriculture, and London transport, but the legislation was not different in principle from a Conservative measure of 1926 which regulated the distribution of electricity. Seemingly, the Labour Party was very little, if any, ahead of its traditional rivals when it came to remodeling capitalist Britain. In foreign and imperial affairs also there were accomplishments. Although Arthur Henderson became Foreign Secretary, MacDonald himself acted as a kind of roving ambassador. He personally persuaded the United States to make concessions in naval disarmament, and he constantly opened or chaired international or imperial meetings. "Prime Minister Visits Britain" headlined the *Daily Mail* on his return from one trip.

In Britain the Prime Minister lived in Hampstead and at his official country residence, Chequers, where his daughter kept house for him. Sometimes he spent weekends in a small cottage he had built for his mother in Lossiemouth. Frequently also he was seen in the London mansions and country houses of the rich and titled, where he was comfortably at home. He had no close friends, only admirers and acquaintances and co-workers. With his colleagues he was distant; he had little in common with most of them. Moreover the ministers of the Labour Government did not have the opportunity to become united by a process of hammering out any great legislative program that would implement the professed ideals of the party. Politically, his Government was not threatened, for neither the Conservative nor Liberal Party leaders saw much to gain by attempting to bring about the downfall of the essentially safe and unmenacing Labour regime. Despite its manifestos, in reality it differed from the other parties very little in program and practice. MacDonald's government thus failed to attempt any radical solutions for the nation's fundamental problems.

It also had no ready socialist, or any other solutions for the crisis of capitalism in the opening years of the Great Depression. Initially, the depression affected Britain less drastically than other Western nations, largely because Britain had not shared fully in the prosperity of the late 1920s. Yet, by 1931 her exports had been reduced by 50 percent, her industries floundered, her shopkeepers declared bankruptcy, and her ships lay idle. More than 20 percent of the work force, $2\frac{1}{2}$ million persons, was unemployed, double the number of 1929. As the costs of unemployment insurance payments increased, tax revenues based on a stagnating economy declined, and it proved difficult to balance the budget.

Later governments were to solve such problems through deficit spending, regulating the currency and the economy, and by inaugurating public works programs. But in Britain only the discredited Liberal leader, David Lloyd George, and Oswald Mosley, then a Labourite and later England's most conspicuous fascist, suggested any such remedies. The leading members of the Labour administration either held to 19th-century economic precepts, as did the Chancellor of the Exchequer, Philip Snowden, or were almost entirely ignorant of economic theory, practice, and reality. Prime Minister Ramsay MacDonald was prominent among the latter. His socialism had always been romantic and idealistic. He had never read Marx, or Engels, or Keynes, nor did he seek counsel from his close friend, John A. Hobson. Accordingly he, like the majority of his party, met the depression unprepared with any socialistic, or even any novel, proposals for solution. This situation constituted his and his party's greatest failure. As Mary Agnes Hamilton, early an admirer and later a harsh critic of MacDonald, wrote cynically in her memoirs, he fell in the "category of eager propagandists whose generalities have not, at some stage or another, been subjected to rigorous translation into concrete fact." Socialism, she further commented sharply, was his religion but never his practice. This, unfortunately, was true, but it was true not just of MacDonald but of the whole movement he led.

Encountering the economic emergency that began in 1929, Labour reacted with less imagination and firmness, even, than the Liberal Party which at least advanced a public works program. MacDonald appointed investigating commissions; he and other ministers spoke in grave, yet hopeful but above all ambiguous, terms. Slaves of their own ignorance and their own conceptions of their roles, bound by Philip Snowden's classical economics and the advice of conservative civil servants and bankers, they could only hope that the solution lay in retrenchment and in waiting for something to turn up. Surely the system would somehow right itself as it always had in the past.

MacDonald and his cabinet were, then, every bit as unequipped to deal with the international financial crisis which flared up in the summer of 1931 as they were unable to cope successfully with other aspects of the depression. A complex situation, compounded of bank failures on the Continent, German inability to meet reparations payments, and the Bank of England's policy of borrowing at short term and lending on long term, meant that the Bank of England and the British Government were unable to meet their financial obligations in the summer of 1931. Default was unthinkable; it was not only un-English, but it would also jeopardize the value of the pound sterling and endanger the hard-won position of the City of London as the financial center of the world. A loan from the United States would provide some assistance, but bankers there and in Britain told the cabinet that dollars would be forthcoming only if the budget were balanced.

Kept to the mark by the orthodox Snowden and ignorant of any alternatives, this was what the cabinet set out to do. It soon appeared, however, that after other legitimate action had been taken, only reductions in government wages and a large cut in unemployment benefits would suffice. For four days, beginning on August 20, 1931, the cabinet wrestled with the problem. Most members agreed to a 10 percent cut in unemployment benefits, but they could not stomach the 20 percent reduction that seemed to be necessary. They were not helped toward solution when the Trades Union Congress firmly opposed the proposed decrease in benefits and the entire policy of retrenchment. Many cabinet ministers had close ties with the TUC and by the evening of August 23 it was clear that MacDonald could not get his colleagues to agree; 11 members would support the cuts, but 9 threatened resignation should the benefits be curtailed by the full 20 percent. Even they, it appears, believed that reductions were necessary, but they refused to accept the responsibility for making them and preferred to pass the cruel measure on to another government.

Conscious that he did not command a majority in the House of Commons, MacDonald consulted regularly with the leaders of the other parties: the Conservative's Stanley Baldwin, and Herbert Samuel, who assumed leadership of the Liberal Party while Lloyd George was undergoing surgery. Baldwin had no desire to assume the blame for an unpopular measure and Samuel preferred not to risk being held hostage in a Conservative-Liberal coalition government as Lloyd George had been ten years before. Samuel suggested that an all-party coalition, a National Government composed of all three parties, be formed under the continuing leadership of the Labour Prime Minister. Baldwin agreed, King George V urged MacDonald to cooperate for the sake of the nation, and he finally concurred.

This was the decision which destroyed MacDonald's reputation. So hungry, it was charged, was he for power and the trappings of power, so far had he removed himself from the needs of the British people, and so completely had he been ensnared by the blandishments of the propertied classes, that he betrayed the masses of the British people whom he professed to lead. The evidence, however, suggests other reasons for his action. Of course he was humanly vain and liked position and power, but he was also dedicated to the welfare of the Labour Party and to his nation. Quite simply, he believed that the necessary and unpalatable measures could be enacted most successfully by an all-party National Government which reflected the unity of the British people at a time of peril. The problem was urgent and immediate action was imperative, so a time-consuming general election was out of the question. If the Labour Party, the largest party in the Commons, should attack the necessary government economy measures from outside another administration, national unity would be placed in jeopardy. Further, his membership in a National Government would, at least partially, rescue the Labour Party from the obloquy of having been unable to solve the crisis alone. As he wrote on August 24, the day his government fell, "Had we simply resigned . . . , the Party would have suffered very severely in the public estimation. We should have been considered as people who had failed our duty." The party, he believed, had failed to live up to the responsibilities of government. If at least a segment of it, especially its leadership, should cooperate briefly with the Liberals and the Conservatives to solve the financial problem, such disinterested action would enable Labour " . . . to recover its position in the public favour more speedily." He hoped, too, that it would have learned from the example of the Prime Minister himself to put national welfare above selfish and narrow party and class concerns.

Obviously, MacDonald was thinking of the war, when part of the party had joined a coalition government. After the war the party had reunited; surely after the short interlude of National Government Labour would unite again. He expected to resign the leadership temporarily, but he had resigned before in 1914, and he had returned before, in 1922.

The new, and supposedly stopgap, National Government enacted an economy budget, including a reduction in payments on the national debt, a recourse which financial specialists had informed the Labour Cabinet was impossible. But financial unorthodoxies not allowed a socialist administration were permissible to a coalition that included parties with more traditional ideologies, and the bankers provided £80 million. Balancing the budget, however, really had nothing to do with the basic causes of the international financial crisis, and the value of the pound soon was threatened again. On September 21, less than a month after the National Government had been formed to shore up Britain's financial stability, Parliament suspended the gold standard. "Nobody told us we could do this!" cried the Fabian Sidney Webb, now Lord Passfield, one of the founders of the Labour Party and Colonial Secretary in the second Labour Government.

As salaries of schoolteachers and seamen were reduced, as sailors on the lower decks even mutinied briefly at Invergordon, the Government which had been formed to save the pound let it fall from $4.80 to $3.40. The coalition also seemed to be losing its temporary character, and the Labour Party reacted bitterly. They advanced no other options, for they had none to advance, but rather they adopted the view that the whole affair had been a bankers' plot against the workers. Vindictively they lashed out against the new administration and the leader who had betrayed his constituency. The branch of the party at Hampstead, where MacDonald lived, expelled him and the national executive of the party followed suit.

The attack increased in intensity during the general election held in October to win a popular vote of confidence for the National Government. As Labour had found excuses for its failures in 1924, so now it covered its failure to deal with the financial crisis of 1931 by charging its ex-leader with treason. Rowdies prevented MacDonald from speaking, he was accused of making secret pacts with the Tories and, most of all, of selling out his people for the sake of his craven lust for power, position, and aristocratic companionship. Paradoxically and tragically, the party that MacDonald had formed and led agreed with him and Keir Hardie that socialism "is not a system of economics." They, like MacDonald, believed what the bankers told them and they, like MacDonald, had no alternative solutions based on alternative economic theory. Thus, MacDonald's critics could argue only from a narrow class basis: unemployment benefits are inviolable. In such a rigid economic context MacDonald was correct when he accused them privately of placing class above nation. That his enemies sensed that he was correct only added to their frustration, which found release in their bitter and vicious attacks on their former leader. They made MacDonald a scapegoat for their own default.

Nor was MacDonald the only Labour Minister who found position and power to be pleasing. Jimmy Thomas, a railway union leader, had shown himself to be every bit as susceptible. Thomas never lost the common touch. But MacDonald had never really possessed the common touch, and association with the traditional ruling classes became him only too well. No other leader of the party looked or acted so much the part of a gentleman ruler of the country. That MacDonald could be convicted of consciously betraying the working classes is doubtful; that he preferred the company of the rich and titled was probably true; that he valued their interests above those of the masses cannot be demonstrated.

In the general election of October 1931 the nation's voters supported the National Government which had faced the emergency rather than the Labour Party which had run away from it, and voted for the National Government that seemed to be standing for national interests rather than those of a class. MacDonald himself won an overwhelming victory. Everywhere, except in the discontented councils of his old party, he was praised as a national savior who had placed the nation's welfare above party and class interests. The fate of Labour in the election reflected this initial judgment of the electorate; its membership in the Commons was reduced from 288 to 46, and almost all of the ministers of the previous Labour cabinet were defeated.

The spitefulness of the election, combined with Labour's humiliating defeat and the recriminations that began in August 1931 and continued until MacDonald's death, all snapped the tenuous bonds of mutual confidence and acceptance which had made it possible for the party to reunite after the divisions of the First World War. The party continued to relive the trauma of 1931. It cherished its bitter rejection of MacDonald and comforted itself by the belief that it had been sold out. "It took years," wrote Mary Agnes Hamilton, "for the Labour Party to get him out of its system." Labour waged the battle against MacDonald until after his death and, for as long as it made MacDonald its scapegoat, it condemned itself to impotence.

If the official Labour representation in the House stood at a powerless 46, MacDonald's personal following, dubbed "National Labour," was even smaller, comprising only 13 M.P.'s. Soon, most of the Labourites who had joined the National Government cabinet under his leadership resigned, and he became head of a cabinet that was composed almost entirely of men from the other parties.

He was Prime Minister, but more and more the power came to be wielded by the man who commanded 471 Conservative votes in the Commons, Stanley Baldwin, The Lord President of the Council. Always an expert on Foreign Affairs, MacDonald concentrated on disarmament conferences, world economic conferences, and League of Nations sessions as he had done in 1924, but Stanley Baldwin and his Conservative majority controlled domestic policy. A life-long socialist, MacDonald found himself presiding over a capitalist administration, but he refused to acknowledge that fact and continued to regard it as a genuinely national government. As a result his speeches became contradictory and frequently contained little substance. Coincident with the increasing ambiguity of his position, his health and his intellect began to fail and he spent longer and longer weekends relaxing as a country gentleman at Chequers. In 1932 he underwent operations for glaucoma in both eyes. When he spoke of resigning, Baldwin found it only too easy to persuade him that he must remain at the helm in his difficult post as a still-indispensable symbol of national unity. Soon the press, and all of his cabinet except Baldwin, began treating him with a contempt they did not trouble to conceal.

In May 1935, he made his last public appearance as Prime Minister during the celebration of the Royal Jubilee. By then it was clear to the Conservatives that he had outlived his usefulness. The National Government could not go to the country with such a leader, so in June Baldwin and MacDonald changed places in the cabinet. The Government, still styling itself "National," won 432 seats in the general election of November. MacDonald, who had won by a majority of 6,000 in 1931, lost to a Labour candidate by 20,000; his National Labour Party now numbered only 8 in the House of Commons.

Although his political career obviously was over, he hung on tenaciously. Politics had been his life for 40 years, he had led the British government as Prime Minister for 7 years, and undoubtedly he looked for a more graceful way of retiring than as a result of a brutal electoral defeat. Baldwin also desired his presence in the parliament and cabinet as a continuing, if faded, sign of the national unity of 1931. Since there was no chance that he would be returned from an industrial constituency, he was nominated for the traditionally Conservative seat representing the Combined Scottish Universities. He accepted, although he had opposed the separate university franchise all his life and had moved to abrogate it only four years before. The university electors of the supposedly safe seat rebelled, and only a personal visit by Baldwin to Scotland, and only after the full power of the Conservative Party machine had been applied, was MacDonald, the socialist, returned in January 1936.

An increasingly shadowy figure, ignored by most of his present colleagues and condemned vindictively by most of his former colleagues, he continued in the cabinet as Lord President of the Council. There seemed to be nothing else for him to do. Finally, when Neville Chamberlain replaced Baldwin as Prime Minister, he relegated his Labour predecessor to the back benches. As MacDonald's health continued to weaken, he vacationed in Canada and then sailed on a cruise to South America. He died at sea on November 9, 1937, a month after his 71st birthday. His body lay in state in the cathedral at Bermuda, and a British warship carried it back to the United Kingdom for a funeral service at Westminster Abbey and burial at Lossiemouth.

The British Labour Party has continued to deny him a place in its pantheon of champions of the people. After 1931 the pitifully small rump of the party in the Commons attacked him unmercifully, ignoring the fact that many of them, as members of the last Labour Cabinet, had also agreed to reduce the unemployment benefits. As they had seized on the Russian scare as an excuse for their inadequacies in 1924, so, after 1931, MacDonald's betrayal became their excuse for their failure to meet squarely the crisis of 1931. MacDonald has been damned further because of his association with the foreign policies of the National Government after 1931 which, operating in accordance with his ideas of international conciliation, built the foundations for the appeasement of the late 1930s. Clinging vainly to the trappings of power to the end, he became not only an object of hatred, but also of ridicule and scorn.

Yet, the fact remains that the party which damned him was a party that he had, in very large measure, created. Eschewing violence and revolution, condemning Marx and Lenin, it was above all parliamentary. In its conscious ignorance of economics and planning, it was critically defective, but that lack was ultimately remedied, and Labour proved very capable indeed of fashioning a new socialist Britain after 1945. That the party eventually was able to construct a socialist Britain was due to the fact that MacDonald had set it squarely within the British constitutional tradition.

SUGGESTED READINGS

Godfrey (Lord) Elton completed only the first volume of his biography, *The Life of James Ramsay MacDonald, 1866–1919* (London: Collins, 1939) and no other complete account exists as yet. Excellent short sketches are in C. L. Mowat, "Ramsay MacDonald and the Labour Party," in *Essays in Labour History*, ed. by Asa Briggs and John Saville (London: Macmillan, 1971); Edward Francis Williams, *A Pattern of Rulers* (London: Longmans, 1965); and Mary Agnes Hamilton, *Remembering My Good Friends* (London: Jonathan Cape, 1944); Ms. Hamilton also wrote, under the pseudonym "Iconoclast," praising MacDonald in *The Man of Tomorrow* (New York: Thomas Seltzer, 1924). L. MacNeill Weir, *The Tragedy of Ramsay MacDonald* (London: Secker and Warburg, 1938) emphasizes and condemns Mac-. Donald's actions in the 1931 crisis. Selections from his writings and analyses of his ideas may be found in Benjamin Sacks, *J. Ramsay MacDonald in Thought and Action* (Albuquerque, N.Mex.: University of New Mexico Press, 1952), and Bernard Barker, ed., *Ramsay MacDonald's Political Writings* (New York: St. Martin's Press, 1972). For background and context, the following are invaluable: J. H. Steward Reid, *The Origins of the British Labour Party* (Minneapolis, Minn.: University of Minnesota Press, 1955); Richard W. Lyman, *The First Labour Government, 1924* (London: Chapman & Hall, 1957); Reginald Bassett, *Nineteen Thirty-One: Political Crisis* (London: Macmillan, 1958); and Robert Skidelsky, *Politicians and the Slump: The Labour Government of 1929–1931* (London: MacMillan, 1967). In his novel *Fame is the Spur* (New York: The Viking Press, 1940), Howard Spring sustains the charge that MacDonald betrayed his party, but the novel is generally sympathetic; it has been filmed under the same title.

Karsh, Ottawa

Chapter **15**

SIR ALEXANDER FLEMING:
English Science in
the Twentieth Century

SHORTLY after the Second World War, when he was touring the elaborate, gleaming, and utterly sanitary laboratory of a great American pharmaceutical company, Sir Alexander Fleming remarked casually that he would never have discovered penicillin if he had worked in such conditions. Taking his comment as a joke, his hosts laughed politely, but Fleming, a dour Scot who saw nothing funny in man's struggle against disease, was merely offering a factual observation. He could not possibly have discovered the penicillin-producing mold under such hygenic conditions, for he had spent his life working in laboratories that many American scientists in the middle decades of the 20th century would equate with a medieval alchemist's workshop. Yet, Fleming's comment reveals a great deal more than the conditions under which he was accustomed to working. It indicates subtly but distinctly a certain unique quality of British scientific inquiry, where great care was taken in stating a problem, developing a methodology to solve it, and proving conclusively the validity of the results; but little time or effort was wasted on the superfluous trappings, such as 10,000 test tubes when ten will suffice, that have occasionally obscured the true goals of scientific investigation. In short, what Sir Alexander underscored with his comment was the unwritten maxim of British science that abhorred pomposity, revered a faultless application of method, and demanded unassailable proof to support conclusions. Although he may never have fully realized it, this maxim governed all of Alexander Fleming's professional activity, and without it his seemingly fortuitous discoveries could not have occurred.

Alexander Fleming was a Scot, born in 1881 on a farm called Lochfield situated at the junction of the counties of Lanark, Ayr, and Renfrew. Although the Fleming farm was extensive, 800 acres, the soil was poor, so Alexander and his brothers spent a good deal of time on the moors hunting and fishing to supplement the family diet with fresh meat and fish. While it cannot be proven conclusively, the claim of Fleming's contemporaries that his moorland experiences sharpened his capacity for observation seems reasonably accurate.

The young Scot began his formal education in a one-room school on the moor with 15 pupils and one teacher, but by the age of eight he had exhausted its possibilities and moved on to a larger school in the nearby town of Darvel. In the course of his career Fleming was to receive degrees and honors from some of the world's finest educational institutions, but he always maintained that his most rewarding experiences were at the tiny one-room Scottish school. Since he showed great promise as a student, Alexander was sent at age 12 to the Academy at Kilmarnock, where the headmaster, very progressive for his era, required the pupils to study two theoretical sciences each year. Fleming stayed at Kilmarnock for only 18 months, and then was sent to London to train for a career under the watchful eyes of two brothers who had

preceded him to the capital. Eventually four of the Fleming brothers
lived together in London in a house near Baker Street Station, and
the eldest brother, Tom, an opthalmic surgeon and optician, supervised
the activities of the others.

Thomas Fleming's medical practice was financially unrewarding, for
he had few patients and many of them were unable to pay. Consequently, he did not mention medicine when he advised Alexander about
a career. Instead Tom persuaded his younger brother to enroll in the
Polytechnic School in Regent Street and study commerce. After the
brief commercial course Alexander Fleming took a job noteworthy for
its long hours and low pay with the American Line Shipping Company.
At the turn of the century Fleming had before him the prospect of
a solid business career, but several events altered the course of his life
drastically.

First, there was the outbreak of the Boer war in 1899. Alexander
enlisted in the London Scottish Regiment, where he became an expert
rifle shot and a star on the regimental water polo team. Fleming was
never sent to the Transvaal, but the reputation as a sportsman that
he established in the regiment had a curious and decisive effect on
his life. Coupled with this, Tom Fleming's medical practice took a turn
for the better, and after he opened his office in Harley Street he recon-
sidered the advice he had given Alexander about a career. Ultimately,
Tom began to put pressure on his younger brother to study medicine,
and that pressure, combined with a legacy of £100 that Alexander
inherited from an uncle, led the shipping company clerk to give up
his job and go back to school.

Medical science at the beginning of the 20th century was at an awkward stage; it had made great progress in the preceding half-century,
but physicians were acutely aware of how little the principles discovered
in the 19th century actually helped them in the struggle against specific
diseases. In surgery, Joseph Lister had proven the value of antiseptic
solutions in reducing infections that in the past had too frequently accompanied operations. In microbiology, Robert Koch and Louis Pasteur
had only recently discovered, classified, and characterized many of the
major disease-causing bacteria. And in diagnostic techniques, Wilhelm
Roentgen won the first Nobel prize in physics for outlining the principles
upon which X-ray technology was developed. As the 20th century
dawned, medicine was clearly becoming more sophisticated in its comprehension of the origins and courses of diseases, but some of the most
common and deadly ailments remained beyond the bounds of successful
treatment. This was especially true of infectious diseases, for while physicians could identify what caused a given illness and how it functioned,
they could not actually do anything to cure the disease. When Alexander
Fleming decided to make medicine his career, the profession was, in

short, usually adept at explaining an illness but all too often helpless to do anything about it.

British medical training reflected the groping state of medical practice. There was no centralized, systematic program of study, but rather a medical school attached to each of the 12 great London hospitals, which were organized into a kind of confederation directed by the University of London. Each school clung tenaciously to as much of its former autonomy as possible, and this characteristic was reflected principally in differences in curriculum and entrance requirements. Like most other medical schools in Europe, the 12 in London had curricula divided broadly into two categories: classroom training in theoretical scientific subjects like anatomy, followed by practical training assisting physicians in the hospital wards. Where the schools differed most sharply was in the theoretical phase of medical training, for some schools emphasized chemistry at the cost of bacteriology while others concentrated on anatomy while neglecting biochemistry. But they were all very much the same in that they placed great emphasis on practical training, and this was to cause serious difficulties for Fleming later in his career. Because of insufficient exposure to the intricacies of chemistry and particularly biochemistry, he was unable to carry his two great discoveries past the initial phases of revelation and preliminary testing.

Alexander Fleming's primary concern was not, however, the haphazard training in theoretical sciences that characterized medical education. He did not have a diploma, and his only chance of entering any of the medical schools rested on earning a high score on the entrance examination. In July 1901, Fleming took the examination and passed at the top of the list in the entire United Kingdom; because of his good showing he could attend the school of his choice. Not knowing anything about the different institutions and thus having no basis for selection, Fleming remembered that when he had played water polo for the London Scottish they had a good game against the team from St. Mary's Hospital in Paddington. That recollection settled it for Fleming. He entered St. Mary's in October 1901 largely because of her water polo team, and he spent the following 54 years there as a student and then as a member of the staff.

Like his entrance into the profession, Alexander Fleming's choice of a medical speciality resulted from chance. Coincidentally with his admission to St. Mary's, the school opened a department of bacteriological study, the Inoculation Department, headed by Sir Almroth Wright. One of the men working for Wright, Dr. Freeman, began searching in 1906 for new talent for the department's shooting team. When Freeman heard of Fleming's feats with the London Scottish he naturally approached the young Scot, who at the time was about to receive his Bachelor of Medicine degree. In order to acquire a crack shot for his shooting team, Freeman persuaded Fleming to join the staff of the Inoculation Department. After some contemplation, Fleming finally agreed. He stayed with the job for the rest of his life.

When Alexander Fleming joined Wright's staff, bacteriology was in its infancy. During the last half of the 19th century many of the basic principles of this science had been articulated by such men as Robert Koch in Germany and Louis Pasteur in France; but when Fleming chose bacteriology it was very much a new science. The Inoculation Department reflected the status of its subject. Occupying two tiny rooms that served as laboratories, Wright and his staff were charged with diagnosing and treating all of the infectious cases in St. Mary's. Moreover, there was little equipment and less money to pay salaries; Fleming and colleagues received £100 a year, and Wright encouraged them to develop private practices to supplement their incomes. It might not have been a very promising way to start a career, but Alexander Fleming was fascinated by the subject and completely overcome by the charisma of Sir Almroth Wright.

The son of a Presbyterian minister, Wright was a complex and controversial figure. He had been educated by private tutors, and loved poetry so much that he memorized 250,000 lines of Shakespeare, Goethe, Browning, Kipling, and Milton. He was even more enthralled by foreign languages. At the age of 62 he learned Russian, and when he was 80 he began a serious study of the Eskimo tongue. His rudeness, ill-temper, and extreme opinions repelled many of his peers; but they all acknowledged that Sir Almroth Wright was a brilliant bacteriologist with outstanding leadership qualities. Cited frequently in textbooks, Wright was internationally known as the man who developed the technique for diagnosing Malta Fever, a serious disease transmitted to humans by goats. He also produced an antityphoid fever vaccine that the British Army was too skeptical to use in the Boer War. Infuriated at military stupidity, Wright resigned his post at the Army School at Netley in 1902 and went to St. Mary's, where he determined to show both the army and the world that the best way to fight infectious disease was through immunotherapy: the artificial stimulation of natural body defenses, such as occurs in vaccination.

When Fleming began working for Wright he was, as a matter of course, enlisted in the struggle to vindicate immunotherapy. Specifically, the young Scot and his co-workers labored almost ceaselessly and to no good purpose over their chief's pet theory: the "opsonin index." According to Wright, opsonin was the substance in the blood that "buttered" bacteria so that phagocytosis, the consumption of bacteria by white blood cells, would be enhanced. Wright and his ten assistants spent long hours every day for years peering through microscopes, tallying the opsonic index of various prepared sera. It was tedious work that demanded a great deal more personal loyalty than it did professional initiative, but it had its advantages. Because Wright headed the laboratory and because he was famous, Fleming and his colleagues made some noteworthy friends during the frequent teas. The European scientists Paul Ehrlich and Elie Metchnikoff proved informative visitors, but Wright's circle extended well beyond science. Arthur Balfour, the political leader, visited the laboratory often, but not as often as did George Bernard Shaw, who immortalized Wright as the principal character in his play, *The Doctor's Dilemma.*

During his apprenticeship at the Inoculation Department, Alexander Fleming discovered nothing of consequence. How could he, saddled as he was with attempting to vindicate Wright's opsonic theory? But he did refine the research skills that were necessary for sophisticated study. His already sound powers of observation were made acute, and he learned to watch closely for unusual developments in all facets of his research. Additionally, Fleming learned the fine art of explaining his experiments and their results in concisely written expository papers. His work was uninspiring, but it served to transform him from a bright medical student into a skillful research scientist.

While Fleming was working at St. Mary's, a German scientist named Paul Ehrlich was struggling with what everyone, especially Wright, considered a crackpot theory about treating infectious diseases. Ehrlich was searching for what he called a "magic bullet," a chemical that would attack infection in the body without harming the recipient of the chemical. As Director of the Institute of Serotherapy in Frankfurt, Ehrlich and his Japanese assistant, Kiyoshi Shiga, began testing innumerable organic compounds in their allegedly quixotic search for a "magic bullet." By May 1909, they accomplished the impossible. Ehrlich and Shiga produced an organic arsenic compound which they called 606, which killed the syphilis-causing *Treponema pallidum* without harming the human body. Ultimately named salvarsan, that which saves by arsenic, compound 606 was to have a profound effect on Alexander Fleming. It proved to him that there was another means of fighting infectious disease than immunotherapy; the application of chemical agents therapeutically.

Shortly after the perfection of salvarsan, Ehrlich visited St. Mary's and gave a quantity of the substance to Wright and his aides. Because it required a great deal of manual dexterity and close control in administration, most of the staff at St. Mary's declined to use Ehrlich's gift, but Fleming viewed the difficulties of using the drug as a challenge. He soon mastered the technique of treating syphilitic patients with salvarsan and found it highly effective. When he had compiled enough data on the drug, Fleming published a report in the leading British medical journal, *Lancet,* explaining this novel method for treating syphilis. As his success was publicized, the number of Alexander's private patients rose dramatically. One of them, an old comrade from the London Scottish, even managed to find some humor in Fleming's work on the dread venereal disease. He drew a cartoon with the caption "Private 606," portraying Alexander dressed in uniform shouldering a syringe instead of a rifle.

Fleming's success with salvarsan irritated Sir Almroth Wright, largely because it was derived from a form of treatment that ran counter to Wright's approach. Claiming that "The doctor of the future will be an immunizer," Sir Almroth heaped scorn on Ehrlich's chemotherapy, indirectly attacking Fleming, but the assistant never argued with his chief about the subject. He simply went ahead with his treatments and kept track of the results. Although there was no confrontation, by 1910 Fleming and Wright had clearly pointed their interests in different directions: Fleming toward attacking invaders of the body with chemistry and Wright toward mustering the natural defenses of the body with vaccines. Wright's natural abrasiveness at the time was perhaps heightened by the fact that his approach to immunotherapy was coming under severe criticism. Many of his colleagues thought that his opsonic indices were dead ends, and some even referred to him openly as Sir "Almost" Wright. Naturally defensive about his professional interests, Wright used Fleming and salvarsan as the most handy targets for his hostility; but the Scot seemed unperturbed by Wright's insults and continued his gravitation toward chemotherapy.

Fleming's interest in chemical treatment of diseases was interrupted by the outbreak of war in 1914. Wright, commissioned a Colonel in the army and ordered to set up a laboratory at Boulogne, took most of his staff to France. At the stroke of a pen, "Private 606" Fleming became Lieutenant Fleming of the Royal Army Medical Corps. At first, the Boulogne operation was not all that it might have been. Located in the basement of the casino, with an open sewer running through the main room, Wright's new facility proved a most unfunny joke to the colonel. Wright's fury about the unsanitary conditions and the stench was soon unleashed on his superiors, and to pacify him they moved the facility to the fencing school on the top floor. Lieutenant Fleming was later to say that this new laboratory was the best one he ever worked in.

The Great War proved to Sir Almroth and his aides the large grain of truth in the old saying that war is glorious only to old men and small boys. The use of high explosive shells drove pieces of steel, clothing, and dirt deep into wounds, and they carried with them millions of microorganisms that caused diseases for which there was no effective treatment. Like his colleagues, Fleming worked throughout the war to find some means of combatting such killing diseases as gas gangrene and septicemia,[1] but nothing proved very helpful. Despite the frustration of having thousands of patients die while the physicians stood helpless, Wright and his staff made some important contributions to medicine during the war. Typhoid fever, for instance, was controlled through the use of Wright's vaccine. Additionally, a discovery was made that, while controversial at the time, eventually helped in the treatment of war wounds. This involved a challenge to the accepted methods of using antiseptics, which caused a storm in English medical circles.

Ever since Joseph Lister introduced the use of carbolic acid as an antiseptic prior to surgery, it was assumed that antiseptics would be beneficial in preventing the infection of wounds. Indeed, today when a child cuts himself his mother immediately douses the cut with antiseptics. But during the Great War Fleming noticed that, especially in cases of gangrene, antiseptics did no good at all. Curious, he determined to find out exactly what happened when carbolic acid was used on a severe wound. By devising an ingenious series of experiments, he learned that it was actually harmful to use antiseptics on war wounds, for the various substances commonly used killed white blood cells, thus reducing the body's capacity to fight microbes while having no effect whatsoever on bacteria. As an alternative treatment, Fleming proposed that wounds be washed with saline solution, for that seemed to elevate the level of white cells and thus promoted the only available means of fighting infection. His discovery of penicillin notwithstanding, Alexander Fleming's colleagues at Boulogne claimed that he was never better as a research bacteriologist than when he debunked the antiseptic myth during the First World War.

Probably because it supported his own views of immunotherapy, Sir Almroth Wright tried to force the army to adopt Fleming's view of antiseptics and stop using them on wounds. The colonel embroiled himself in a bitter quarrel for his trouble. In 1915, Wright addressed the Royal Society of Medicine in London on the subject of antiseptics, hoping that the society would support his opposition to antiseptics before the Army Medical Corps. Instead of support, he received abuse and argument. Sir William Cheyne, President of the Society and a disciple of Lister, said in effect that Wright and his staff were demented, and that the great Scottish surgeon had proven once and for all that antiseptics were absolutely necessary in treating wounds. It was in vain that Wright tried to explain that there was an immense difference between treating infections and preventing them, so the debate deteriorated into personal insults followed by an exchange of letters in *Lancet*. The army

---

[1] Commonly called "blood poisoning," septicemia is an invasion of the bloodstream by pathogenic microbes. Before antibiotics, a patient stricken with septicemia had little chance of recovery.

declined to adopt Fleming's discovery officially, but brass-hat orders had little status in the field hospitals of France. There, the army doctors saw for themselves that Fleming was right, so they simply stopped using antiseptics and used a saline solution instead.

Although Fleming was gratified to learn both that his discovery was being adopted and that it helped, he realized that it was little more than a stopgap measure. To rely on the natural defenses of the body was all very well, but in severe wounds the natural defenses simply were not capable of doing their job alone. What was needed, Fleming said repeatedly, was something that could be injected into the blood that would destroy the microorganisms of disease, just as salvarsan killed the spirochetes of syphilis. Such a substance was never found at the Boulogne laboratory, but the concept was firmly implanted in Fleming's mind while he was in France. Indeed, by 1916 it so dominated his thinking that everything else seemed scientifically inconsequential.

At the height of the antiseptic controversy in 1915, Fleming, now a Captain, went on leave to England. There he met Sarah McElroy, who owned and managed a nursing home in York Place, Baker Street. Before his furlough was over, Alexander Fleming married Sarah, and beyond giving him a happy home life, the marriage had a significant impact on Fleming's career. Because Sarah believed strongly in her husband's research ideas, she sold her nursing home. The profits were used both to provide an independent income for the Flemings and also to buy a country house, the Dhoon, at Barton Mills in Suffolk. Sarah Fleming's generosity allowed her husband to return to the laboratory at St. Mary's after the war rather than go into private practice to support his family. Thus Sarah Fleming underwrote Alexander's vital research in the postwar years.

In January 1919, Captain Fleming was demobilized from the army and returned to his work at St. Mary's in Paddington. He still worked on Wright's pet projects of immunotherapy, but the war had changed Alexander Fleming's views on the purpose of bacteriological research. Despite salvarsan, Fleming in 1914 operated on the premise that his goal should be finding techniques of helping the body defend itself against disease. By 1919, his premise had changed, for he perceived the nature of his work to be more along lines of finding a substance that would attack microorganisms without harming their host.

As Fleming changed, so did Great Britain and her people. The postwar era brought a false prosperity followed by economic depression and huge unemployment rolls. It also brought the rise of the Labour Party in political life, a desperate search for social pleasure, and myriad other alterations indicating that a new Britain was arising from the cataclysm of 1914–1918. The microcosm of St. Mary's hospital reflected these broader changes. Sir Almroth Wright, an unabashed misogynist who had written a book denouncing women's suffrage, returned to St. Mary's to find, much to his disgust, women attending the medical school. As the Inoculation Department grew, its administrative demands required that Wright appoint an Assistant Director. In 1921, this new post went to Fleming. His appointment caused a deep split in the laboratory staff, for Freeman and his supporters bitterly resented the Scot's elevation over the man who had recruited him. To complicate matters, St. Mary's experienced financial difficulties after the war, and the hospital might well have closed had it not been for the good work of the medical school's dean, Dr. Charles Wilson, later Lord Moran.

Wilson, as well as being a physician good enough for the fussy Churchill, seems also to have been a fund-raiser extraordinaire. Using his social contacts, he persuaded Lord Revelstoke, then chairman of the Baring Brothers financial house, to donate £25,000 to the hospital. But the man who really saved St. Mary's was the press magnate, Lord Beaverbrook. When Wilson approached Beaverbrook, who happened to be one of the dean's patients, the press baron decided to investigate rather than simply hand over a contribution. Touring the hospital, Lord Beaverbrook stopped in the outpatient cafeteria and, incognito, asked how much a bun cost. He was told 3½d., but if he had no money, it was free. This attitude more than the hospital's financial statement impressed Beaverbrook. A few days later he summoned Wilson to his office and handed him a check for £63,000 to rebuild the medical school completely.

As the buildings were refurbished and Fleming began his new duties as Assistant Director, he adjusted well to the dramatic changes all around him. He was particularly pleased, however, to discover that the hated opsonic index of Wright was rapidly losing credibility with the chief. Instead, there seemed to be a tendency in the laboratory, now renamed the Pathology and Research Department, to allow the staff to pursue their own interests, and nothing could have suited Alexander Fleming more. By 1921, reasonably free from the domination of Wright, Fleming was able to make his first really important discovery.

As a laboratory worker Alexander Fleming had two characteristics that proved immeasurably helpful in his work. He had no predilection toward tidiness; his desk and tables were always littered and he would keep cultures for weeks, sometimes piling them on top of each other. Moreover, he had a genius for observation and would examine everything carefully before discarding it. In 1921 these traits made Fleming's first research breakthrough possible.

Studying a large, yellow, nonpathogenic coccus,[2] Fleming worked for months determining its physiology and its reaction to various com-

---

[2] A bacterium which does not cause disease (nonpathogenic), and is oval or spherelike in shape (coccus).

pounds. Since he believed in total commitment to a project, he naturally followed his inclination to keep the dozens of Petri dishes in which the bacterial colonies were cultivated. Eventually he reached the point where he had to dispose of some of the Petri dishes, but before he did he examined them with an eye toward unusual developments. One dish immediately caught his attention. In it he had grown a colony and added some of his own nasal mucous, and a glance showed him that the mucous seemed to inhibit the growth of the coccus. Reasoning that there must be something in his own mucous that had antibacterial power, he launched a series of experiments to learn more about this extraordinary phenomenon.

First, he cultivated the coccus in a tube of nutrient broth and then added some nasal mucous. The opaque bacterial suspension quickly cleared after the addition of mucous, showing that something produced by the body was destroying the microorganisms. Next, Fleming decided to try the same experiment using a different body fluid, tears. The result was the same, but the destruction of the coccus occurred much faster, in less than five seconds. Naturally excited by what could be the greatest medical discovery since salvarsan, Fleming decided to concentrate on using tear fluid and find the exact mechanism of bacterial destruction.

Completely immersed in his project, Fleming soon made a pest of himself at St. Mary's. He needed an immense quantity of tears to carry on his experiment, and obviously could not provide it all himself, so he cornered first the staff and then the patients demanding that they give up some tears for the cause of science. Almost everyone cooperated, at least in the beginning, but they soon began to go to extremes to avoid Fleming, for it was both tiresome and painful to have him squeeze lemon rind into their eyes while he collected tears with a pipette. Eventually, he had to resort to paying people for their tears, but he did secure enough to make extensive and revealing experiments. Before long, Fleming realized that he had been extremely lucky in his discovery, for his work revealed that the yellow coccus was by far the most sensitive bacterium to tear fluid. Other microbes, some of them pathogenic, displayed varying sensitivity to the fluid, but Fleming was struck by his incredible good fortune in picking the right bacterium and the right substance to apply to it quite accidentally. What came to be called "Fleming's luck" was to serve him well throughout his career.

By simple deduction, Dr. Fleming extended the range of his discovery. He reasoned that if tears and mucous attacked bacteria, then other body substances must also, and he set about finding out if this were the case. In rapid succession he learned that nails, hair, tissues, and virtually all other parts and products of the human body had the same power as tears in attacking microbes. From these observations Fleming concluded that he had uncovered one of the body's basic defense mechanisms against disease, and he was correct. While this discovery was later obscured by his work in antibiotics, it nevertheless was of fundamental scientific importance. It was dubbed "lysozyme" by Wright because it lysed or disintegrated bacterial cells and also had the chemical properties of an enzyme, but the discovery did not get the reception that it deserved in British medical circles.

Following the usual means of presenting new information to his colleagues, Fleming read a paper on lysozyme to the Medical Research Club in December 1921. It was coldly and insultingly received. No questions were asked by the audience, which meant that they considered the paper boring and insignificant. Undaunted, Fleming persuaded Wright to read a similar paper to the Royal Society in February 1922. Again, there was no reaction. Despite the two categoric rejections of his work in two months, Fleming was undeterred. Confident in the importance of his work, Fleming refused to be intimidated by the ignorance of his peers. From 1922 until 1927, Fleming published five papers on lysozyme, all of them virtually ignored by scientific circles. While lysozyme was eventually recognized as the significant agent that it is, Fleming's determination throughout the ordeal of rejection proved more important than the discovery. Had he not believed so completely in his work and been so convinced that it was worthwhile, he surely would have given up when his early reports on penicillin were treated similarly.

By 1928 Fleming decided that he had done everything that he could with lysozyme. He did not, of course, know at the time that in two years his work would be hailed by the Belgian Nobel laureate, Jules Bordet, at the First International Congress of Microbiology. Nor could he know that lysozyme was destined to be the subject of 2,000 separate scientific papers and also to be a substance of extensive commercial use in protecting packaged foods from infection. On the brink of recognition, Alexander Fleming shifted his research interest from lysozyme to chemotherapeutic agents. Specifically, he began investigating the effects of mercuric chloride on pathogenic streptococci. His general aim remained what it had been for 15 years, the discovery of another "magic bullet" like the one Ehrlich had found; but his research was to turn up something far beyond his greatest expectations.

Like many other microbiologists of the era, Fleming hoped to find a chemical compound that would, in the right dosage, kill infecting bacteria without harming the patient. Quite by accident, he opened the door to a whole new arsenal of medical treatment instead: the antibiotics.[3] One day in 1928 when he was examining his streptococcal cultures, Fleming noticed that his assistant, Dr. Pryce, had exposed some of them to the air and contaminated them. Berating Pryce and examining

---

[3] Substances that inhibit the growth of or destroy bacteria and other microbes.

the damaged cultures at the same time, Fleming suddenly stopped his tirade and began peering intently at one Petri dish. What caught the irate scientist's attention was a colony of mold that, growing on the agar[4] with the streptococci, appeared to be inhibiting the bacterial growth. Although Fleming certainly needed no reminder after his experiences, Pryce immediately pointed out that this was the same way that Fleming had discovered lysozyme.

Excited by the obvious antagonism between the mold and the bacteria, Fleming picked off a tiny bit of the mold and placed it in a tube of broth for growth and preservation. He then put the Petri dish aside, not knowing that it was to become his most treasured memento and·one of the principal artifacts of modern medical history. Abandoning all of his other work, Fleming concentrated on the mold, first learning how to grow it on agar. He then devised a simple but ingenious experiment to outline the principles of its effect on bacteria. In an agar-filled Petri dish he hollowed out a core in the center and filled it with mold. Then he streaked various bacteria away from the core rather like the spokes of a wheel and incubated the culture. The results were more tantalizing than he had expected. All of the Gram-positive[5] microbes were unable to grow near the core, while the Gram-negative bacteria remained unaffected by the mold. Fleming then decided to grow it in broth to secure greater quantities. After some groping for the right technique, he finally learned how to cultivate the mold in broth and produced a yellow liquid that had the same effect as the mold itself. Diluting it to find the range of its power, Fleming soon learned that even in the weakest strength it still could inhibit the growth of many dangerous pathogens. Although he could not know it at this early stage, his most potent broth solution contained only one active part per million in the solution.

Satisfied now that he was not wasting his time, Fleming finally decided that the next logical step was to find out exactly what the mold was. Knowing little about molds, this problem sent him to the textbooks where, through pictures and descriptions, he identified his mold as being of the genus *Penicillium* and the species *chrysogenum*. One of the young staff members at St. Mary's, Dr. C. J. LaTouche, when asked for a confirmation of the identification, told Fleming that he was wrong. According to LaTouche, the mold was a *Penicillium* for sure, but the species was *rubrum* rather than *chrysogenum*. As it turned out, both were wrong. In 1930, an American mycologist, Dr. Charles Thom, cor-

---

[4] A gelatinous substance used as the principal growth medium for bacterial cultures.

[5] Derived from a bacterial staining technique developed by Christian Gram, the terms Gram-positive and Gram-negative indicate the general characteristics of the two broad groups of bacteria. Pathogens of the genus Streptococcus, for instance, are Gram-positive, while those of the genus Salmonella are Gram-negative.

rectly identified the mold as *Penicillium notatum*. When Fleming read Thom's report, he noted that the mold had first been discovered by a Swede on a specimen of decayed hyssop. Alexander Fleming, physician and Scottish Covenanter, was reminded of the 51st Psalm, "Purge me with hyssop and I shall be clean."

In later decades, when antibiotics were as familiar as aspirin, it was difficult to appreciate Fleming's incredulity at what he had found. But in 1928, when patients died from septicemia induced by an infected scratch, Fleming was understandably overwhelmed by the potential of his discovery. What he seemed to have blundered onto, thanks to a mold spore floating into his laboratory from Praed Street, was something viewed as a remote theoretical possibility in 1928: a phenomenon of antibiosis. Granted, there was nothing very new about antibiosis even in the 19th century. Lister in 1875, Pasteur in 1877, and Duchesne in 1897, all made observations of antibiosis resulting from the action of molds on bacteria. But none of them had investigated further. Only Alexander Fleming, inspired by Ehrlich's salvarsan and his own wartime frustrations in treating infection, carried antibiosis to the experimental stage.

In the process of developing a drug there were two qualitative tests that it had to pass before it could be made available for general use. One was the determination that it had the desired effect. In the case of Fleming's mold the desired effect was the destruction of pathogens, which he had primitively but verifiably established. The other test was one of toxicity. Was the drug harmful to the patient? If so, did the benefit outweigh the damage? This test Fleming had yet to perform with his mold juice, and he approached it with some apprehension. So far all antibacterial drugs except salvarsan had failed this test. Fleming first injected the juice into a rabbit, watched him carefully, and concluded that the rabbit tolerated the injection well. Then he tried it on a man by irrigating infected skin areas with the juice. Again, there were no indications of adverse reaction. Finally, Fleming injected a massive dose of the juice into a mouse and observed that there were no undesirable effects. Moreover, Fleming determined that the juice did not inhibit white blood cell function. The only conclusion that could be reached was that the mold juice both killed bacteria and was nontoxic. Fleming's enthusiasm for his discovery increased proportionately.

Thinking that something much better than salvarsan was within his grasp, Dr. Fleming was soon jolted back into the hard reality of biological research. A woman who had lost her leg in a bus accident was brought to St. Mary's, where she soon developed an infection that reduced her chances of survival to virtually nothing. Certain that this would be a good trial for his mold juice, Fleming began treating the woman by soaking her bandages with the *Penicillium* solution. The infection was too advanced, his solution was too weak, and Fleming soon lost his patient. Although the experience was very disappointing, it served a useful purpose. It brought into sharp focus the next step that needed to be taken in developing Fleming's drug: to extract the active principle of the juice so that it could be used in concentration. Simple as this sounded, it proved to be an immensely complicated obstacle that was to keep penicillin, as Fleming came to call the drug, out of general use for well over a decade.

Since penicillin has, over the past 30 years, proven to be of immeasurable value in saving lives, it is difficult to explain why it took so long to develop as a therapeutic agent. Part of the blame must rest with Britain's scientific community, for Fleming's discovery was studiously ignored or casually dismissed by nearly every scientist who should have had his professional curiosity aroused by the test reports. The few researchers who showed an interest were either too involved in other projects or were too poorly trained in biochemistry to approach the problem of refining penicillin with any hope of success. Considering the great social consequences of the drug, British governments of the inter-war period must also accept part of the responsibility for penicillin's agonizingly slow development, for official support of scientific research was effectively limited to programs that related to national security. The financial problems of the governments during the 1930s account at least in part for this lack of support, but they do not excuse it. There was, for instance, public money spent on scientific projects much less worthwhile than penicillin, and when the drug promised to contribute to Britain's war effort after 1939 there was widespread administrative backing to get it into production. Yet, the fundamental reasons that penicillin took so long to develop were that Alexander Fleming could neither convince his peers that his discovery was vital nor refine it himself because of his inadequate training in biochemistry. The result was that Fleming had to live for over ten years convinced that his drug could revolutionize medical treatment but unable to make it available to physicians on even the most limited scale.

Since Fleming was no better a chemist than he was a mycologist, he enlisted the aid of two young staff members at St. Mary's to help him concentrate the mold juice. These two young scientists, Frederick Ridley and Stuart Craddock, had at least a nodding acquaintance with biochemistry, and when they started their attempts at extracting the active principle they were optimistic. Following standard textbook procedure, they first combined the juice with a solvent and then heated the mixture in a vacuum at very low temperature. This process gave them a brown, syrupy, molasseslike mass ranging from 10 to 50 times more powerful than the original juice. Ridley and Craddock were unable, however, to refine the substance beyond this initial stage, and after several frustrating months they gave up the project. Ironically, Ridley's reason for dropping the project was that he had a bad case of boils, which he hoped to cure with a sea cruise. Had he purified the mold juice, he could have cured his boils and probably would have received a Nobel prize as well.

Thwarted by his inability to concentrate the juice, Fleming nonetheless decided to inform his colleagues of his discovery. On February 13, 1929, Fleming read a paper on penicillin to the Medical Research Club, which responded to penicillin with the same lack of interest it had shown toward lysozyme. Naturally disappointed by his failure to impress upon his colleagues the importance of his discovery, Fleming decided to try another approach. He published a paper in the *British Journal of Pathology* in June 1929, explaining the most important features of the substance: it was antibacterial, nontoxic, and was soluble in alcohol but had not been purified. This paper too was ignored, but Fleming's tenacity assured that the subject of penicillin would not be consigned to oblivion.

Since Fleming and his colleagues at St. Mary's were unable to refine penicillin, the fate of the substance shifted to another London location: the School of Tropical Medicine and Hygiene. There, Professor Harold Raistrick developed an interest in molds generally and *Penicillium* especially; he organized a team consisting of himself as biochemist, Dr. P. W. Clutterbuck as chemist, and Dr. R. Lovell as bacteriologist. Securing strains of the mold from both Fleming and the Lister Institute, the Raistrick team began experimenting with it. In a matter of months they had learned how to cultivate the mold in a synthetic medium and had also isolated the yellow pigment that gave it a distinctive color. Off to a promising start, the Raistrick team was disbanded before it could make a major breakthrough. First the mycologist who had joined the team was killed in an accident, and then Clutterbuck died of a mysterious illness. Finally, Lovell left to take a post at the Royal Veterinary College, and Raistrick abandoned the project because he could not stabilize the penicillin in the refining process. Although he did not know it at the time, Raistrick could hardly have been closer to solving the puzzle of purification, for all that was needed when he gave up was to make the solution more alkaline so that the penicillin would not be destroyed.

Despite his own failure and that of the Raistrick staff in attempting to refine penicillin, Alexander Fleming continued year after year to work with his promising mold juice. In 1932, for instance, he demonstrated the power of the compound dramatically. A Dr. Rogers joined the staff at St. Mary's and contracted a disabling eye infection. After all other treatment failed, Fleming treated the infection with his mold juice and cured Rogers. Two years later, Fleming was still hard at work on penicil-

lin, although he had made no real progress with the substance in over
five years. He appointed as his assistant a Dr. Holt, who was trained
as a biochemist, and naturally Fleming set Holt immediately to work
on the problem of extracting pure penicillin. Working largely on his
own, Holt got as far as the entire Raistrick team, but like all other
early penicillin researchers, Holt could not go beyond the critical point
in the extraction process where the penicillin disappeared, never to be
recovered. Holt, too, finally gave up, but not Fleming. In 1935 he was
just as committed to the mold as he had been in 1928. Unfortunately,
he was just as unable to purify penicillin and prove its utility
therapeutically.

If Alexander Fleming ever had good reason to abandon penicillin,
it came in 1935, for in that year Hitler's Germany announced to the
scientific world that many bacterial infections could be controlled with
a "wonder drug" produced by Nazi science. Resuming where Ehrlich
left off, in 1932 a German bacteriologist, Dr. Gerhard Domagk, began
experiments for the Bayer Company using dyes on mice infected with
Streptococci. He soon noticed that one red dye seemed to protect the
mice from the bacteria, and while he did not understand the mechanism,
he knew that he had made an important discovery. Naming the dye
Prontosil, Domagk proved its efficacy under the most dramatic circumstances. His daughter contracted a septicemia from the *Streptococci*
while working in his laboratory; as a desperation measure he treated
her with Prontosil and saved her life. For the following three years
Domagk and other Bayer scientists tested the drug under the most secret
conditions, and finally they announced it. When Fleming heard Domagk
explain the drug as a meeting of the Royal Society of Medicine, he
was impressed; but he maintained that penicillin could do a better
job if only it could be refined. Many of Fleming's colleagues took his
comments to be peevish, but he was quite right.

Prontosil was not really an antibiotic substance, but, unknown to the
Germans, it worked rather through a bacteriostatic mechanism. Many
microorganisms, most notably *Streptococci*, use para-amino-benzoic acid,
PABA, in their metabolism, and if they are deprived of it they cannot
grow. This weakness of many bacteria proved to be the strength of
Prontosil, for although Domagk was unaware of it, his drug simply
combined with the PABA in the human body, thus making it impossible
for PABA-reliant pathogens to grow and do damage. Ironically, the
French taught Domagk and the Germans a lesson in scientific research.
Working at the Pasteur Institute, four French bacteriologists began testing Prontosil, which had been patented by Bayer. They soon learned
that while it worked fine in the body, it did not work at all in test
tubes. They then unraveled the mystery of Protonsil's action and learned
that only a part of the dye molecule was of consequence in bacteriostatic

activity: para-amino-phenyl-sulphonamide. By completing Domagk's work, the French thus revealed the sulphonamide class of bacteriostatics, made Bayer's patent on Prontosil a worthless scrap of paper, and broke the German monopoly on worldwide distribution of the drug.

A whole new era of medical treatment resulted from the introduction of "sulfa," for it was the first really important chemotherapeutic agent. In England, before the introduction of the sulphonamides, cases of puerperal sepsis at Queen Charlotte's Hospital carried a mortality rate of 20 percent in spite of preventive measures. Using "sulfa," the mortality rate was lowered drastically to 4.7 percent. It soon became apparent that several dangerous pathogens were vulnerable to the sulphonamides, for spectacular results were recorded when the drug was used on infections ranging from "strep" throat to gonorrhea. The mortality rate in meningitis infections, for example, dropped from 70 percent to 10 percent with the advent of sulfa treatment. Holding out the hope of salvation from many of the most dreaded diseases, the sulphonamides captured the imagination of millions of people from all walks of life. It was the first drug in history to rise to nearly heroic status. Yet sulfa had its disadvantages. Most notably, there were many dangerous pathogens that did not respond to it, and others, originally susceptible, that developed genetic changes to escape sulfa's effect.

While physicians all over the world were noting the proven powers of the sulphonamides, Alexander Fleming feared that his mold juice would sink into even greater obscurity. In 1936, his fears seemed justified when, at the Second International Congress of Microbiology, he read another paper on penicillin that left his sulfa-conscious audience utterly unimpressed. But, at about the same time two scientists began working together who were ultimately to overcome the main obstacle to penicillin purification: Dr. Howard Florey and Dr. Ernst Chain.

These two men, who built the famous Oxford penicillin team, were as dissimilar in background as can be imagined. Florey, an Australian-born Rhodes Scholar who had studied extensively in America and Britain, was appointed to the Chair of Pathology at Oxford's Sir William Dunn School in 1935. Chain, in contrast, was a German-Jewish biochemist who had fled his homeland in 1933 when the Nazis came to power and was working in relative obscurity at Cambridge in 1935. Through the medium of Sir Frederick Hopkins at Cambridge, Florey and Chain were brought together at the Dunn School, for Hopkins recommended Chain for the biochemical post open in Florey's department. Thus when the Germans announced Prontosil to the world in 1935. Florey and Chain began a relationship that was soon to dwarf Domagk's feat.

Ernst Chain was the catalyst in solving the puzzle of penicillin. When he first went to Oxford, he was given a free hand in research. He decided to work on Fleming's long-neglected lysozyme as well as on the mechanisms of snake venom. A literature search on lysozyme soon led Chain to over 200 papers on antibacterial substances, and of those essays he found Alexander Fleming's 1929 paper on penicillin to be most provocative. Discarding lysozyme and snake venom, Dr. Chain elected to concentrate his efforts on penicillin, more specifically on the problem of purification, and with Florey's support he applied to the Rockefeller Foundation for a grant to buy equipment. Receiving $5,000 from the Foundation to support three separate research projects over a ten-year period, Chain began his intensive experiments on penicillin early in 1939.

By a peculiar quirk of fate, a strain of Fleming's *Penicillium* had made its way to Oxford through the means of a Dr. Dreier, who had studied it briefly and kept samples of the mold. By cultivating the *Penicillium*, Chain soon amassed enough material to begin some preliminary experiments in refining. Chain was struck by the peculiar instability of penicillin under normal purification techniques, but, being a first-rate biochemist, he wisely decided to treat the substance as though it were an extremely delicate enzyme. Moreover, he utilized a novel laboratory technique that had not been available when Fleming and Raistrick had struggled with purification: lyophilization or freeze-drying. Through this means, where substances pass directly from a solid to a gaseous state and the component compounds cease to act on each other, Chain produced a brown powder composed of several proteins, salts, and partially-purified penicillin. Then, Chain refined the powder by dissolving it in water and freeze-drying the solution once again. This produced an even more purified residue powder, and Chain was heartened when, after injecting 30 milligrams of the substance into a mouse, no toxic effects resulted.

From the foundation of his initial encouraging experiments, Chain joined forces with a Dr. Heatley; together they worked out the first effective technique for extracting the active principle of penicillin. The process was complex and difficult, and its crucial stages proved to be working with the solution at a low temperature and then freeze-drying the neutral residue in solution to get a penicillin salt. Slow, crude, and time-consuming, the Chain-Heatley method of extraction was the only one available for any kind of penicillin production until 1946.

Naturally, Chain and Heatley began testing the bactericidal power of penicillin as soon as they had refined a sufficient quantity for experimentation. They were stunned by the results of their tests. The partially purified drug was 1,000 times more powerful than Fleming's original mold juice, and the pure compound proved to be 1,000 times more powerful again. Further, as Fleming had predicted, penicillin was more active than sulfa; so much so that there really was no comparison, for even the partially refined drug was ten times more effective than the sulfonamides on the same microorganisms.

On May 25, 1940, as France prepared to surrender and Britain contemplated standing alone, a critical test was carried out at Oxford University that seemed in the face of probable invasion to be of marginal consequence. The Oxford team infected three groups of mice with three different bacterial diseases and then treated half of each group with penicillin. The results were spectacular, for all of the untreated mice died while most of those injected with penicillin survived. Six weeks later a decisively similar test was conducted using 50 white mice infected with virulent *Streptococci*. Twenty-four of the 25 treated mice survived, while all of the untreated controls perished. The results of these tests appeared in an article titled "Penicillin as a Chemotherapeutic Agent" in the August 24, 1940, issue of *Lancet*. Alexander Fleming, who had discovered penicillin and had worked on little else for 12 years, was probably the most surprised physician to read the article, for he had no idea that anyone else was interested in his molds. Florey and Chain were no less surprised when Fleming came to Oxford to see them, for they had thought that he had been dead for several years.

Shortly after Fleming united with the Oxford team, his penicillin was subjected to the test that would decide whether or not it was really a medical marvel. Protecting mice was one thing, but would it cure a mortally infected human being? The answer to that question came in February 1941 after the Oxford team had collected enough penicillin to use on a human patient. An ideal test case presented itself when an Oxford police constable was reported to be dying of a septicemia which began in a scratch at the corner of his mouth. Since the man was in a terrible state with abscesses all over his body, in a coma, and in an obviously hopeless condition, Florey and Chain were given permission to administer penicillin as his only chance. Identifying the infecting organism as *Staphylococcus aureus*, a bacterium known to be sensitive to penicillin, they began treatment with considerable optimism. On February 12, intravenous injections of 200 milligrams of penicillin were begun and continued every 3 hours; at the end of 24 hours the constable had improved dramatically. His wounds began healing, he regained consciousness, and he was clearly well on the road to recovery. The meager stock of penicillin, so painfully collected, was quickly used up in the course of the treatment, and just as the constable approached complete recovery the supply ran out. The patient suffered a relapse, and Florey and Chain had to watch helplessly as he died on March 15, 1941. Their only consolation was the knowledge that if they had collected a large enough supply he could have been completely cured. In the grim tradition of medical humor, the experiment was a success but the patient died.

With the efficacy of penicillin clearly proven experimentally, the next hurdle was to mass-produce the drug for domestic and military use.

Since this was obviously beyond the capacity of Oxford University, Fleming and the Oxford team approached the government and industry with their problem. It quickly became apparent that British industry, staggering under the burden of wartime orders, could not possibly undertake the production of penicillin, so Fleming and his colleagues turned toward America as their only alternative. In June 1941, Florey and Heatley flew to the United States with strains of *Penicillium,* hoping to convince the Americans of the importance of the drug and also to persuade them to produce it.

Luckily, soon after he landed, Florey met an old friend, Dr. Charles Thom, who headed the mycological research section of the Northern Regional Research Laboratory in Peoria, Illinois. This facility had been built principally to develop uses for organic by-products of agriculture, and Thom learned that one of these by-products, corn steep liquor, provided an ideal medium for producing penicillin. With this discovery and the agreement of two American drug firms to produce penicillin, the industrial focus of the drug shifted to the United States. Historically, the impact of this shift has been to mislead the public into thinking that penicillin was an American creation, but during the war this misconception never troubled the British scientists. They were properly concerned with making it available, not with establishing credit for its development.

Somehow, in the shuffle of purification by the Oxford team and production by American industry, Alexander Fleming's seminal work on the drug was overlooked. Indeed, several researchers actually published papers on penicillin describing exactly what Fleming had written and talked about years earlier. On August 27, 1942, however, the confusion about this "wonder drug" and where it came from was cleared up. The *Times* published a lead article entitled "Penicillium," explaining what it was, how it worked, and how much better it was than the sulphonamides; but they neglected to give credit for its discovery to Fleming. Four days later, Fleming got his due when Sir Almroth Wright, 81 years old and living in the country to avoid the irritation of air raids, wrote a letter to the *Times*'s editor explaining Fleming's role in the development of penicillin. Thereafter, no doubt remained about who was responsible for the antibiotic. Like sulfa seven years earlier, penicillin and its discoverer were elevated to heroic proportions by the public. Fleming, perplexed by his own fame and amused by public fascination with his mold, speculated on the commercial possibilities of an advertisement for penicillin lipstick. "Kiss who you like, where you like, how you like. You need fear no tiresome consequences if you use our penicillin rouge."

The acclaim that Alexander Fleming received because of penicillin carried its share of honors. In 1943, he was elected to the Royal Society,

Britain's oldest and most distinguished scientific organization, which counted among its earliest members Hooke, Boyle, and Newton. In the following year Fleming was honored with a knighthood by a grateful British government. The Royal College of Surgeons awarded him their coveted gold medal, which had been conferred only 20 times in the preceding 144 years. But the greatest honor of all came on October 25, 1945, when Fleming received a telegram from Stockholm notifying him that he had, along with Florey and Chain, been awarded the Nobel prize for medicine. Curiously, Fleming never profited materially from his discovery or his fame. To this day the drug penicillin is not governed by a patent controlled by Fleming's heirs or anyone else. Only the processes by which the drug is produced are patented and regulated for profit by the lucrative drug industry that Fleming's discovery spawned. Apparently unaffected by the pomp and adulation that accompanied his fame, Alexander Fleming maintained his perspective by keeping a scrapbook containing all of the untrue information printed about him in the press. He titled the book "The Fleming Myth."

After the war, Sir Alexander Fleming replaced Wright as Director of the St. Mary's department which soon became the Wright-Fleming Institute of Microbiology. Though he continued working at the laboratory, his professional activity never led him again to the heights of discovering another lysozyme or penicillin. In reality, he was more of a roving ambassador of British science than a serious research microbiologist, traveling all over the world as the foremost representative of Britain's spirit of scientific inquiry. On the morning of March 11, 1955, Fleming awoke anticipating a luncheon at the Savoy with Eleanor Roosevelt and Douglas Fairbanks, Junior. He died, apparently of a heart attack, before he could keep the appointment. Buried in the crypt of St. Paul's cathedral, near the remains of Admiral Nelson, Sir Alexander Fleming lies today, symbolizing the strange blend of fortune and professional commitment that is the essence of scientific discovery.

It would be preposterous to claim that Alexander Fleming was the single most important British scientist of this century. Over the past 75 years British science has given the world such diverse gifts as nuclear energy, antibiotics, jet propulsion, radar, and perceptions of the DNA structure of human cells. In some cases, particularly that of Francis Crick, James Watson, and Maurice Wilkins, who articulated the double helix of DNA, careful planning and exhaustive experimentation produced an important result. In others, such as R. J. Mitchell's idea for the design of the Spitfire fighter plane, romanticism in the form of a fascination with gulls in flight led to a significant revelation. Yet, with Alexander Fleming, whose discoveries of lysozyme and especially penicillin were of fundamental biological importance, fortune in a piece of nasal mucosa and a mold spore from Praed Street and the hard work of a dedicated physician completely changed the course of applying science to the everyday lives of ordinary people. Millions have lived and shall continue to live because Alexander Fleming was struck in 1928 by an observation of natural bacterial antagonism. Had he been less alert, "blood poisoning" would still have the deadly ring that it had to generations before the Second World War. Much of what is taken for granted in medical treatment would be only a hazy, theoretical possibility.

SUGGESTED READINGS

Although there are several biographies of Sir Alexander Fleming, most of them are brief, popular works rather than scholarly studies. The best biography is André Maurois, *The Life of Sir Alexander Fleming* (New York: Dutton, 1959) which tends to be uncritical and contains errors relating to scientific subjects. Other worthwhile books dealing either with Fleming or his discoveries are: Laurence Ludovici, *Fleming, Discoverer of Penicillin* (London: Dakers, 1952); David Masters, *Miracle Drug* (London: Eyre and Spottiswoode, 1946). Because there is no comprehensive history of British science in the 20th century, background material for Fleming's career is virtually nonexistent. Perhaps the best source of information on the tempo of scientific activity, its importance, and the role of the government in channeling the direction of scientific inquiry during the 1939–1945 war is Angus Calder, *The Peoples War*, (London: Jonathan Cape, 1969).